John A. Welsh, D. Sc., was founder and chief executive of Flow Laboratories, Inc., which is now a major operating division of Flow General Inc. (NYSE). Prior to that he was treasurer of Thermo Electron, Inc. (NYSE) and president of Joseph Kaye & Co., Inc.. In 1970 he became the founding Director of the Caruth Institute of Owner-Managed Business, Edwin L. Cox School of Business, Southern Methodist University. He received his education at MIT and taught engineering courses there for four years. He began his career as a pilot in WWII.

Jerry F. White is a management consultant specializing in new, fast-growth business. He is also chairman of the Owner-Managed Business Center, Inc. in Dallas, Texas which produces and markets innovative management development programs for owner-managers. He is associate director of the Caruth Institute at Southern Methodist University. Mr. White has presented more than 300 seminars on Profit & Cash Flow Management throughout the United States and Canada to more than 5,000 entrepreneurs and owner-managers. During his earlier career he was associated with Westinghouse, IBM, and Collins Radio.

Dr. Welsh and Mr. White are co-authors of many publications including *Administering the Closely Held Company* (Prentice-Hall 1980) and "A Small Business Is not a Little Big Business," Harvard Business Review, July-August, 1981.

THE ENTREPRENEUR'S MASTER PLANNING GUIDE

How to Launch a Successful Business

John A. Welsh
Jerry F. White

A SPECTRUM BOOK

PRENTICE-HALL, INC.   Englewood Cliffs, New Jersey 07632

Library of Congress Cataloging in Publication Data

Welsh, John A.
  The entrepreneur's master planning guide.

  "A Spectrum Book."
  Includes index.
  1. New business enterprises.   2. Entrepreneur.
I. White, Jerry F.   II. Title.
HD62.5.W45   1983   658.4′2   82-18112
  ISBN 0-13-282814-6
  ISBN 0-13-282806-5 (pbk.)

This book is dedicated to *The Caruth Institute of Owner-Managed Business at the Edwin L. Cox School of Business, Southern Methodist University, and its founder W. W. Caruth, Jr. of Dallas, Texas.*

This book is available at a special discount when ordered in bulk quantities. For information, contact Prentice-Hall, Inc., General Publishing Division, Special Sales, Englewood Cliffs, N.J. 07632

10   9   8   7   6   5   4   3   2   1

Printed in the United States of America

ISBN   0-13-282806-5 {PBK.}

ISBN 0-13-282814-6

Editorial/production supervision and interior design by Cyndy Lyle Rymer
Cover design © 1983 by Jeannette Jacobs
Manufacturing buyer Cathie Lenard

Prentice-Hall International, Inc., *London*
Prentice-Hall of Australia Pty. Limited, *Sydney*
Prentice-Hall of Canada Inc., *Toronto*
Prentice-Hall of India Private Limited, *New Delhi*
Prentice-Hall of Japan, Inc., *Tokyo*
Prentice-Hall of Southeast Asia Pte. Ltd., *Singapore*
Whitehall Books Limited, *Wellington, New Zealand*
Editora Prentice-Hall do Brasil Ltda., *Rio de Janeiro*

Contents

Contents

Preface

The lessons in this book have been burnished in the hot coals of the competitive marketplace where what counts is successful achievement. And that is what we wish for our readers, successful achievement in making their business bigger or starting their own business. We recommend planning before acting and describe how to create an effective business plan.

There are many facets to a plan including production, marketing, administration and finance. These facets are discussed within a larger context. There are three components to success in building a business, each of which changes with time:

- the entrepreneur progressing along a career path
- a business concept and the competitive strategy which has a chance of winning a niche in the marketplace, and
- financing in an environment of constantly changing economic conditions and regulatory constraints

There is a short period in time along each of these components when the probability for success is enhanced. These components are viewed pictorially as being at right angles to each other. When the optimal periods for success along each component come together they become the edges of a cube. This portrayal provides a graphic image which helps to grasp the admonishment that to improve the probabilities for success you must move inside the cube.

We have chosen to prepare short but meaningful chapters in bite-size pieces. Each chapter addresses a single concept. Related concepts are grouped together under five parts. Part I answers questions about what a business plan is, what it looks like, what is in it, and how best to present it to a busy investor.

Part II examines the profile of successful entrepreneurs. The characteristics found to be common among successful entrepreneurs throw light on how they view the world around them and how they deal with people. The implications are profound. These characteristics provide the strength, tenacity, and leadership needed to guide a business during the volatile and uncertain times it must endure. But, they also lead to turmoil and trouble for most entrepreneurs as the business grows and takes on the formalities of a management structure. Knowing of these implications beforehand leads successful entrepreneurs to build on their strengths and overcome the impending management problems.

Part III deals with the product or service offered for sale, the industry within which it competes, and:

- the three available marketing strategies: focus, differentiation, and cost leadership,
- the five powerful underlying market forces: rivalry, threats of new competitors or substitute products, the bargaining power of suppliers or customers, and
- the inescapable phenomenon that prices, measured in constant dollars, decline in proportion to accumulated experience.

Knowledge of these factors greatly improves an entrepreneur's skill in selecting a product or service and choosing a strategy to make it succeed.

Part IV deals with venture capital and examines how:

- venture capital differs from investment capital,
- economic conditions and regulations of government encourage or discourage venture capital investment,
- to cope with the securities and exchange laws, and
- to choose the legal form for the business to make it a more desirable investment opportunity.

Part V describes a critical management skill. Entrepreneurs and owner-managers need many skills. With most, help is available from specialists as in marketing, research, finance, or administration. There is one skill, however, which entrepreneurs cannot delegate. This is the skill of visualizing and portraying the future operations of the business in terms of profit and cash flow. Help is available from clerks and computers, but the skill is not in the manipulation of numbers. It is in understanding how present management decisions and actions will be portrayed by the financial statements to be prepared by clerks and computers after the decisions are implemented.

The appendices include three sample business plans, one for a manufacturer, one a contractor, and the third a retail service business. These examples are based on actual plans, although the names and places have been changed. The format of business plans is as varied as the entrepreneurs who write them. The illustrations provided here are the stories told by three different individuals.

The book is the first comprehensive publication of the content of a program that evolved over a 12-year period at the Caruth Institute of Owner-Managed Business. It has been presented to more than 5,000 people of all ages and educational backgrounds. The degree of their subsequent success in business which they attribute to this program has been extraordinary. The diversity of the audience led to the "plain English" style and basic, but fundamental, description. The material in Part V is from a separate program which has been presented to another 5,000 entrepreneurs and owner-managers across the country since 1975 in a seminar format. That seminar, presented in dialogue by the authors, evolved into a series of 30-minute instructional programs made for television and available on film and videocassettes, and a more advanced management book, *Administering the Closely Held Company* (Prentice-Hall, 1980).

ACKNOWLEDGMENTS

The authors would like to acknowledge five individuals who made important contributions to the development of the ideas presented here. Dr. Byron Williamson and Dr. James C. Hörger contributed a meaningful psychological profile of successful entrepreneurs. Dr. Richard F. Tozer first proposed the model of the successful entrepreneur's career path and provided insight on the experience curve strategy for entrepreneurs. Giffen H. Ott and Randy J. LaMotte made invaluable contributions in the area of practical business planning.

1

Why Prepare a Business Plan?

Why prepare a business plan? Successful entrepreneurs advocate it. Venture capitalists require it. Bankers desire it. New venture specialists suggest it. Suppliers admire it. New managers need it. Consultants recommend it. Why, indeed, prepare a business plan? Because it improves the probability of succeeding.

The business plan is a concise summary of the detailed activities surrounding the creation or expansion of a business. It is typically prepared in the form of a booklet, 8½ by 11 inches, about ten to thirty pages, professionally typed and enclosed in a simple binder. It describes the product or service, the customers, the competition, the production and marketing, the management and administration, the financing, and all the things needed to make and sell the product or service at a reasonable profit. There may be, and probably will be, extensive supporting data. This information will be available in appendices or other supplementary reports. The business plan is the capstone to all the detailed plans and forecasts.

As this book shows in the chapters that follow, there is a strategic framework for a plan for the birth or growth of a successful business. Its dimensions are: (1) the entrepreneur (see Part II), (2) a business concept that has a chance of winning in the marketplace (Part III), and (3) the entrepreneur's access to venture capital for this particular business concept (Part IV). And the entrepreneur needs one critical skill, the ability to describe the future operations of the business in a language of simple numbers (Part V).

The dimensions of the strategic framework are not static. Like the dynamic economy in which we live, the entrepreneur, the business concept, and access to venture capital all change with time. If you know this and know something about how each dimension should be positioned to improve the probabilities for winning, your business plan leads to the successful launch of a new business.

Someone has said, "It is easy to write a one-hundred-page

document, but it is tough to write a good ten-page report." There is some truth in this, especially when preparing a business plan. A person who has great confidence in what is going to be done and how it is to be accomplished can describe the plan clearly and simply. Turning that thought around suggests that if a person can't state clearly and simply what he or she is going to do, that person probably isn't sure how he or she will do it.

Therein lies one of the main reasons for preparing a business plan—to convince yourself and others that you know what you are doing. Few would attempt to build a multimillion-dollar building without first preparing detailed plans. The same is true for an entrepreneur building a multimillion-dollar business. The principle also applies for a $100,000-dollar business.

A plan has several valuable properties:

1. It is the way to get your act together.
2. It is a great technique for evaluating how good a business idea might really be.
3. It is a necessary exhibit when trying to raise capital.
4. It can be surprisingly effective in getting favorable treatment from suppliers.
5. It is a valuable recruiting tool when hiring key employees.
6. It is an orientation document for those new key employees you expect to help make it happen.

It is easy to get into business, especially if your credit is good or if you have the personal net worth to support the investment. You don't need to show graduation certificates or pass tests. Once you have incurred the liabilities, however, things can become very sticky. Bills come due with relentless regularity and remorseless frequency.

A business, even a very simple one, has enough complexity that a person cannot mentally encompass all its facets. The many parts of the business compete for the entrepreneur's time and energy. If all goes well, you can handle these demands. If anything goes wrong, however, you, as manager, can very quickly become absorbed by one part of the business and neglect others. But the other parts won't go unattended for long without trouble. You may then feel like a juggler with five balls in the air riding a unicycle in a strong wind.

Planning provides a carefully thought out course of action to achieve a goal. In carefully thinking through the course of action you can't help but consider alternatives. You are quite naturally led to consider what might be done if things don't go exactly as planned. Becoming aware of some things that might go wrong provides an opportunity to "scheme" around the difficulty before it arises.

The business plan includes a best judgment of how much time and money will have to be put into the enterprise. It also includes a best estimate of what can be expected from the business and how soon.

Comparing the two provides a measure of whether the business is worth the investment of a big piece of your lifetime and most, if not all, of your personal assets. If it is good enough, perhaps other people will find it worth investing their money, time, and effort to help make it happen.

If you have to raise capital to build the business—and most entrepreneurs do—negotiations with investors and bankers won't get very far without a business plan. Imagine asking someone to let you spend their money. That's what you are doing. It will take a pretty good story to win consent. That story is the description of what you are going to do, how you are going to do it, and why you are sure it will work out the way you describe it—your business plan.

Some enterprising entrepreneurs have found a good business plan worth many dollars when negotiating with suppliers. Consider the business that will need six word-processing machines: one now, two in nine months, and three more in eighteen months. Trying to buy one machine now won't excite the sales representative. But suppose you can show him or her an order for six machines with periodic shipments over the next eighteen months. Many salespeople lose their objectivity in those circumstances. Even landlords and stationery store owners can be swayed.

Recruiting key people can be a very difficult problem for a new or unproven business. Good people are generally already employed and have other job choices. They may be interested in the opportunity for rapid advancement and the degree of freedom and control a new business offers, but they will also be concerned about job security. They will want to know that you have more to offer than just a good story. A well-prepared business plan can have considerable authority. It carries the kind of weight associated with silver stars on a soldier's epaulets.

The plan also provides key employees with an idea of where they fit in the overall organization. The enthusiastic story told by an entrepreneur often sounds good, but it lacks the realistic perspective of the employee or partner who is expected to bear the burden of some key part of the venture. A clear written story allows entrepreneur and key employee to discuss the proposed effort with some objectivity.

What is a business plan? It is a tool to improve the probabilities of successfully building a viable business of your own. Why prepare a business plan? To improve your chances for achieving *financial independence* and the *freedom* of being your own boss.

2

Recipe for a Winning Business Plan

The business plan tells a very special story. It is the story of a unique business enterprise, the one you, the entrepreneur, will create. Telling this story will reveal how knowledgeable and competent you are, how certain the outcome is, and how desirable it is to proceed with the project.

There are similarities among all good business plans, but no two are exactly alike, because no two businesses are exactly alike. Even if they make and sell the same thing to the same market, two businesses will have different personalities. The behavior and attitudes of the managers will be reflected in the businesses. Even the decors will be different, just as the homes of the managers will reflect their individual taste and style. Each business plan is unique.

The written description of a business will carry the imprint of the author's personality. When comparing a plan prepared by a lawyer with one prepared by a salesperson, their imprints are clear even to a novice. The words they choose and the sentence structures they use are very different. Because the business plan describes what a particular entrepreneur intends to do, you don't want to hide that individual's personality. The entrepreneur should prepare the plan. The entrepreneur's personality, taste, and style are a fundamental part of the story.

There is no formula for preparing a good plan, but some clear guidelines exist. First of all, recognize what the substance of business is:

> The substance of business is people parting with their hard-earned money in return for whatever you have to offer them.

Business consists of a series of transactions in which one thing is given up in return for another. The crucial transaction is the one in which customers give up money for the product or service provided by the enterprise. Therein lie several topics that deserve consideration in the plan: what, how, where, and when. You would expect to see topic headings like the following:

1. *The Product.* What product or service is being offered? How is it made ready for sale?

2. *Target Market.* Who will part with their money? How many of them are there? Where are they?

3. *Competition.* Where do the customers obtain the product or service now? How does that product or service differ from yours? How strong is the competition?

4. *Marketing.* How will the customers learn about your product? Where can they buy it? How does it get to where they buy it?

5. *Management.* Who will coordinate the activities of production, administration, and marketing? Who will decide what is to be done and when?

6. *Financial Performance.* How much profit will be made and when? How much capital is required? What will the business's net worth be a year from now? two years from now?

Before preparing the plan it is wise to decide to whom it is written. The plan may be read by many people, each with a different perspective. All, however, will be busy people with many other things on their minds and too much to read in the normal course of their day. Most will probably also be skeptics.

Experience in writing, reading, and evaluating business plans leads us to suggest that you assume the reader to be a *busy investor.* That person would be knowledgeable, realistic, and very conscious of time. And it can be hoped that these qualities also describe the entrepreneur. As the business planner you can ask, how do I present this story to that busy investor so that he or she will provide money and other support to my business?

Imagine walking into the investor's office. Sit down, look around. Note the investor glancing at a wristwatch. See how many reports and letters are on the desk waiting to be read. Now, tell your story in a way that will get that person's attention, interest, and consent to finance the business.

Choosing an investor as the assumed reader is important. It is one thing to ask someone if he or she likes your proposed venture. It is quite another to ask for money. As long as you are just asking for people's opinions they will want to be nice to you. When you ask for their money they don't mind hurting your feelings. The decision to start or expand a business has potentially grave consequences. You should want a cold, objective evaluation of your plan's merits before making that decision.

The plan begins with a brief overview, the introduction. It is probably better to write this section last. In a sense it is saying, "OK, now that we have this story, tell me what it is going to tell me." It is more than that, however. It is the counterpart to your first few minutes of a visit with the reader. It is the handshake, the hello, and the exchange of words that lead the reader to listen with interest.

Once the reader finds the anticipated story of interest, it must be well told. It needs structure, continuity, and organization. Each storyteller will know how best to organize the specific presentation, but a logical sequence follows.

INTRODUCTION

The purpose of the first page or two of the plan is to introduce the reader to the story and provide assurance that it is going to be worth reading. The introduction provides quick answers to the most obvious questions of that busy investor. The plan represents the business. The reader asks that business

> Who are you?
> What are you?
> Where are you from?

The answers are likely to sound like, "We are Welsh and White from Chicago, Illinois. We provide entrepreneurs the help they need to build a successful business." This leads to other questions.

> Are you a corporation or proprietorship?
> Who owns the company?
> When did it start?
> Have you made any sales?
> Do you have any track record?

Answers to these questions provide the background of the business, if it has one. They give the reader a feeling for where the business and its key people are coming from. With some satisfaction in this area, the reader will want to know more about what is going on now:

> What does the company do?
> Is that like anything already familiar to me?
> What are you trying to accomplish?
> What do you want from me?

The objective of the introduction is to entice the reader to turn the page and read on. Your story can't be told on one or two brief pages, but the introduction can present the highlights and capture the reader's imagination. The information should have a tantalizing, but realistic, flavor. If you don't capture the reader's imagination the interview is over.

Consider the following introduction to a business plan we once read, (specific names are altered):

> Stoneburg Enterprises, Inc., a Montana Corporation founded two years ago, was formed to develop and market the high quality patented product known as the Stoneburg Magic Bed Massager. The Company

has successfully designed, maufactured and sold its widely praised product and is now seeking equity financing to begin a mass marketing campaign designed to achieve annual sales of $2 million, with an after-tax profit of 10 percent, in 24 months.

Consider for a moment how much introductory information has been conveyed in only two sentences. You know what the company does, how long it has been in existence, something of its history, its major objectives, what it seeks from the reader, what the product is, and so on—and in only two sentences.

What will the reader learn by turning the next page? That depends on your story. If you propose to offer customers something that seems unusual or incredulously clever, perhaps the next question in the reader's mind would be, "What is a Stoneburg Magic Bed Massager?"

PRODUCT (OR SERVICE)

The purpose of the section on your product or service is to describe it and to convince the reader that there is something unique about it. A busy investor knows that potential customers will see your product or service as one among many. It needs something to make the customers perceive it as better than what they can get anywhere else.

Perhaps you propose to sell something readily available elsewhere, but with a new kind of financing or a new kind of ownership. Leasing living room furniture, renting the television set, or buying the telephone headset, for example. You will want to extol the virtues of this new kind of financing or ownership as perceived by the potential customers and explain in detail how it works.

Sometimes the success of a new business rests on its unique location. In that event, this part of the story will dwell on how successful the product or service is somewhere, why it is successful there, and how the proposed location has the same characteristics as the location of the existing business.

If the proposed product or service requires something special in its preparation, this is the place to describe it. The something special may be machinery or access to a particular labor skill, a particular source of supplies, or a unique talent. These set the proposed business apart from the potential competition.

If the proposed product or service is very technical or complex, this part of the story may require careful analysis of its key elements. The reader of the plan, like the customer, does not have to know how to make the product or deliver the service, but he or she does want to feel assured that you know. The reader wants to be treated as someone who could understand your complex story if you would take the time to explain it simply. Avoiding an explanation as if it is too technical may be perceived as doubting the reader's ability to understand.

7

Photographs or a carefully drawn exhibit can often be extremely helpful. The most useful pictures are simple; they make their point at a glance. Intricate diagrams that require study frustrate the reader. It may be true that a picture is worth a thousand words, but not ten thousand words.

TARGET MARKET

The purpose of the target market section is to identify precisely and describe in detail your potential customers. If among the potential customers there are primary and secondary targeted segments, they should be specified. In our world so many products and services are offered that even minor differences in customer choices are satisfied by different products. Each business, and each product or service of the business, serves the interests of a segment of the population.

The more clearly that population segment can be identified, the greater the probability of reaching them and selling to them. Great masses of statistical data about people are available. If the potential customers can be identified with the characteristics used in the statistical data, then finding them and counting them is easier. Also, your claim to knowledge of how many there are and how to locate them is supported by statistical documentation.

Products and services usually serve some part of a larger market. For instance, automobile rearview mirrors sell to the automotive market. Within that greater market, however, is a market segment of interest. There are rearview mirrors mounted inside the car and those mounted outside. There are mirrors for trucks and mirrors for automobiles. There are detachable mirrors, adjustable mirrors, and mirrors that dim out bright lights. Within each of these is a segment of interest to this particular business plan.

Within the market segment of interest will be the target market, the specific objective of this business's sales effort. Detachable mirrors might be our product. Then users of detachable automotive mirrors would be our target market. They would be the drivers of vehicles that need or want such mirrors. Why would they want them? Because something is blocking their view. What could that be? Trailers, perhaps.

This line of reasoning might lead to people who own or rent a detachable trailer to be pulled behind their automobile or light truck. One large group of these people might be members of certain travel clubs or readers of certain recreational vehicle magazines. Another might be renters of trailers whose customers must have the rearview mirror. Again, these people might belong to a particular trade association and read its monthly magazine.

This statistical information is usually called *demographic data*. Your ability to describe the potential customers in your target market with demographic characteristics conveys the authority with which you understand your market. Identifying the data sources relevant to the target customers suggests that this business knows what it is doing and how it is going to do it.

COMPETITION

The purpose of the part of the story on competition is to demonstrate a realistic knowledge of the obstacles to success created by competitors. Knowledge of competitive products and services provides a basis for comparison to show why your proposed product or service is likely to be selected by customers. If past experience with the competitive products or services can be cited, that adds to the authority of your business plan.

It is nearly impossible to conceive of a new business concept that doesn't compete with something. And to have a concept so unique that it doesn't have some competition raises doubts about whether the proposed customers will recognize anything of value in it.

Most business concepts that have a chance of winning their niche in the marketplace are improvements on something already familiar. Familiarity implies that someone is already providing a competitive product or service. A realistic business plan should demonstrate detailed knowledge of that competition.

Whatever the existing competition is providing, it must be satisfying its customers enough to induce them to spend their hard-earned money to buy it. It must have good qualities and characteristics. The proposed business must compete with the best of those qualities. You must recognize the best in what is already offered and then demonstrate how your business proposes to offer a product or service that is even better.

Sometimes the proposed product or service is not expected to be better than the competition's. Then it must be offered in a way that distinguishes it from the others. A discount store is usually large, to handle large volume. It also operates with low overhead. There are few salespeople and the customers participate in providing the sales service. That makes the discount store different from its competitors. To describe this difference requires knowledge of what stores selling the same products are *usually* like.

Managing a business means competing. As in football, boxing, or running the mile, the winners get to know a great deal about their competitors before the contest begins. They assess their strengths and weaknesses and establish a strategy for winning that particular contest. This section of the business plan should make that kind of assessment. For more on competition and competitive strategies, see Chapters 16, 19, 20, 22, and 23.

9

MARKETING

The purpose of the marketing section of your plan is to describe the activities that will convince the customers to spend their money for what you have to offer. These activities include promotion, advertising, distribution, and all the direct and indirect elements of selling.

In the world in which we must compete customers are deluged with messages about products and services. Most of the mail handled by the U.S. Postal Service is advertising and solicitation. Roads, streets, and highways are often cluttered with billboards. Radio and television derive their revenue from purveyors of goods and services advertising their wares. This assault on the mind is telling us about the 450,000 active trademarks registered at the U.S. Patent Office and the 25,000 new ones added each year. The communications media are introducing us to the more than 5,000 *significant* new products being offered each year by those 1,500 companies listed on the New York Stock Exchange alone. There are more than 175 brands of cigarettes on the market today and more than 100,000 prescription drugs.[1] In the midst of all this you must devise a method for finding your customers, telling them about you, and convincing them to seek you out. Effective positioning in the marketplace is crucial.

This effort requires spending time and money. A busy investor wants to know how much money is required, where it is to be spent, when, and how often. Money spent on advertising may be a necessity, but it is very different from money spent on equipment. When you buy equipment there is something tangible that can be resold, even if at a loss. When you buy advertising there is no assurance that anything will be obtained.

Consider also that the per capita consumption of advertising in America is about $200 a year. If you plan to spend $1 million per year on advertising, you are hitting the average consumer with less than a half-cent of advertising spread over 365 days. A consumer is already bombarded with 40,000 times that amount of advertising from other companies.[2]

Knowing much about the identity of the potential customers and how the competition is reaching them provides a basis for proposing a marketing plan of action. Being very knowledgeable about existing channels of distribution improves your chances of finding a channel for the new product or service. Personal experience in the distribution network may be necessary to gain knowledge of the subtleties of that element of business.

With this background the entrepreneur can describe how the business will go about marketing its unique product or service. The proposal should be specific. How much money will be spent for brochures, catalogs, mailings, advertisement, samples, and demonstrations? Who will make the demonstrations and give away the sam-

ples? Will they be paid salary or commission? Will they have to travel?
How will they pay for the travel? These questions lead to a schedule of
marketing expenses based on a timetable of market effort.

To be convincing about the validity of the proposed marketing
plan it is helpful to name the individual who will be responsible for the
program. That person's credentials and experience should support the
conclusion that the plan will work.

MANAGEMENT

The purpose of the section on management is to point out the essential
management functions needed to make this business succeed and to
identify the competent individuals who will be responsible for those
functions. A business consists of people. People make the decisions and
conduct the activities. People can turn a good situation into a bad one or
a bad situation into a good one. Given that the product or service of the
business has a reasonable chance of selling and that there is a viable
market, the people who guide the affairs of the business will determine
whether it succeeds.

Several functions of business must be covered, even if by only
one person. Basically, a business must prepare something to be sold,
production, and then sell it, *marketing*. In the process of doing these two
things there is a need for *administration* to purchase materials and
supplies, keep records, and provide financing. Over these three is a need
for one final arbiter, *management*.

If a new business is to grow to a viable size before exhausting its
resources, it must grow rapidly. A small business undergoing rapid
growth is characterized by constant change, a shortage of resources, and
the need for quick decisions. In these circumstances there is little time
for considered judgment by consensus or staff study. Somebody has to
make a decision and get on with its execution.[3]

Experienced investors in new businesses have learned that the
probability of success is improved when one person is clearly in charge.
They have also learned that the odds are improved when that leader has
knowledge and experience in, or at least a good grasp of, the administrative functions of business. The question is asked, "Who is your business
person?"

If a board of directors or management advisory committee is to
be part of the proposed management team, this is the place to name them
and summarize their background. Do not include their resumes or those
of the key managers at this point. Lengthy resumes belong in an appendix.

The kind of leader who is more likely to succeed as an entrepreneur is discussed at length in later chapters. In particular the characteristics of successful entrepreneurs are described in Chapter 8.

FINANCIAL PERFORMANCE

A busy investor and the entrepreneur will want to examine the proposed series of transactions in sufficient detail to feel confident that this business will thrive. This part of the business plan is usually called the projections. Its purpose is to present a summary of these projections.

Part V of this book describes how to prepare projections. Chapters 34 and 35 forecast, or project, the profit and the cash flow. Chapter 37 illustrates how these projections fit into the total record-keeping process in business. The result of these projections is a calculation of the capital required by the business, how much time it will take to regain that investment, and how great the reward will be. The sample business plans in the appendices provide specific examples of projections and their use.

The projections begin with a sales forecast. The entrepreneur brings together past experience, data from sources of information, and knowledge of the growth characteristics of the industry to arrive at a prediction of sales (see Chapter 39). Then the expenses that will be incurred to achieve those sales are listed and subtracted from the sales to see if the business concept is viable.

Projections are usually prepared month by month for the first two or three years. They may be quarterly thereafter, if needed. The decision about how far into the future to forecast depends on how long it will take this particular business to (1) become profitable, and (2) achieve consistently positive cash flow. It is common for a business to show profit before there is more cash flowing into the bank account from operations than out of it. The criteria for business survival are both net profit and net cash flow into the bank account. Figure 2-1 depicts the normal relationship between profit and cash flow during the start-up or rapid expansion of a business.

The projections are usually presented with totals for each twelve-month period.The format is month-by-month details in twelve

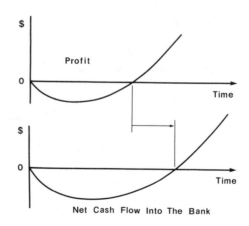

FIGURE 2-1 Profit and Cash Flow in a New or Rapid Growth Business.

columns and the twelve-month totals in a thirteenth column. This provides an easy way to check the arithmetic by adding vertically and horizontally. The term *cross-footing* is used to describe this checking process.

A balance sheet is normally prepared at the end of each twelve-month period. An entrepreneur may feel the need for assistance in preparing the balance sheet, but Chapter 37 will be sufficient for most readers.

There is one more extremely important aspect of the projections, the footnotes. For every row of sales, expenses, receipts, and disbursements numbers in the forecasts there is a footnote describing the logic for choosing the numbers. The detail in the footnotes should make it possible to reconstruct the numbers if they were lost.

What the entrepreneur proposes to do and how it is to be accomplished is found in the projections and footnotes. This is where the entrepreneur specifies the activities that will lead from a well-told story to an actual business enterprise.

The amount of capital required to start the new business is calculated—not guessed at—from the projections. Figure 2-1 shows how profit and cash flow vary as time passes. Figure 2-2 shows how the bank balance changes with time. This is plotted from the cash flow forecasts. When the initial bank balance is chosen to be zero on the cash flow forecast and the calculated bank balances are allowed to go negative, then the biggest negative bank balance in the forecast is the minimum capital required to ensure that the business won't run out of money. That point is identified in Figure 2-2.

The projections are prepared in great detail. A summary of the detailed projections is presented in this part of the business plan. The summary may be annual or quarterly or whatever makes the most sense in your particular business. The detailed projections are usually made available on request. They may be enclosed in a separate binder. They should be organized so that they may be read easily by someone with knowledge of projections. If the projections are not too bulky, they may be included in the business plan as an appendix.

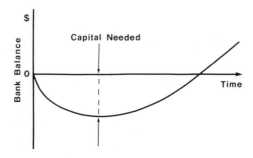

FIGURE 2-2 Capital Required to Support New or Rapid Growth Business.

APPENDICES

The purpose of the appendices is to provide the reader with easy access to detailed information that supports the story told in the business plan. It is important that the reader of the plan get the overall picture before being distracted by too much detail or overemphasis on one part. The reader makes a tacit assumption that the writer can back up claims made or conclusions drawn. The appendices are presumed to provide the evidence for those claims and conclusions.

Appendices are best arranged in the same order as the plan. We have suggested section titles: product, target market, competition, marketing, management, and financial performance. Supporting material falls logically into the same sequence. It is helpful to choose a numbering system for the appendices and use that system when making reference to appendix material in the text of the business plan. For appendices bound with the plan it is helpful to provide page numbers as well as appendix numbers.

A busy investor, or anyone else interested in learning about the business, will not have the time or the inclination to read and study something that looks like a textbook on economics. The written story about this business and all the supporting documentation must be packaged so that it is easy to grasp and verify.

A large and voluminous business plan can be intimidating. A reader does not easily make the commitment to read something that looks like a lot of work. Appendices provide a writer a way to package the presentation in bite-size pieces so that the potential reader never has to make a commitment to more than what appears to be easy reading.

3

Building In That Magic Ingredient: Credibility

To a busy investor, reading a business plan may seem like visiting a fortune-teller. The future is always going to be portrayed as very bright. There will be blessings of fame and fortune. The hero of the plan will perform great deeds. All the investor must do to reap the bountiful harvest of this glorious experience is part with money.

Most investors, lenders, and suppliers have heard that story all too often. Knowledgeable and experienced readers of business plans have had the opportunity to make investments. They know how the impartial tides of fate and luck can tarnish the most crystalline vision of the future. *Knowledgeable* and *experienced* are often synonymous with *skeptical* among busy investors. They have developed a "feel" for a plan worth looking at and an entrepreneur worth listening to. They sense credibility in a business plan. They are tuned in to the symbols and symptoms or a lack thereof.

How do they judge a business plan's credibility? How do you build credibility into your plan? The judgment of credibility is subjective and complex. There is no simple, all-inclusive formula. But there are clues.

A credible story has internal consistency. Each part of the story supports and confirms each other part. There are no conflicts of facts or logic. The reader's own experience confirms the facts and representations where that experience applies. The written language supports the stated words. The plan and its entrepreneur portray a single image that is not blurred by unsaid or half-said claims and implications. It has clarity and openness.

Our perception of a *credibility criteria* may be stated in five parts. After listing them here we will discuss each in more depth for you to grasp their meanings. The credibility criteria follow.

15

1. Business plan personality
2. Business plan balance
3. Track record—Credentials
4. Evidence of integrity and realism
5. Easily verifiable personal references

BUSINESS PLAN PERSONALITY

A business plan prepared by an entrepreneur is an example of the kind of work to be expected from that entrepreneur. There is a great deal of evidence in this work sample to suggest whether the entrepreneur can successfully produce and sell the product or service proposed.

Entrepreneurs would be expected to put their best foot forward in presenting their plans. To find anything less on reading the plan will raise questions about the entrepreneur's work when that foot is not forward.

A report that demonstrates by its content that it required diligent work suggests that its writer is capable of diligent work. Broad knowledge and thoroughness in the plan imply knowledge and thoroughness in the entrepreneur. Research supported by documentation in the plan illustrates the writer's ability to seek out the facts to support important decisions. When a plan is well organized, easy to read, and professionally presented, it is easier to believe that its author can organize and execute what is described in it.

A busy business manager receiving a letter in the mail will quickly read the text looking for some required action or needed reaction. A curious thing happens, however, when the letter contains obvious misspellings, strikeovers, or other typographical errors. While one channel in the manager's brain is trying to decipher the intended message, another is musing on the kind of secretarial help the sender employs. When misspellings have been hand corrected by the person who signed the letter, even further musings occur. The reader's second channel is feeling sorry for the letter's author, who obviously has poor secretarial help and doesn't have what it takes to get the work done right.

Most of us have multiple channels working at all times. On occasion it is difficult to "turn down the volume" on the second channel. When the second channel provocation is strong, the first channel gets turned off. Business plans can include many examples of second-channel provocations. They include illogical, disorganized, and overly wordy presentation. Poor English suggests poor communication skills. Misspellings and typographical errors are the results of negligence and carelessness. Inaccuracies display ineptitude.

In Chapter 8 the characteristics of successful entrepreneurs are described in detail. If you have them they will appear in the personality of your business plan. It would be unfortunate if the reader of the plan overlooked them because of second-channel provocation.

Balance refers to internal consistency. The reader weighs each new statement in the story against what has already been said and against the reader's knowledge and experience. When each seems to support and confirm the others, they are in balance. When a new statement seems to be in conflict with something said before, the scales tip precariously.

Consider the professional football placekicking specialist who claims the ability to put the ball through the goalposts eight out of every ten tries from the thirty-yard line. Is that credible? Would you bet money on it? Whether you are an avid fan of the game or not, you feel that a placekicker would not be on a professional football team with less than an eight out of ten record from the the thirty-yard line.

Suppose the same placekicking specialist claims an eight out of ten record from the fifty-yard line. Is that credible? Everyone knows that fifty yards is halfway down the football field. Would it seem reasonable that a player, even one on a professional team, could put the ball through the goalposts eight out of ten times from the middle of the field?

In these two situations we find the same highly competent individual. One is credible and the other is not.

A student from the local junior high school's varsity squad claims a placekicking record of eight out of ten from the thirty-yard line. Do you believe that? Do you feel a need to check the record before accepting that claim?

Here are two situations in which the circumstances are the same, but with different individuals. One is credible and the other is not.

There is a balance between what people believe they can do, no matter how genuinely they believe it, and what is statistically or realistically possible. The reader of a plan is continually balancing, consciously or unconsciously, the elements of the story against what the reader believes to be statistically or realistically possible. Whenever the reader runs into elements of the story about which he or she has no knowledge, the story must provide convincing evidence for the reader to put on the scales.

In the context of a business plan, three major elements weigh heavily in enhancing or denying credibility. They are

People
Market
Money

Consider the plan prepared by a 20-year-old with no management experience at all, facing tough and entrenched competition, projecting first-year sales of $3 million and asking for $1 million in start-up venture capital. There is no balance among any of the elements—people, market, and money.

Suppose a business plan describes a mature individual with twenty-five years of management experience, saturated with outstanding achievement, including building two other successful businesses in a related field, entering a virgin market and projecting first-year sales of $3 million. The entrepreneur claims to have devised a way to reduce the needed venture capital from $1 million to $250,000.

The balance is better here. At least the people part seems balanced and the market does not have entrenched competitors. But what of the money? Three million dollars in first-year sales and only $250,000 investment? Your gut, or your instincts, tell you that this requires more investigation. A financially oriented reader would immediately expect $500,000 to be needed for accounts receivable alone—sixty-day receivables at the end of the first year. Even with $1 million in capital, generating sales of $3 million in the first year from a standing start is cause for the comment, "That's incredible!"

Some key elements to be balanced would include the entrepreneur's experience, training, competence, and background. Others would be the size of the market, needs of the customers, and accessibility of the target market. Or the sales forecast, the financing required, and the profits that are possible. Or the size of the product and the number to be in inventory compared with the square feet in the proposed warehouse. Or the number of administrative and clerical employees compared with the proposed number of desks needed.

TRACK RECORD—CREDENTIALS

Thousands of years of lending experience have taught bankers that one of the best indications of a person's future behavior is that person's past behavior. The same concept shows up in all matters of personnel recruiting and selection. A professional person's resume, or anybody's job application form, attests to the general acceptance of this hypothesis.

The same thing shows up in the business plan. A person who has worked up the corporate ladder from stock clerk to president of a Fortune 500 company and performed brilliantly in that position has enormous credibility regardless of the other elements of the plan. The same is true, if to a lesser extent, of anyone who has a Nobel Prize, an honorary doctorate, a Pulitzer Prize, or an MBA from a prestigious university. Similarly, a person who has started and built three businesses to more than $25 million in annual sales has great credibility just because of this track record.

Credibility of the business plan is enhanced by the degree to which its author can acquire a track record or respectable, substantial credentials that are effectively related to the proposed business. This doesn't mean that you can't do something you haven't yet had the opportunity to try, like being president of a company. Nor does it imply that you need a college education. It suggests that, like the bankers considering a loan prospect, the busy investor reading your plan is looking for evidence of past behavior that will confirm your proposed behavior.

EVIDENCE OF INTEGRITY AND REALISM

In preparing a business plan you, the entrepreneur-author, make a statement of what you will do. The reader's reaction is to ask, "Do you do what you say you will do? Is it possible for you to do what you say you will do?" The reader is looking for data and evidence on which to make a judgment.

How do we judge today the likelihood of tomorrow's experience? Skillful investors, bankers, and suppliers instinctively feel comfortable making judgments of bigger importance based on small pieces of data. For instance, did you keep your appointment on time? Or did you arrive late and offer explanations and excuses? Successful entrepreneurs get there on time regardless of the traffic problems and the unforeseen event. They get to the building early, take a few minutes to compose themselves, and then walk into their appointment exactly on time.

When you ring your bank at 9:15 A.M., having promised to call at 9:00 A.M., don't be surprised to find that the banker spent the first five of the intervening fifteen minutes waiting for the phone to ring, then dismissed you as unreliable and became absorbed in more important business. Sophisticated and experienced investors and bankers have memories like vises. Little tidbits of data can come back to haunt you many years later.

In the business plan it is assumed that the author has verified the market statistics, checked the accuracy of the arithmetic, confirmed that all of the significant competitors have been identified, and done everything with thoroughness. If any single instance is found where that is not true, a cloud of doubt is cast over the entire plan. After all, the entire plan is what you say you will do.

Because a busy investor is looking for evidence of your integrity and realism, provide some. Don't let your enthusiasm and optimism in telling the story allow little flaws to creep in. Build in items that can be verified by observation and research and provide the information needed to make the observation or the research easy.

EASILY VERIFIABLE PERSONAL REFERENCES

In the business plan the entrepreneur-author is asking the busy investor to "trust me, believe me, place your money in my hands, and have faith in me." The same is being said to bankers, landlords, suppliers, employees, and customers. A prudent investor will want to talk to some people who have known you in the past to justify placing that much confidence in you. Any hint of difficulty in obtaining that information will cause apprehensions about finding it at all. When information concerning you is verified, but with qualifications, it is the qualifications the sophisticated investor will remember.

Knowing in advance that these things are happening and that these feelings are being evoked, the entrepreneur may want to take steps to improve the investor's confidence. For instance, your resume might say you graduated from MIT in 1975. Dial information and get MIT's number. Then call that number and ask if they would verify that the person named in your resume graduated from MIT in 1975. Do the same with an important former employer. Don't be surprised to find the record is not clear or not readily available or that the new employee with your old employer never heard of you. Clear the channels before asking someone to use them.

Although a single instance of inconsistency will put the entire business plan in doubt, only a few confirmations of facts give the entire plan credibility. Unfortunately, you don't know in advance which few facts, claims, or relationships will be checked. The only way to ensure that the plan is judged credible is to make it so in the first place.

4

Tips on Professional Presentation: Convincing Investors and Lenders

The manner in which a business plan is presented may have as much influence on its reader as the facts in it. As many messages may be conveyed by style and design as by the written words. The time and place chosen by the reader to examine the plan can effect the response to it. The successful entrepreneur will be concerned about the aesthetics of the plan document, the setting where it is to be received, and the circumstances in which it will be read.

Commercial real estate developers understand that to lease their property it must be appealing to the potential client. They include an attractive landscape design in their architectural planning. Professional chefs are as much concerned about the appearance of the dish they serve as about its taste.

Professional presentation takes into consideration some of the artistic and theatrical aspects of telling a convincing story. It may be true that you can't tell a book by its cover, but most books in the bookstore have a cover specifically created to help you make the purchase decision. Professional presentation considers the audience and provides every possible assistance to make the interaction with the plan and the entrepreneur a pleasant and satisfying experience.

MAKE THE PLAN EASY TO READ

Select a typewriter with a standard, businesslike type font. If the typewriter has interchangeable fonts, pick a typeface like some you have seen in professional business correspondence. Fancy, ornate, or unusual type styles, or type that is either too big or too small, presents a subtle impediment to ease of reading. Although calligraphy and early Gothic may be pretty, they are not what the eye is trained to interpret.

Use a standard, letter-size paper. Different sizes are standard in different countries. In the United States 8½ by 11 inches is standard in commerce. Being the standard size means that it is familiar in appearance and fits into standard binders, file folders, and the file drawers of standard office furniture. It also fits nicely into a standard-size briefcase.

Number the pages. The reader will probably make notes with questions to be asked later. Provide a system for easy reference to pages so the reader can locate the subject of a question or comment at some later time. It is not unlikely that two people will be discussing copies of the plan, perhaps over the telephone. A numbering system helps the parties identify the material they are discussing.

Provide ample borders on the sides, top, and bottom of the pages so the reader can make notes. Recognize that the plan will be a working document to an interested reader. Center the typed area in the space left after a binder is attached or holes are punched.

Use white space liberally. It adds to the aesthetic value of a page and makes it less intimidating. A report that has solid typing from border to border, top to bottom, creates the impression that reading it will be an unpleasant chore. Single-spaced or double-spaced typing is a matter of the author's choice, but recognize that a solid page of single-spaced typing is likely to appear forbidding.

Add eye appeal by changing the page layout. A single-spaced paragraph of about six lines extending from border to border might be followed by one, two, or more short columns of information or data. Titles on the left with text on the right for some segment of the story might add variety. There is no need to overdo layout change, but it may help you make the report more interesting to be aware of the possibilities.

Bind the plan in a simple but secure cover. Busy people in business travel frequently. They often read reports on airplanes and in hotel rooms. A plan in a convenient binder that slips neatly into a briefcase is more likely to make the trip.

Use a binder that locks in the contents. Some attractive binders only exert pressure to hold the pages together. Quite often the pressure of rough handling or accidental dropping is greater than that of the binder. Binders that secure the contents with holes in the paper are more likely to withstand normal use and occasional misuse.

Avoid bulky or heavy binders. A standard, three-ring binder may be very practical for many applications, but it takes up too much space to bind only twenty or thirty pages. If the reader of your plan has no other reports or plans to examine, perhaps the three-ring binder is suitable. If your reader has many three-ring binders to handle, you might want to choose something lighter.

We know a venture capital investor who examined a business plan and liked it but was unable to follow up with an investment. The entrepreneur had not included a name, address, place or phone number in the report. It is normal to place the identity of the writer on the first page inside the cover of a report or plan.

Wherever numbers in the plan can be associated with other numbers, check for accuracy. Some people are surprisingly adept at recognizing errors in arithmetic, as in adding a column of numbers. Typographical errors are more prevalent in numbers than in ordinary text.

Forecasts and projections involve a great many numbers. The opportunity for errors is ever-present. The numbers on the different forms of financial reports are interdependent. The income statement forecast, the cash flow projections, and the pro forma balance sheet all describe the same business entity. The figures presented in each must be consistent with those in the other two (see Chapter 37).

Typographical errors interfere with easy reading no matter where they are. Misspelling has the same detrimental effect. For some readers, grammatical errors cause consternation. There is no need to write with the correctness of a Ph.D. in English, but generally accepted English usage improves the smooth flow of communication.

LEGAL PRUDENCE

Be aware that delivering your business plan to a potential investor makes you subject to some fairly tough laws, the *securities laws*. They are often called the blue-sky laws. There is a securities law for each state in the United States and a federal securities law.

If you solicit investment only from residents of the state in which you will be, or are, operating the business, then you must satisfy the securities law of your state. When seeking investment from residents of other states you must satisfy the laws of those other states and the federal law simultaneously.

The securities laws are a very serious matter. Before showing your business plan to a potential investor, it would be prudent to discuss it with an attorney who has recent experience in securities law. He or she will provide guidelines for your use of the plan and will supply a *disclaimer* to be prominently displayed in it.

Keep control of all copies of the plan. A common practice is to use a library checkout system. An envelope pasted to the inside back cover can accommodate a 3-by-5-inch card, which can be used to identify who received a copy and when. Potential investors who choose not to invest should return their copies of the plan.

Chapter 30 discusses further the constraints placed on entrepreneurs and their business plans by governmental authorities. The free market economies of the Western world are only relatively free. There are still numerous regulations, and to ignore them or be unaware of them can cause problems later, when the business can least afford them.

PLAN YOUR PRESENTATION STRATEGY

The entrepreneur who has just completed a business plan usually can't wait to tell others about it. If there is no need for capital from investors, the purpose in presenting the plan is to discover any flaws in it. The questions raised and the opinions expressed help to refine the entrepreneur's grasp of the proposed endeavor. It is not unusual to find that the entrepreneur's concentration on preparing the document has caused some conspicuous facet of the endeavor to be overlooked.

If the plan is to be used as a means to obtain investment, the manner of its presentation becomes very important. Normally the first interaction with investors is a meeting in which the entrepreneur introduces the concept of the business. This may be a conversation with one or a small number of persons. If the potential investors are interested in pursuing it further, they will probably ask for a more elaborate presentation to some of their colleagues.

A presentation to one person sitting across the desk is quite different from a formal presentation to a group, where charts and graphs may be displayed. Between those extremes is a conference room with people seated around a large table.

When talking across a desk there is little opportunity to present exhibits other than standard stationery size, like pages from the business plan. But exhibits can be prepared in this size. People who are good at making presentations think through what they will say and how they will say it beforehand. They prepare exhibits to enhance their prepared remarks. A good interview seldom just happens. One of the parties prepares and makes it happen.

The conference table setting presents a greater challenge because you can't have continual eye contact with several people, some of whom may be sitting at your side, simultaneously. The challenge is to make the presentation lively and fast paced enough to maintain everybody's attention. It is easy to be sidetracked with premature questions before the overall story has been told. Unless an exhibit is needed to make a point, it is probably best to make the point first and then distribute the exhibit.

The more formal setting, where there are chalkboards or facilities for projecting exhibits on a screen, is probably the most interesting. The entrepreneur can prepare a lively story with professional-looking tables, charts, and pictures. Obviously, this presentation is not ad-lib. People who make this kind of presentation for a living, like big company contract proposal teams, rehearse their delivery many times.

When you pick up potential investors at the airport, your business plan presentation begins at the airline terminal. The drive to the plant or office needs to be pleasant and comfortable with a minimum of distractions. If lunch or dinner is to be included in the agenda your choice of location will be read as representative of your habits. It might be wise to reserve a table, preferably in a relatively quiet restaurant, and arrange for preferred service.

There is nothing wrong with staging the presentation. Better to use theatrical preparation than to have unforeseen events ruin the one chance you will get to win over a potential investor. Besides, if you can manage a great presentation it suggests that you are a good manager.

THE INVESTMENT DECISION

The venture capital investment decision is emotional. Chapter 32 illustrates how both the conscious and subconscious of the potential investor contribute to this decision. Facts, figures, and carefully laid plans provide part of the basis for the decision. Personal impressions gained from talking with the entrepreneur also provide some basis. In the end, the decision is based on the totality of interactions with the entrepreneur and the business plan. In the matter of presentation, no stone can be left unturned in an effort to influence the potential investor favorably.

5

The Plan as a Fluid Document

A business plan is a summary of how the enterprise would be built based on all of the information available at the time it was written. But circumstances change continually. New contacts emerge. Fresh data becomes available. The entrepreneur's perception improves. As time passes parts of the plan will change.

When the plan is shown to potential investors and lenders they will ask questions and provide opinions. This feedback may suggest ways to improve the plan or change the presentation to be more clear and responsive to their questions. An entrepreneur will want to incorporate his or her latest thinking into the plan before showing it to the next busy investor.

Knowing in advance that the plan may change suggests organizing it to make it easy to revise sections. Having lots of white space adds to the aesthetic quality of the presentation, but it also permits adding to or changing pages without renumbering the entire plan. Starting each major titled section at the top of a page may provide some space at the ends of sections for later revisions or additions.

Even if the plan is not going to be presented to strangers it should be viewed as subject to change. As the process of putting together the business proceeds, some of the best estimates will prove only partially correct. As more data emerges the plan should be reviewed and updated.

A plan is a guide. When an undertaking is complicated enough that you can't contain all the parts of it in your head, a written plan holds them for ready retrieval while you work on one or a few of them. But the parts interact. A change in one may affect others. The more complex the undertaking the more likely that a change in one part will have a ripple effect.

This is especially evident in the projections. As the actual figures are identified they have to be compared with the forecast figures. A series of small increases in expenses can easily add up to a significant number. Profit is a small percentage of the overall revenue or expense. A small change in either the overall revenue or expense can dramatically alter the profit.

Those who have used a detailed plan in building their business report that the greatest benefit came from revising the plan. After all the time and energy that went into preparing the plan in the first place they felt satisfaction and accomplishment. They had a heightened sense of self-confidence. But when they revised the plan on the basis of later data, they learned for the first time how the many parts of a business interact to produce a functioning whole. In fact, it is possible to improve your management of an enterprise you have never run before through this revision process.

Curiously, writing a plan does not in itself make the writer fully knowledgeable of its contents. While writing you concentrate on the parts. Once a part is written it is dismissed from your mind while another is completed. Even the writer of a plan must study it and work with it to become fully aware of what it says. For the entrepreneur, who will be bombarded with information, data, and new problems, the usefulness of the plan is increased when he or she internalizes its contents and can visualize the ripple effects of changes.

6

The Entrepreneur's
Launch Window

There are three principal components to success in the birth and growth of a new business. Each is constrained in time.

First, there must be a competent entrepreneur. The entrepreneur has a particular set of physical, mental, personality, behaviorial, and emotional characteristics. These, however, are not enough to identify a potentially successful entrepreneur. That person progresses along a career path. Sufficient experience and business skill need to be acquired to ripen the potential entrepreneur and prepare him or her for the adversity that will certainly arise in the business.

Second, there must be a viable business concept. A business concept is not a bright idea. It is a proposed series of transactions and behavior that can be described in terms of cost, space, equipment, labor, promotion, transportation, and all the items in the complete detailed financial report. It, too, is constrained by time, for to begin too soon may preclude success; to wait too long may deny it the opportunity to grow to a viable size. Changing technology and economic conditions are only two of many forces imposing time constraint.

Third, there must be access to adequate capital. Capital comes in many forms. One of the most important is the time and labor of the entrepreneur. Another is the credit extended by landlords, lawyers, accountants, and other suppliers. Eventually, however, there remains a need for some hard cold cash. It may be provided by the entrepreneur, friends and relatives, or professional purveyors of capital in the form of debt or equity. This access to capital, too, is constrained by time. Sometimes it is readily available. At other times there just isn't any.

These three components may be imagined as celestial bodies, like comets, wending their way through cosmic space. To create a new business, three different kinds of comets, each with a particular set of characteristics, must meet and combine in the vastness of the night sky. Unlikely as this meeting may seem, in the time and distance dimensions of the universe there is a finite probability that it has happened, is happening now, somewhere, and will happen again. If this analogy is compressed into the time and distance dimensions of the world in which we live, these wandering, dissimilar bodies would have a better chance of finding one another.

Such is the world of commerce. In different economies, different places, and different times, the conditions for the emergence of entrepreneurs, concepts, and capital wax and wane. At times the conditions produce an abundance of each and a cascade of entrepreneurial events that survive, thrive, and grow. And then there are times and places where the number of events is minimal.

In this context it is less difficult to grasp the cause of the disheartening business mortality rate. It is also possible to conceive of a means to improve the odds of success. This analogy may be used for a pictorial representation of where to position yourself to increase the probability of winning, how to put yourself in a position to be lucky.

COMPONENT ONE: THE ENTREPRENEUR

The first component is a particular kind of person. This, of course, assumes that not everybody is, or can become, one of these people. In some egalitarian circles this thought may be repugnant, but the observation is not made to exclude anyone. It is a recognition of the fact that among the many people in any population there is a veritable rainbow of talents, aptitudes, and means to self-satisfaction.

In every population there is some small percentage of people who want full responsibility, accountability, and the freedom to choose the course of their destiny. Likewise, there is a percentage who would abhor that life. We may think of those who desire responsibility as blessed or cursed, depending on our perspective. There is no need to judge the right or wrong of the personality with which they find themselves. They just are that way.

Entrepreneurs are people whose presence is clearly evident in the setting of an entrepreneurial event. They stand out like the man at the baseball field's pitcher's mound. If they are that different from those about them, there should be some words to describe them, to indicate their differences from, and perhaps their similarities to, the general population.

Although people may be equipped with all the characteristics of the entrepreneur, they change with time. Certainly the entrepreneur as a child is not ready to create an entrepreneurial event. Nor is the entrepreneur in the twilight of life likely to start a business. The leader of a new business would be a responsible adult with adequate experience to make judgments to the benefit of the business. The entrepreneur has to complete some maturing before beginning.

On the other hand, if that person waits too long, other constraints may arise that would diminish the probability of winning. Some

29

of these might be family responsibility or commitment to a work activity that is emotionally and intellectually consuming.

COMPONENT TWO: THE BUSINESS CONCEPT

The second component describes a business concept that has a chance of winning its niche in the marketplace. Business concepts have characteristics that can be identified and classified.

In the developed countries of the twentieth century the artifacts of civilization are too numerous to be listed. Technology is growing at a startling rate. Each new increment of scientific knowledge and engineering capability produces whole families of artifacts not known to our parents, never mind to our more distant ancestors. Opportunities to create and produce new products and services abound.

But with the diversity of products and services offered comes greater diversity of choices available to the consumers. Some products may strike the fancy of a great many consumers; others will find few people who prefer them to the alternatives available. Variety in choice creates competition among the producers to gain the attention and the affection of the consumers who, in the end, decide the life or death of each new artifact made available in commerce.

The terms used to characterize a business concept must relate the concept to the perceptions of consumers. The chance to win in the marketplace must match the qualities of the product or service and the perceptions of value held by consumers. These perceptions of value will change with time. Each decade seems characterized by different values. The press characterizes decades with titles such as the Roaring Twenties or the Gay Nineties. Some decades are more somber, as the 1930s; some witness great changes in moral values, as the 1960s. A product or service that might succeed in one decade could be a total failure in another.

Technology and manufacturing capability place stringent time constraints on any particular product or service concept. Electronic banking or the multiple-listing service provided by realtors could not have emerged until communication, computer, and printing technologies could permit mass production of their artifacts at prices within the reach of a great many people. At the other end of a product or service life is its replacement by newer technologies. Who could successfully market mechanical adding machines once electronic calculators became available at a price within the reach of children?

COMPONENT THREE: ACCESS TO VENTURE CAPTIAL

The third component is venture capital available to an entrepreneur who already has a business concept, both of which are in that state of readiness that enhances their probability for succeeding in the marketplace.

Venture capital is cash placed at the disposal of an entrepreneur to start or build a business. Because of business mortality statistics, it might better be called *adventure capital*.

If potential investors know you very well, trust you, or love you, they may be willing to help you in an endeavor that they comprehend only slightly. Their affection for you may induce them to provide financial support without seriously considering the investment nature of their action. This is usually the case in the earliest stages of financing a new business, when venture capital is seldom available from professional investors but comes from relatives and friends.

Even friends and family cannot provide financial help if they do not have an excess of idle cash. When Uncle George has just sold the farm and paid the taxes, he may be magnanimous in helping a promising niece or nephew. If Mother has just lost a third of her assets in that blue-ribbon mutual fund, it isn't likely she would help her daughter. The same is true for dispassionate venture capital investors. When they are "invested up" and have no liquid assets, they can't invest. On the other hand, when they have just cashed in their chips on an outstanding investment they may be seeking a new opportunity.

Access to venture capital depends on the availability of the cash and the investor's intimate knowledge of the entrepreneur. Only intimate knowledge breeds trust sufficient to move people to part with their cash on your behalf. Professional investors gain this knowledge by prolonged investigation. Uncle George and Mother have watched the baby become a promising and responsible adult.

There is, in the nature of this relationship, one time constraint related to the entrepreneur's maturity and another that waxes and wanes with the economic fortunes of the potential investors. If this component to the success of a new enterprise were portrayed pictorially, it, too, would be like a projectile passing through a region in which it may be effective.

THE LAUNCH WINDOW

If these three components were portrayed as lines having segments identifying the period in time when they are ripe, so to speak, they might be viewed as the three axes or coordinates of a time-space. The entrepreneur might be viewed as rising along the vertical axis. The business concept might be viewed as passing to the right on the horizontal axis, and the entrepreneur's access to venture capital might be portrayed as perpendicular to these two axes.

Each of the axes would have a short segment indicating its time of usefulness in contributing to the success of a new business. If the three beginning points were shown at the origin of the axes, then these time segments would circumscribe a cube. If the entrepreneur, the business concept, and access to venture capital were located within this cube, the three components would be meeting when each is ready to create an

31

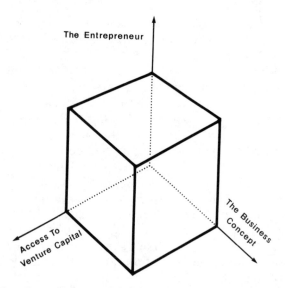

The Entrepreneur

Access To Venture Capital

The Business Concept

FIGURE 6-1 The Three-Dimensional Launch Window for a Successful Entrepreneurial Business.

entrepreneurial event. Figure 6-1 portrays this entrepreneur's launch window.

This picture implies that if aspiring entrepreneurs could position themselves within such a cube they would greatly increase the probability of succeeding in the attempt to create a new business. To do so, they would have to understand the three components, be able to identify the position of themselves and their business concept along these time lines, and then time the launching of their new business within the cube.

Having worked with this concept for many years, we are convinced that a new business born within this cube has a much greater probability for survival and growth than the mass of new business start-ups which have contributed to the statistics on failure.

Recognizing the cube and placing yourself within it requires planning. The effort to identify your position requires gathering much data, analyzing it, and improving your position to move into the cube. The result is a clearer picture of where you are, where you are going, and how you are going to get there. Also, the analysis is of sufficient magnitude that the tendencies to gloss over important facts or to be superficial are reduced. The components are more than a recipe or questionnaire. They require thought, study, and scheming. They engage those learning circuits of your gray matter.

CRITICAL SKILL

One more aspect to starting and operating a business needs special attention. It has been mentioned as part of the entrepreneur's preparation and maturing, but it is more than that. It is crucial to success in managing the new enterprise as well as in the planning process. It is the management skill of describing business operations with numbers. This skill permits you to visualize future financial results of present management actions.

Bookkeepers and accountants communicate reasonably clearly with each other. Sometimes, however, they are so intent on the exactness of their art that they are unable to state their thoughts in the lay language of the owner-manager. Their training is dominated by the perspectives of tax planning, auditing, and the sophistication attributed to the "big eight" accounting firms examining the records of the Fortune 500 corporations.

The focal point of this miscommunication lies in their portrayal of the conditions and operations of the business with a historical income statement and balance sheet, often prepared only annually. The owner-manager's perspective requires a portrayal of the future, not the past, and a focus on liquidity, not return on investment. Portraying the future operations of the business in terms of profit, a mathematical concept, and in terms of cash down at the bank, a very tangible asset, provides two entirely different pictures. A business survives or dies with that hard tangible asset. It can exist a surprisingly long time with no profit.

Understanding this difference between profit and cash flowing into the bank, and being able to portray the future operations of the business in terms of each, is a critical skill for aspiring entrepreneurs. Without it, positioning themselves within the cube is merely putting themselves in a position to be lucky. With it they control and direct their fledgling enterprise and capitalize on positioning to manage their future.

To be your own boss you have to put it all together yourself. To put it all together you need all the parts. For a beginner, it helps to know what the parts are and how you get them. The remainder of this book describes the major parts. For your unique business you have to learn many other things. No matter how detailed and descriptive we are, you will run into situations we didn't cover. But the framework of the cube will give you the alphabet and the arithmetic. You can write your own story and count your own blessings.

7

Entrepreneurs
Are Different

Entrepreneurs are outstanding individuals. Why else would they be identified with such a distinctive word? Like many other words, however, the term is frequently used without being precise about its meaning. To some people the word *entrepreneur* conjures up images of a tall man on a black horse wearing a black shirt and black hat. To others it conjures images of a person who makes things happen, puts it all together, overcomes great odds. To still others the word connotes one who simply does things differently from the rest of us.

DEFINING ENTREPRENEUR

In France the word *entrepreneur* is used to denote the owner of a very small business, someone who employs five or fewer people. The English language provides a broader meaning. The protagonist in the Horatio Alger stories is thought of as an entrepreneur. People who start and operate their own businesses are thought of as entrepreneurs. Many attach the name to people who are doers and achievers.

We were surprised one day when explaining why a particular entrepreneur was unable to make a viable business out of the resources available in the face of obstacles surrounding the situation. Our listener said, "But isn't that what entrepreneurs do?" We later found that this attitude is unexpectedly common. It is the presumption that entrepreneurs are people who overcome all obstacles. Entrepreneurs, however, are not magicians. They may appear to overcome great obstacles, but it must be granted that there are situations in which even an entrepreneur cannot put it all together.

In new entrepreneurial businesses it is very clear which individual is running the show. Someone is leading and the leader is directing the decision making. Leadership is characterized by style and charisma. Some successful entrepreneurs have much charisma and great

34

style in management. Others have little of either. Directing the endeavor, by whatever style, seems closer to describing the activity of the person who stands out in an entrepreneurial endeavor.

You don't need to be near an entrepreneurial event for very long, before you can identify the entrepreneur. One individual is making the decisions, is aware of all that is going on, and is the person to whom everyone else turns for direction. Whether he or she is soft spoken or outspoken that individual's presence and dominance is clearly evident. The conclusion is quickly drawn that entrepreneurs are different. Being that different, they must have a set of identifiable characteristics.

THE ORIGINS OF A LIST OF ENTREPRENEURIAL CHARACTERISTICS

Many lists of characteristics of entrepreneurs have been proposed. Some are very long and contain many adjectives. All too many of these are superficial. We have felt a need to seek a reasonably short list of fundamental characteristics that we hope will describe a personality and provide a profile that will remain consistent as the entrepreneur travels through life. Such a list emerged a few years ago from a study by an outstanding entrepreneur in collaboration with his company's industrial psychologist.

In 1946 there were two brothers working for the DuPont Company in Wilmington, Delaware.[1] They had been raised on a chicken ranch in El Paso, Texas, and migrated to New York, where both received their Ph.D.s in chemistry from Columbia University. Both were doing very well in their employment, working with agricultural pesticides. Both, however, longed to return to their native Texas.

At a New Year's Eve party the brothers were discussing their possible return. When asked what they would do for a living, they glibly responded they would start their own business. As the party wore on the conclusion that they would move to Texas and start their own business grew from that glib statement to a serious intent.

During the ensuing months their concept grew. In reading chemical reports the brothers learned of a new pesticide that controlled lice on poultry. From their knowledge of raising chickens, they knew that this new chemical would cut by 50 percent the time spent by poultry farmers in controlling lice. In June, six months after that fateful New Year's Eve party, they resigned from DuPont, leaving the field for which they had spent seven years preparing themselves.

The brothers opened a partnership with the savings they had ($2,000) and called it Agricultural Specialties. It was later incorporated under the name Thuron Industries, a word extracted from the first names of the brothers, Thurmond and Byron. Thurmond was the more conservative and introspective; the presidency fell to Byron.

Their concept of a poultry insecticide was viable. Sales expanded, and larger volume products were added. With every available penny directed toward producing profits, the business survived and became an ongoing success.

After ten years the business was doing extremely well. Sales were up, profits were good, the business had grown to over one hundred employees, and all the outward signs of success were clearly evident. But something was wrong. There was turmoil and turnover among the employees. Despite the success of the business there was dissatisfaction and excessive bickering and griping. Time required to handle these problems was reducing the time available for productive work.

At this point Byron Williamson invited an experienced consultant in business organization to examine the company and tell him what could be the trouble. As Byron describes it, the consultant arrived on the site and for two days interviewed the managers reporting to the president and numerous other employees. When finished, the consultant presented the results to Byron. After reviewing what had been done, who had been interviewed, and what had been found, the consultant presented the conclusion, stating, "Dr. Williamson, there is nothing wrong with your business. The problem, sir, is you."

You would think such a conclusion might jeopardize the consultant's fee. You might expect that short of anything else the consultant would be dismissed along with the report. This was not the case, however. Byron calmly replied, "Tell me about it."

What Byron had run into turns out to have been a classic experience of many successful entrepreneurs. While struggling to build their business they and their people enjoy the thrill and excitement of putting it all together, hardly noticing the inconvenience and turmoil in the face of what they perceive to be their achievement. As the business grows and more people are employed, it becomes necessary to structure an organization. Classically, when the organization assumes a management structure, the entrepreneurial style of management is insufficient for the task.

The consultant's reply to "Tell me about it" was, "You must learn more about how your behavior affects your people and make some changes, or you should sell this company and start a new one."

The reaction of the brothers to this news was to follow the consultant's advice—they explored both options. They checked out possible buyers for the company, and Byron enrolled in a course for behavioral change designed for company presidents.

Six months later the decision was made. Byron's experience with behavioral change had been positive. The company was not sold. Byron shared his experiences with the managers. Similar personal learning experiences were offered to them, at company expense, if and when they were interested. The movement spread. Considering the people along with the profits became a cornerstone of the company's philosophy, which they called "Partnership for Profits."

During this phase of the company's progress, a firm of industrial psychologists was employed on a permanent basis to help employees throughout the company.[2] The firm's representative to Thuron was Dr. James C. Hörger.

Dr. Hörger became intimately acquainted with Byron's psychological makeup. He was equally acquainted with other entrepreneur-clients. Byron had similar acquaintances. Most of Thuron's direct customers were businesses founded and operated by single individuals—entrepreneurs. Byron had spent ten years or more with these owners, in their businesses, in their homes, traveling, and he came to know them intimately. This circle of acquaintances provided the basis for a study undertaken years later.

In 1970 Thuron was sold, and in 1971 Byron joined the business faculty at Southern Methodist University. In this new position he surveyed the existing literature on the behavior and characteristics of entrepreneurs. Then, with the participation of Dr. Hörger, a list of characteristics common to successful entrepreneurs was developed. It originally numbered ten. When studies were begun on "unsuccessful entrepreneurs," an eleventh characteristic was added. These characteristics have come to be known as the "Profile of the Successful Entrepreneur."

Our work with Williamson and Hörger and their studies of the entrepreneur has convinced us that their set of characteristics is valid, useful, and fundamental. Their conclusions although derived independently, build on the extensive work of David McClelland[3] and of Collins, Moore, and Unwalla,[4] as well as the work by students and colleagues of McClelland and the many serious efforts in this direction by other researchers.

HOW MANY ENTREPRENEURIAL INDIVIDUALS ARE THERE?

In the general population few individuals stand out as clearly recognizable entrepreneurs, although a larger number of people stand out as being like entrepreneurs. We have chosen to identify the characteristics of those individuals who are clearly entrepreneurs. All others are viewed as entrepreneurlike to a greater or lesser extent.

It would be helpful to have some sense of what percent of the population would be included among these entrepreneurs and entrepreneurlike people who could be expected to succeed in starting or building a business.

The Internal Revenue Service receives about 15 million business income tax returns annually.[5] Obviously, some of these businesses are very large. On the American and New York stock exchanges, approximately 3,500 companies' stocks are publicly traded. In the over-the-counter market stocks from approximately 5,000 companies are actively traded. Further, there are many substantial firms whose stock is not traded in the public market, but there is no indication that this number is larger than the number whose stock is traded.

The smallest company in the list of Fortune 1,000 largest corporations in America has sales of about $100 million, although inflation may change this within the decade. Many of the companies traded in the over-the-counter market have sales of less than $10 million. This suggests that there may be 10,000–20,000 big businesses among those that file income tax returns. By subtraction, there are still far in excess of 14 million small businesses.

We cannot leap to the conclusion that there are in excess of 14 million entrepreneurial businesses. However, small businesses do tend to be entrepreneurial. Census data claims that more than 98 percent of all businesses in the United States have annual sales of less than $1 million.[6] These small organizations tend to be owner-managed and entrepreneurial.

These figures include about 2.5 million independent farmers.[7] When they are excluded, the total number of independent small businesses in the United States is still in excess of 12 million.

In the present age distribution of the United States population 50 percent are between 18 and 65 years of age. In a total population of 220 million about 110 million adults have not yet reached retirement age. If there are approximately 12 million small businesses in this country, and approximately 110 million adults, then we must conclude that more than 10 percent of the population is already engaged in an occupation that would identify them as entrepreneurs or entrepreneurlike businesspeople.

It is interesting to speculate on the number of people who have the characteristics of entrepreneurs but are not yet in business. For instance, since until recently women have been discouraged from starting and operating their own businesses, half of the adult population with entrepreneurial characteristics may not yet have displayed them. This could imply that approximately 10 percent of the 55 million adult women less than 65 years of age have entrepreneurial characteristics. If those 5.5 million people were in business for themselves we would find that more than 15 percent of the population could be entrepreneurs.

This may be weak evidence upon which to draw a conclusion, but we believe that about 15 percent represents the portion of Americans who have sufficient entrepreneurial characteristics to include them among the entrepreneurs and the entrepreneurlike. What little evidence is available from foreign populations suggests that this percentage is a reasonable approximation for every population, except where cultural taboos and social mores preclude the development of such aspirations.

By choosing to define the entrepreneur as we have done, it is possible to identify a few individuals and study them in depth. Their characteristics may then serve as a reference when examining the characteristics of the large population of people who have started and built a business. This provides a more firm basis on which to consider the characteristics of people who have not yet started a business, but hope to. It may, possibly, help to inform some that they have the characteristics, and hence the potential, for an entrepreneurial career. And it may forewarn some who aspire to such a career that they are not likely to find satisfaction in that choice.

8

How Entrepreneurs
Are Different

Entrepreneurs who start glamourous businesses which grow rapidly and become listed on the New York Stock Exchange within five years are clearly outstanding individuals. They are also stand-out individuals. In the setting of the new business they don't need a name tag to identify them. They are readily identifiable by their presence. They are at the hub of the activity and they are very obviously in charge.

Proprietors of small businesses are like these outstanding individuals, but to a lesser extent. It is easier to see the similar characteristics in the proprietors once you know what you are looking for. With very outstanding entrepreneurs it is less difficult to identify the characteristics.

The successful entrepreneur whose profile follows is an individual who is clearly the leader in the setting of an entrepreneurial event.[1] The individuals studied to determine these characteristics had each started an ongoing business where none existed before. Each had achieved sales of more than one million dollars per year, had been in business at least five years, and showed all the signs of an ongoing business which could be expected to continue for at least another five years.

These characteristics do not predict that a person is, or is not, going to be a successful entrepreneur, but they are found to be common among the successful entrepreneurs examined. It would seem reasonable to suggest that a person having these characteristics has a probability of success in proportion to the degree to which they are present. Chapter 6 described how these characteristics are only one out of several criteria indicating probability of success for an entrepreneurial event.

As with any list of short titles there is the danger that this list will be used in place of what it is meant to identify. The titles alone are not sufficient to describe what they represent. They are memory joggers, tools to help order our thoughts. The understanding of these characteristics is in the text, not the title.

40

We have attached no scale to these characteristics. We are firmly convinced that any short list of true-false questions or any of the myriad of "test yourself" questionnaires so popular in the media are inadequate. The existence of the characteristics and the degree to which they exist in any individual can be most reliably determined by an in-depth, structured interview by an experienced and trained psychologist.

It is useful to know about the characteristics. After working with entrepreneurs and entrepreneurlike individuals, lay people can become adept at recognizing positive or negative symptoms of these traits. For investment purposes, however, including the intent to invest your own time and money in a new business venture of your own, we would suggest engaging the services of a professional before drawing conclusions.

THE PROFILE OF THE SUCCESSFUL ENTREPRENEUR

1. <u>Good Health.</u> Successful entrepreneurs are physically resilient and free of illness. They are able to work for extended periods of time. Entrepreneurs in the throes of building their businesses seem to deny themselves the luxury of illness and will themselves well. Successful entrepreneurs who have suffered chronic health problems, such as hay fever, often report that the symptoms disappeared when they started building their own businesses. It appears that psychosomatic symptoms are also suppressed by concentration on achieving business success.

In a small business where there is no depth of management, the leader must be there. In a starting business there is never sufficient revenue to support the staff needed for all the business functions that must be filled. In lieu of paying others to fill the functions, entrepreneurs fill them with personal effort over extended hours. The work is relentless. The entrepreneur almost never gets sick.

We all know people who utilize at least part of their sick leave each year. We all know people who every year come down with sneezes and sniffles of some sort for three to five days that keep them in bed and out of work. The successful entrepreneurs are not found among this group. Entrepreneurs may have colds and headaches, but they will not allow themselves to admit it. More than that, at the end of the eight-hour day, when their employees return home, the entrepreneur typically continues to work either at the office or at home for nearly another eight hours so that all that must be accomplished for the survival of the business will be completed in time.

We conducted a series of sixty-four seminars over a four-year period in which distinguished entrepreneurs were asked to tell an audience candidly how they did it. At the conclusion of these sessions each entrepreneur was asked to list, in his or her own words, the characteristics essential to success in an entrepreneurial career. Curiously, among

41

the first four characteristics mentioned by every one of these distinguished entrepreneurs was good health.

2. <u>A Basic Need to Control and Direct</u>. Entrepreneurs do not function well in traditional structured organizations. They do not want authority over them. They believe they can do the job better than anyone. They need maximum responsibility and accountability. It is a need for freedom to initiate the action that they see as necessary. It is not a need for power, especially not a need for power over people. They enjoy creating and executing strategies. They thrive on the process of achieving. Goals achieved are superceded by greater goals. They see the future in their life as within their control and they strive to exert their influence over future events.

In a large structured organization you will recognize these people by their statements, such as "If they wanted that job done right they would give it to me and *leave me alone.*" You may also hear them say, "As long as *they* are running this job, it will never get anywhere." Entrepreneurs behave as if they believe that they are at least as smart as their peers and certainly smarter than their superiors.

It is our conviction that this characteristic is primary and dominant in the behavior of entrepreneurs. They have a compelling need to do their own thing in their own way. They need the freedom to choose and to act in accordance with their own perception of what choices and action will result in achievement.

Entrepreneurs just don't fit well in a highly structured environment. They are often referred to as mavericks. It is not unusual to find that they have changed jobs frequently. When a large number of entrepreneurs are asked about the circumstances surrounding their decision to start their own business, it is surprising how frequently they say they quit their job that morning knowing they were going to be fired that afternoon.

3. <u>Self-Confidence.</u> Entrepreneurs are ebulliently self-confident in what they believe possible when they are in control. They tackle problems immediately and directly. So long as they are in control they are persistent in their pursuit of objectives. They are at their best in the face of adversity. Conversely, with loss of control, their involvement and constructive participation diminishes.

Entrepreneurs who are starting, building, or running their own business exude self-confidence. Curiously, a small gain in control seems to result in a large increase in self-confidence while a small loss of control seems to result in an unduly large loss in confidence that a shared objective can be achieved. Entrepreneurs are very self-confident in what they can accomplish when doing it themselves, but they have an uncomfortable feeling working as a team member. Loss of control seems to result in frustration, and sometimes anger. Greater control seems to result in greater direct action and the appearance of greater self-confidence.

Several years ago we had a number of interviews with MBA candidates nearing the end of their educational experience. Each entered the office with downcast eyes and a dejected demeanor. Each said, "They told me to take those courses," followed by, "They want me to get an interview and a job." "They" remained some undisclosed third party. The next statement was, "I know how to get an interview and a job." And there the communication stopped. They were not able to say what they wanted or why they were visiting our office.

In each instance, these students were in their late twenties, had built successful businesses in real estate, and then lost their businesses in the 1973–1974 recession. Each had returned to school to learn how to do it right the next time. But now each was being ushered into the typical career path of graduating MBA students. The result was serious depression.

After some discussion it became clear that these people, each in his or her own way and own time, had displayed the characteristics of the succesful entrepreneur. They had lost their business success because of the economic downturn. And they had submitted themselves to the traditional structure of the university in search of some explanation for their loss and some guidance for their future. Now they were being faced with submission to a larger and more lasting structure in a corporation.

With each of these individuals we discussed the characteristics described here, particularly the need for control and its relationship to self-confidence. In each case the students seemed to grasp quickly their personal position and its implications. Every one of them decided not to listen to advice about interviews and jobs, but to get back out into the world they knew best and do their entrepreneurial thing again. Each left the office with chin high and a smile of self-confidence on his or her face. They finished their MBA program with internships, independent studies and other nonstructured courses. And they felt good about themselves and the world about them.

4. Never-Ending Sense of Urgency. Entrepreneurs seem to have a never-ending sense of urgency to do something. Inactivity makes them impatient, tense, and uneasy. When in control, and especially when building their enterprises, they seem to thrive on activity and achievement.

Entrepreneurs are not likely to be found sitting on a creek bank fishing unless the fish are biting furiously. They may enjoy fishing, but while in the entrepreneurial mode, that is, while in charge and trying to accomplish something, they are more likely to be found getting things done.

Entrepreneurs usually prefer individual sporting activities, for instance, golf or tennis, over team sports. You may often find them to be downhill skiers. Entrepreneurs prefer a game in which their brawn and brain directly influence the outcome and the pace of activity. They don't

43

seem to enjoy waiting for the fish to bite or for the rest of the team to pass the ball in their direction.

These people usually have a high energy level. They are frequently characterized as having drive. They have an achievement orientation and a constant, uninterrupted pattern of behavior toward that achievement. They seem tireless in the pursuit of the goals they have set for themselves.

5. Comprehensive Awareness. Successful entrepreneurs have a general overview of the entire situation when they plan, make decisions, and work in specific areas. They have a constant awareness of the effect of a single event upon the whole undertaking. They have distant vision and simultaneously an awareness of important specific immediate detail. They are continuously aware of the possibilities and alternatives.

Entrepreneurs maintain their distant vision but they devote their energy to the step immediately before them. They see the distant mountain, but they concern themselves with the creek in front of them. They are not confused about seeing the forest for the trees.

An illustration of this characteristic is seen in the treatment of the monthly financial report. The accountant and the accounting staff spend hours balancing the accounts and closing them out. The achievement, for them, is to have balanced the books and demonstrated that fact with the delivery of the Balance Sheet. The entrepreneur, on the other hand, wants to know generally what the order of magnitude of the numbers came out to be and their *significance* to the business operations, and that is enough.

6. Realistic. Entrepreneurs accept things as they are and deal with them that way. They may or may not be idealistic, but they are seldom unrealistic. They want to know the status of things at all times. They want to measure and be measured. News is neither good nor bad so long as it is timely and factual. They seek firsthand, personal verification of data, often bypassing organizational structure. They deal with people the way they deal with functions and things. They say what they mean and assume everyone else does too. They are good to their word. Honesty and integrity flow from this characteristic.

Entrepreneurs are persistent in pursuing their goal but realistic enough to change their direction when they see that change will improve their prospects for achievement. They are able to handle a lack of structure and organization. They are comfortable in what appears to others as chaos. They can accept a disarray of information for what it is, information.

When someone makes a statement, entrepreneurs accept the statement at face value. In the same manner, when entrepreneurs make a statement they assume it will be accepted as stated. During our distinguished entrepreneur seminars another of the first four characteristics mentioned by each entrepreneur as needed for success was *integrity*.

This characteristic sometimes gets entrepreneurs in trouble. They are often surprised to find that some of the people they deal with say one thing and actually mean something else. Contrary to the image frequently attributed to them, they are often overly trusting and not sufficiently suspicious in their business dealings.

7. Superior Conceptual Ability. Entrepreneurs possess that peculiar raw intellectual ability to identify relationships among functions and things quickly in the midst of complex and confused situations. They identify the problem and begin working on the solution faster than other people around them. They are not troubled by what appears to be ambiguity and uncertainty because they perceive order. They are accepted as leaders because they are usually the first to identify the problem to be overcome. This conceptual ability applies primarily to functions and things; it does not often appear when inter-personal problems need resolution.

Superior conceptual ability is not the same thing as high IQ or education. It is an ability to relate functions and things in seemingly complicated and confusing situations. Being realistic, entrepreneurs accept an array of disorganized information and find no discomfort with it. Having a comprehensive awareness enhances this ability.

In the entrepreneurial mode entrepreneurs seem to be extremely clear in describing their immediate goals and how they will be achieved. If it is pointed out to them that their means to achieve a goal is precluded for some reason, they will almost instantaneously enunciate an alternative means to achieve the same goal with the same precision and confidence they used for the newly abandoned means. Their achievement orientation and their problem-solving ability overwhelm obstacles.

8. Low Need for Status. Successful entrepreneurs find satisfaction in symbols of success that are external to themselves. They like the business they have built to be praised but are often embarrassed by praise directed toward them as individuals. Their status needs are satisfied by achievements rather than clothes, office decor, or the automobiles they drive. Their egos do not preclude their seeking facts, data, and guidance. They don't hesitate to say, "I don't know," especially in areas outside their own expertise where they are not expected to know.

During the period of struggle for survival and growth, successful entrepreneurs concentrate their resources and energies on essential expenditures for productive assets. They want to be where the action is and do not often find this in an office. It is not unusual to find the entrepreneur's office moved frequently. Likewise, in entrepreneurial enterprises, the organization chart is changed frequently. Entrepreneurs' focus is on the relationship between functions and things and toward achievement. Symbols of achievement and position seem to have little relevance to them.

The significance of these characteristics may be overlooked by

45

casual observers. As will be discussed later in this book, a business consumes all available assets faster than it can produce them when it is growing rapidly. In starting and building a business rapid growth is essential to achieve the size needed for stability and equilibrium. During this period of growth the entrepreneur with high status needs will misuse the meager resources available. Successful entrepreneurs find their satisfaction for status needs in the performance of the business, not in the appearance they as individuals present to their peers and the public.

9. Objective Approach to Interpersonal Relationships. Entrepreneurs are more concerned with people's accomplishments than with their feelings. They generally avoid becoming interpersonally involved. They keep themselves at a distance psychologically. They don't hesitate to sever relationships to help them progress toward established goals. During the period of building the business when resources are scarce, they seldom devote time or assets to satisfying people's feelings beyond what is essential to achieving operational effectiveness and efficiency.

As the business grows and assumes some management structure, entrepreneurs go through a management crisis so predictable that it is classic. Their need for control and its associated relationship to self-confidence make it nearly impossible to divest the authority required by a structured organization. Their strong, realistic approach induces them to seek information directly from its source, bypassing the structured chains of authority and responsibility. And their apparent lack of sensitivity to people's feelings often causes turmoil and turnover in the organization.

Successful entrepreneurs drive themselves and their organizations, think clearly, and are usually mentally ahead of their associates. They are impatient and just don't have the tolerance and empathy necessary for team-building interpersonal behavior. They run their own show and delegate very few key decisions. They choose experts rather than friends for associates.

This is not to say that good interpersonal skills are detrimental to the entrepreneur. As the organization grows and there is a greater need for management, the entrepreneur with better interpersonal skills will survive longer as the manager. Most entrepreneurs, however, seem to have only moderate interpersonal skills. Before a new organization has assumed a structure, moderate interpersonal skills are adequate.

10. Sufficient Emotional Stability. Entrepreneurs have considerable self-control and are able to handle the anxieties and pressures of the business and other problems in life. In stress situations having to do with functions and things, entrepreneurs are cool and effective. They are challenged rather than discouraged by setbacks or failure, but this does not extend to problems involving people's feelings. Entrepreneurs tend to handle these problems by suggesting an action plan. This is seldom perceived as addressing the "feeling" problem.

Entrepreneurs frequently have strong emotional feelings and reactions. They are able, however, to control these at least to the degree necessary to achieve success in their entrepreneurial enterprise.

Where people are concerned, entrepreneurs' superior conceptual ability with functions and things, moderate interpersonal skills, and emotional stability are often inadequate to provide a warm and reasonably stable relationship. On the other hand, in our experience and contrary to some published reports, the divorce rate among successful entrepreneurs is no higher than that for people in general. One published study reports only half as many divorces among successful entrepreneurs as in the general population.[2]

Entrepreneurs appear to vent their frustrations in achievements involving functions and things. It is not unusual to find that when things are going well entrepreneurs are uncomfortable and dissatisfied. They will frequently stir up something new, some activity on which they can vent their pent-up energy. They are not content to leave well enough alone.

11. Attraction to Challenges, Not Risks. Entrepreneurs are neither high nor low risk takers. They prefer situations in which they can influence the outcome. They are highly motivated by a challenge in which they perceive the odds to be interesting, but not overwhelming. They seldom act until they have assessed the risk. In one sense, they may appear to take great risk. They play for high stakes. In entrepreneurland, all personal assets are at stake until the business becomes a very substantial enterprise.

Entrepreneurs are often thought of in terms of the risk they assume. Even the dictionary describes an *entrepreneur* as one who assumes the risk of business. Like all prudent businesspeople, however, entrepreneurs know that high risking is gambling, not business. They are not gamblers. Entrepreneurs calculate their risks. In fact, they will sometimes appear to be inactive or coasting for extended periods of time. They act only after they have convinced themselves that little if any risk remains in the endeavor.

The characteristics found to be dominant in entrepreneurs enables them to succeed at a "risk level" at which others would fail. They are realistic, persistent, make sense out of complexity and they are confident in the face of adversity. These are traits which carry them on to success where others would be confused and disillusioned, and would give up and quit.

THE COMPOSITE PROFILE OF CHARACTERISTICS

Some successful entrepreneurs lack one or more characteristics. They will usually have someone influencing their judgment who is strong in the characteristics in which the entrepreneur is weak. This individual

47

may be a partner or a member of the management team. On occasion, this individual is found on the board of directors or among the investors. There are instances when the individual is a mentor, totally divorced from the business, such as a minister, priest, or rabbi. Sometimes this person is a spouse or a relative. On occasion there may even be more than one such individual.

There will very likely be competent, experienced production, marketing, administration, and finance people on the functional management team. They, too, may influence the entrepreneur's management decisions, but these individuals are subordinates on the team. Their advice cannot be perceived by the entrepreneur as decreasing his or her freedom to control and direct the operations. Their role is supportive under the entrepreneur's direction.

ASSESSING AN ENTREPRENEUR'S CHARACTERISTICS

There is no scale applied to the intensity of the entrepreneurial characteristics. There is no thermometer on which to say that at 212° Fahrenheit you are an entrepreneur. Rather, individuals are viewed as having spoonfuls of the characteristics.

The characteristics cannot be viewed superficially. Although most of us will observe these characteristics in the outstanding entrepreneur, their existence and extent in any individual cannot be determined by a layperson's examination. To identify the interaction of the characteristics and the extent to which they lie latent at any moment requires an examination in depth by a trained psychologist with experience and knowledge of these characteristics. Such an examination would normally take a half day and cost about as much as one good ready-made suit of clothing. The entrepreneur will probably find the experience worth an entire wardrobe.

9

Fate, Luck, and Innovation

Fate is a concept that the entrepreneur can accept. Being realistic, the entrepreneur accepts the fate of the stars or the fate in an insect's life cycle. The entrepreneur does not accept, however, that fate is a powerful third party controlling his or her destiny. Among the manifestations of the entrepreneur's realism are the acceptance of the regulated economy in which we operate. While some may decry the regulations and complain of how they prevent us from achieving our desires, the entrepreneur merely asks, "Tell me how they work."

The entrepreneur does not ask the world to change to provide an opportunity for achievement but rather asks, "How can I achieve in the world as I find it?" An entrepreneur, operating in the entrepreneurial mode, in control and with consequent high self-confidence, displays a clear disdain for fatalism.

Studies by Albert Shapero[1] find that successful entrepreneurs have a strong internal locus of control. This is to say they believe that they control their destiny. People with an external locus of control seem to believe that their destiny is controlled by people and events over which they have no influence. Entrepreneurs in the entrepreneurial mode clearly demonstrate their confidence in their ability to bring about a desired result independent of any external influence.

Most entrepreneurs will allude to some luck when describing how they built their enterprise. All who have been through the entrepreneurial experience know very well that when the best-laid plans have been executed there are still many factors beyond our control. Success or failure may depend on how those external factors interact with our plans. We accept a favorable interaction as luck.

When speaking to successful entrepreneurs about luck and listening to them recite their experiences and examples of good luck, it becomes evident that probabilities of success or failure vary greatly, depending on how the entrepreneur reacts to bad luck. People with the characteristics of entrepreneurs react to bad luck in the strongest

49

possible positive fashion. The person with the entrepreneurial profile rises to the occasion in the face of adversity. Entrepreneurs are skillful and perceptive in finding ways to cope with a setback. With their superior conceptual ability they are expert problem solvers. They are persistent and versatile. A challenge is highly motivational to them.

Entrepreneurs do not take "no" or "it can't be done" as answers. Their immediate reaction is, "Why not?" When in a position to control and direct with its accompanying self-confidence, entrepreneurs find the challenge of bad luck an opportunity to vent their emotional frustrations and exercise their conceptual ability. It is common to hear successful entrepreneurs report, "Yes, I've been very lucky. On the other hand, I find that the harder I work, the luckier I get." It is also common to hear the entreprenuers say, "They told me it couldn't be done, so I did it."

Entrepreneurs are often thought of as innovative and imaginative. Perhaps they are. Entrepreneurs, being realistic, with comprehensive awareness and a superior conceptual ability, are people being challenged with a problem on which emotional anxieties and frustrations can be vented. Entepreneurs are willing to entertain far-fetched ideas, especially their own, without seeing them initially as filled with impossible problems. Their high self-confidence and their persistent strong drive give their far-fetched ideas an opportunity to be tested. While all about them seem to see the impossible problems, entrepreneurs are busy seeking possible solutions. Having comprehensive awareness, they frequently propose solutions involving relationships not apparent to those with a more restricted perspective.

The degree to which successful entrepreneurs are innovative and imaginative seems to vary widely. Some are highly innovative and convert their imaginative ideas into ongoing businesses. Others are far less imaginative and simply take advantage of opportunities they perceive as the basis for their businesses. But even in these cases, their innovativeness and imaginativeness appear in their handling of inevitable adversity.

The terms *fate* and *luck* arise in another context among people who wish to help entrepreneurs. In this group the question of fate is often asked, Are entrepreneurs born or made? We are not able to answer that. It appears that many of these characteristics are evident at a very young age. Some may be modified by experience. Some, however, require emotional and behavioral changes in the individual that can be accomplished only with great difficulty and, in some cases, not at all. Whether born or made, entrepreneurs exist in abundant numbers and often display their characteristics when they are very young.

The entrepreneur's perception of luck is displayed in reported results of the ringtoss game.[2] A large pin, about the size of a broomstick and perhaps eight inches long, is placed on the floor. Individuals are then given six rings or hoops about six inches in diameter. They are told that the objective is to pitch the rings onto the pin. There are no rules regarding how far away you stand from the pin when you make the toss.

In a random sampling from the population, there are always some who will stand directly over the pin and drop their six rings in place. There are also some who stand back from the pin and attempt to toss their rings from a distance that makes it nearly impossible to succeed. The entrepeneurs in the group will stand a little distance away from the pin, enough to make the toss challenging, but not so far as to deny them the probability of putting that ring on the pin.

10

Entrepreneurs
As Managers

Their strong need for control and accompanying high self-confidence thrust entrepreneurs toward doing everything themselves. The same job done by different people will probably be done in different ways. Different is not necessarily less well done. But whether in the entrepreneurial mode or working with and for others in a structured organization, entrepreneurs perceive the job done by others as a job done less well than they could have done it themselves.

When queried about the circumstances surrounding formation of their new businesses, successful entrepreneurs frequently relate a story of dissatisfaction and inability to function in a structured environment; they quit or walk away from that environment to gain the freedom of running their own organization. With growth and success in their new enterprise, it is not long before they need a management organization and structure. Typically, entrepreneurs are engulfed in the same kind of structure from which they escaped and find the same dissatisfaction and inability to function.

So long as there are functions and things to work on, and no time to get involved in people problems, entrepreneurs can operate at the top of a structure. However, a slowdown in growth, even temporary, brings people problems to the attention of the entrepreneur and his or her moderate interpersonal skills, along with the need to control, may be inadequate to the task. Entrepreneurs' emotional stability permits functioning coolly and effectively in stress situations with functions and things, but where people's feelings are involved they tend to give orders or treat the situation as of little importance. Unless there are stress situations involving functions and things to consume the entrepreneur's attention, turmoil and turnover often result.

Entrepreneurs who have more than moderate interpersonal skills and those who can divest themselves of some control may continue to grow with the organization. Although it is unusual to find entrepreneurs who remain at the top of their structures from inception through listing on the New York Stock Exchange, some have done it. More typically, when the organization reaches a size where the entrepreneur finds a compelling need for management structure, an inability to function in that structure causes trouble. This was the classic situation in which Byron Williamson found himself after ten years of successful growth with Thuron Industries. It took considerable effort on his part and the consultation of industrial psychologists to help him change his behavior and divest sufficient control to remain as the head of the organization.

ORGANIZATIONAL GROWTH OF A NEW ENTERPRISE

When a new enterprise is formed, it may include one to five individuals. There is little organizational structure. It will be clear that someone is the entrepreneur and the captain. On the other hand, there are so few people and so many functions to be filled that everyone wears several hats. Also, with so few people there is little need for physical separation or formal communication. Everyone knows what everyone else is doing and usually overhears what everyone else is saying. There is a shared excitement in the moment-by-moment achievements and frustrations. There is a full sense of participation and appreciation for individual contribution. Because there is so much to be done and so few to do it, everyone has the opportunity to initiate action and to discover and display talents and aptitudes.

With a little success and the passage of time, the organization will begin to form. Individuals in the small group crystallize their areas of responsibility and function based on their talents and aptitudes. There is still no need for any real sharing of authority.

With a little more success and the passage of still more time, the organization may begin to look like Figure 10-1. As the work load increases, some members of the small founding team begin to acquire help to perform their tasks. The organization chart begins to imply some segmentation of responsibility and authority. At this point, there is sufficient growth in the organization for one of the entrepreneur's key characteristics to begin to emerge as a problem.

An entrepreneur in an organization portrayed by Figure 10-1 will be curious about the activities and achievements of the people at the lowest level in the management structure. When hearing an interesting report from the top management level, the entrepreneur's reaction is to display pleasure, satisfaction, and curiosity and to march off to visit the lowest level in the management chain to view the achievement. Being realistic, the entrepreneur wants firsthand information.

The entrepreneur may view this behavior as expressing interest, participation, and appreciation to the immediate subordinate. In talking with the lowest level on the management chart, the entrepreneur may

53

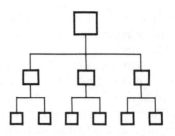

FIGURE 10-1 Organization Chart with Sufficient Structure that Entrepreneurs Begin to Interfere with Management Tranquillity.

feel a sense of egalitarianism. He or she is often oblivious to the effect such behavior has on the organization. The entrepreneur has bypassed a management level and confused the lower-level employees about whose wishes they are to satisfy.

With still more success and the passage of more time, the organization chart will begin to resemble Figure 10-2. Now the picture portrays a chain of management responsibility and authority; it appears to be a road map showing channels through which information must flow. Even with this kind of organization, the entrepreneur's behavior does not change. Now, instead of bypassing one level of management, the entrepreneur bypasses several. He or she freely enters the chain at any point, seeking information and dispensing guidance and direction.

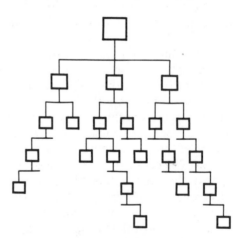

FIGURE 10-2 Organization Chart Describing a Management Structure Conducive to the Parlor Game.

DISADVANTAGES OF BYPASSING THE STRUCTURE

John Welsh was surprised to discover examples of this behavior in his own actions. When Flow Laboratories was founded in 1961 it consisted of a makeshift laboratory in a basement garage in Roslyn, Virginia. By

1965 the company was quartered in four buildings in Rockville, Maryland, supplying biological materials to the research and diagnostic community. Whenever he was in town, Welsh made a point of visiting each of the four buildings at least once each day in order, he thought, to be seen by the employees and to make himself available to their needs.

On one of these excursions into the plant, he arrived on the shipping dock at approximately 5 o'clock. While strolling along, being friendly and helpful to anyone in sight, he found a very large shipment ready to be placed on a truck. It aroused his curiosity, because this was not a typical shipping day. He recognized the shipment immediately and recalls saying out loud, but to no one in particular, "I didn't know that was supposed to go out today." He then strolled off smiling inwardly with satisfaction that the important order was being completed.

This shipment was a very special preparation of tissue culture substrate in which an experimental batch of vaccine was going to be manufactured to be tested in infants. Welsh was not only aware of but concerned about this important material and had considerable pride that Flow Laboratories had been chosen to prepare it. Two days later when he received a phone call from the customer asking where the shipment had gone he could hardly believe what he was hearing. The shipment had not arrived in Chicago. He assured the caller that something had happened at their end of the line. Certainly it had left Flow; he had seen it with his own eyes.

After a brief telephone conversation, Welsh asked to be given a few minutes to investigate and promised to return the call. He then began tracking down through the chain of command to gather all the facts and information about the shipment. Within thirty minutes the organization located the shipment. It was in the freezer in the warehouse. One of the minimum-wage employees on the shipping dock reported, "The president was here, and he said that shipment was not supposed to go, so I put it back in the warehouse."

ADVANTAGES OF BYPASSING THE STRUCTURE

The entrepreneur's behavior may be detrimental to the smooth functioning of the organization, but it provides an advantage not usually available to managers content to utilize the channels of the organization chart for information and communication. The basic relationship described in Figure 10-2 identifies the individual who must be satisfied for the subordinate to get a raise and a promotion. Each individual, knowing the structure, can establish priorities and interpersonal relationships to improve the probability of a favorable evaluation. On the other hand, this kind of structure and channel of communication is very much like an old-time parlor game.

In the not too distant past, in the days preceding radio and television, one of the popular games for half a dozen or more people

55

consisted of one person whispering a short story to the person on his or her left. The story would continue to be whispered from one party to another until everyone in the room was involved. Then the last person to hear the story would stand up and tell the story as it had been heard. The fun in the game was then to have the person who initiated the story repeat the original story told. With as few as six people, the two stories were always so different that it was hilarious.

Looking at Figure 10-2 and imagining a story being passed from the lowest level of the management structure to the entrepreneur through the chain of command, the similarity to the parlor game is evident. Worse than that, information being passed from the lowest level up to the entrepreneur is conveyed by each individual talking to the person he or she must satisfy to get a raise and a promotion. A story can always be told in more than one way. Obviously, when conveying a story to the person from whom you hope to get a favorable evaluation, you will select words and inflections to put yourself in the best light.

An organization such as that in Figure 10-2 with a half-dozen layers through which information passes, is a parlor game with a biased one-way filter. Entrepreneurs bypass this information system to the benefit of the enterprise, but at the expense of organizational tranquillity.

Entrepreneurs are builders of new businesses, but are seldom good managers in large structured organizations. Conversely, good managers in highly structured organizations are seldom successful at building a new business. Perhaps if entrepreneurs could be made fully aware of this before starting their new enterprises, they would be realistic enough to accept a graceful departure after achieving the success of a structured organization.

11

The Entrepreneur's Career Path

Our distinguished entrepreneur speaker series hosted sixty-four out-standing entrepreneurs over a four-year period. These sessions were arranged to be off the cuff and off the record. Tape recorders were excluded, representatives of the media were asked to confine their reporting to human interest stories, and members of brokerage firms were pledged to refrain from buying and selling stock on the basis of what was discussed in these sessions. The result was an extremely candid, open presentation by these entrepreneurs of how they started their businesses.

Dick Tozer reported in 1974 on the first 41 of these speakers, finding that 11 had built New York Stock Exchange firms, three were listed on the American Exchange, 10 had stock publicly held and traded over-the-counter, and 17 were privately held.[1] Their businesses had sales ranging from $100,000 to $3.5 billion and represented, collectively, more than $10 billion in sales in 1974. Twelve had sales in excess of $100 million in 1974.

Tozer, who hosted these sessions, first observed a career pattern among these speakers. Subsequent study with Williamson, Hörger, and ourselves enumerated seven significant steps in the pattern. Other steps preceding and following these seven have been observed, but these appear to be essential to entrepreneurial success. Curiously, the steps are sequential. A subsequent review of the career path of individuals who started and failed revealed that they skipped at least one of the steps in this sequential career path.

This career path has been surprisingly consistent among the entrepreneurs we have met and worked with. On occasion it is somewhat difficult to isolate the steps as discreet time segments. For instance, Steps 2 and 3 sometimes appear to occur simultaneously. Step 4 does not always appear in the entrepreneur's retelling of the events surrounding the beginning of the business until some provocative questions are asked in a setting where the entrepreneur feels a sense of trust. Nonetheless, probing questions with the intent to verify or deny the career path usually results in confirmation of the suggestion that there is sequential progress along the path.

1. Decide They Might. This abbreviated title for Step 1 is intended to identify a significant turning point in the perception entrepreneurs have of themselves. Many people have thought they might someday like to start a business of their own. At some point in entrepreneurs' careers, however, the possibility becomes a reality. Usually quite suddenly they realize that the prospect is not idle dreaming. Some bright idea or business opportunity emerges to make the possibility a probability. Sometimes entrepreneurs observe someone they know personally, from their own socioeconomic and educational level, who has started a business that appears to be succeeding, and they relate to this role model. Frequently, entrepreneurs have been placed in the position to control and direct a significant undertaking and discover, usually within a very short time, three to six months, the real possibility of their creating an enterprise.

This is a time of profound change in entrepreneurs' perception of themselves and the world around them. It is a change from idle observer to active participant. It is a change from vicarious enjoyment and perhaps envy of the achievements of others to personal experience and activity.

Two important things occur at this point. First, the entrepreneur subsequently views all information and data in a new light—how it will influence his or her business concept. There is no further idle fantasizing. Specific data is sought and cataloged. The entrepreneur's learning circuits are switched on and grasp all information and contacts in the context of how they fit together to describe the emerging business concept.

The second important occurrence at this point is that the entrepreneur has selected the boss. The entrepreneur's experience at this point in the career path is, "I might do it." This does not permit a selection of the most qualified or most experienced individual for the task. Without professional advice or counsel the entrepreneur has made a final and absolute decision as to who shall be the boss. In the context of the entrepreneurial characteristics, who else could control and direct the enterprise?

2. Gain Product and Market Knowledge. Entrepreneurs are very realistic. They gather information, data, perceptions, and feelings firsthand. Typically the successful entrepreneur gains customer and product knowledge while working for an established competitor, at or very near the interface between the customer and the product.

Ross Perot, who founded EDS, has a typical experience. While working for IBM he was the best salesman in his territory. He was out there shaking hands with the customers, looking them in the eye as he listened to what they said. He worked at being the best at what he was doing, and he listened carefully to learn what products and services would cause his customers to part with their hard-earned money. From his vantage point he was able to recognize a viable business concept and gain realistic market information about his prospects.

Another example is Herman Lay, who founded Lay's Potato Chips, later to become Frito-Lay and in time merge with Pepsi-Cola. Herman Lay eventually became chairman of the executive committee of PepsiCo, Inc. He began driving a secondhand truck, selling potato chips door to door. He handled the product and talked to the consumer. His information was clearly firsthand.

Our brief title to this significant career step can be amplified to the statement, "They gain product and market knowledge near the interface between the customer and the product or service." Viable new business concepts seldom emerge from the fortieth-floor office of a Manhattan skyscraper. They usually emerge from entrepreneurs working as engineers with their hands on a design or craftspeople with their hands on a product of which they have a very intimate knowledge. Or they emerge from salespeople who shake hands directly with the consumers.

3. Develop a Business Concept. The entrepreneur uses product and market knowledge to develop a business concept that is a business idea rather than just a bright idea. Bright ideas are clothed in words like, "If you did this you would make a million dollars." Business concepts are clothed in words like, "Four people working in 1,000 square feet can produce enough to generate $30,000 in sales per month." Customers and suppliers are identified, and key employees are solicited. A plan emerges. The entrepreneur begins to identify terms of sale, capital required, cost, square feet, equipment, transportation—many facets of business.

Typically entrepreneurs will cycle back and forth between Steps 3 and 2. They gain product and market knowledge and develop a concept. They then gain additional product and market knowledge and modify the concept. In fact, they may go on for many years modifying and improving their business concept.

Successful entrepreneurs are seldom secretive about their business concepts. They try out their ideas on anyone and everyone they think might have something to contribute. They also find a certain satisfaction in talking about their business concepts. Sometimes at a social gathering you will find people looking at them in awe and talking about them admiringly. Some potential entrepreneurs clearly enjoy this respect and can continue the pattern for a long, long time. In fact, typically the next step in the career path does not happen without an external influence.

4. Experience Career Displacement. The initiation of a new business enterprise seldom occurs in an orderly, well-planned fashion. When you listen to many successful entrepreneurs discuss the circumstances surrounding the initiation of their enterprises you repeatedly hear, "They wanted to send me to a small town and I just wasn't going to move." Another refrain is, "I worked for twelve months preparing that plan for the new division, and management turned it down." Or another, "I was laid off in the reduction in force that year." Apparently it takes some external influence of sufficient importance to the entrepreneur to make action imperative.

59

Being fired, laid off, asked to move, passed over for a promotion, or having management turn down a proposed new product or plan are negative forms of displacement. A positive form of career displacement might be, for instance, having a large government contract in hand before starting the enterprise. It was not uncommon during the 1960s for technical people to obtain substantial government contracts from the Department of Defense either before or coincident with the formation of their new enterprise. Being offered a sizable capital investment is also a positive career displacement. One entrepreneur's company was started after he had lunch with a friend who happened to mention that he had just made a half a million dollars from a recent investment and was looking for a place to reinvest it. There are positive career displacements, but the truth is they are not abundant.

Being displaced geographically or isolated ethnically are negative career displacements. Shapero provides evidence of this displacement, citing the examples of the Cuban population in Miami, Florida.[2] Other examples are the Jews in many parts of the world, the Chinese residents of Malaya, and the Indian residents of Thailand.

Cooper has found that entrepreneurial companies undergoing the strains of growth while being managed by entrepreneurs appear to become incubators for new entrepreneurial enterprises.[3] The frequency of career displacement events and the number of personally known, credible role models are significantly higher in these businesses. These firms also provide a reservoir of partners who face the dilemma of an almost inevitable parting of the ways. Head skis and Hart skis are the results of that kind of negative career displacement.

Negative displacement is very effective. It is a highly motivating challenge to the person with entrepreneurial characteristics. With a negative displacement entrepreneurs become galvanized for action. They have set out to prove that they are right and the world is wrong. Once they have made their commitment it is nearly impossible to stop them. Their goal orientation is overriding and their superior conceptual ability, along with their comprehensive awareness, rise to support that orientation. Needless to say, at this point entrepreneurs are in control and active, factors that enhance strong drive and self-confidence. They are in that emotional state in which they rise to adversity—what we have been calling the entrepreneurial mode.

It is interesting to note that women active in the movement to provide women with equal opportunity in business have decided, after a few years of more equal opportunity, that necessity is the best motivator. They report that just having the opportunity doesn't motivate to the extent needed for success in business. To overcome the adversity that will strike and strike again takes the commitment that results from a career displacement.

5. Make It Work Once. Successful entrepreneurs do not market nationwide or industrywide or with a full product line in the beginning. They

concentrate their market and their product or service into the smallest viable size, and they build a small business with positive retained earnings. The business with $1 million sales from its four divisions likely has not yet completed this step. The successful entrepreneur makes one division in one business, but makes it work very well.

Entrepreneurs get to know more and more about their little business and all of its facets so that in a very short time they know more about their business than anyone else. Successful entrepreneurs are experts about their own business. They are high on their expert curve.

In a sense the expert curve is not a curve at all, but rather a ladder on which we perceive those who have more expertise to be higher. When you think about expertise you realize that for everybody there appears to be someone else who is more expert about any particular subject. On the other hand, a person does not have to know very much about a particular subject before he or she knows much more than some other people and to those people appears an expert. We are all experts in some subject relative to some people. To portray this relationship we have chosen to imagine a line going straight up.

An interesting characteristic of the expert curve is its scale. When you begin to gather information and gain knowledge about any particular subject, you very quickly gain a position of expertise relative to many others. With additional information and knowledge you find that small gains in your understanding reduce dramatically the number of individuals who are still expert relative to you. This makes the scale on the expert curve exponential. Rather than going from 0 to 100, the scale on the expert curve leaps from 10 to 100 to 1,000 to 10,000 and so on for equal gains in increments of additional knowledge and information.

Successful entrepreneurs get to know more and more about their little business and move themselves up the expert curve for their business. Having accomplished this step in the career path entrepreneurs face the first major impasse: the crisis of the "big head." They have done it once, and all things now seem possible.

When starting you own business you perceive that all about you are people saying it cannot and will not work, that starting a business is a foolish career decision. Banks won't lend you money for lack of a track record. Potential customers want to know how they can be assured that the business will be around next year when they want to reorder. Needed employees talk about the security of their positions as they join the endeavor. Even worse, in the beginning everyone appears to assume an attitude of wait and see while you, the entrepreneur, are in desperate need of all the help you can get.

The entrepreneur often feels alone and gets the impression that the only way the business is ever going to work is for him or her to make it happen. When it does happen, the entrepreneur may be forgiven for believing that he or she alone deserves the credit.

61

Unfortunately, the entrepreneur's attitude at this point is all too often related to a perception that having made this small business work very well he or she can make almost any new business opportunity work very well. Opportunities appear in abundance, and the clichés of the business and financial community encourage growth. With the entrepreneur's newfound self-confidence the opportunities seem irresistible.

6. Perceive Growth Opportunities. Successful entrepreneurs who perceive growth return to the earlier steps before initiating growth. They recognize that expansion and growth represent a new and different business concept, one that requires careful study, planning, and understanding to make it potentially viable.

To operate one restaurant and do it well requires a restaurateur. To operate two or more restaurants successfully requires a manager. Too few entrepreneurs recognize the significance of their presence to the success of the venture. As in the case of operating two or more restaurants, growth implies success of the venture even in the absence of the entrepreneur.

A classic dilemma emerges for the entrepreneur. Growth implies a management structure, but entrepreneurs do not function well in a structured environment. Divesting some control is necessary to the health of the management structure. Divesting some control, to the entrepreneur, threatens self-confidence and appears to deny the opportunity to vent frustration in solving new and interesting problems.

One other problem emerges at this point—the relationship with investors. The money placed with the entrepreneur was viewed, consciously or subconsciously, as a ticket to the Irish Sweepstakes. Investors know that the enterprise may or may not work, and if they lose their money they are prepared to accept that consequence. When the entrepreneur has created a successful viable entity and perceives growth, however, the investors see a real and valuable asset being placed at risk. They may have had little to lose in the beginning, but the entrepreneur has now created something of value for them, and they do not want to lose it.

During the start-up of the new business, investors typically allow the entrepreneur a relatively free hand in operation. When the entrepreneur has created something of value, they find it nearly impossible to avoid staying in contact and being fully informed about their investment. They express concern for the welfare of their asset. The entrepreneur perceives this new interest as interference and reduced confidence in his or her ability. Very often a conflict emerges between the investors and entrepreneur.

7. Expand Significantly. Having gained additional product and market knowledge and prepared a viable business concept for the expansion, successful entrepreneurs proceed on their growth pattern. They don't take on other people's headaches. They don't mistake astro turf for green pastures. They build on the

knowledge and experience they have acquired in the creation of their viable little business. Having risen on the expert curve, they use that expertise.

At this step the entrepreneurial profile so essential to the creation of the business becomes a problem. Moderate interpersonal skills are not adequate for the task at hand. They tend to interfere with the chain of management responsibility.

With the success of the initial venture and opportunities for growth, entrepreneurs find it easier to gain loans from banks and equity financing from venture capital investors. They seldom recognize the strength of the strings attached to such capital. People with entrepreneurial profiles often have difficulty maintaining interpersonal relationships with investors. If the investors have sufficient voting control, it is not unusual for the entrepreneur to depart at their insistence. Should the entrepreneur maintain sufficient voting control to preclude this, the relationship often turns sour while the investors attempt to extricate themselves.

A survey of venture capital firms in 1975 by Tozer indicates that few founding entrepreneurs have remained with their businesses as they grew.[4] Among more than 600 venture capital firms queried, over 100 responded with information about founding entrepreneurs. Among the portfolios held by these firms, 97 percent reported that all or most of the founding entrepreneurs have been replaced by managers. As Tozer stated, "Life as a founder/chief executive in a venture capitalist's portfolio company is apparently hazardous."

Those entrepreneurs who have successfully carried their new business through the growth phase have somewhat better interpersonal skills than the average entrepreneur, although their skills are not necessarily equal to those of professional managers. We have also found that those who remain as chief executives through the growth phase have a warm and open relationship with at least one dominant investor or a key investor who communicates with most of the others. Of those who do not survive this phase of the entrepreneur's career path, few seek a position with a large firm. Regardless of the circumstances of their departure, they go out and do it again. Even entrepreneurs who have apparently failed typically try again. It is not unusual to find among successful entrepreneurs career paths that included several failures before they finally found a viable business concept they could nurture to fruition.

One of our entrepreneur-friends has summed up the attitude of the entrepreneur who started and built a business entity. Our 42-year-old friend became a paraplegic at age 22 in a motorcycle accident. When faced with the possibility that his present entrepreneurial enterprise may have to be closed and asked about future employment, his response was adamantly against employment and single-mindedly in favor of trying again. He said, "It tastes too good."

12

The Entrepreneur's Time Line

The first ingredient, and by far the one of foremost importance, in the birth and growth of a new business is the person who makes it happen, the entrepreneur. Policies of government, incentives by the state, esoteric studies by academia, and a host of political, social, economic, and cultural barriers or gateways may contribute to the circumstances surrounding the birth of a new business. But in both the cold of a competitive marketplace and the warm embrace of a corporate subsidiary, some person must launch into the wind and tide of that time and place and race for economic survival.

A business is a group of people working together to satisfy their individual needs, goals, and aspirations. The group includes the producers, consumers, suppliers, and community in which they find themselves. They don't just work in concert. They respond to the concertmaster. And the concertmaster is constrained by time and resources, to say nothing of the whim and fancy of the people. As our own lives survive within a narrow band of temperature, altitude, atmosphere, and nourishment, so too the economic entity survives within a narrow band of transactions whose kind, quality, and timing are unique to that economic species.

Some businesses appear to survive in spite of their managers, and indeed they sometimes do. Too often, however, new businesses find themselves among the mortality statistics. In the French military school of St. Cyr at the dawn of the twentieth century the molders of military tactical thought and belief focused their admiration on the French heroes who displayed the reckless abandon of élan. They concluded that élan alone was needed to win battles, and they cultivated that heroic, if thoughtless, philosophy among their officers. By 1918 a generation of French manhood was sacrificed to that philosophy in the trenches of their eastern border.

We have little interest in encouraging a similar sacrifice in pursuit of economic freedom. To be among the mortality statistics is to have lost that freedom. Our goal is to achieve economic freedom and hold it. To that end our interest is in those who have earned their station, not won it. We hope to improve your probability of success if you give it a try.

Not all of us can aspire to the freedom of owner management. Some will prefer the freedom from choice provided by those who prefer the freedom to choose. Our heritage is the freedom of equal opportunity under the laws of the state. Within that estate we have the freedom to know ourselves, to discover our talents and aptitudes, and to aspire to the greatest heights within our grasp.

IDENTIFYING POTENTIAL
SUCCESSFUL ENTREPRENEURS

For those who consider starting a business an attractive career choice it would be helpful to know if they have a reasonable probability of succeeding. Some of us have a flair for foreign languages, others an instinctive grasp of mathematics. Some have a natural facility with musical instruments, others can't carry a note. The same is true for starting and operating a business. Among those who might like that career choice some have all the necessary attributes, and then there are those who have few if any. As with almost every aspect of characterizing people a spectrum of talents, aptitudes, and attributes among us will range from one extreme to the other.

One measure of our attributes for a successful career in entrepreneurship is found in those who have done it. We can find a sufficient number of identifiable characteristics to improve our recognition of the extremes of the spectrum. That would at least permit us to help the hopeless to avoid the trauma of failure. At the other end of the spectrum we might find reason for encouragement among some and cause for caution among others. Even if our examination does not provide clear guidance to all who seek to be entrepreneurs, a portion will gain insight.

There have been many contributors to a better understanding of the attributes or characteristics of successful entrepreneurs, including Benjamin Franklin in our American literature and Paciolo in fifteenth-century Italian literature.[1] We feel confident that a search of the printed word of early Egypt and Mesopotamia would display references to improving the chance for success in business predating the biblical references. Most of the more recent contributors have sought a simple description in the manner of Newton's Laws of Motion and Einstein's Law of Mass-Energy Conservation.

We have presented a list of eleven characteristics that appear to be common among individuals who have started a new successful business. Each has survived at least five years, has achieved sales of $1 million per year and has displayed outward symbols of a reasonable expectation that it will survive another five years. We hypothesize that to

65

the extent that an aspiring entrepreneur shares those characteristics he or she has a better than average probability for success in a similar undertaking.

Creating a business is a venture into the unknown. It bears many of the characteristics of what Abraham Maslow described as a prominent action of the self-actualizing person.[2] Few things in life are certain. Change is ever present, everywhere, and in every time. To manage a business is to maintain its health and vitality in the face of ever-changing conditions. Managing a new business is much like the problem facing a young child. Even with the help and guidance provided by concerned adults, both the young child and the new business must learn for themselves how to survive in their environments.

COMMITMENT SPARKED BY ADVERSITY

The potentially successful entrepreneur needs life experiences that provide practice in solving problems when the question is not stated, the key information is nowhere in sight, and the relevant textbook hasn't been written. The entrepreneur needs to be ripened, honed, and readied for the entrepreneurial event.

Career displacement turns on the switch. Adversity is inevitable. Commitment is essential. Dedication, persistent and consistent, is a fundamental element of success. Problems don't arise in orderly single file—they come out of the trenches in waves. It would be so tempting to abandon the field that the perceived availability of that option must be concealed.

Lenders, such as bankers, have learned from years of experience that the probability of a loan being repaid is improved by placing the borrower in a position in which he or she has too much to lose to consider abandoning the obligation. It doesn't always work, but it improves the probability of repayment.

Lenders gain the borrower's commitment with collateral and down payment. Prudent lenders are selective in the collateral they accept. Long-life assets with a ready resale market, like real estates and automobiles, are preferred. Curtains and carpets don't excite the lender because they don't excite the borrower either.

The same is true for the entrepreneur. Personal commitment, completely internalized by the individual, improves the probability of the intended or desired outcome. Typically, the new business starters have little to lose in the way of assets. But they commit it all. And they publicly proclaim, verbally and by their actions, to friends, relatives, and associates that they intend to succeed in their endeavor. What they really risk is ridicule by the people from whom they need and want acceptance, reassurance, praise, and esteem. That peer pressure adds tenacity to their commitment and improves the probability of surviving adversity.

This is why negative career displacements work. Being placed in an untenable position, such as being fired, moved to an undesirable location, passed over for an expected promotion, or politically expelled from one's homeland, arouses great emotional reactions. For the person with entrepreneurial characteristics these reactions are manifested in single-minded determination to survive and to rise to heights that reveal how incorrect the perceived oppressor was. The person with this mind-set and adequate preparation for business will be formidable in competition.

Beyond the time required for the entrepreneurial person to be ripened are time constraints that may make it too late to begin. As life proceeds we garner the liabilities imposed by our biology. Like all living things we need to procreate. For most of us the combination of our instinctive needs and relationships with the opposite sex impose constraints on our opportunities to work long hours for an uncertain income.

When we have the benefits of a good job and a reasonably certain future to support our certain obligations the desire to step out into the fray and enter the competition of the commercial world can be easily suppressed. Time and experience strengthen these constraints. A comfortable salary and satisfying position take time to acquire. They arrive at about the same time that the obligations to provide for our offspring reach their zenith. Employers add to the constraints with pension plans, bonuses, and stock purchase opportunities. And the offspring themselves develop relationships at school and in the community that further suppress the temptation to venture into the unknown.

Later in life liabilities are reduced and the opportunity to build an enterprise of our own becomes more viable. Many individuals facing early retirement do, in fact, choose to make the change to a small business of their own. But another constraint arises. Nature, in its immutable way, begins to demonstate that in time we must make way for our progeny.

Age itself is no obstacle to beginning an entrepreneurial career. There are outstanding examples of individuals who began at age fifty-five or even age seventy. The condition of the individual, the obligations as perceived by the individual, and the need or desire to have economic freedom determine the possibility and the opportunity to launch an entrepreneurial career.

Career displacements can overcome all these constraints. The probability of the balance being tipped in favor of starting a new business, however, is strongly influenced by these external forces.

TIMING OF OPPORTUNITIES

We have observed another form of time constraint on the entrepreneur. We worked with a very talented electronics and computer engineer in his midthirties. He and a partner had started a business to fill a contract with a large city newspaper for automating delivery of newspaper bundles from the presses to the trucks backed up to the loading dock. A computer determined how many bundles of what size would be placed on each truck depending on the routes the truck served.

The partner had twenty years' experience in the newspaper industry. He described the operations of the newspaper production and posed problems to the engineer. Between them they designed a very advanced system for preparing copy, placing it in the newspaper pages, and making the final printing plates for the presses. Their system would have dramatically reduced the cost of producing a newspaper. Unfortunately, they were unable to find financial backing during the 1973–1974 recession, and the newspaper owners were reluctant to entrust such a dramatic change in their operations to two obscure entrepreneurs. Upon the very successful completion of their first contract, they were forced to close their operation.

A short time later the partner with newspaper experience was involved in a fatal aircraft accident. The engineer decided to continue seeking an opportunity to start his own business. He refused employment opportunities and supported himself by consulting and short-term work assignments with senior-level offices of large, well-known, technical firms.

For four years our friend devoted day and night to looking for the product opportunity that would allow him to start his own business. Somehow, opportunity after opportunity arose only to prove ethereal on serious investigation. His reputation was outstanding with the technical community, and in trying to find his niche he gained a high reputation among some of the country's most reputable venture capital firms. But he couldn't find the vehicle he was seeking. In the end he found an opportunity to start and build a department within an existing firm, and he accepted it.

Our friend was given considerable freedom in this new position, and he is utilizing all of his talents and aptitudes to the fullest. But his dedication to building his own enterprise didn't materialize. A total of six years were devoted to preparing for that dream. The time came, however, when the frustration of seeking his dream was greater than the frustration of working for someone else.

This man is still young enough and ambitious enough to step out and do it if the opportunity presents itself. But the time when he was ripe came and went without his finding the other necessary ingredients to starting a successful new business.

In the career of the successful entrepreneur there is a period during which the individual is ready. That time passes, however, and a time comes when it is too late. Another time may come along when once again the individual is ready. And that time, too, will pass. This might be expressed as a time line representing the career of the prospective entrepreneur, which was described in Chapter 6 as a vertical line. In the context of this book, this time line is the first of the four major criteria for success in starting and building a business.

13

The Competitive Marketplace

Going into business means entering a competition. The free enterprise economy permits each of us to compete to the best of our ability. Even with the degree of government intervention that exists in the western democracies we have enormous freedom to choose our product (or service) and the way we offer it to potential consumers. The requirements for licensing or permits, if they exist at all, are minimal. The constraints on our opportunities to enter into business are usually related to our own talent, aptitude, work experience, and our ability to muster the needed financial resources. The constraints on our potential success are within ourselves; our ability to manage the many facets of business within the time limitations available. The limits on the degree of our potential success, however, measured in profit margins or return on investment, are imposed by the *competition* in the marketplace.

Some products seem to fare better than others. (We use the word product to mean "product or service.") Are there characteristics of products which would indicate which are more likely to succeed in the marketplace? The answer is a qualified yes. The product provides a starting point for identifying the many factors that might indicate the possibility for succeeding in the marketplace. But, the product itself does not determine its probable success or failure; it must be offered for a sale to potential consumers who are free to choose from among a great many products.

A product is only a part of a business concept. Success depends as much on the production, marketing, distribution, financing, and administration as on the product itself. The business concept includes all of the factors which make up the repetitive cycle of events that result in customers transferring some of their money to the business.

Business concepts do not enter the marketplace to win or lose on the strength of their own merit. The marketplace itself has very compelling forces that interact with the business concept. Management must guide the business concept into a competitive position that permits it to

69

survive and thrive. Having succeeded in achieving stability and profit-ability, management must then continually guide the business through the changing conditions that exist in the dynamic marketplace.

Within the marketplace a business concept will be in competition with other businesses selling products that perform the same function. The collection of competitors who supply these products performing the same function are called an industry. Industries develop characteristic profit margins and returns on investment. Different industries have different characteristic margins. The reasons for these differences are reasonably well known. The problem is that there are so many forces woven into the fabric of the competitive marketplace that an immense intelligence organization may be needed to monitor them, correlate the data collected, and interpret it to the benefit of the business. What is more, the forces may change, either slowly and undetectably or quickly and overwhelmingly.

Knowing that the data is complex and changing does not provide a reason for ignoring it. The fact that the data is available provides an advantage to the manager who is able to obtain it and interpret it. Since knowledge of the competitive forces in the marketplace and their probable effect on the industry's performance is available to all the competitors, entrepreneurs must assume that some of the competitors are using it.

COMPETITIVE FORCES

Competitive strategy has become an area of specialty among management researchers and consultants. These specialists find that the competition within an industry is constrained by an underlying structure consisting of five powerful driving forces:

1. Rivalry among existing firms in the industry
2. The threat of new firms entering the industry
3. The bargaining power of suppliers to the industry
4. The bargaining power of the buyers from the industry
5. The threat of substitute products or services

These underlying forces determine the profit margins that are characteristic of the industry. They limit the prospects for greater than normal profit margins. They influence the intensity of the competition and the long-term probable outcome of the competition. To entrepreneurs who are not familiar with these forces they represent *fate*.

We often attribute the success of an entrepreneurial venture to its entrepreneur. We shouldn't detract from the importance of the leader in a new venture, but it is very important to recognize that there are other forces that contribute to the success. A super individual with a good product entering an industry with an adverse underlying structure may have little success. A lessor individual entering an industry with a more favorable structure may succeed despite mistakes and misjudgments.

There may be many factors that influence a business firm's performance in the short term. These factors are transient such as economic conditions, material shortages or strikes. In the long term, however, the five underlying structural forces determine the potential returns achievable by the industry. The various firms competing within an industry are thereby limited in their potential profit margins and returns on investment.

The field of competitive strategy has a professional journal where its members publish their research.[1] Strategic planning consultants have their own international association.[2] An excellent summary of the state of the art was published in 1980 by Porter.[3] A serious entrepreneur would be wise to become acquainted with these resources.

COMPETITIVE STRATEGIES

Competitive strategists observe three fundamentally different strategies for competing within the structural framework of the five underlying forces in an industry. They are:

1. Focus
2. Differentiation
3. Cost Leadership

Sustained commitment to one of these strategies is usually necessary to achieve success.

The three strategies differ in more than their functional distinction. Implementing them requires different skills, resources, organizational arrangements, control procedures, and incentive systems. They may also require different styles of leadership and can lead to very different corporate cultures. Different kinds of people will be attracted to each.

We will provide a brief review of these strategies in this chapter. First, we want to examine the underlying forces in order to provide some recognition of their importance. This may shed some light on the fundamentals of competitive strategy. It is not intended to substitute for reading in the literature of the field, however. This summary is intended to encourage further reading and study before undertaking so serious an endeavor as starting a business.

RIVALRY

Rivalry is the behavior of competitors to gain increased sales as in holding a sale, offering discounts, featuring particular items in advertising, providing free delivery, and such normal competitive actions. Increased rivalry will result when there are numerous competitors. Service stations sell gasoline on so many corners in many parts of the country that the rivalry may be fierce. Gasoline price wars are a familiar sight. Photofinishing is another overly populated industry. Faster and faster service is offered while free film and extra prints eat away at the profit margins.

The same increase in rivalry results when the existing competitors are equally strong. Without a dominant competitor to establish acceptable rules the competitors jostle each other for market position. An added service offered by one is quickly matched by the others. A price incentive by one is matched and bettered by the others. Having offered more for less it is nearly impossible to regain the lost profit margins.

When the growth of the market is slow or non-existent the competitors are faced with the same lack of growth. Some will find the need for growth despite the market condition reason enough to increase promotion, cut price, and offer greater service. The other competitors cannot sit back and watch if these strategies begin to gain customers. Meeting and exceeding the competitive offers is a necessary reaction.

When there are high exit barriers the weak competitors may be unable to withdraw from the competition. This usually results from assuming excessive debt to finance a heavy capital investment. Some equipment manufacturers have been warm and willing when financing a new competitor to buy their expensive machinery. They can turn cold and indifferent when the new competitor is unable to attain or sustain the sales needed to service the debt.

Some industries have high entry barriers. One obvious example would be the automobile industry. Many high technology industries require a scarce scientific or engineering talent. On the other hand, many industries have low entry barriers. Auto repair shops or paint and body shops require a relatively plentiful talent and very little capital investment. House painters and lawn care services have the same ease of entry.

Barriers to entry and exit provide one relatively easy way to understand how strong forces beyond the control of the entrepreneur limit the potential for success in business. Four combinations of entry and exit barriers may be considered.

1. Low entry and low exit barriers. The condition produces an industry in which there are many new competitors. The weak firms among them retire from the competition quickly. The total number of competitors is likely to remain about constant. Retiring weak competitors are quickly replaced by new ones. Since the new ones are jostling for recognition and a market share, rivalry is likely to be intense. Profit margins will be low even for the oldest and strongest competitors.

2. Low entry and high exit barriers. This condition produces a most unpleasant competitive environment. When transient factors like economic conditions are favorable many new competitors enter the industry. When these same factors turn adverse the weak competitors find themselves unable to

withdraw. Being unable to extricate themselves they turn to savage rivalry just to meet their debt commitments. Whether the transient factors are favorable or adverse, this kind of industry is stuck with small margins at best.

3. High entry and high exit barriers. This condition creates an industry in which there may be few competitors, but the weak among them cannot withdraw. If the number of competitors is not too large the industry may enjoy good profit margins, but the competition is unstable. The addition of just a few new competitors can spark intense rivalry and low margins. Or adverse transient factors can provoke the weaker competitors to increased rivalry with the same result.

4. High entry and low exit barriers. This condition creates an industry with a high probability of stability. There are few new competitors, and when the going gets rough, as in a down economy, the weak competitors retire. This permits the survivors to achieve good profit margins. High entry barriers also tend to select more sophisticated and knowledgeable new competitors who will support stability rather than rivalry. This is a desirable industry for the aspiring entrepreneur.

THREATS AND BARGAINING POWER

The threat of new firms entering the industry depends on the barriers to entry and the reaction the new entrant can expect from existing firms in the industry. When past experience suggests that the existing firms will deal with a new entrant swiftly and forcefully few entrepreneurs will care to challenge them. Even when entry barriers are low, but existing firms are known to retaliate quickly to new competition, new entrants are easily intimidated.

The threat of substitute products is often a much greater problem for existing firms. The threat arises from other products that can perform the same function. They may emerge from new technologies or from changes in economics. When the tradeoff between price and performance is sensitive to small changes a substitute product with an improving price history may displace an industry product.

Potential substitutes produced by an industry enjoying high profit margins can be especially threatening. If for any reason that industry experiences increased competition it may find itself forced to reduce price and pursue new markets. Reduced price may improve its desirability as a substitute. Increased promotion may bring this fact to the attention of the consumers.

The bargaining power of suppliers becomes troublesome when industry competitors are unable to obtain selective treatment. The differing treatment might be in price and payment terms as for quantity purchases, or it might be in specially prepared supplies. One of the competitive tools available to management is in selecting suppliers who provide something special. If all the suppliers provide the same thing at the same price and terms a manager loses this valuable competitive tool. When an industry has little choice but to deal with its suppliers on their terms its growth and competitive strength are strongly influenced and, to some extent, controlled by the supplier.

Increased bargaining power of buyers usually results in lower prices. A buyer's market that persists for long can sap all of the profit margin from an industry. Suppliers to large dominant competitors like the automobile industry find their margins squeezed while their powerful customers become more demanding about terms, quality control, and requirements to warehouse minimum supplies. Proprietary labelers for bottled goods, spray can packaging, or pills find themselves in the same predicament.

THE ENTREPRENEUR'S PERSPECTIVE

When considering the creation of a new business most entrepreneurs are found to be enthralled with their business idea, their product, or their service. It is often hard to get them to consider the obstacles to their success realistically. Knowing that there are strong forces beyond their control may help lead them to consider the distinct possiblity that the industry they intend to enter could help or hinder their prospects for survival and growth.

The underlying forces do not suggest that some industries are off limits to an aspiring entrepreneur. Within every industry there is the possibility for some competitors to thrive. What they do suggest is that there is a means to a more realistic assessment of the new firm's probabilities for success than just the entrepreneur's unbounded self-confidence. Entering into a business endeavor is entering into a competition. As with all competition there are rules for playing the game and specific rewards and penalties. The underlying forces limit the rewards and indicate the potential penalties.

Success for an entrepreneur means first survival, then growth to a stable size with at least average profit margins. Further success is described by greater than average margins. For some it means continued growth with above average profits. In some industries these achievements are more difficult to obtain. Within the limits imposed by the industry, however, most of these achievements can be obtained.

THE FOCUS STRATEGY

This strategy implies concentrating the marketing effort on a particular buyer group, a particular geographic territory, or a segment of the product line. The entire focus strategy is built around serving a particular target market very well. Each functional component of the business, production, distribution and so on, develop their policy to support this strategy. While the differentiation and cost leadership strategies are aimed at achieving their objectives industrywide, the focus strategy is aimed at achieving its objectives with only its target market.

Although the focus strategy may preclude a firm's growing beyond its target market, it carries the potential for above average profit margins. It also provides opportunities to build defenses against each of the competitive forces. Focus can be used to select target markets least vulnerable to substitutes or where competitors are weakest.

In the paint industry there is one firm that has focused on serving the professional painter only. In the paper industry there is one firm which has specialized in providing industrial papers only. In the restaurant industry there are a few who have chosen to serve only gourmet dishes in the most elegant surroundings at a price which targets a small, but affluent clientele.

The entrepreneur with a strong talent or aptitude, but limited financial resources might find the focus strategy attractive. Especially when a firm is new and small it may find advantages in focusing its attention as well as its meager resources on doing an outstanding job of serving a small, well defined market segment. Later, having achieved recognition and reputation, the entrepreneur might consider building on those assets in a wider target market.

THE DIFFERENTIATION STRATEGY

This strategy involves creating something that is perceived as being unique in the industry. It may be achieved by technology or by creating unique features or outstanding performance. It may be identified with a brand name that has gained general acceptance and recognition. Or it may result from customer service known for its quick and reliable response to customer needs.

In the higher education industry, some universities have used the differentiation strategy with obvious success. In the field of engineering there are a few universities known for their outstanding programs. MIT is always mentioned among the best. In business schools there are a few outstanding programs with Harvard always mentioned among the best.

Differentiation can be achieved with special features. Among the ample variety of countertop kitchen ranges the Jenn-Air range has a special feature that makes it stand out as clearly different in the eyes of the consumers. Most consumers recognize the picture of a smoky barbecue grill with the smoke appearing to flow dutifully back into the range.

Among automobiles there are several manufacturers who have used the differentiation strategy. Among American manufacturers Cadillac has long held a distinction that other manufacturers have been unable to break. Among foreign automobiles the Mercedes surpasses even the Cadillac in its distinctiveness. And the name Rolls-Royce has become synonymous with quality and elegance worldwide.

The fast-food restaurant industry contains several trade names with sufficient distinctiveness to stand out even among their copiers.

75

McDonalds and Colonel Sanders Kentucky Fried Chicken are two of them. Howard Johnson's enjoyed that distinction for three decades with a not-as-fast sit-down restaurant.

The popular marketing strategy called "positioning" aims at differentiation.[4] It generates brand loyalty. Customers are less concerned about price. The bargaining power of buyers is thereby reduced. The threat of substitute products is reduced dramatically and the uniqueness perceived by the consumers erects an entry barrier to new entrants to the industry.

The differentiation strategy may preclude gaining a large market share. Distinctive differentiation implies exclusivity which may not be consistent with large market share. It does, however, provide the means to achieve better-than-industry average profit margins and a more readily defensible position against the underlying market forces.

THE COST LEADERSHIP STRATEGY

This strategy is based on the concepts of the learning curve. Fully allocated expense per unit, in constant dollars, has been observed to decrease with each doubling of cumulative experience in a consistent and persistent manner. The implications of the curve are far-reaching and profound. Their greatest value falls to the competitor who enters the competition early and establishes the dominant market share. The strategy is most attractive in growth industries. The dependence on cumulative experience doublings lends itself to industries involved in mass production of manufactured or assembled products.

Once cost leadership is achieved it provides strong barriers to new entrants who must invest heavily in plant, equipment, and marketing strength. It reduces the power of suppliers who can exert downward pressure on prices until the next lowest cost producer is threatened. It reduces buyer power by permitting price incentives and standardization. And it raises barriers to substitutes by maintaining its cost leadership against them.

Examples of firms that have successfully applied this strategy are Black & Decker with portable electric tools, Texas Instruments Incorporated with hand-held calculators, and Briggs & Stratton with small gasoline engines. During the first two decades of this century Henry Ford applied this strategy to the Model T automobile.

We will devote much time to understanding the implications of the learning curve in the chapters which follow. This emphasis is not to suggest that the cost leadership strategy is the most desirable. Rather, it is because even in applying the focus and differentiation strategies the affects of the learning curve are at work. In the relatively free and open competitive economies of the western democracies innovation and creativity are rewarded by the marketplace. Innovation and creativity continually drive prices down and efficiency up. A business which does not strive for reduction of its unit costs does so at its peril.

Inventors are often so intent on the form and function of their new device that they have difficulty conceiving of the complex organization of resources needed to carry their product to the marketplace. Entrepreneurs are all too often similarly intent on the form and function of their business idea. In the conventional wisdom the Horatio Alger story can be relived by merely going into business. The terminology is unfortunate. Few who just go into business survive.

What we go into is the competitive marketplace. We challenge the existing competitors with our organization of resources, talents, and aptitudes. We seek the favor of the consumers, but not just their nod of approval. We need their money. Meanwhile our competitors in the industry are equally in need of the consumer's money. The resulting rivalry is not just a friendly game. The outcome affects the lives and livelihood of the people who are party to the rivalry.

Starting and building a new business is an exciting and thrilling experience with the potential for great rewards, both psychic and monetary. It is an experience that puts life into a normal existence. It is worth the trials and tribulations, the frustrations, anxieties, and relentless demands on your energy and stamina. It is an experience we advocate for those with the characteristics of the entrepreneur.

Although there is no such thing as guaranteed success, or even just assured success, enough is known, or can be learned, about the strengths and weaknesses of new business concepts and their competitive environment that the fraction of new business which succeed can be improved dramatically. The means to this end is to avoid just going into business, to stop and consider where do I want to go, how am I going to get there, what obstacles will I find along the way and what resources do I need to overcome them.

14

The Business Concept

Entrepreneurs are not magicians. They cannot just make anything happen. They need a business concept that has the opportunity to succeed. The best entrepreneur at the best time along a career path, with a business concept with no chance of success, has no chance of success. Even a good entrepreneur with a good business concept has no assurance of making it happen. To improve the probability of winning, the entrepreneur needs a business concept with a good probability of succeeding.

CHOOSING A BUSINESS CONCEPT

A business concept may be built on a new product or just an improvement on an existing product. It may be a new or improved service. But it need not be either. It can be a new or better delivery method or a better financing method. For example, automobiles, houses, and appliances would not be sold in such great numbers and available to so many people were it not for the availability of financing with relatively small periodic payments over an extended period. The fast-food restaurant is an example of a better delivery method. It provides food at a lower price and in less time because of the method of serving.

Another example is the tire store that is only open four days a week. Its founders noted that most tire stores are open six days a week, including two or three evenings. They then noted that most of the tires are sold only during a short period among those many hours. In fact, they plotted sales volume versus time during the normal store hours. They found that most of the sales occurred during a particular forty-to-fifty hour period.

The founders also noted that a retail store employs many people, some of them part-time, to cover the large number of hours that the store is open. This creates a substantial management problem in finding, training, scheduling, accounting for, and keeping good help. During the time the founders were making this analysis there was much talk in the media about the American worker going on a four-day workweek. It dawned on them that by matching the full-time employees' regular work schedule to the hours during which most of the tires were sold they could come up with a new business concept. They combined this delivery system with quality tires and superior service in a stand-alone building. This business concept has grown to a substantial chain in a very few years.

Two additional kinds of business concepts come to mind in which there is no new product, service, financing, or improvement. One is reproducing an existing concept to satisfy increased consumer demand. The other is duplicating an existing business in a new area.

When a distinctly new product with broad application is introduced to the marketplace, such as the double-knit fabrics of the 1970s, it is not uncommon to find that the existing suppliers cannot satisfy the demand. This situation is always followed by the entry into the field of many new suppliers who merely duplicate what is already being done. We will have more to say about the competitive advantages and disadvantages of choosing such a business concept in Chapter 23.

Duplicating an existing business in a new geographic area has many desirable qualities. This is probably the most common kind of concept among new business start-ups. New population centers need access to existing services and supplies, more conveniently located. New shopping strips and malls follow new housing developments into the suburbs.

Duplication in a new geographic area is the essence of franchising. It is not necessary to find a new population center. It is only necessary that the business concept be new to the population it serves and that the delivery system be geographically limited, as with a restaurant, retail store, or ready-mix concrete plant.

A viable business concept may fill a need; this would seem to be the most desirable kind of concept. It may be just as successful, however, if it satisfies a want or a frustration. Many successful businesses satisfy a desire that buyers explain with somewhat dubious reasoning, for instance, executive toy stores. Although many collectors may describe their activity as a hobby or avocation with investment possibilities, it is sometimes hard to explain logically spending large amounts of money for the things they collect other than to say they just want them. Frustrations are satisfied by games, chewing gum, and the like. Many sporting activities appear to be satisfying a frustration as much as a need.

BUSINESS TRANSACTIONS

The best way to get a picture of a viable business concept is to think of what happens in business, what is the very substance of business. This is easier to see in a very simple business. In the very smallest and most primitive business we observe a transaction, an exchange between two people. It is a selling encounter. Mark Twain recalls exchanging string and things for frogs and penknives. In any business encounter there is the exchange of one thing for something else.

In today's complex culture, what is exchanged may be less tangible than string and penknives. Service businesses sometimes exchange things that are difficult to define precisely. The service of cleaning your house is identifiable, but the service of selling advice often leaves the buyer wondering what was bought.

The very essence of business is exchanging one thing for another, but long ago it was recognized that making a deal is often prevented by not having something to trade with an incremental value. Exchanging eight blankets for one horse implies an incremental value of one blanket, but if you own horses and want to exchange for one blanket, you can't make the deal. The incremental value of horses is eight blankets.

Some of the original inhabitants of the American continent solved the problem by using beads to represent an incremental value. In ancient Athens and Rome they made small decorative pieces of attractive metal. In ancient Egypt they used decorative pieces of attractive stones. Today we use decorative pieces of paper and some distinctive pieces of metal.

When we decided to use decorative items to represent incremental value we removed the item of value itself from one side of the transaction. In fact, we substituted two transactions for every one. Any and all of these decorative items used to represent incremental value we call *money*. The very substance of business has become "people parting with their hard-earned money for whatever you have to offer them in exchange."

The substance of business is the transaction itself. If that doesn't happen there is no business. The business transaction is between two people or a collection of people acting as two. You may dig minerals out of the ground or chop down trees for lumber, but until they are used in a transaction with someone there is no business. Business involves a transaction between people in which something perceived to be of value is exchanged.

DISTINCTIVE PERCEIVED CONSUMER VALUES

What are the words spoken during a transaction in the making? What does the seller say? What does the buyer say? Close your eyes and think of someone trying to sell you something. What words do you hear? It's cheaper. It will last longer. You don't have to service it. It's better, prettier, softer. You don't have to pay now. If you don't like it you can send it back. You can't get it anywhere else. Twenty billion of them have been sold. It is the latest fashion. It's smaller. It's lighter. It's easier. It's faster.

These words describe *values.* They may be real or only perceived values, but they induce people to part with their money. Remember the commercial showing three automobiles that look very similar? One is foreign, one is expensive, and one is comparatively cheap. The advertisement is by the seller of the least expensive automobile. Has that ad decreased the sales of the expensive car or of the foreign car? Not at all. In fact, all three have a history of increased sales during the time that commercial was shown to millions of viewers on television.

Whether the claims of the advertiser are true or not, what induced people to part with their money was something more than just price, although price did induce some people. What induced people to buy the expensive auto? Probably prestige. What induced people to buy the foreign car? Probably the reputation for better engineering and crafting, whether the reputation is deserved or not. What induced people to buy the inexpensive car? Probably their inability to afford either of the other two.

The words that induce people to part with their hard-earned money list values as they are perceived by the buyer. The facts of the real values are relatively unimportant. What counts is what the buyer thinks. We call these *distinctive perceived consumer values.* We can list some: price, service, prestige, pleasure, entertainment, education, financing, efficiency, quality, style, durability, resale value, investment, safety, location.

It would be very helpful if we could prepare a profile of a business concept comparable to the profile of the entrepreneur with a short list of descriptive words. We are unable to do that.

The list of words that describe a business concept is long and varied, and it changes with time. During the early 1970s the road we used while driving to work each morning passed through a low-lying area that was flooded each time there was a heavy rain. One year a pickup truck was swept into the flooded stream, resulting in the death of two passengers. Immediately after the waters receded on that occasion we observed large construction equipment on both sides of the road and a supply of huge concrete pipes. As one might expect with any public works, a large sign was erected at the approach to this construction bearing the name of the construction project and that of the mayor of our city. This time, however, the sign conveyed a different message. It proclaimed in large bold letters, "Pollution Control Project."

In prior years this would have been referred to as a flood control project, but during the 1970s the mayor's name had to be associated with those good words, *Pollution Control.* Those words had become a new distinctive perceived consumer value. You may recognize some perceived values that were relevant in the 1970s: organic, biodegradable, energy saving, solar powered. In other fields you may recognize words such as electronic, bionic, hydroponic.

In the late 1940s and throughout the 1950s the United States government provided educational benefits for the veterans of World War II. At the same time the country was experiencing a baby boom and

81

economic growth. The veterans were children during the Great Depression preceding the war. They wanted something better than hard times and war for their children. For themselves, education held the promise of a better future. And for their children higher education seemed a necessity. The marketers of children's toys responded by providing toys that were "educational."

In the 1960s and 1970s the country shifted some of its concern to the environment and consumer protection. Safety and health became important to both children of the baby boom and their parents. And the marketers of children's toys responded by providing toys that were "safe." You may have observed another change in the 1980s. Toys reflect the new infatuation with electronic technology and computers. Batteries are an integral part of most toys.

As you can see, the descriptive words that induce people to spend their money change with time. There can be no closed list of perceived consumer values to describe a business concept; it must be a timely list. Business managers might be well advised to keep attuned to what words are in fashion and alert to the new ones appearing in the media, the literature, and popular music.

MAKING THE CONCEPT VIABLE

There is more to the description of a business concept than a list of its perceived values. Another important criteria is that the perceived value to the buyer must be more than the actual value to the seller.

A business concept must be a viable economic entity. A business must produce more than it consumes, and it must produce it in such a way that the business can meet critical payments as they come due. The value is determined, as in any free market transaction, by what a willing buyer will pay a willing seller. The value is not intrinsic in the thing being given up. It is intrinsic in what the parties are willing to agree to at the moment. But the established value at which the transaction will take place must be more than the cost to the seller. In addition to the price being right, payment must be made in a timely manner or the seller will go broke.

It is not necessary to prepare balance sheet forecasts to describe a viable business concept. They are not so complex that an entrepreneur can't understand them, but they are the end product of the forecasting process. From the perspective of the manager the intermediate steps toward preparing the balance sheet are more understandable and of more significance.

The intermediate steps are a description of what money flows in and out during a period of time. These are related to what the manager can and does do directly or indirectly through other people. The formal names for these presentations are the *income statement forecast* and the *cash flow forecast*. The former relates the time and the magnitude of obligations to transfer money. The latter relates the time and the magnitude of the obligations fulfilled. They are described in detail in Chapters 34 and 35.

Preparing these two forecasts forces consideration of all the economic factors of the business concept. They cannot be prepared without determining, or at least estimating, sales, salaries, rent, insurance, depreciation, advertising, and all the other expenses incurred in conducting the business. These forecasts are a precise and concise description of the business activities and their results. You can add all the words that seem appropriate to dress up the picture or make it interesting to someone else, but to someone who can read financials the numbers tell the story.

Distinctive perceived consumer values are related to the starting point in preparing forecasts. They begin with *sales*. All of the activity of the business is built around preparing what is to be sold, selling it, and getting paid for the sale.

Whether sufficient sales will develop to permit the business concept to be viable depends on the consumer's perception of value in what is being offered. Without sales the basic transaction describing a business doesn't exist. With sales there is at least the opportunity for the concept to be viable. To confirm that viability it is necessary to portray the future operations of the business in terms of the forecasts.

Copious footnotes describing how each item in the forecasts was derived are an integral part of the description of a viable concept. If some logic may be too involved or lengthy to confine to footnotes it can be described elsewhere. For instance, and in particular, the description of the product or service, the customer, and the channel of distribution to the customer deserves more than a cryptic remark in the footnotes.

It is evident that a business concept that has at least a chance of succeeding in the marketplace is described by much more than a brief press release statement. A superficial description implies superficial knowledge by the describer. To those who provide financial support to a new business, superficiality also implies risk. And they are right.

15

Distinctive
Business Functions

The spectrum of kinds of businesses is so great that we quite naturally want to classify them into groups. Our dealings with a retail establishment are so different from our interaction with a large manufacturing corporation, usually from the position of an employee or a customer, that we see them as different things. If we are in the business world we see manufacturing as entirely different from retailing, to say nothing of a service business.

CLASSIFICATION BY
HANDLING OF GOODS

The conventional way to classify businesses is related to their handling of goods. Wholesale is differentiated from retail in that the wholesaler handles bulk quantities and the retailer handles individual units. Manufacturing differs in that it assembles finished goods from bits and pieces. Service businesses usually handle few or no goods at all.

In this conventional classification system are the following categories:

1. Manufacturing
2. Wholesale
3. Retail
4. Contracting
5. Service

In this spectrum the manufacturing firm assembles parts into a whole product. The wholesaler receives large quantities from the manufacturer and distributes smaller quantities to the users of those smaller quantities. The smaller bulk users may be retailers who distribute the goods to the end consumers or they might be contractors who install the goods for the benefit of the end users. Service firms repair and maintain the goods in the hands of the end users. They may also provide advice and counsel, function as an intermediary, or supply labor of a specialized kind.

Immediately you observe that within each of these classifications is a spectrum of business types. There are job shop manufacturers, who make one or a few of any product, and production line manufacturers, who make thousands, if not millions, of a single product. There are process manufacturers, as in the chemical and petroleum industries, and there are batch manufacturers. There are wholesalers, who stock an inventory of goods, and distributors or manufacturers' representatives, who do not hold any inventory.

The term *contracting* covers a multitude of businesses from building houses, offices, highways, and bridges to plumbing, painting, television repair, and air conditioning. They are related by the need to perform their work at a place of the customer's choosing and by the job shop characteristic of a clear beginning and end to the task.

To say you have a service business provides very little idea of what the business is. It does say what the business is not. But service may imply providing advice or providing repairs to existing products, or it might imply selling gasoline. The organization of those who sell gasoline is the Association of Service Station Operators.

We find it curious that when bankers are asked what they sell, most reply, service. The same is true of insurance agents. Accountants and lawyers are usually more specific. They say they sell accounting service and legal service.

There are also similarities among businesses of different classifications. Wholesale, retail, and service businesses are heavily oriented toward selling. Contracting and job shop manufacturing are characterized by a heavy bidding effort, a different kind of selling effort. And then there are the portions of the spectrum between these clear classifications. A tire store is like a retailer in that the customers come to the store and buy in small quantities, but like a contractor in that it repairs and installs tires.

CLASSIFICATION BY BUSINESS FUNCTION

We need a classification of businesses for the purpose of discussing a business concept. A means to this end is to think of business functions:

1. Raw Materials
2. Manufacturing
3. Distribution
4. Sales
5. Service
6. Administration
7. Finance
8. Research and development

These may be viewed as major functions within a fully vertically integrated business; for instance, a company that owns forests, lumber mills, railway cars and trucks, warehouses, and the retail stores to sell the finished wood product. In this array of functions a construction contractor may be viewed among the manufacturers. A plumbing contractor may be viewed as a service. The intent, however, is broader than that.

A construction contractor must obtain raw material to build something. There is the distribution function of getting materials, labor, and supervision to the job site. Sales is a bidding effort of the contractor. Finance and administration are essential functions of this same construction contractor.

Let's examine an example. In his heyday Henry Ford had an integrated business including rubber plantations at one end of the spectrum and automobile dealers at the other. He had an acceptance corporation to finance sales and vast machine shops to manufacture engines. Although Henry Ford's managerial style has been questioned, it is clear that his vast empire must have had extensive administrative control. And building such an industrial giant required financing of major proportions.

Imagine a visit to the rubber plantation. What kind of people do you see? What are they doing? How are they dressed? What language do they speak? What can they hope to give their children?

Now imagine a visit to the Ford Motor Company assembly plant. Ask the same questions of this situation. Also, are the people different from those on the plantation? Do they have a different educational background? Are they physically bigger? Are they likely to have a suntan during the winter months?

Imagine another visit, this time to the administrative offices of the company. Are you surprised to find a large number of clerks? Do the people here dress differently from those in the prior two places? Do these people look like they would enjoy a deer hunt in the Canadian Rockies?

Try just one more visit in your mind's eye. Go to the loading dock at the back of the plant where raw materials are being delivered to the assembly plant. There are big tractor-trailer trucks and a railroad siding. How would you like to have a difference of opinion with the people who work there?

This is not an attempt to stereotype people. It is a fact of life that people will seek and find employment where they can feel comfortable with their coworkers. They will seek work that provides them the opportunity to use their talents and aptitudes. Or they will find employment in an area close enough to their innate qualities and adjust to the environment in which they find themselves. The result is that when you visit an established organization you find different kinds of people in the different business functions.

The mode of operation in different business functions is quite different. It is normal for business offices to work from nine to five, granted that many work from eight to five. It is also normal for production workers to work from eight to four, four to twelve, and twelve to eight. It is not unusual to find that production workers begin at seven. Research people are more likely to work the hours of office people, but with surprising disregard for the five o'clock whistle.

The methods of managing these different functions can be almost foreign to one another. Think of managing salespeople versus managing assembly line workers. One entrepreneurial company built a sophisticated biological research laboratory in the same building as the production facilities. Within a year it became evident that they had to be separated. The different behaviors of the two groups caused friction between them. A special research laboratory building had to be constructed more than a mile from the production building.

Remunerating these different groups is also not done the same way. Salespeople want and need immediate tangible rewards for their accomplishments. Research people take a much longer range view. They usually get paid monthly. But imagine telling the production workers they will be paid monthly. Managing in each business function is very different; experience in one function does not prepare a manager for service in another.

These functions in the vertically integrated business may be separate businesses. Raw materials as a function is usually a business in its own right. A term now in vogue to describe this kind of firm is *extraction industry*. It may include strip mining, deep-hole mining, harvesting the forests, shallow and deep gas or oil wells, offshore wells, quarrying, and similar pursuits.

Manufacturing may include light assembly or heavy production, jobbing or processing. A manufacturer might make trucks or women's skirts. Distribution refers to moving things physically from one place to another. It is usually accomplished by trucks, trains, or airplanes. It may include local delivery or long haul, warehouse transfer and storage, or pipeline and conveyer belt transportation.

Sales, in the context of a business function, includes all the marketing and selling efforts, whether they be wholesale, retail, door to door, mail order, national service, or local service. Service is frequently assigned to the sales function for administration; however, it is a different function. In this context it refers to keeping that which was sold in working condition after the customer has acquired it.

Administration is a function apart. It is usually viewed by people in the other functions as a necessary evil at best and an unnecessary interference at worst. It is characterized by paperwork, often appearing to be created by the administrators without regard for the burden it imposes on the productive functions and without clear knowledge of its usefulness. The clerical function, which occupies the time of a large proportion of the administrative people, is designed for a narrow perspective. And frequently clerks hold positions that influence people's very lives and livelihood.

Finance is a world of banking. In any organization accounting

87

and financial control may or may not be associated with those responsible for finance. Accounting is an administrative procedure. Finance has to do with providing the capital required by a business. It deals with banks, underwriters, insurance companies, commercial finance companies, investors, brokers, auditors, and the legal assistance needed to conform to the rules and regulations of the Securities and Exchange Commission. There is a whole industry devoted to the world of finance and within that industry a myriad of business types of all sizes and complexions.

Research and development is another world apart with a spectrum of activities from the achievement-oriented product development to pure research. Research is characterized by a large proportion of very intelligent and well-educated people. They introduce their own intellect and logic into management decisions, disregarding their often limited perspective. Where administrative people live by the book, research people try to rewrite the book continuously.

There are obvious differences in managing the different functions in business, and there are even more subtle differences. To recap but a few, the differences are in the types of people involved, the modes of operation, managing these people in these modes, selling the services or the products of each function, and financially supporting each.

DECIDING TO EXPAND INTO NEW FUNCTIONS

A common difficulty for entrepreneurs during the growth of their businesses is expanding into another distinctive business function. We visited a proprietary label bottler and tablet maker for the drug trade with a view to acquiring the company. The business had small profit margins because the buyers squeeze the last penny out of their proprietary suppliers. It also had to contend with a large number of labels, 9,000 in this case. It served a market having about 150-mile radius and had grown to the point where it frequently shipped in truckload lots.

This enterprising entrepreneur observed the number of eighteen-wheel tractor-trailers leaving the plant and made a calculation of the cost to operate those trucks. When this cost was compared to the freight bill it appeared that the margins in the distribution business were phenomenal compared to those in bottling. The obvious next step was to buy a few eighteen-wheel tractor-trailers.

Within a year the business was available for acquisition and unable to command a price comparable to similar businesses in the area. The problem, as it turns out, was not in the lack of better profit margins. It was in the management time consumed in learning how to deal with a different kind of people, a different set of regulatory constraints, a work force that wasn't on the premises, and a host of other differences in the new business function.

We have a friend who built a multimillion dollar business with outlets across the country providing swimming pool supplies. This entrepreneur observed that one item that moved well had a very small profit margin when compared with the rest of the pool supplies—the pumps. Our entrepreneur-friend determined to acquire the pump manufacturer and thereby add the maker's profit margin to the seller's. As you might guess, within a year our friend was looking for a way out of an incredible dilemma. The manufacturing subsidiary had consumed all the cash the pool supply business could generate and was in need of still more.

When the stories of successful entrepreneurs are examined, one consistent thread is that they started in one distinctive business function and stayed there. You might immediately point to some example of an entrepreneur who built a vertically integrated business. How do we reconcile these examples?

Some of the speakers at our distinguished entrepreneur speaker series had large integrated businesses. An interesting perspective emerged, however, from their record of sales versus time. They have a very long period of slow but steady and consistent profitable growth financed from within. At some point they became what is termed "of investment quality" by the finance community, and they went public. From that point on their growth was typically exponential.

When we read or hear about these outstanding entrepreneurs we see the exponential portion of their record. The long, slow foundation building is not interesting to the investment community or the media. But the truth is there was a long period of solid building within one distinctive business function.

A new business or a young business can barely support the management, administration, and marketing it has to have to operate in one distinctive function. Different business functions require different handling in each of these areas. This imposes an additional nonproductive burden on an already overburdened revenue-generating segment of the business.

Successful entrepreneurs start the smallest possible viable business concept and concentrate on it until it works very well. They get to know more and more about their little business until they know more about it than anyone else. They become *the* expert about their business.

While discussing the entrepreneur's career path we pointed out that having made the business work well they then perceive growth opportunities. At this point it is very easy for them to conclude that having made this business work they can make any business work. They frequently see green pastures on the other side of the fence. The successful entrepreneurs go back to Steps 2 and 3 on the career path; they develop and refine a business concept for the growth they will undertake. Then they expand their little business. They don't leap after someone else's headaches. They build on their own experience and expertise.

There will be more to say about these distinctive business functions in Chapter 22. There is good fundamental reason why the most successful entrepreneurs are those who have, for whatever reason, chosen to build their castles in their own backyards.

The Economic
Experience Curve

The words used to describe a business concept are an open-ended list and they change with time. In dealing with a business concept and its chances of success in the marketplace, it would be helpful to have something which, in a sense, stands still. A model emerged in the recent past that provides just that kind of help. It is derived from some very common experience plus a somewhat surprising observation of how prices change with time in the marketplace. It is a relatively simple tool to construct strategy and tactics for a business concept.

THE LEARNING CURVE

We have all observed that when we perform a repetitive task we get better at it. Those daily practice sessions on a musical instrument when we were young were an excellent demonstration. So was learning to drive an automobile.

The Industrial Revolution precipitated the creation of many repetitive tasks in manufacturing. Following the Civil War in the United States and the introduction of mass production of interchangeable parts, workers were given a part to produce and allowed to make it in the best way they could. With repetition of the task, they got better.

Somewhat later, Frederick W. Taylor observed that some workers managed to complete a task in less time than others.[1] He proposed that if the slower workers were shown how the faster workers did the job it would be possible for the entire work force to increase its productivity. To this end he began studying and timing the body motions of workers.

Many startling improvements emerged from Taylor's work. The locations of on and off switches were changed. The height of workbenches was adjusted. Unnecessary reaching for parts was eliminated. In time all of this resulted in conveyors to bring the work to the workers and to take away the finished pieces. By the end of the 1800s, Taylor's work led to improvements in productivity that helped this country to become the leader of the Industrial Revolution.

During the first decades of the 1900s it was a general practice in progressive production firms to make time and motion studies of repetitive manufacturing tasks. By the time the fledgling aircraft industry came along these studies were routine.

In 1925 the base commander of Wright-Patterson Air Force Base in Ohio observed a curious trend in the total man-hours required to build aircraft.[2] This observation was first reported publicly eleven years later when T. P. Wright noted that the direct labor required to construct an airplane decreased 20 percent each time the number of airplanes manufactured had doubled.[3] The second plane was manufactured with only 80 percent of the labor required for the first. The fourth plane required only 80 percent as much labor as the second, and the eighth took 80 percent of that consumed to make the fourth.

It is surprising how much time passed between this report and subsequent publications of significance. Frank J. Andress speculated on a general theory of learning in the *Harvard Business Review* in 1954.[4] Winifred B. Hirschmann published an article in the same journal in 1964 providing a more general discussion on this theory and its application to industries that appear to have little labor content.[5] In 1968 the staff of the Boston Consulting Group, Inc., published the results of a series of studies relating price decline to accumulated total production experience.[6]

Time studies on a wide variety of production tasks have revealed that the time required to perform a repetitive task is decreased by an equal percentage each time the worker doubles total accumulated experience performing the task. The size of the decrease appears to be about 15 percent. Surprisingly, the phenomenon continues for as long as the diligent worker continues the task.

When these results are plotted on a graph they form a curve that decreases in value exponentially, as shown in Figure 16-1. The cumulative number of times the task has been performed is shown as one to four. These represent hundreds, thousands, or dozens, whatever unit is applicable. If the repetitive task is thought of as resulting in the creation of a unit of some sort, then the curve suggests that, on the average, the time required to produce the last unit made is always less than that required for any prior unit.

If this same curve is plotted on a logarithmic scale, on log-log paper, it becomes a straight line and its slope is a direct measure of the reduction in time required to perform the task each time the total accumulated experience doubles. Figure 16-2 shows the data from Figure 16-1 plotted on log-log coordinates. Again, the horizontal axis may represent hundreds, thousands, or whatever.

The horizontal scale of this figure suggests the major limitation to progressing down the curve forever. When total accumulated experience is 100 it may not be difficult to achieve experience totaling 200. By

91

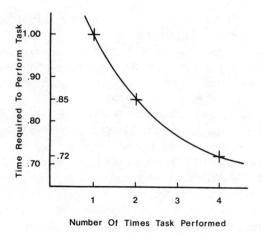

FIGURE 16-1 The Learning Curve.

the time accumulated experience becomes 1 million it may take a long time to achieve 2 million. Eventually the total past experience will be so great that it could take nearly forever to double one more time. Nonetheless, although the absolute decrease in time required to perform the task is small, the percentage decrease continues.

The exponential curve in these two figures has become very well known and is called the *learning curve*. During World War II government contracts for tanks, planes, and ships were priced on the basis of this anticipated learning.

Hirschmann's work suggested that the learning curve applied even to industries with little direct labor content. This report, which seemed hard to justify, was followed by a very significant extensive study from the Boston Consulting Group, Inc.

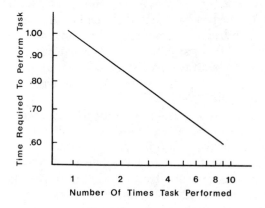

FIGURE 16-2 The Learning Curve on Log-Log Coordinates.

The Boston group attempted to go back and determine historically the time consumed to produce a broad range of products. That information was nearly impossible to find. Instead it chose to examine the price of products versus the total number of such products ever produced. Price and quantity information is generally available from annual reports, trade association data, government statistics, product catalogs, and promotional materials.

There were several opportunities to observe new fast-growth products during these studies. The electronics industry was just beginning its explosive growth with the introduction of silicon transistors, germanium diodes, and integrated circuits. A surprising picture emerged. Figure 16-3 shows the characteristic shape of the graph plotting the sales price of these products versus the total accumulated industry experience, measured in total units manufactured to date. The data is plotted on log-log coordinates, and the price is in constant dollars, that is, adjusted to remove the effect of inflation.

The line connecting the data points has three characteristic segments. The first very gently slopes downward, the second has a dramatic downward slope, and the third has a slope between these two. After some investigation it was found that the first segment is associated with the introduction of a new product, such as the transistor, and the entry of many producers into the market to satisfy the great demand. The second segment illustrates the shakeout when overcapacity of the manufacturers causes prices to tumble in the marketplace. Weak competitors fall by the wayside during the shakeout. The third segment represents the price history in the stable industry that emerges when supply and demand are approximately in balance. This portion of the curve is long and consistent. It has a gentle slope downward, indicating decreasing

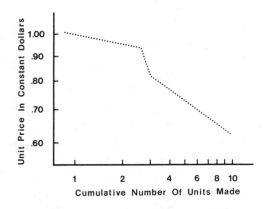

FIGURE 16-3 Price versus Cumulative Experience.

price with the accumulation of experience, provided the effects of inflation are removed.

Stable industries generally have characteristic net profit margins as a percentage of sales. For instance, grocery supermarkets usually net 1 percent to 2 percent of sales on high volume. These characteristic margins are, of course, subject to change with the general economic conditions and the changing tides of competition. Still, when viewed over long time periods in a stable economy, industry margins vary within their own characteristic ranges.

Because the third segment in Figure 16-3 represents price per unit in a stable industry, we can subtract the characteristic net profit margin from it and obtain a characteristic expense. The result is a line parallel to the third segment, as shown in Figure 16-4. If this expense line is extrapolated to the left, it turns out that the industry achieved this acceptable profit margin shortly after the new product entered the market. In response to the law of supply and demand the producers increased their margins in a seller's market. This induced other producers to join the competition, while reducing some of the demand that would have existed if prices were lower.

As the number of producers increases they find that their salespeople are running into interference from the salespeople of other producers. No matter how many perceived consumer values there may be, price is always a value to contend with in the marketplace. When a buyer's market develops, competition for sales produces lower prices. With overcapacity among the producers the result is inevitable; prices tumble and the producers with higher expenses have to retire from the competition.

Figure 16-4 suggests that in a stable industry the competitors are reducing their expense by an equal percentage each time the total cumulative experience doubles. That sounds very much like a manifestation of the learning curve.

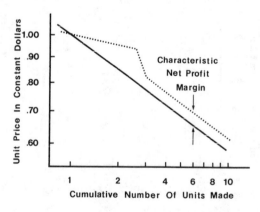

FIGURE 16-4 Typical Expense Curve Derived from Price Data and Characteristic Profit Margins.

Figure 16-5 illustrates a portion of the price curve plotted on log-log coordinates. A segment of the horizontal axis would represent the units produced during some time period, such as one month. The height of the slice indicates the price of the units produced during that period. That price multiplied by the number of units sold is the total sales for the period, or the *revenue* that would be reported on an income statement.

The height of the column made by this slice is composed of a variety of expenses, usually beginning with the direct materials and the direct labor to work on the materials. These are like building blocks in the tower, as shown in Figure 16-5. The next block would be the indirect expense associated with the workers doing their job, the overhead. Then a block must be added for the front office—the purchasing, personnel, accounting, and, collectively, general and administrative expense.

Having made the units it is necessary to sell them—marketing is another brick on the pile. Then there may be the effort to improve the present product or to generate the next product, research and development. After all these expenses necessary to make the product and convey it to the customers there is the overall expense of having a country in which there is sufficient law, justice, safety, and means of travel to operate. The expense of this burden is reflected in the income tax, another brick.

The final brick, lying between revenue and the total pile of expense bricks, is the profit. This picture is exactly the same as an income statement or a profit and loss statement. It is the *accrual accounting* representation of what a product or service sells for and the expenses attributable to the product or service sold. The accrual method of accounting makes the curve relatively smooth and consistent.

The expense of having a country in which to operate is not fully covered by income taxes. The remainder of this expense is included in

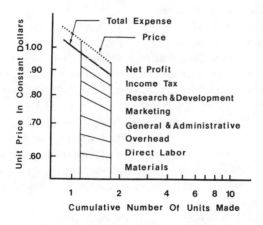

FIGURE 16-5 Price and Expense Curves and Their Relationship to the Income Statement.

the other bricks; for instance, part of the price paid for the materials covers taxes paid by the materials supplier. Part of the labor wages will be taxed in many ways, including income tax, Social Security tax, sales tax, and the city, county, and state taxes paid by the wage earner. Part of the overhead will include taxes on fuel, power, purchases of supplies, and the employer's contribution to Social Security taxes for the laborers. General and administrative expense will include taxes on fuel, power, Social Security, sales tax on purchases of supplies and equipment, plus city, county, and state levies on things like water, sewer, inventory, and so on. Research and development and marketing will include their share of similar taxes.

Interest paid on borrowed working capital will appear in both overhead and general and administrative expense. The expense of using expensive plant and equipment will show up as depreciation under the same headings. Improvements to existing facilities will be evident in these same categories as amortization, and so will employee training and fringe benefits.

The expense of the capital contributed by the owners comes out of the top brick, the profit. It is usually called *dividends* in corporations and *owner's drawings* in proprietorships and partnerships. This brick supplies the working capital to support larger inventories and accounts receivable as the business grows. And it provides the means with which to make investments in tools and fixtures, to acquire new plant and equipment, or to improve existing facilities.

The implications of this expense curve are profound and fundamental. The fully allocated expense per unit in constant dollars decreases by a characteristic percentage each time total cumulative experience in producing the unit doubles. Like the learning curve, the decrease continues for as long as experience is accumulated. The limitation is, as with the learning curve, the dimensions of the horizontal axis. In time the total cumulative experience becomes so great that it will take nearly forever to double one more time.

This fundamental relationship has been called by various names, including *progress function, learning curve,* and *experience curve.* We refer to it as the *economic experience curve* because it portrays the fully allocated expense in constant dollars.

The Boston Consulting Group has published economic experience curves for a broad range of industries, including germanium transistors, silicon transistors, germanium diodes, silicon diodes, integrated circuits, crude oil, motor gasoline, ethylene, polystyrene, polyvinylchloride, primary aluminum, primary magnesium, titanium sponge, monochrome television receivers, free-standing gas ranges, free-standing electric ranges, facial tissue, Japanese beer, electric power, and refined cane sugar.[7]

The results of these studies are impressive. Price, in constant dollars, declined with experience in a consistent and persistent pattern in each industry examined. The percentage decrease with each doubling of experience varied over a range with 20 percent to 30 percent being dominant. It appears that 30 percent is achievable.

WHAT MAKES THE CURVE POSSIBLE?

Our initial reaction to this phenomenon is to ask how it can be. We accept the learning concept with its approximately 15 percent improvement, but where and how do we obtain approximately 30 percent decrease in the fully allocated expense?

The answer lies in the behavior of organizations. Learning by the individuals in the organization contributes a dominant part of the expense reduction. Greater volume permits organizations to take advantage of specialization. In small-volume production a worker may perform several operations. With larger volume the job can be broken down so that each worker performs only one operation, but performs it many more times per day. Thus each worker doing a specialized task proceeds down his or her individual learning curve faster. It takes each worker fewer weeks or months to achieve another doubling of cumulative total experience measured in number of times the repetitive task has been completed.

With specialization comes *scale*. We often hear of scale in production as though it meant size. We have met many managers who assume that being bigger, as by acquiring another business, will provide economies of scale. This is a patent misinterpretation of the terminology. Scale means jigs and fixtures. It means dedicated specialized equipment. It is related to size only in that such special jigs, fixtures, and dedicated equipment require sufficient production volume to amortize their cost in a reasonable time. Scale refers to bigger size only to the extent of bigger production quantities of an individual product.

Scale requires investment, and this in itself becomes a contributing factor to the decrease in fully allocated expense. Producers without access to investment capital are severely constrained in continuing down their economic experience curves. Producers with access to the public market for investment capital have a decided advantage on the same curve. Investment provides the ability to take advantage of technology and innovation.

Probably the most dramatic improvements in reducing expense come from refining the design of the product and its method of manufacture, employing new materials and new techniques. Continuing advances in technology provide a stream of opportunities. Experience with manufacturing provides insights on how to produce more easily. New materials, new methods of using materials, and new methods of joining materials continually refine products so that they are easier to make. Just

97

as welding replaced bolts, cements and adhesives replace welding. We call this process *redesign*.

The factors that permit a producer to decrease expense per unit along an economic experience curve are learning, specialization, scale, investment, and redesign.

To move down an economic experience curve requires an aggressive management devoted to expense improvement. This is not a condition of management, however. The marketplace imposes more than enough pressure on management to be aggressive in this area. If only one competitor improves expenses more than the others, the conditions are created for instability in the marketplace as in the first two line segments in Figure 16-3.

If the producer with lower expense reduces price to maintain the industry profit margin, the producers with high expenses will go broke competing. The producers with the higher expense must aggressively pursue expense reduction or be continually threatened with price competition and loss of their share of the market.

On occasion a dominant competitor will emerge who gains cumulative experience far greater than the other competitors, resulting in much lower expenses. The dominant competitor may then set the market price high enough that the other competitors can stay in the competition, but low enough that they don't interfere with the dominant competitor's market share. The dominant competitor will then use the greater profit margin to build the next product and create another new economic experience curve.

Where does a curve end? It doesn't really. It gets replaced. Technology produces a step change in the product or service offered, and something new displaces the product described by a curve. For instance, slide rules were used for generations, and a dominant competitor held sway in the marketplace until integrated circuits made possible the hand-held calculator. The curve describing slide rules is no longer in the competition. Instead some very dynamic producers who fully comprehend and appreciate the economic experience curve provide calculators that are quicker and easier to use, will print the answer, and have a built-in memory.

Other examples of displaced curves are kerosene stoves replaced by gas or electric stoves, horses replaced by the internal combustion engine, and, for some applications, internal combustion engines replaced by jet engines.

It is not often that scientists, engineers, or inventors can come up with an entirely new product comparable to the office copier or the telephone. On the other hand, almost everybody can see how to improve an existing product or service. You can always improve on an existing methodology utilizing technology and innovation. This prolongs the life of an economic experience curve. The curve is killed when it is displaced by a new economic experience curve.

98

The Boston Consulting Group has applied its findings to its big-business clients. Some large corporations have applied the concept of the curve to their new products. Texas Instruments, Inc., is one of the most outstanding examples with its calculators and wristwatches using integrated circuits and microprocessors. It turns out, however, that the significance of the curve is greatest when applied to a new business concept.

If the expense curve of Figure 16-4, plotted on log-log paper, is plotted on ordinary coordinates, it looks like Figure 16-1. Although the percentage decrease in expense is the same for each doubling of experience, the biggest absolute dollar improvements are in the first few doublings. And to double from one to two or from 100 to 200 is not unreasonable for a new business. There are ten doublings in going from the first unit to the one-thousandth unit.

The economic experience curve describes fully allocated unit expense in constant dollars versus total cumulative number of units made for a group of competitors, as in an industry. It may also be used to describe the same relationship for the individual competitors. It provides a basis for comparing your business concept's position with that of your competitors. If you can identify which curve you are on, you can learn much about the strategy and tactics that will give your business concept the opportunity to succeed in the marketplace.

Although most entrepreneurs and aspiring entrepreneurs of our acquaintance are not familiar with the experience curves, some have read articles on the subject in the popular business magazines. A number of consulting firms have emerged that apply experience curve theory to decision making for managers of very big businesses, multinational companies, and, more recently, the global firms.[8] A body of strategic planning knowledge is emerging, and these curves are an important part of that knowledge base.[9]

The banner headlines in some magazine articles occasionally cast doubt on the validity of the experience curves, but the text of these articles does not. While advanced thinkers in strategic planning learn more about the fine points of applying the theory to very large companies, they sometimes find that the application is not as simple as the fundamental description of the curves might suggest. But that does not alter the facts presented by plotting price data versus cumulative experience. On the contrary, investigations since the Boston Consulting Group first published its findings only confirm the existence of experience curves.

Curves similar to those described in this chapter have been constructed for the wholesale price of a standard basket of goods and services for a country, in noninflated currency, versus that country's cumulative growth in gross national product, again in noninflated currency. It appears that for most countries the resulting curve looks like the economic experience curve, with the same 20 percent to 30 percent decrease in cost for each doubling of cumulative gross national product.

Until your new or growing business becomes very large, there is little need for concern about the global implications of the curves. The realm of the entrepreneur is the far left end of the curve. The strategy for the entrepreneur will be discussed in the next few chapters—know which curve you are on, and be farther down your curve than anyone else.

17

The Economic
Productivity Curve

Fully allocated expense per unit, measured in constant dollars, declines with the accumulation of experience in a consistent and persistent pattern. Fully allocated expense includes all expense, the total *input* needed to produce the unit. The unit itself is the *output*. Output divided by input is *productivity*.

The economic experience curve implies an *economic productivity curve*. If the data used to plot the former curve, expense in constant dollars to produce the last unit made, is used to plot the units produced per constant dollar consumed in making the last unit, the resulting curve describes productivity, the number of units produced per fully allocated unit of expense.

Figure 17-1 is an economic experience curve plotted on log-log paper showing 25 percent decrease in expense per doubling of accumulated experience. Figure 17-2 is the same information plotted as output per unit of input, an economic productivity curve. On this 25 percent curve a unit produced at an expense of $1 at some point in time will have an expense of 75¢ when total accumulated experience has doubled. The output per constant dollar input will have increased from 1 to 1.33 (1.00 divided by 0.75). An organization that has a 25 percent expense reduction has a 33 percent productivity improvement with each doubling of accumulated experience.

The same reasoning applied to the learning curve demonstrates that a worker performing a repetitive task and reducing the time to perform the task by 15 percent with each doubling of accumulated experience has a productivity improvement of 18 percent (1.00 divided by 0.85).

The United States government's published figures on productivity of the American worker fluctuate with the condition of the economy and relate year-to-year or quarter-to-quarter change. Its definition of productivity provides a manager with limited help in managing a business. The economic productivity curve provides managers and workers

101

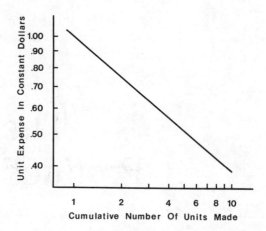

FIGURE 17-1 An Economic Experience Curve.

with an objective measure of efficiency and attainable goals and objectives for planning.

When considering a business concept and describing it in the precise language of what comes in and what goes out, income statements and cash flows, the implications of these two economic curves suggest what you can do and what you can expect of the competition.

IMPROVING PRODUCTIVITY

These curves can be more readily understood when applied to production examples where large quantities of identical units are produced. The underlying principles, however, apply to all businesses. For instance, commercial artists would seem to be creating something new

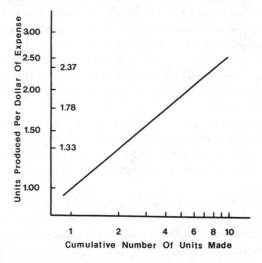

102

FIGURE 17-2 An Economic Productivity Curve.

with each assignment, and that is true. But faced with competition, they have had to specialize to some extent, as in concentrating on annual reports or logo designs. And they have taken advantage of technology and innovation. They no longer print or paint letters of the alphabet. These are available in a myriad of type styles and sizes on easily transferred rub-off paper. A veritable rainbow of transparent and translucent films are available for cutting and pasting in lieu of painting. Even pencil sharpeners and erasers now have electric motors.

The dry cleaner's retail outlet now has a conveyer that allows the store clerk to dial a customer's order number. The finished garments are automatically brought to the clerk. Fast-food outlets make hamburgers on a conveyor belt. Paper cups and plates along with plastic knives and forks have eliminated the dishwasher. The floor and furniture in a recently constructed McDonald's are an inspiration if you imagine yourself doing the housekeeping.

Productivity is improved by the same factors as the economic experience curve: learning, specialization, scale, investment, and redesign. Learning occurs with extended experience. This would suggest keeping employee turnover to a minimum. Of course, other factors enter the decision to keep an employee, but the curves suggest that having found a good employee, the wise management option is to hold him or her.

Specialization suggests reducing the number of tasks assigned to an individual employee. In a new business the few people employed have to do everything. With growth in volume the tasks can be divided into smaller and smaller pieces so that individuals can specialize and increase their rate of progress down the learning curve. Granted, there are limitations to this effort. When specialization produces boredom, progress may cease or even be reversed. Also, the volume of work needs to keep everyone fully occupied. Nothing to do is as boring as too much of the same thing.

Specialization increases the opportunities to take advantage of scale. Even without specialization, jigs and fixtures can be designed to make the task easier, simpler, and faster. With specialization the cost of special jigs and fixtures can be more easily justified and amortized. In general, it is easier for people to conceive of gadgetry to improve the way a job is done when the task is more specialized, less complicated. Very often the jigs that make a simple task easier can be made by anyone in the house who is handy with his or her hands.

When investment is needed to improve productivity, the manager of a new or small business faces an entirely new problem. External financing is hard to come by. It is constrained by the need for a track record demonstrating profitable growth, the cash flow to service debt, and the collateral to guarantee repayment. There is enough demand for external financing to support growth in accounts receivable and inventory that there is little opportunity to find additional money to provide specialized equipment.

Successful entrepreneurs are not averse to using secondhand furniture and equipment or makeshift facilities until their businesses become big enough and strong enough to afford something better. Even then they tend to be tight with their money. By the time they can afford new furniture and equipment they have learned what excellent quality items are readily available at a good price from other entrepreneurs who started out needing only the best. Successful entrepreneurs don't commit their meager resources to anything but productive assets.

Redesign often provides the greatest improvement in productivity. The implications of this factor are simplification of the production process, substitution of materials and supplies that cost less or may be assembled more cheaply, and improvement of the yield from a given input of resources.

One example of redesign is the hand-held quarter-inch electric drill. A few brand names, like Black & Decker, are common in the marketplace. Before World War II the drill had a cast-iron casing. After the war the casing was made of die-cast aluminum and had a dull gray appearance with a pitted surface. By the 1950s the same die-cast aluminum had a polished mirror finish. Since then some parts of the casing have been replaced with molded plastic material. Inside the drill the roller bearings have been replaced by porous metal sleeves, which have no moving parts and never need oil or grease. Despite the inflationary effects of the economy over a thirty-year period, the quarter-inch electric drill was priced in 1980 at one-third to one-half its price in 1950.

Texas Instruments, Inc., is an example of a company that understands and uses the principles of the economic experience curve. Its management accepts the principle and vigorously pursues the strategy it dictates. The company includes in its employee training a videotape instructional program called *Design-to-Cost*.[1] In the introductory training manual the president states that this design-to-cost concept must permeate the company and become second nature to those who design, manufacture, and market the company's products.

In the design-to-cost concept, unit cost is a primary design parameter, equal in importance to performance. The process begins with estimating price elasticity, that is, how the market will expand as price is reduced. This provides a basis for judging the volume and price at which an adequate share of the market may be obtained. Then, working backward, cost objectives are obtained by subtracting reasonable profit and indirect expense margins from price. This permits plotting cost versus cumulative production in the form of an economic experience curve. Finally, estimating volume to be shipped in successive time periods establishes dates on which cost objectives are to be met.

An article in *Business Week* suggests the results of this management dedication to the concept.[2] It reports that in integrated circuits Texas Instruments had beaten the Japanese at the low price end of the product line and Hewlett-Packard at the high end. The company was the dominant competitor worldwide in integrated circuits.

One of the greatest impediments to progress in improving productivity is communication between people. Whether attempting to pass along instruction or merely trying to make people feel good, as in providing praise for a job well done or a sympathetic ear, it takes time to talk to people. There is hardly any substitute for personal eye contact and verbal communication. A bigger paycheck helps for a little while. The gift of a gold wristwatch helps, again for a little while. But tangible items and mechanical memoranda, rules, and regulations, do not substitute for that innate human need for personal attention.

Abraham Maslow described this as the third step in the hierarchy of needs, the one immediately following the needs for the survival of the organism, the physiological and safety needs.[3] It is generally termed *love*, but it is not the moonstruck love of popular music, advertising media, or romantic journalism. It is the plain and simple expression of caring, concern, and interest for one person by another.

This caring and interest are communicated by words spoken directly to the person, but the message communicated depends as much on the arch of the eyebrows, the twinkle in an eye, and the turn of the lips during delivery as on the words themselves. This is what consumes the time. And there really cannot be a substitute. A conversation by telephone, even if accompanied by a video transmission, still leaves out the gross body language. The parting handshake confirms or denies the integrity of good words. The shrug of the shoulders as the speaker departs may impart a more lasting message than all the words.

As a new business begins few people are available. There is no need for formal communication. Everyone knows everything that is going on. As a business grows some people are separated from others, usually with good reason. Some, like the bookkeeper, need a workplace with peace and quiet. The office workers are separated from the production workers, because they need different environments to do their job. In time, the owner-manager needs lieutenants to assume responsibility for segments of the business. This separates those reporting to the lieutenants from the owner-manager.

When people no longer see, hear, and feel what is going on, they have to be provided with the knowledge and information pertinent to their function in the business. This leads to feelings of alienation, which demand the personal attention of some person perceived to be concerned, interested, and able to improve the pay and the position of the alienated employee.

This area of interpersonal communication does not lend itself very well to progress down a learning curve. But some examples exist where progress has been achieved. They derive from observation of the activities of people in two different situations, the small, new business and team sports.

In the small, new business everyone involved knows what everyone else is doing, why they are doing it, and how the group as a whole is progressing. They know what everyone else is saying, both verbally and nonverbally. This is usually an exciting and satisfying work environment. People feel participation, appreciation, and achievement. The environment is usually characterized by openness in human relationships, diligence in work effort, and satisfaction in achievement. The work is paced by the fastest worker, and the slower workers like it.

In team sports there is a hierarchy of authority and responsibility as in a business. The athletes perform their tasks to the best of their abilities with the encouragement, guidance, and control of the coaches. They also work under the threat of being replaced if their individual performance doesn't satisfy the objectives of the group as determined by the coaches. As in the business, even the coaches work under the threat of being replaced by the owners. But the group is small. Even in a complex team sport like football the number of players, coaches, and supporting personnel is sufficiently small for everyone in the group to know everyone else to the fullest extent that they have an interest in knowing them.

As in the case of an infantry platoon or a bomber crew, the closeness of a small group of people striving to achieve an objective breeds trust, sharing, and caring. The more difficult the objective the better. And progress is clearly evident to all the parties involved in the small group. In sports there is usually a very large scoreboard prominently displayed at the edge of the playing field. In a small business the number and size of the orders coming in and the satisfaction of the customers is known immediately by everyone. The infantry platoon occupies a hill, and the bomber crew returns home safely.

This array of observations suggests that small, cohesive work groups with clear and challenging objectives and a continuously displayed measure of progress can and do overcome the communication impediment to mounting the economic productivity curve. And the size of the cohesive group would seem to be no more than 150–300 people. Is there any need to mention that athletic groups, like football teams, continuously better their own performance statistics?

It is interesting to learn that Texas Instruments, Inc., management's philosophy is to maintain small profit centers, each acting as if it were a small company. They call these units *product-customer centers*. They range in size from $10 million to $100 million per year in sales; the management objective is to reduce their size to $10 million to $30 million.

In the research laboratories of this company there are only three levels of title or position. The director of research occupies the top level and the lowliest researcher has only one level of management between his or her position and that of the director. This is referred to as a *flat* organization. It has the characteristics of the small business, the athletic team, and the product-customer center.

There may still be examples where it is hard to imagine progressing down the curve, for instance, in the sale of residential real estate. In considering the sale of residential real estate it is helpful first to choose a unit measure of progress. There may be many activities involved in the business, but only one causes the customer to part with hard-earned cash. That is the "closing," where the buyers, sellers, realty agent, title company, and all the parties to the agreement sign their names and cash changes hands.

Bringing about this event involves some very time-consuming activities. Homes available for sale must be found by the realtor. Then proper descriptions of the properties are prepared with relevant data about schools, taxes, zoning, shopping, and so on. Next, potential buyers must be found, qualified as capable of purchasing a property, shown the property, and allowed, with some persuasion, to conclude that they want the house. Then there is the exchange of offers to determine the price and the offering of earnest money. The determination of whether the buyers can in fact obtain the financing follows. Finally, when each of these activities, and more, is successfully completed, a closing can be scheduled. Even then the sale is not over until the closing is completed.

Almost all of these activities involve people talking to people, an impediment to progress in improving productivity. But think a moment. Some of these activities have already been improved. The practice of multiple listing by groups of realtors has reduced the time consumed in finding homes for sale and in preparing descriptions of them. Multiple listing directories, complete with a photograph of each property, allow potential buyers to select the properties of most interest without leaving the realtor's office.

Split commissions allow a realtor to send the agent most familiar with the property to accompany a client to see it. And more recently national networks of multiple listing agencies make it possible to choose the few houses of interest before visiting a distant city. Prearranged financing and association with title companies and insurance agents further speed the flow of activities.

The economic productivity curve is composed of the same elements as the economic experience curve. The productivity of the workers represents a small portion of the slice, or column, shown in Figure 16-5. The overall productivity improvement results from improved effectiveness and efficiency everywhere in the column of expenses. Each function performed throughout the business must reduce expense in a consistent and persistent pattern. The expense of salaries for officers must decrease per unit produced. The expense of the accounting department must decrease per unit produced. Everything, including heat, light, rent, insurance, and business lunches must decrease per unit produced to remain competitive.

107

Adding new machinery to aid or replace workers may reduce the direct expense to produce the units, but if the added expense of interest payments, depreciation, maintenance, and better paid operators is equal to or greater than the savings in labor, the business has made no progress up its productivity curve.[4] Productivity improvement is not an expression of just the diligence or industriousness of the workers. Productivity improvements are the net result of managers, workers, suppliers, designers, financiers, and administrators, all moving down their experience curves simultaneously.

18

Dominant
and Subordinate
Competitors

The economic experience curve was first obtained by plotting price per unit in the marketplace versus total accumulated production volume industrywide. It thus represents price and volume for the group of competitors in the industry. Some competitors will have accumulated more experience than others, which suggests that some will have lower expenses than others. Price will be what the marketplace is willing to pay to support the total volume offered by all the competitors.

The curves resulting from the Boston Consulting Group studies suggest that fully allocated expense in constant dollars often declines 20 percent to 30 percent with each doubling of accumulated experience.[1] To understand the implications of this phenomenon Tozer examined an expense curve that declines by the more conservative 20 percent.[2] Such a curve, plotted on ordinary coordinates, is shown in Figure 18-1.

This curve is shown for two doublings, that is, from one to two and from two to four. These digits may represent tens, hundreds, thousands, or whatever unit is reasonable for a particular instance in the marketplace. The expense is chosen to be one dollar when accumulated experience is one to have a convenient starting point for the arithmetic. The one dollar could also represent whatever unit is applicable.

Three points on the curve of Figure 18-1 are marked for significance. When experience equals one, the fully allocated expense is $1. When experience doubles to two the expense is 80¢. When experience doubles again to four the expense is 64¢.

In stable industries where profit margins are characteristic of the industry and most, if not all, of the competitors are well down the curve, each competitor must be reducing expense according to the curve; those who do not will become weak competitors, lose their margins, and be forced to abandon the competition. It may be less evident, but the same expense declines occur throughout the life of the competition.

The effects of expense declines on competitors can be more dramatically demonstrated by looking at the beginning of the competi-

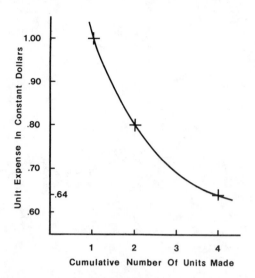

FIGURE 18-1 A 20 Percent Economic Experience Curve.

tion, a new entrepreneurial enterprise. In fact, although the theory is generally applied to large and established industries, its dollar impact is greatest for the new business or the entry of a new product or service into the marketplace.

TWO NEW COMPETITORS

Suppose that two competitors enter the marketplace with identical products on the same day. Suppose, further, that for whatever reason one sells two units each time the other sells one. If we look at them traveling down their curves at any point in time, one will have made and sold twice as many as the other. One has become the dominant competitor and might be identified by the letter D. The other has become a subordinate competitor, S.

Figure 18-2 shows these two competitors when S has made one unit. D, of course, will have made two. If the cost to S is $1.00, the cost to D will be 80¢. If both are selling their units at a profit, the price is probably in the vicinity of $1.10. From Figure 18-2 you can see that when S has a profit margin of 10¢, D has a margin of 30¢.

A new business, with all the demands on its resources, would clearly be better off in the position of the D competitor. Growth consumes cash and financial resources. Being the dominant competitor improves opportunities to increase financial resources. High growth rate is a normal characteristic of a new business. Month-to-month sales increases must be large in a new business if it is to reach the break-even point before its resources are gone. Beyond that, high-growth rate is probable, because the business is building on a small base of sales.

110

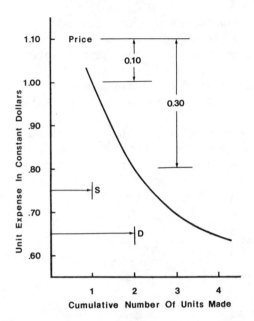

FIGURE 18-2 Two Competitors, One Dominant, D, and the Other Subordinate, S, on the 20 Percent Economic Experience Curve.

Doubling $5,000 in sales per month is achievable. Doubling $5 million in sales per month is cause for a cover article in a business magazine.

Suppose that our two competitors continue selling at the same two-for-one ratio while they double sales again. Now S will have cumulative experience two and D will have four. Their difference in expense will be diminished from 20¢ to 16¢, but D will be even further out in front in accumulated experience. The opportunity for S to catch up has diminished. Although the absolute difference in their expense has diminished, D continues to have expenses 20 percent less than S. Under any circumstances that is a significant figure.

TWO COMPETITORS: NEW VS. ESTABLISHED

Consider another scenario. It is very common for would-be entrepreneurs to observe a business concept that seems to be doing well and decide to do exactly the same thing. Even large companies jump into the competition when they observe that a market is not being completely satisfied by existing suppliers.

Suppose that our competitor D has been in the marketplace and has reached the cumulative experience of one when S decides to enter the field with the same product or service. Now suppose further that S is a super competitor, capable of selling one unit every time D sells one even from the first day (a most unlikely prospect). Watch them compete down the curve, as shown in Figure 18-3.

At some point in time, S will have made and sold enough to accumulate experience of one. Because D sells one every time S sells one, D will then be at two in accumulated experience. They are in exactly the same position as if both started at the same time and D sold two each time S sold one.

Look at the competitors at some later time when S has sold two. D will have sold three. S is still the same distance behind D in progressing down the curve. True, S will have reduced the gap in their relative costs, but D still has costs 10¢ less than S. Ten cents out of eighty is 12.5 percent, a significant difference.

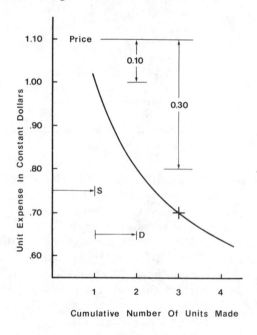

FIGURE 18-3 The S Competitor Joins the Competition after the D Competitor Is Well Established on the 20 Percent Economic Experience Curve.

THE ADVANTAGE OF DOMINANCE

Consider another aspect of this competition. Because S sells one each time D sells one, they have equal current market shares. If D holds 18 percent of the current market, S also holds 18 percent. To observers of the competition S and D are equals. But because D got into the marketplace first and cornered greater accumulated experience, D has a cost advantage.

This cost advantage may be useful in many ways. Suppose the demand for the product of S and D softens. The D salesperson will be talking to the same potential customer as the S salesperson. Remember that price is always a significant perceived consumer value. Even the very rich like to buy at a good price. The two salespeople facing the same potential customer will bring up the question of price or the potential customer will bring it up for them.

When the competitors are in the positions shown as experience one and two on Figure 18-2 or 18-3, the D salesperson can offer a generous discount to close the sale. If D offers 10 percent, S can match the offer and lose 1¢ on the sale while D makes 19¢.

Consider the case of S and D having equal current market share as shown in Figure 18-3 at the time when S has achieved experience of two. D can offer the product for cost, 70¢, plus 10 percent, a total of 77¢. S can meet the competition and lose 3¢ on the sale.

These results may dismay some, but we suggest to realistic aspiring entrepreneurs that a dominant competitor controls the subordinate competitors and determines their survival in the marketplace.

Dominant is a relative term. In Figure 18-3 the D competitor has double the accumulated experience of S when D reaches an experience of two, but only 50 percent more experience when D reaches three. As they progress down the curve, the lead held by D will diminish to insignificance. For instance, if one and two represent hundreds, then when D has experience of 1,000, S will have 900. When D reaches 10,000, S will have 9,900. If S can hold on to the same market share as D for long enough, in time the difference in their expenses will be small compared to the characteristic profit margin in the industry, and D will lose its advantage.

On the other hand, in the examples of Figure 18-2, D holds twice the market share of S. As they progress down the curve D will always have twice the accumulated experience of S. The percentage difference in their costs will always equal or exceed the characteristic profit margins in the industry. In this instance, D does control S. The subordinate competitor provides the dominant competitor with an acceptable excuse for maintaining greater profit margins than D might otherwise justify.

For the aspiring entrepreneur the message should be clear: dominate your market. Get in first and reduce price in proportion to expense to increase the rate of market penetration, to increase the depth of market penetration, and to make it more difficult for competitors to join the party. Strive for dominant market share.

START-UP LOSSES AND BREAKING EVEN

The expense of making a prototype and the expense of the initial production unit are almost invariably much greater than any customer would be willing to pay. It is normal to hear of start-up losses. The first task in producing a new product or service must be learning how to make it for less than the acceptable selling price. It may be necessary to sell at less than cost initially to accumulate the experience needed to reach that break-even.

Some years back there was a story making the rounds about David Sarnoff, chairman of RCA at the time television was first introduced to the public. The picture was black and white, and the television tube was encased in a large piece of furniture, usually containing a radio and record player and called a home entertainment center. It sold for approximately $1,500 per set.

As the story goes, Sarnoff was playing golf with some business friends when one of them suggested that he would like one of those new TV sets, but he wondered if Sarnoff would let an old golf buddy have it at cost. Sarnoff gladly obliged and the following week the delivery truck pulled up to the Park Avenue apartment, the driver and his helper delivered and installed the latest TV console, and the delivery men left an invoice for $2,500.

The old golf buddy was in a bit of a huff that evening when he got the bill, and the next morning he called Sarnoff. "David," he said, "I thought you said you would get me one of those new TV sets at cost?" To which Sarnoff calmly replied, "I did."

There is a lesson here for those who would enter someone else's market. The first step in entering the market is to buy enough of it to break even. If there is already an established competitor, you must take the second step, buy a share of the market sufficient to give you a toehold. If a D competitor observes an S competitor interfering with D's sales, it must retaliate to preserve its position in the marketplace. Price is a powerful weapon at D's disposal.

At times during the recent past the automobile industry found itself hard pressed to maintain sales at levels that would support the massive necessary investment in plant, equipment, and people. You may remember that when the cars had to be moved the automobile companies came through with rebate checks direct from the manufacturer.

You may buy into an existing market as did our S competitor in Figure 18-3, but it can be very costly. Promotion and advertising will no doubt loom large among your expenses. Unfortunately, promoting and advertising your brand of a product can promote the product independent of the brand name. An S competitor challenging a D competitor with advertising and promotion may help the D competitor as well as itself.

Characteristically, competitors entering the market with a new product establish their relative market shares very quickly. It is then very difficult to change the relative shares of the major competitors. This is especially evident in the soap, pharmaceutical, and cosmetics industries, where new products are presented to the market rather frequently, the number of units sold is large, and consumers are many and widely dispersed. It is also true of gasoline retail brands, which are supported by a well-established distribution system and highly visible name identification.

HIGHLY FRAGMENTED MARKETS

There is an exception to this scenario worth consideration by the entrepreneur. Suppose that there are many competitors and no one of them is clearly dominant. As they increase experience by many doublings the absolute dollar difference in their expenses will diminish to insignificance. The competitors would then appear to be clustered together on the curve. This is known as a *highly fragmented market*. In such a market all the competitors are so close to one another on the curve that no one of them stands out as dominant. None of them can get far enough down the curve from the others to have a cost differential that would permit controlling the competition with price.

The marketplace is replete with highly fragmented businesses. Dress shops are an excellent example. Barbershops and convenience stores, specialty bakeries, florists, and custom photofinishers all share highly fragmented markets. So do insurance agents and realtors. Frequently doctors, dentists, lawyers, and accountants find themselves in such a market, as do automobile dealers. One indication of this condition is the proximity of similar businesses, such as an office building housing several lawyers or several dentists or a shopping mall housing several shoe stores, several dress shops, and several fast-food restaurants.

The best position for the entrepreneur is that of the dominant competitor. Figures 18-2 and 18-3 illustrate how difficult it is to overtake an established D competitor. We have discussed the cost of buying into an established market and the means at the disposal of D to retaliate. We have also alluded to the help provided to D by an S competitor trying to advertise and promote the product.

Having attained the position of a dominant competitor you have all the odds in your favor. How do you get to be a dominant competitor? Figure 18-3 strongly suggests that the best way is to start there—be the first competitor on a new curve. Following someone else down a curve makes you an S competitor on day one, with all the attendant obstacles to changing that position. Beginning as a D competitor provides all the advantages and the greatest probability of succeeding to the extent you wish.

115

19

Strategies for Competitors

The economic experience curve provides a graphic guide to competitive strategy. The picture is easier to portray if the curve is drawn on log-log coordinates so that it becomes a straight line. Figure 19-1 is the same information plotted in Figure 18-1, but on logarithmic paper. Fully allocated expense of the last unit produced in constant dollars decreases 20 percent for each doubling of total accumulated experience in this example.

MANIPULATING PROFIT MARGIN

When a new product or service enters the market, its cost is typically more than the price it will bring. With repetition of the task in producing the unit, its expense is decreased until the price it will bring equals its cost. With further repetition of the task expense declines further and provides a profit margin to the business.

This portion of the history of a new product is shown in Figure 19-1. The beginning of the curve is magnified to show a price of $1.10 and expense declining through this to $1.00 when experience equals one. At this point the profit margin is 10¢ on a sale for $1.10.

The curve suggests that the margin can be increased dramatically from this point on if the price in the marketplace will hold at this level. The initial curve representing the findings of the Boston Consulting Group and shown in Figure 16-3 suggests that some producers in this position attempt to maintain price and increase their margin.

It might be well to remember at this point that the break-even point and the point indicating a desired margin are dependent on rate of sales as well as cumulative experience. The vertical axis of the graph represents fully allocated expense. That means rent, insurance, the president's salary, and all other expenses. If the rate of sales, for instance the volume per month, is inadequate to support the minimum indirect

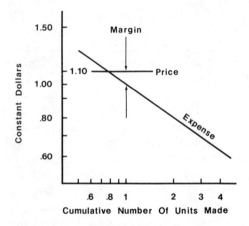

FIGURE 19-1 A 20 Percent Economic Experience Curve on Log-Log Coordinates.

expenses necessary to the operation, then the business may not survive long enough to bring the cost down to break-even and beyond. The curve, when extended to these early beginnings, represents a business with the *opportunity* to succeed.

Suppose that the competitor in Figure 19-1 is the first on a new curve. Having reached a desired margin the producer may decide, based on knowledge of the economic experience curve, to hold the desired margin constant. That means that the vertical distance between the expense curve and the price curve will remain constant. The price curve must parallel the expense curve, as displayed in Figure 19-2. Price becomes expense plus a fixed percentage of expense.

Once again, sales volume has a bearing on progress. If sales are 100,000 units per year for two years in a row, the reported sales and profits in dollars will be much less in the second year. Though the

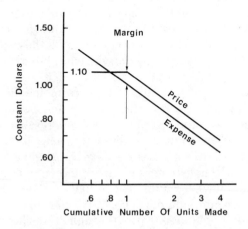

FIGURE 19-2 Pricing Strategy When Price Is Reduced along with the 20 Percent Expense Reduction.

117

long-range objective may be dominant market share, the rate of growth must be sufficient to keep management looking good in the eyes of the investors. To maintain growth in reported sales and profits, the area under the curve representing successive reporting periods, like successive years, must increase.

Suppose that the competitor in Figure 19-1 decides to maintain the initial price level for as long as possible and reap the greater margin. The short-term results are rewarding, but they are short-lived. We don't live in a vacuum. Others will observe the bountiful profits being made by this *D* competitor—the news cannot be concealed. After all, the bookkeeper knows about it, the banker knows, the suppliers know, the technicians know, and the investors know. And they also know the management well enough to conclude that there is nothing godlike about it. Even lesser mortals like themselves could produce the product or service.

Even if you could pledge these people to secrecy, the manager is down at the club, having driven there in a late-model luxury car, and he or she can't keep quiet. You don't have to be successful to attract the attention of eager copiers. You only have to behave as if you are. Satisfying the ego with house, car, clothes, meals, travel, and entertainment will do the trick.

The inevitable response to excessive profit margins is competition. Initially the price may hold while the *S* competitors accumulate experience and the praise of their investors. In time, however, the *D* competitor's salesperson will encounter the *S* competitor's salesperson talking to the same potential customer. Then price will enter the discussion and the shakeout will be precipitated.

The *S* competitors will not withdraw without a tenacious fight. They and their investors have tasted the sales, growth, and profit. They will be convinced that they need only hold on a little longer. Good money will follow bad as the investors in the weak competitors struggle to salvage what they thought they had. All the while price will continue to fall as the buyers revel in the plight of the producers. New customers will emerge at the lower price who could not buy at the higher price, but they provide no solace to the producers, who would like to raise prices to cover costs.

The weak competitors don't retire from the field. They are crushed into submission. Prices may have to fall below the *D* competitor's total expenses before supply and demand reach an approximate equilibrium. Prices then gyrate up and down seeking their equilibrium. In due time they will settle to a reasonable margin over expense, and an objective observer will note the price history shown in Figure 19-3. The price fluctuated about what would have been the price had a reasonable margin been chosen and held constant in the first place.

The *D* competitor does not pass through the shakeout unscathed. Weary and wary investors and bankers impose their own influence on operations, frequently changing management as if *it* were the problem.

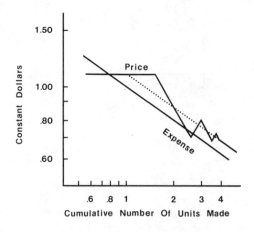

FIGURE 19-3 Price History of the Industry When Price Is Held Constant While Competition Develops.

Decreasing price to maintain constant margins would seem the more desirable of the two pricing options. One other option emerges, however, from observing those who successfully apply the strategy suggested by the curve. Richard Rogers described how he applied this option in his mother's business, Mary Kay Cosmetics.

The first competitor on a new experience curve chooses to lower prices after the desired margin is achieved, but not quite in proportion to the expense decline. Prices are allowed to decline a few percentage points less than expense. Reported margins are maintained constant. The difference is spent on institutional advertising, employee incentive and reward programs, long-range product improvement and renewal, and other things to strengthen the business. This is called *creative spending*.

Figure 19-4 illustrates the area of creative spending on the experience curve. Price is chosen to permit target margins in excess of what is desired. Then management observes the actual performance and spends down to the desired margin to be revealed in the financial reports. Creative spending amounts to only 1 percent to 3 percent of sales. It is just enough to cover any unforeseen fluctuations in performance, so that even under poor conditions the company can maintain its targeted reporting margins.

Creative spending can be turned on or off in response to company performance. Mary Kay provides Cadillacs and mink stoles to outstanding sales performers. Creative spending is the cushion management provides itself above its profit objectives; to report the excess to investors would raise their expectations for the future. Reported excess at one time and the lack of it another would raise questions about the consistency of management's performance. Creative spending allows management to appear consistent while improving and strengthening the business.

119

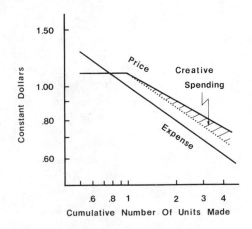

FIGURE 19-4 Creative Spending Strategy: The Result of Price Reduction Following, But Not Equalling, Expense Reduction.

After a long time in the marketplace a dominant competitor may hold such a commanding lead down the curve that there is little need to decrease price to prevent competition or increase market penetration. A dominant competitor may choose to stop decreasing price and let margins widen. Of course, by this time enough experience has been accumulated that the next doubling may be a long time in the future. When market share is dominant and growth rate has peaked, this is a much safer time to hold price and reap the rewards of being the D competitor.

A subordinate competitor has some difficult choices to make. Unless the S competitor's market share is close to that of the D competitor, the gap between their expenses will remain like a permanent tax on earnings. The first and most desirable option is to increase market share.

We have already pointed out the magnitude of the investment needed to win this game with price, promotion, and advertising. Another path to the same end is to concentrate on a segment of the market where S has more experience than D. Ford Motor Company was second in automobiles, but had more experience in pickup trucks. Ford decided to go for the light truck market and successfully became the dominant competitor in that segment. General Motors Coach, on the other hand, has dominated the intracity bus market.

CARVING OUT A MARKET SEGMENT

The automobile industry is often thought of as a monolithic giant dominated by a few large automakers. This is far from the case. Rubber belts and hoses are dominated by different competitors. Batteries, spark plugs, and tires are dominated by others. Big trucks, tractors, and trailers are dominated by still other competitors. Axles are made by suppliers to motor companies.

The automakers manufacture engines and bodies and assemble automobiles. They are dependent on a vast array of suppliers for most of the components of their product. And they are dependent on a vast array of services in the aftermarket, including the fuel and lubricants needed to operate their product.

If an S competitor is unable to find an area in which it has more experience than the D competitor, it might look to the segment where it has its most past experience. If this can be matched to a market with potential for growth, there is a possibility for becoming the D competitor in something.

Despite their fickle nature, customers behave as if loyal to their present suppliers. In truth, they are reluctant to face an existing supplier providing satisfactory service with an excuse for switching to a new source. On the other hand, when their supplier lets them down or can't match something available elsewhere, customers can be outspoken about their feelings.

It is difficult to take customers away from an existing supplier, but in a growing market many potential customers have not yet established a supplier relationship. S has as much chance as D to obtain a share of the new customers. Therein lies the reason for S choosing a segment in which it has both past experience and opportunity for growth.

Having identified such a possible area of concentration, S could seriously examine the product or service of that area, the methods of packaging, delivery, financing, servicing, and even pricing. A minor innovation, the application of a recent new technology, or a redesign could provide the means to penetrate the market segment.

While concentrating on a small segment of the market, S might also ask how else its unit could be used, by whom, instead of what, or in conjuction with what. In a sense this is brainstorming.

Much of the experience and learning go with the people. When you are looking for ways to improve operations you look for good, experienced people. You may be willing to pay a high price for them. And where do you find these good, experienced people? Usually working for an established competitor. Although they may not bring trade secrets, they can bring knowledge and a different perspective. Frequently people in key positions with an established competitor feel stifled, unable to make the changes they see so clearly from their vantage point. Given a little freedom and encouragement, such people often bring new life to an existing product or process.

In general, the most desirable option for subordinate competitors is to build on their experience in a narrow market segment with growth potential so they can become dominant competitors in something.

Some subordinate competitors prefer to rely on the federal regulatory agencies to protect the rights of the poor lil' old small competitor. You may choose to do this if you please—and take your chances with the legal expense.

Another option for a subordinate competitor is to choose an area characterized as a highly fragmented market. When there are many competitors, none of whom is clearly dominant, there is at least the chance to be an equal among subordinates. No one competitor has the clout to give you much trouble. All the competitors have the chance to break out of the pack.

The highly fragmented market also lends itself to choosing an area where the S competitor has much experience and then examining the product or service for improvement. The application of technology, the satisfaction of a current perceived consumer value, new packaging, distribution, financing, redesign, combination, or specialization can alter the perception of the consumer and give an S competitor the chance to challenge for dominance in some segment of the market.

Of course, there is the option of keeping a low profile in hopes that the dominant competitor will not notice the competition. This may also imply being satisfied with a smaller share of the market, although it is possible to dominate a small geographic area. If the territory is not of interest to the D competitor it might provide a satisfactory market for an S competitor whose ambitions are not too great.

Noting what the economic experience curve describes provides another option for S competitors, although admittedly this one may be more difficult to effect. The curve describes a group of competitors providing what is perceived by the consumer to be the same product or service. If by the application of changes the business concept can be modified enough that it is perceived as different from what is being provided, then you may have a new curve of your own. Possibilities along this line are convenience stores that sell only beer and cigarettes or shops that only tune automobile engines.

New business start-ups are in the subordinate competitor position in the beginning. Even the business concept that represents a new curve must initially convince customers to spend their money on the new concept instead of where they would otherwise spend it. This is all the more reason to incorporate experience, technology, and redesign into the concept to increase the perceived distinctive consumer values. And because price is always an important consumer value, the business concept should begin with as much accumulated experience as can be assembled. People retain what is learned by experience. Start with people who have accumulated experience as directly related to the concept as possible.

Step 2 in the career path of successful entrepreneurs, as described in Chapter 11, is gain product and market knowledge as close as possible to the interface between the product and the market. It is usually obtained while working for an established competitor. Successful entrepreneurs learn all they can about the business. They are very good at what they are doing. The economic experience curve and strategies for competitors lend credence and add weight to the importance of this step in the career path.

20

Strategy for Entrepreneurs

Among the entrepreneurs appearing at our distinguished entrepreneur speaker series the most successful went down their own economic experience curves.[1] As W. W. Caruth, Jr., has said, the best way to get to the top is to start there.[2] The best way to be the dominant competitor is to start there. Being first on a new curve provides the opportunity to build the business you start.

Joining the competition on an existing curve necessarily means being a subordinate competitor, at least in the beginning. Attempting to overtake a dominant competitor is difficult to say the least. Even in a highly fragmented market a dominant competitor seldom emerges.

The current market share for competitor A is A's sales divided by total sales in the marketplace. For competitor B the market share is B's sales divided by total sales in the marketplace. Because the denominator is the same for both, the ratio of their market shares is the ratio of their sales relative to each other. These figures determine which competitor is advancing down the curve at the faster rate, but they are not sufficient to determine their relative positions on the curve. The horizontal axis measures total accumulated experience to date.

A subordinate competitor must obtain and hold a greater market share than the dominant competitor to catch up in accumulated experience. Figure 18-3 illustrated the relative positions of S and D competitors who have equal market shares. S is always behind in the race. Even a competitor with the largest current market share may be a subordinate competitor while overtaking the competitor who started down the curve first.

The strategies suggested by the curve and the constraints imposed by it strongly recommend that the entrepreneur try to find a new curve and be the first one to start accumulating experience. The curve, when drawn on ordinary coordinates, also suggests that the big gains are to be made at the beginning of the race. The magnitude of the cost reduction when measured in dollars is much greater at the beginning of the curve. The ability to obtain successive doublings is greatest at the

123

beginning. And until the new curve has demonstrated its value by the success of the first competitor, imitators don't know it exists.

There is a pattern to the strategy followed by entrepreneurs who have clearly succeeded in building a business where none existed before. For those who wish to build a business it may be helpful to be aware of the strategy associated with their success.

STEP ONE

Pick an Area of Activity in Which You Have the Most Experience. This usually comes quite naturally. The opportunities to perceive an unfilled need or a specialty area in the market usually arise from interaction with suppliers and consumers. Studying a market or a business possibility, or researching a product or market, can provide considerable data, knowledge, and insight. The fact remains, however, that we learn more, quicker, with more depth of understanding and better retention when we are butting heads with others who are striving for similar achievement.

The entrepreneurs of the speakers series were very good at what they were doing while working for an established competitor. They were often the best in the company. For instance, Sam Wyly was one of IBM's best salespeople. Later as a sales manager with Honeywell, he attained sales with five salespeople that other offices made with thirty. One day he decided that if he could sell that well for Honeywell he could sell just as well for Sam Wyly. The result was University Computing Corporation.[3]

To be good at what you are doing, it helps to like it. Many people say they would like to start a business, but they don't know what business to start. Our advice is to consider whatever turns you on. Start looking in the field or area of commerce you find interesting, preferably exciting. It doesn't matter which area so much as that you like it. There are enough distractions and impediments to progress in problem solving without adding subconscious feelings of discontent and dissatisfaction.

If no business concept seems evident at the moment, an entrepreneur can start finding one by being very good at whatever job is available. As with the opportunities that emerge for the business at Step 5 on the career path, opportunities for individuals flow to those who have demonstrated success at something. Successful achievers are few enough in number that they stand out like big red barns in snow-covered fields.

STEP TWO

Devise a Business Concept. A concept can evolve from striving to do a better job than is presently being done. It may involve improving on an existing occupational task. It may consist of adding to an existing service or providing a product or service not yet available. It may be just helping potential customers to buy something already available.

Morris Zale, whose jewelry store chain and other enterprises now gross more than a billion dollars a year, began selling diamonds out of a small display counter in someone else's drugstore in the mid-1920s. He loved the diamonds, and he loved to see other people thrill in owning them. He also felt saddened that so many good people who dearly wanted to own a diamond couldn't accumulate the money for the purchase. He wanted to help them acquire the jewelry they clearly adored. Morris Zale is credited with being the first to offer diamonds for sale on a time payment plan.[4] In the mid-1920s selling diamonds and jewelry on credit was a new business concept, representing a new economic experience curve.

Before 1970 good, fresh seafood from the Gulf of Mexico was hard to find in midwestern cities. During the 1970s airline service was introduced to the Rio Grande Valley, making Port Isabel within two hours of most major midwestern airports, and fresh gulf seafood became readily available, if at a premium price. Then with the inflationary trend in restaurant food prices and the introduction of many nonstop airline flights to Boston and Seattle, fresh Puget Sound salmon and Maine lobster became available at prices within reason.

The availability of good seafood didn't just happen. Some enterprising individual recognized the possibilities introduced by the new airline service, assessed the probabilities that midwesterners would enjoy fresh seafood, took a trip to the seaports to establish sources of supply, found or created an outlet for that very perishable commodity, and took the chance. It worked. Salmon sold on the Seattle piers at 6:00 A.M. is available for dinner in restaurants at 6:00 P.M. in most midwestern cities.

STEP THREE

Describe the Business Concept in Terms of Distinctive Perceived Consumer Values. Because the list of distinctive perceived consumer values is open-ended, you have to search for all the values that may be important at the time (see Chapter 14). Price is always a pertinent value and probably the first to be considered.

The improved airline service and the inflationary rise in food costs brought Puget Sound salmon to major inland cities. The continuing inflationary rise in airline fuel costs and dockside prices for seafood may send the salmon back to Seattle.

The list of perceived consumer values describing the concept should be as long as possible. Better to list doubtful values than to overlook even one that may be perceived by the potential consumer.

A successful entrepreneur is seldom secretive about his or her concept. He or she talks to everybody, listens well, and looks for values he or she hadn't perceived, trying out possible values on people who might be buyers. Talking about the concept and trying to explain it, to justify it, to convince others how good it is, helps to formulate the list of perceived consumer values. At the same time these discussions lead to clarification of many other facets of the concept, such as sources of supply, methods of delivery, size of packaging, kind of help needed, cost of help needed, and so on.

STEP FOUR

Compare the Proposed Business Concept to the Competition. Competition comes in many forms. Some forms are inconspicuous, but no less competitive.

One way to get a handle on who or what is competitive is to explain to what the proposed product or service is similar. Do this both in writing and orally, to an interested listener. The description usually begins with, "It is like, but . . ." Or imagine the people who will buy the product or service and list the other suppliers who will be talking to them about buying a similar thing. Still another way is to list substitute products or services. Push that thinking a little further and list the products or services you could "make do with" to avoid buying the proposed new concept. Push it still further and ask what you would use if you *had* to do without purchasing the new concept's product or service.

The list of competitors should include everything that competes for the same customer dollar. A high-fidelity sound system may not seem to compete with a good color television receiver, but many people in the marketplace have to choose which of the two they will buy first, next, now, or ever.

Once you have listed the competitors, describe each with its distinctive perceived consumer values. Again, it is better to list dubious values than to overlook consumers' perceptions. It is worth the time and effort to learn a great deal about each competitive product or service. This provides insights that improve the description of the business concept.

Now it is possible to compare the proposed business concept with the competition. Use any measure or scale that helps to rate and rank the competitors. And remember, being realistic is one of the characteristics of successful entrepreneurs.

STEP FIVE

Change and Improve the Concept in Light of Its Comparison to the Competition. You may remember the second and third steps on the career path: gain product and market knowledge and develop a business concept. Successful entrepreneurs cycle back and forth between these steps. They keep improving the concept with additional product and market knowledge. The key improvements are those that make the concept different from and better than the competition.

In effect, the proposed business concept is massaged and sculptured to make it more and more unique. If it can be improved to the point that when compared it isn't like the competition, then it could be a new economic experience curve.

Not very many years ago secretaries wasted a lot of time erasing errors on the original and carbon copies of their typing. One secretary, who also happened to be an artist, found the task of erasing very distasteful. It occurred to her that if she were painting instead of typing she could remove the offending error with a single brush stroke. Then she did, in fact, paint out an error with pigments that matched the surface of the stationery.

This enterprising young woman soon began mixing paints in her kitchen. So many of her friends liked the paint that she began selling it. For many years Bette Clair Graham became better known as the founder of Liquid Paper Corporation, and her little concept became an accessory to the typewriter around the world.

Imagine Ms. Graham trying to explain what she was doing back in the days of mixing paint in the kitchen. Try to describe Liquid Paper as an eraser. It is like an eraser, but it isn't an eraser. Actually it isn't like an eraser, but it does the same thing. Does it erase? Well, no, you see it's like paint. Needless to say, that was a new economic experience curve and Liquid Paper Corporation enjoyed all the benefits of being the first competitor on the curve.

STEP SIX

Test the Market to Be Sure the Consumer Agrees with You. It's one thing to have your spouse and your parents think you have a great idea. It's something else to get money from strangers. Sometimes it is hard to make a real test. For instance, a new retail establishment really has to open to make the test. In a manufacturing business that needs $2 million worth of equipment to make item one it is difficult to make the test. To the extent possible, however, the test is almost mandatory.

Market analyses, surveys, and studies rely on circumstantial evidence. Most include a questionnaire for purported potential customers. The problem with this kind of test is that it can't ask the real question: "Will you give me $xxx for this?" It is quite another question to ask, "If I had this would you buy it for $xxx?" The usual survey questions are even further from the mark.

When people receive a survey questionnaire in the mail it is easy for them to express their annoyance. They can throw it away. When asked by another person to answer a few questions it is a little more difficult to express displeasure. Most people get out of the situation as quickly and easily as they can. They are pleasant and brief with their answers. They want to make the questioner go away. The easiest way to do that is tell them what they want to hear and get on with it. Besides, what does it cost to be nice? But when you ask for their money people don't mind offending you.

The test should involve selling a few units of the product or service. If this can't be done through someone else's store or by going from door to door, then make the initial effort as small and inexpensive as possible. Keep the overhead and the up-front investment to a minimum. It is a curious fact that when the speakers at the distinguished entrepreneur series were asked how much money they put into their business to get started, they almost invariably said less than $10,000.

When entrepreneurs so often say that they started in a garage or a basement they are being quite literal. John Welsh was a junior associate to the founding group of Thermo-Electron, Inc., now trading on the New York Stock Exchange with sales of more than $100 million. It began in the basement of an auto body and paint shop in Belmont, Massachusetts.[5] Welsh was also the founding entrepreneur of Flow Laboratories, Inc., which after several mergers is now traded on the New York Stock Exchange as Flow General, Inc., with sales over $100 million.[6] Flow Laboratories started in the basement garage of a four-story office building in Roslyn, Virginia.

STEP SEVEN

Examine the Market to Be Sure You Have Room to Travel a Long Way Down Your Curve. We have a friend who expanded into an economic recession. We have another friend who took a restaurant that had failed twice in a bank building in a suburban town. On the other hand, we have a friend who supplies blood test kits and chemicals serving a growing health-care industry. He found some room to travel.

It takes time to nurture and grow a business. It takes time to accumulate experience. It takes repetitive sales to build up doublings of experience. A business that satisfies a whim, a fancy, or a fad can often make a satisfying profit, but it is short-lived. It seldom returns the invested capital, never mind some reward to the investors.

STEP EIGHT

Step 8 is an addition to Step 7. When there appears to be a market that will last for a long time, check to be sure there are no new things on the horizon that would change the situation. For instance, is there a new technology in the laboratories that could make the concept obsolete? Microprocessors and hand-held calculators obliterated slide rule sales. Transistors did the same to vacuum tubes.

Are there economic conditions that could change the prospects
for the concept? Are there changing consumer values? Are there prospects for zoning changes in the community? Is the neighborhood changing? Are freight costs rising?

The best laid plans of mice and men are known to go awry. Change is certain. An aspiring entrepreneur doesn't want to be myopic. A desirable curve catches a change just beginning.

STEP NINE

Conceive the smallest possible economically viable business utilizing the concept. You can always build on success. It's a mess digging out from under a failure.

STEP TEN

Step 10 is the same as Step 5 on the career path: Make it work once, or make your business concept work very well. Generate positive retained earnings on the balance sheet. Put yourself in a position to take advantage of the growth opportunities you will certainly perceive.

21

Finding Your Own
Experience Curve

If an economic experience curve is so desirable, how do you find one? Where are they most likely to be? Is there any systematic approach to the search?

EXTERNAL SOURCES
OF NEW EXPERIENCE CURVES

There are clues. New curves occur in instances of change. The change may be in anything that has a bearing on commerce. Because commerce is so pervasive and affects everyone, the areas in which change provides opportunities are almost limitless. Certainly some conspicuous areas would include economic, social, or cultural change; political or regulatory change; technological change, and changes in transportation, communications, and information. Geographic changes, population changes, and educational changes interact with one another to provide abundant opportunities. Growth in almost anything provides commercial opportunities.

The opportunities to find historically significant curves, like transistors or microprocessors, are not abundant. In fact, compared to the number of people seeking them and an ordinary life span, they are relatively rare. On the other hand, the opportunities provided by these few signficant technological changes expand and multiply as the new technology is applied.

Perhaps few of us are equipped with the aptitudes of scientists and engineers, facility with mathematics, and three-dimensional conceptual ability, but many of us have enough of those aptitudes to comprehend the products of their technology. Often another set of aptitudes is needed to perceive the applications. Very often a different set is needed to execute the practical applications.

Technology is a fertile field for new concepts, but no more fertile

130

than the area of population change. As you drive through any town or city it is evident that the largest number of businesses are retail establishments serving the end consumer. As the population grows, the number of these retail establishments grows. When the population moves, as to the suburbs, these businesses move in lockstep.

The big shopping malls are very desirable retail locations. But they know their strengths, and they are very selective in choosing tenants. Malls seldom take chances on new, untried, unproven establishments. They may demand a track record before leasing to a new client. The opportunity to build that track record is out in the suburbs or in a changing neighborhood.

A business concept that represents a new curve may be geographically limited. A business with a fixed location dependent on customers coming to that location has an effective radius beyond which it may as well not exist. An identical establishment far enough away that their radii do not intersect is like a new business concept with its own curve.

Some businesses are limited geographically because of local taste or custom. More often this kind of limitation is regional or related to an ethnic influence. On the other hand, ethnic and local cultural uniqueness are gaining more emphasis as the nation becomes more like a single large province. Businesses that have been geographically limited in the past are finding their limits expanded by the national scope of news and entertainment, the fluidity of the population, and improvements in national transportation.

Many entrepreneurs have observed a new business in one region of the country and duplicated it in another. Other enterprising people have started a business of publishing lists of businesses emerging around the country, urging their readership or membership to copy these concepts in different locations. This kind of business is not new, but a new twist appears to be combining it with a magazine and how-to publications available at an attractive price.

Geographical limitation is the basis for franchising. A business with a limited radius in the marketplace must be duplicated to reach a greater market. Franchising is usually found in highly fragmented markets. As a result, it is not unusual for a franchisee in a particularly receptive market territory to grow rapidly and become stronger than the franchisor. There are several instances of the press identifying a franchisee as though that individual were the franchisor.

Occasionally an individual can see in someone else's establishment the opportunities for growth and replication. Charles Tandy found such an opportunity in his father's leather supplies store. After World War II Tandy went to work for his father, who provided for the needs of shoe repair shops. While reviewing the monthly invoices, he noticed a few unusual addresses, penal institutions.

Tandy visited these institutions to find out what they were doing with the leather. It turned out they used it for arts and crafts as occupa-

131

tional therapy. He then began visiting other institutions with a view to introducing leathercraft for occupational therapy. In a short time sales for this purpose far exceeded sales to shoe repair shops. He used this leathercraft business as a base to build the bigger businesses for which he is better known, Radio Shack and the Tandy Corporation.

Transportation is a key factor in almost all commerce beyond cottage industries. The civilization of the Tigris-Euphrates Valley used the camel and the river. The ancient Egyptians used the Nile River. The seamen of Carthage carried their trade the length of the Mediterranean Sea. During the bloom of international commerce in Venice, Genoa, and the ports of northern Italy, the sea routes of the Mediterranean connected the camel caravans in the East and pack routes throughout Europe in the West.

Transportation is just as key a factor today. In the early days of this country cities sprang up at seaports and river junctions. Later came a golden age of canal building throughout the northeastern corner of the country. Railroads supplanted the rivers and canals, often following the same routes, but they freed transportation to leave the natural waterways and venture out into the Great Plains.

In the early days of this country the vast open spaces were divided into square-mile sections on maps long before settlers saw the land. Many years later the states built a network of farm-to-market roads along the boundaries of these sections. When flying across the United States today you can see that pattern of one-mile-square sections blanketing the ground with a patchwork quilt extending from the Appalachians to the Rockies and beyond to the Pacific Ocean.

During the administration of President Dwight D. Eisenhower, the Congress committed this country to build an interstate system of limited-access, high-speed divided highways. Cities that had been an overnight trip away have become an easy drive for a dinner engagement. More recently, the airline industry has matured to the point that many cities a day's drive away are accessible by hourly flights with a minimum of ticketing and reservations. In some instances you buy the ticket on the plane as though you were traveling on an intracity bus.

The truck came into its own with the creation of the interstate highway system. Although it did not totally displace the freight train any more than the train totally displaced barge traffic on our waterways, the changes it brought were fundamental to commerce. And then the automobile became the great people mover, bringing with it a whole new concept of mobility.

One of the distinctive business functions of Chapter 15 was distribution. Picking up at one place and delivering to another adds value to what is carried. Changes in transport routes and vehicles provided new and abundant opportunities for commerce throughout the ages. Changes today occur at an even greater pace. Aircraft are not the only emerging area of transport. Conveyors, whether for people or for products, are becoming more common and productive. Horizontal elevator systems are emerging where trains or buses once held sway. The aerial tram cable car once found only at ski slopes has appeared in downtown New York City.

Cities and towns in the path of population growth create planning boards and councils before the growth is very evident. One of their main concerns is transportation routes and congestion. Along with planning for these, they map out far in advance the desired zoning for residential, commercial, and industrial construction. These plans are supported by extensive forecasts of population and the services needed to support it. The city administrators are happy to provide this detailed information to anyone prospecting for a new business idea.

The opportunities are not only for new retail outlets. The first call may be for real estate planning and development, which requires bulldozers; ditchdiggers; wire and pipe suppliers; paving, grass, and shrubbery suppliers; building supply and hardware stores, followed by furniture, drape, and gift shops. These are quickly matched with grocery stores, stationery stores, beauty salons and barbershops, gas stations, plumbers, appliance stores, and the full array of services culminating in the shopping mall.

New communities need fire trucks and police cars. They need offices in which people may work. Education and entertainment follow. And in one way or another, manufacturing and assembly plants will emerge along with warehouse and transfer terminals.

As you can see, there is no dearth of opportunity. It is probably evident also that there is no dearth of enterprising individuals to take advantage of the opportunities. Entrepreneurs race to open their businesses at desirable locations in a timely manner. In that race there is little time to learn the tricks of the trade. The competition is among the already competent. As suggested in Chapter 19, you should build on your experience.

Economic, social, and cultural change, which is occurring constantly, provides opportunities of many kinds. Apartment complexes advertised for adult living are not seeking senior citizens. The adults they seek may at times appear adolescent, depending on your viewpoint. During the last generation the two-income family has become so prevalent that services once provided by one member of the family have to be purchased. Child care, laundry, dry cleaning, fast food, and preprepared food respond to these new needs.

The rising cost of housing has changed the prospects of owning your own home to owning your own condominium. An extended period of inflation has changed the perspective of ownership of a home and what is in it. Ownership is measured more in the size of the monthly payment than the net worth of the asset.

Cosmetics for non-Caucasian men and women are a recent addition to the marketplace and promise as much growth and variation as cosmetics for people of ruddy or other more prevalent complexions. Styles for both men and women are being influenced by the greater acceptance of one race by another.

With the dawn of the 1970s came the realization that our natural

133

resources are not limitless. By the end of that decade petroleum shortages had driven home the hard fact that humanity, a mere speck in the cosmos, could deplete the riches of one of the most prominent planets in the solar system. Until the beginning of the 1970s the oceans and the atmosphere were considered infinite by comparison with human creations, but that conception changed dramatically. Even the seemingly innocent spray can is capable of changing the atmosphere, the temperature, and the solar irradiation of the whole world.

Along with these revelations have come opportunities galore. Efficiency in the use of resources has taken on a new perceived value. Recycling our resources has become a necessity. And the greatest change of all is in the field of energy production, consumption, and conservation.

New methods of heating water, heating and cooling homes, powering electrical appliances, and lighting homes must be found. Opportunities lie in all the areas. And each will bring change in other areas. Solar systems require pumps, valves, meters, and tanks. Conservation of heating requires new uses of insulation of all kinds. Conservation of cooling requires more than insulation; under a hot sun a home needs shade and ventilation—more pumps, valves, and meters.

If the 1970s saw a revolution in computers and communications it was a mere ripple compared with what is to come. The Christmas toys of the late 1970s were a hint of the power and influence of the cathode ray tube in our television set. When connected to a computer, which may be accessible over the telephone, with software programs in easy-to-change cassettes and access to huge libraries of information, the illuminated screen that so captivated us in earlier decades could become both our slave and master.

The computer keyboard is likely to become as commonplace as the scratch pad and pencil. Isn't it curious that typing and tabulating skills, so recently associated with clerical duties, should loom so large as communication skills? Being able to talk with your fingers may create a new separation of the able and disabled. For the masses, reading, writing, and arithmetic may be replaced with reading and typing.

The educational system of the twentieth century is an anachronism from an earlier age when the basic knowledge needed for a lifetime could be transmitted to the young while they were still young. The rate of change in useful, and many times necessary, knowledge is now so great that education must be a lifelong experience. Part of our work time, playtime, and leisure time must be allocated to learning, not as passive observers in a motion picture theater, but as active participants, probably at a keyboard.

To accomplish this educational function in competition with the new galaxy of information and entertainment, the methods of providing education themselves need to be replaced. Seminars of one-, two-, and three-day duration are better suited to the needs of the knowledge seeker. Film and television reveal the dreadful redundancy in conversational communication, to say nothing of that in the classroom lecture.

Where do you look for your own economic experience curve? Look around you. It is most likely to be where there is change. The more rapid and dramatic the change, the more likely there are new curves. Is there a systematic approach to the search? By all means, yes.

PERSONAL SOURCES
OF NEW EXPERIENCE CURVES

Ideas for new business concepts emerge from many areas of endeavor.[1] For instance,

1. Hobbies. The stories of mama's cooking becoming a successful restaurant chain are legion and so are those about mechanics, radio hams, photography buffs, and so on. The common thread in these stories is that the hobbyists are superior at what they do.

2. Specialized talent, aptitude, or experience. Designers and drafters who are very good at some particular segment of their craft often find greater satisfaction in an independent business. An aptitude for comprehending a complex subject, like tax regulations, provides a variety of opportunities to sell services. A unique experience and an aptitude for public speaking have led many into the seminar business.

3. Proficiency in current employment. In sales, manufacturing, designing, administering, or whatever function of business, people who are superior at what they do often find greater satisfaction and reward doing it for themselves.

4. Discovering opportunity. It is not unusual to hear owner-managers say they started some little enterprise only to discover opportunity. One orthodontist began supplying T-shirts, campaign buttons, and other rewards to patients to encourage compliance with his instructions. Other orthodontists asked for some of these products. In a few years the dental practice was dwarfed by this behavior modification business.

5. Invention. The originators of significant new patentable inventions seldom become successful entrepreneurs. There are exceptions, of course, like Dr. Edwin Land, who invented the Polaroid camera and built the Polaroid Corporation. But inventions involving less technology are often the basis for a business. One entrepreneur put an electric motor on the pencil sharpener. Bette Graham decided to use a soluble pigment instead of an eraser for the typewritten page and thereby introduced the world to Liquid Paper.

6. Acquisition. Many times a reasonably good business concept has been found by another person who seems unable to manage the resulting business wisely. This is the opportunity for someone who knows how to run a business to buy out the present owner and build on the concept.

In each of these areas new business concepts seem to be associated with individuals being very good at what they do, having superior understanding of a complex subject, or being very practical at solving problems. New concepts are the result of

1. Discovering a need or a want that is not adequately satisfied
2. Striving to solve a problem or mollify a complaint
3. Responding to wishes for things presently perceived to be unattainable.

The search for a business concept begins with gaining knowledge and experience in something that interests you. It is important to be interested and enthusiastic. We have natural defenses to an unpleasant situation that close our eyes and ears to opportunity. Interest and enthusiasm encourage learning and the self-confidence to support open-mindedness. An open mind actively involved in striving for something is surprisingly able at finding new ways to accomplish objectives and reach goals.

Finding a product or service that fills a need is certainly desirable. Most products or services, however, seem to fill a want. The potential consumer is heard to say, "I wish . . ." The entrepreneur responds with, "Why don't you . . . ?" A person seeking a new business concept becomes attuned to the casual remarks that express dissatisfaction with things as they are.

The search proceeds with striving to solve problems, mollify complaints, or grant wishes. The result is improved by bringing into the scheme something new, different, and, it is hoped, better. Experience suggests that almost every product or service has been improved on continuously over time. There seems little reason to think this won't continue.

The search need not be in your field of educational specialty. Experience is what counts, interaction with reality. Education and the influence of social and cultural background flavor reaction to experience, color the interpretation placed on experience, and broaden the responsive options to experience, but the experience provides the stimulus as well as the opportunity to recognize a new business concept.

Accumulated experience provides advantage. Broad and varied experiences aid the individual with comprehensive awareness, but in the segment of commerce that is interesting, if not exciting, enough experience needs to be accumulated to understand the subleties of the business.

Identifying a new curve results from striving to do a job better, to provide an improved service, to change the way things are being done now. It comes from combining new things in new ways to give more satisfaction to consumers. People make the purchase decision. Ask yourself, "What can I offer people that will make them willingly give their hard-earned money to me?"

136

22

Economic Experience
and Distinctive Functions

The economic experience curve is a relationship between fully allocated expense of the last unit produced, in constant dollars, and the total cumulative number of units produced to date. It was deduced from historical data relating price in the marketplace to the total cumulative number of units produced, again in constant dollars. After a period of relatively level pricing followed by a shakeout, a stable industry emerges with supply and demand in approximate equilibrium and characteristic uniform decline in price with each doubling of cumulative production experience. Because stable industries report characteristic profit margins, a line may be drawn parallel to the declining price line and separated from it by the characteristic reported profit margin of the industry.

Constraints on the validity of this hypothesis are (1) that the extensive data collected and reported on this relationship is factual; (2) that stable industries do, in fact, have characteristic profit margins; (3) that the measurement of value be in a currency free of the effects of inflation; and (4) that there be competition. Given that (1) and (2) are substantiated by experience and (3) can be achieved arithmetically, the condition for the existence of economic experience curves is that there be competition.

If a segment of the curve representing price data in the region of a stable industry is examined, the area under the curve represents total revenue for the period portrayed by the segment. Revenue is the first item at the top of a profit and loss statement or income statement. Revenue less profit equals total expense. Such a segment is shown in Figure 22-1.

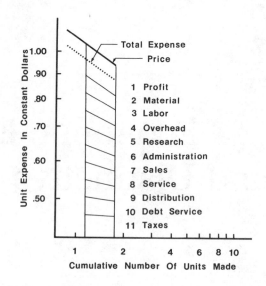

FIGURE 22-1 An Income Statement, or Profit and Loss Statement, Portrayed as Part of an Economic Experience Curve.

APPLYING THE EXPERIENCE CURVE TO ALL ASPECTS OF BUSINESS FUNCTIONS

The enlarged segment is a graphic representation of the income statement. The major items composing the income statement are listed on the right, and their graphic segmentation is shown on the left. Expense is detailed with typical and representative items, showing income tax at the bottom.

Figure 22-1 shows that the expense per unit produced for each of the *business functions* composing the total expense must decrease in some consistent and persistent pattern similar to the decline in price with each doubling of accumulated experience. If this logic is portrayed for the entire expense curve on log-log paper, the picture in Figure 22-2 emerges. The segments under the total expense curve are numbered to correspond to the items on the income statement in Figure 22-1.

In Chapter 16 we listed five phenomena as probable contributors to the consistent pattern of declining price and hence expense: learning, specialization, scale, investment, and redesign. These were described with relationship to a product. Figure 22-2 suggests that the decline occurs in areas other than the product. In particular, it applies to things like administration, which would include management, accounting, purchasing, personnel, communication, publication, training, and financial control.

At first glance it may seem difficult to apply learning, specialization, scale, investment, and redesign to areas in which repetitive tasks are not so clearly in evidence. A moment's reflection, however, will

138

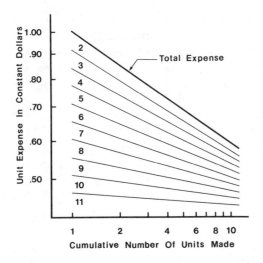

FIGURE 22-2 Detailed Components of an Economic Experience Curve.

reveal opportunities in administration to apply each of these. In the accounting departments of large organizations the accounts payable function is located in an area separated from the other accounting functions, such as accounts receivable. That's specialization. The mere division of the accounting journal into a sales journal, cash journal, expense journal, and general journal is a manifestation of specialization. Calculators and computers represent scale. Continual revision, consolidation, and streamlining of the record-keeping system is redesign. Preparation of multicopy, preprinted carbon forms is redesign. Calculators, computers, and forms require investment.

When considering a new business, the portion of the price versus cumulative experience curve of interest is the far left of the graph. Once again price times units, represented by a segment of the curve, equals sales. An enlargement of this segment also portrays an income statement. There is a difference from the graphic representation for a stable industry, however. In a new business the distribution of the total expense among the individual items may omit some items, others may be far more dominant.

Consider a small group of technical people who create a new electronic device in their basement, probably using their employer's facilities at odd hours for some of the development work. Initially they make a breadboard model. Then they make a prototype. In time they assemble a few copies of the device. It is not unusual to find that they can sell the few copies with little difficulty. Often they can sell far more than they can make, and they launch a new business in meager industrial quarters.

In this early stage of their business the components of expense are materials, labor, overhead, and a little debt service. Administration is insignificant, and the other items listed in Figure 22-1 are almost nonexistent.

139

As their business grows, they accumulate experience in producing the unit, but not much in the other components of expense. In time, however, they will be able to produce more than they can easily sell, and more selling expense will arise. In a little while they will discover that checkbook accounting is inadequate to the task, and greater administrative expense will creep into the distribution. Much further along in their history all the items of expense will become prominent. This phenomenon may be portrayed as in Figure 22-3.

In this figure the vertical line segment labeled *a* represents start-up. Segment *b* shows some sales expense in the distribution. Segment *c* includes some administration. Segment *d* includes all the expense items. In this figure the numbered components of expense are the same as in Figure 22-1.

SHIFTING EMPHASIS AMONG BUSINESS FUNCTIONS

In Chapter 15 we discussed the different distinctive business functions and pointed out that people with different aptitudes, talents, and even personalities gather in these different areas of commerce. They respond to different motivation techniques, different reward structures, and different management methods. Management experience in one distinctive business function is seldom adequate preparation for managing another.

The shifting of emphasis among functions within a new and growing business provides the entrepreneur with adversity and challenge. One of the dominant characteristics of successful entrepreneurs is

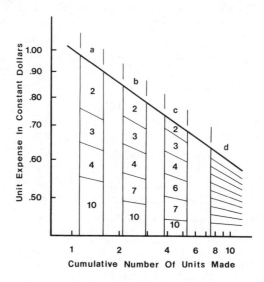

FIGURE 22-3 Economic Experience Curve Components for a Growing New Business.

a need to control and direct. They find it difficult to relinquish control of the new area of the business needing attention, but they have been accumulating experience in a different area.

Entrepreneurs seem able to handle this shifting focus of attention while the business is small and growing. Almost invariably they *must* handle the additional responsibility. A small enterprise can seldom afford additional expertise. Being realistic, however, entrepreneurs recognize the desirability of bringing in help in new areas. Also, entrepreneurs tend to choose people of competence as associates; this selection may carry the business a considerable distance down the experience curve.

When a business is viewed in a broader context, the segments in Figure 22-3 illustrate another frequently observed phenomenon of small, growing, new businesses. It is often said that big companies allow small entrepreneurial companies to try out new ideas, new products, and services. Once the small companies make them work and the business is of proven interest, the big companies enter the competition and crush the little ones. There are sufficient examples of this apparent action by large competitors that the comment gains some credence.

Figure 22-3 suggests that something else may be happening, which to the outside observer appears to be big company vengeance. Let us go back to our small group of technical people who create a new electronic device in their basement. Suppose the electronic device is an appliance used in the kitchen. Initially the technical people are fully occupied with improving the design and the production technique. Choosing the materials to be used and the colors to be made available, finding reliable suppliers, and packaging will consume the team's attention.

In time the design and production problems will begin to settle down, but marketing will become a problem. Finding channels of distribution, including wholesalers, distributors, and retailers, will become a major task. Already the technical people are out of their realm of expertise. But in true entrepreneurial spirit they press on, learning quickly as they progress.

As a little more time passes they must face the problem of keeping their appliance in working order after it is in the hands of the consumer. Repair and maintenance are as much a part of marketing as are retail outlets to display and sell the appliance. Service becomes a significant part of the total package offered to the consumer.

Repair and maintenance is more a job shop operation; manufacturing and assembling the appliance are more a production-line or process operation. Again it is normal to find people with different aptitudes, talents, motivations, and satisfactions in these different operations. The entrepreneur and technical team may be still further from their area of expertise.

When sales and service begin to dominate the constraints on continued growth, the technical people find that they are the D competitor in making their appliance, but the S competitor in sales and service. Many competitors specialize in sales and service of electrical appliances. Some of them are well established and a long way down their experience curve.

The entrepreneurial team is faced with the options of creating a sales and service organization or contracting with someone else's organization to supply that function of business. The entrepreneur, with a strong need for control and distaste for structure, all too often chooses to build the sales and service organization.

Building a sales and service organization is, for our technical team, like starting a new business. And this time they don't have the advantage of experience and expertise. As the appliance business grows, it consumes cash, financial resources, and management's time and energy. Starting a sales and service business also consumes these resources. This dilution reduces the entrepreneur's effectiveness in both appliance manufacturing and the sales and service business.

Meanwhile, one or more of the established sales and service organizations will be hearing from its salespeople that there is now an unfilled need in the marketplace. All these sales and service organizations will have well-established relationships with manufacturers capable of producing the appliance. Some of the manufacturers will be well financed, well equipped, and well staffed with technical people. It isn't difficult to buy one of the appliances and copy it, making changes and improvements.

Before long one or more competitors to the appliance will appear in the marketplace, supported by a superior sales and service organization. At this point the composite of accumulated experience in producing, selling, servicing, financing, administering, and so on will shift from our technical team to the new competitors, who are already well down their experience curves in the dominant components of the total economic experience curve describing the competition.

In the resulting competition the technical team that introduced the new appliance will appear to be a weak competitor. In time they will, in fact, be the weak competitor. They are very likely to be driven from the competition. And then observers of the competition will repeat that old refrain about the big companies walking all over the little ones.

There may be a lesson in all this: It might be better to join them than to fight them. Some entrepreneurs manage to build their additional business functions, like sales and service, but this discussion may provide a realistic appraisal of their odds. Being forewarned provides the opportunity to improve the accuracy of the appraisal.

Once again the message of the economic experience curve is, build on your experience. In areas where you lack experience, bring it in.

23

Alternatives to Finding a New Experience Curve

The evidence for the virtue of finding a new experience curve and being the first competitor on it has been offered in several ways in the last few chapters. But suppose you are just unable to find a new curve of your own? What then can you do to improve the probabilities of winning?

The alternatives to having your own experience curve are many and varied. They share one characteristic, however. They are competitors in highly fragmented industries. The competitors are bunched together on the curve describing them. No single competitor or group of competitors has achieved such a commanding lead that it or they can dominate the field.

Dominance requires being far enough ahead in cumulative experience that the expense advantage to the dominant competitor is significant when compared with the profit margin characteristic of the industry. Holding twice the market share of the next largest competitor gives the dominant competitor an expense advantage equal to the characteristic expense decline associated with one doubling of cumulative experience. If the curve is declining 20 percent with each doubling, the dominant competitor could be expected to have unit expense 20 percent less than the next competitor. Because characteristic profit margins usually lie in the 2 percent to 10 percent range, this competitor would clearly have a position of dominance, as portrayed in Figure 18-2.

Figure 23-1 is that same figure, showing that if D sold 50 percent more than S, then when S had sold one, D would have sold one and a half, and the expense to the larger competitor would be approximately 88¢. D would have an expense advantage of 12 percent, still significant compared with the profit margin.

If the same logic is applied to the situation where D sells only 25 percent more than S, D's expense advantage from Figure 23-1 would be approximately 7 percent. This may still be significant. If there are many competitors with the largest holding 12.5 percent of the market and the

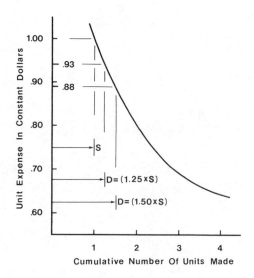

FIGURE 23-1 The S and D Competitors on an Economic Experience Curve as D's Dominance Fades.

next largest holding 10.0 percent, the result would be a 7 percent expense advantage to the largest competitor.

CHALLENGING THE DOMINANT COMPETITOR

When the expense advantage is small, the dominant competitor becomes vulnerable to challenge by another competitor, inadvertent adversity, and slippage caused by its own management's temporary laxity. The challenging competitor can put itself in a position to be lucky. If the dominant competitor makes a mistake in the marketplace, the challenger may leap ahead.

In John Welsh's business there were two principal competitors, each holding the same share of the market. The product was predominantly living animal tissue cells cultured in test tubes and bottles. These cells had to be grown and delivered under the most fastidiously sterile conditions. Unless the producers maintained continuous stringent quality control and security of the sterile production facilities, the cells would be contaminated with bacteria, yeast, mold, virus, and a rainbow of other diseases.

Even with the best of controls and vigilance each producer would occasionally lose a whole week's worth of product to inadvertent contamination. On these occasions the customers would call the remaining producer for a supply of material. In time the producer who had the fewer number of incidents acquired the greater share of the customers. Being a reliable supplier allowed Welsh's laboratory to become the lead

144

competitor, although under the circumstances the business never achieved the advantage of the D competitor in Figure 18-2.

There is more to this story that may prove of value. The two principal competitors sold their products by catalog, personal relationships, and displays at the annual meetings of pertinent professional associations. After several years of this competition, a third supplier appeared on the scene with a new philosophy of selling. The new competitor was managed by people with sales rather than technical background. They decided that covering the country with six to eight salespeople who would call on customers and aggressively promote sales would be their strategy.

In three years the marketplace found itself with three principal suppliers, each holding about one-third of the market and each covering the country with six to eight salespeople. The expense structure of the industry had to change to permit a significant redistribution to the expense of selling.

The two original competitors were managed by entrepreneurs who complacently ignored the challenge until it struck them where it hurt, their bottom line. Then both retaliated with the advantages they held. In the end they prevented the new challenger from gaining dominance, but the damage had been done. Now there were three principal suppliers and an even more fragmented industry.

ENTERING A HIGHLY FRAGMENTED INDUSTRY

In highly fragmented industries small but perceptible differences can allow a new competitor to gain a position in the marketplace that permits establishment of a viable business. The fast-food industry is a segment of the restaurant industry characterized by specialization. There are chicken places, fish places, and taco places, but the greatest number seem to be purveyors of beef.

Not far from our office is a McDonald's restaurant. Next door to it is a Bonanza Steakhouse. And next door to that is a Denny's. Across the street is a Jack-in-the-Box, and on the same side of the street but in the next block is a Howard Johnson's restaurant. At the other end of that block is a Jo-Jo's.

These names may not be familiar in every part of the country, but they are familiar in most cities coast to coast. Their menus are different in distinctive ways. But they have one thing in common—they all serve the ubiquitous hamburger in all its varied guises. The hamburger business appears to be so fragmented that changing the environment in which it is served is sufficient distinction to the consumer to permit the creation of a viable business.

Theme restaurants offer another example of how a business can

145

be viable in a highly fragmented industry. In theme restaurants the menus vary only superficially. Their distinctive difference appears to be in the decor of the building and the dining room.

In a highly fragmented industry an entrepreneur can readily aspire to be an equal among equals. Often the competitive advantage is one of personality, matching a friendly, warm, caring proprietor with the clientele. Or it may be in the personality of the manager and the manager's relationship and rapport with employees who reflect the manager's warmness in dealing with the customers.

Have you ever walked into a department store, selected the item you wished to purchase, and then stood around waiting for the sales clerks to finish their frivolous conversation before they would deign to recognize your presence? How often have you wanted to put the item back on the shelf and walk out? Or even more, wanted to dump the item at the feet of the clerk and stomp out of the store?

At the other end of the spectrum is the experience of walking into a hardware store and being greeted by someone who asks, "May I help you find something?" So often when you enter a hardware store you are looking for something you can't describe precisely. To look for it is to wander through endless shelves cluttered with strange items. Isn't it comforting to find someone who can help when you say, "I'm looking for something that's like a . . ."

An even further extreme on the sprectrum does not always work. That is the overly friendly sales clerk who won't give you the time to browse and collect your thoughts. Or the restaurant server who greets you with "Hi, I'm Joe." The customer expects, and *needs*, respect, what Maslow called esteem. Consumers don't part with their hard-earned cash for friends. They seek what at least appears to be objective assistance in weighing the perceived value of what they are buying. They consider spending money a serious matter and they want it treated seriously.

Few businesses serving the end consumer find themselves free of the burden of several competitors. Usually there are so many competitors that all are struggling to remain viable. In these businesses the key to survival and growth is in the transaction that is the very substance of business, the interaction between the salesperson and the customer. Granted that a desired product or service is essential, as are a convenient location and an adequate number of consumers. But among equal competitors that have these essentials the deciding difference is in the interpersonal behavior of the proprietor and staff.

This emphasis on a warm and caring proprietor is not limited to retail establishments. In John Welsh's business, fragmented into two and then three suppliers, even under the best conditions the living tissue cells would occasionally arrive in the hands of the consumer with contamination. If not that, they would freeze in winter or "cook" in summer and be delivered DOA—dead on arrival. This entrepreneur and his staff wanted to be part of the solution to the customer's problem, not part of the problem. After the first two years in business it was very common to hear customers say, "You make mistakes, but you are nice people to deal with." The customers became loyal even in adversity, and the good things they said to their colleagues were worth far more than any promotion program could have been.

ASPECTS OF FRAGMENTATION

In Chapter 21 more opportunities in a fragmented industry were mentioned. Markets can be fragmented geographically, by specialty, or by consumer taste, convenience, or price.

Geographic fragmentation is usually the result of a fixed selling location serving a population that must come to the business. The fixed location serves a radius. Beyond that radius people just won't travel that far to visit the store. Different kinds of stores have different radii. Different population densities create different radii, as do transportation facilities.

It is common to see billboards along our interstate highway system that say, "Easy off—easy on." Shopping malls require a sufficient population density to be viable. They are usually near main transportation arteries and offer ample convenient parking and a comfortable, air-conditioned environment. They often provide a place to park the kids and a fast-food area. Skating rinks in shopping malls are common, usually surrounded by a myriad of food outlets.

Less dense population centers are usually served by a strip of retail outlets, again located on main transportation arteries and providing convenient parking. In very low population density rural areas, a whole town may consist of merely a crossroads with a commercial establishment on each corner.

Fixed location selling or service establishments must be duplicated outside their customer radii. Therein lies an opportunity. A map, the Yellow Pages, and the census tract data available at the nearest federal building can provide a fruitful beginning to the search for such an opportunity.

Fragmentation may also result from provincial differences. Colonel Sanders demonstrated that southern fried chicken could be enjoyed in the North, the East, the West, and even Australia, Japan, and Europe. Western attire has found acceptance in the eastern states. Colorful Hawaiian shirts have turned out to be popular in all areas of the country with climate similar to that of the islands.

Ethnic differences also provide opportunity. French cuisine is popular in all population centers. In every city of any size there is at least one German restaurant. In most cities, even of only moderate size, there is at least one Italian restaurant. And the list may be extended to include Greek, Jewish, and so on.

Fragmentation by specialty has created a shower of oppor-

147

tunities. Shoe stores and paint stores are examples of specialization. The degree of specialization has reached far beyond these old-line examples. There are now establishments that only tune automobile engines, or only fix brakes, transmissions, tires, or front ends. There are pants stores and hat stores and necktie stores. Kiosks only develop photographic film or only make keys or only sell recordings.

Fragmentation by specialty also appears in manufacturing operations. An individual with knowledge and experience may obtain manufacturing equipment relevant to that knowledge and become a supplier. A good machinist in possession of one good automatic screw machine or turret lathe or centerless grinder can find other manufacturers very much in need of his or her service.

This provides an opportunity for someone who does not have the knowledge and experience of a machinist. From time to time the government will provide special assistance to classes or groups of people. Sometimes the groups are ethnic minorities, sometimes people disadvantaged by sex, economic deprivation, or physical handicap. These people are sometimes able to obtain expensive production equipment easily. They may then form a team with individuals who have the knowledge and experience to operate the equipment and sell its output.

Herein lies another clue to the aspiring entrepreneur. It is not necessary to own the specialized and expensive production machinery. It is only necessary to have access to it. An individual with the means to lease, rent, buy on a long-term loan, or just borrow equipment can form a team with people who have the knowledge and experience to exploit it. We have one friend in southern California who enjoys her work as an administrative employee and is well paid. She used her savings and her good credit to purchase a tractor-trailer unit, hired a driver, contracted with a company in the agribusiness for its use, and is now the president of a company about to buy its second eighteen wheeler.

Sam Wyly, the founder of University Computing Corporation, reports that to found his business he purchased a large used computer at a price less than the bank was willing to lend against the computer as collateral. From time to time the marketplace is overstocked with expensive productive equipment. A good place to look is in an industry undergoing a shakeout. Often the mistakes of one entrepreneur provide opportunities for others.

People who have demonstrated the ability to build a business usually encounter more opportunity than they can prudently handle. One way to increase the number of opportunities available to you is to start or build any business of interest to you. You might want to start in some highly fragmented industry with a geographic radius. Perhaps a franchise would seem suitable. Your first endeavor need not be your last. Consider building whatever is within your means at the moment and view it as a stepping-stone to bigger and better things.

24

Dominance:
A Working
Capital Advantage

The competitive advantage lies with the dominant competitor. Creative spending, market identity, and momentum are but some of the advantages. But for the growing business there is still another great benefit. Dominance provides a working capital advantage.

Growth consumes cash. Small businesses typically grow at greater rates than large businesses. Small, nonpublic businesses have meager financial resources and limited opportunity to gain them from financial institutions and investors. Growth must be financed, in large measure, from internally generated cash.

Cash is generated from profit, credit, loans, and investors. In a growing business cash is consumed much faster than profit and credit can support. Debt and equity financing are necessary adjuncts to continued growth. However, a dominant competitor, using a subordinate competitor's expense structure to justify profit margins can, and often does, find that the needed working capital can be generated internally.

Dominance implies a clear and resounding outdistancing of the nearest competitor (see Figure 18-2). This clear dominance illustrates how being first on the experience curve and furthest down the curve may provide working capital adequate to support growth.

NEED FOR WORKING CAPITAL

In Chapters 37 and 38 we will discuss in greater detail the definition and origin of working capital and the balance sheet. For the moment we want to examine only a part of the balance sheet. Working capital is the excess of cash and assets that will turn into cash shortly over the obligations to pay in cash in the near future. In more formal language it is the current assets less the current liabilities.

Dominance   In a growing business items in the current assets that consume most of the cash are growth in accounts receivable and inventory. On the obligation side, suppliers of the materials that go into inventory are often the only ones who will extend credit. The promises to pay suppliers who provide credit are called accounts payable.

Accounts payable usually represent the largest portion of the current liabilities, although they are much smaller than the accounts receivable in normal operations. Payables and receivables can be expected to increase by about the same percentage when growing, but the absolute size of the growth in receivables is greater. The same percentage increase of a larger number is itself a larger number.

THE WORKING CAPITAL
ADVANTAGE OF DOMINANCE

To illustrate the working capital advantage of the dominant competitor let's examine the growth in the current assets side of the balance sheet.[1] Inventory and receivables are not cash. They are boxes in the warehouse and invoices in the bookkeeping department. It is hoped, and expected, that they will turn into cash soon, but not while they remain inventory and receivables.

Suppose we examine Figure 24-1, where we find our old friends *D* and *S* competing on an economic experience curve on which expenses decline 20 percent with each doubling of cumulative experience. The

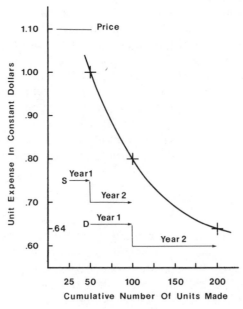

FIGURE 24-1 *S* and *D* on an Economic Experience Cuve as Each Doubles Sales Annually.

150

figure is very similar to Figure 18-2. Here, however, we show the prog- *Dominance*
ress of the two competitors during two successive years of competition.
Also, we have put more substantial numbers along the axis representing
accumulated experience. As before, the number 100 could stand for
whatever unit is appropriate.

The dominant competitor sells two units every time the subordinate competitor sells one. Otherwise they are equal in performance.
Each doubles sales annually. Each carries a sixty-day inventory and
holds accounts receivable equivalent to sixty days' sales.

Now we'll demonstrate the growth in working capital required
by inventory and accounts receivable for each competitor during the last
year. In the last year D's shipments have been 100 units, and experience
has grown from 100 to 200 units. This is indicated with an arrow marked
Year 2 on the figure. We can determine the growth in inventory and
accounts receivable by calculating the total at the end of the year and
subtracting the total at the beginning of the year. (You may skip ahead to
the three conclusions if you find the numbers too trying.)

For the D competitor at the end of Year 2 the inventory was equal
to sixty days' sales. That is two-twelfths of one year's sales. Because D
produced 100 during the year it has $2/12 \times 100$ in inventory.[2] The unit
expense of that inventory is very nearly the expense for the last unit
produced that year or, from the figure, 64¢. The value of the inventory is

$$2/12 \times 100 \times \$0.64 = \$10.67$$

At the beginning of year 2 the inventory was two-twelfths times
the fifty units produced in year 1. The unit expense of the inventory at
that time was very nearly the expense for the last unit made that year,
80¢. The value of the inventory at the beginning of the year would have
been

$$2/12 \times 50 \times \$0.80 = \$6.67$$

The growth in inventory value over the year would have been $4.
For the same competitor the accounts receivable at the end of the
year would be equivalent to sixty days' sales or two-twelfths of the units
shipped during the year multiplied by their sales price. If we assume that
the price holds at $1.10 throughout this two-year period, then the ac-
counts receivable at the end of Year 2 would be

$$2/12 \times 100 \times \$1.10 = \$18.33$$

Using the same logic, and examining Figure 24-1, the accounts
receivable at the beginning of the year would have been

$$2/12 \times 50 \times \$1.10 = \$19.17$$

The growth in accounts receivable would have been $9.16. The combined growth in inventory and accounts receivable would have been $13.16.

For the S competitor at the end of Year 2 the inventory would be two-twelfths of the year's output of fifty units. The unit expense of this inventory would be very nearly the unit expense of the last unit produced that year, or 80¢. The value of the inventory at the end of the year would be

$$^2/_{12} \times 50 \times \$0.80 = \$6.67$$

In the prior year S would have produced twenty-five units, and the unit expense of the last unit produced in the year would have been $1.00. The value of the inventory at the beginning of Year 2 would have been

$$^2/_{12} \times 25 \times \$1.00 = \$4.17$$

The increase in the working capital needed to support the inventory would have been $2.50.

The accounts receivable for S at the end of Year 2 would be two-twelfths of the units produced that year multiplied by the sales price:

$$^2/_{12} \times 50 \times \$1.10 = \$9.17$$

At the beginning of that year the accounts receivable would have been

$$^2/_{12} \times 25 \times \$1.10 = \$4.58$$

The growth in working capital to support the accounts receivable would have been $4.59. The combined growth in inventory and accounts receivable would have been $7.09.

CONCLUSION 1

Growth consumes cash. And more growth consumes more cash. S needed $7.09, while D needed $13.16 to support growth equal to doubling in one year.

One source of this additional money is profit, although as you will see in Chapter 35 profit is not cash and when it turns into cash it is found in many places besides accounts receivable and inventory. But profit is a source of financing. Let's see how much profit is generated by the competitors compared to how much financing they need to support inventory and accounts receivable.

During the year in question, D sold one hundred units at a price of $1.10 for a total revenue of $110. The expense during that year varied from 80¢ per unit at the beginning of the year to 64¢ at the end of the year. From Figure 24-1 it would appear that the expense of the median unit produced, unit number 150, was about 70¢.[3] The one hundred units would have had an expense of about $70, giving D a profit of $40 for the year.

During the same year S sold fifty units at a price of $1.10, receiving total revenue of $55. The expense varied from $1 per unit at the beginning of the year to 80¢ at the end of the year. From Figure 24-1 it would seem that the expense of the median unit produced, the seventy-fifth unit, would be approximately 88¢. Fifty units would have had a total expense of $44.00, and S would have reported $11.00 in profit.

CONCLUSION 2

With $13.16 needed for working capital and $40 profit, D would have had enough left over to buy the equipment needed to continue growing and reducing expense by scale, investment, and redesign.

For S the $11.00 profit seems adequate to cover the growth in inventory and receivables of $7.09, but it leaves little to provide for the expense of scale, investment, and redesign to continue down the curve. It also provides too little to consider rewarding the investors.

Let us examine this logic supposing that price had been declining with expense. If the profit margin of 10¢ when the expense was $1.00 was characteristic of the industry (this is the point where cumulative experience is fifty units in Figure 24-1), then the revenue would be 10 percent greater than the expense. The S competitor had expense for the year of approximately 88¢ per unit. For S to get 10 percent above that the price would have averaged 97¢ and S would report a profit of $4.50. If S can average 97¢ per unit, presumably D can also. Then D would have revenue of $97.00, expense of approximately $70.00, and a profit of $27.00.

It may be easier to comprehend all this arithmetic in a single table with the key points on the figure more clearly marked, as in Figures 24-2 and 24-3. They illustrate this second example, in which the average sale price is 97¢ each.

With price at 97¢ per unit the accounts receivable would be reduced. For D the receivables would be

$$^2/_{12} \times 100 \times \$0.97 = \$16.17$$

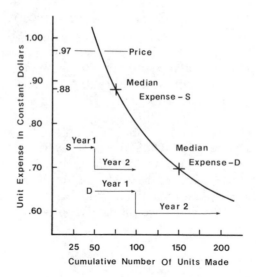

FIGURE 24-2 S and D Compete as Each Doubles Sales Annually with Price at 10 Percent above S's Expense.

instead of $18.33 at the end of the year, and

$$^{2}/_{12} \times 50 \times \$0.97 = \$8.08$$

at the beginning of the year. The cost of increased inventory would be unchanged at $4.00, and the combined growth in receivables and inventory would have been $12.09 compared to profit of $27.00.[4]
    For S the receivables would be

$$^{2}/_{12} \times 50 \times \$0.97 = \$8.08$$

instead of $9.17 at the end of the year, and

$$^{2}/_{12} \times 25 \times \$0.97 = \$4.04$$

at the beginning of the year. The growth in cost of the inventory would be unchanged at $2.50. The combined growth in inventory and receivables would have been $6.54 compared to a profit of $4.50.[5]

CONCLUSION 3

154

Should price decrease in proportion to the expense of S, then D would report profits of $27.00 while needing $12.09 to cover growth in receivables and inventory. S would report profits of $4.50 and need $6.54 for growth in inventory and receivables.

Competitor D		Competitor S	
End Of Year (2)			
Inventory			
2/12 × 100 × 0.64 = $ 10.67		2/12 × 50 × 0.80 = $ 6.67	
Receivables			
2/12 × 100 × 0.97 = 16.17		2/12 × 50 × 0.97 = 8.08	
Total	$ 26.84		$ 14.75
Beginning Of Year (2)			
Inventory			
2/12 × 50 × 0.80 = 6.67		2/12 × 25 × 1.00 = 4.17	
Receivables			
2/12 × 50 × 0.97 = 8.08		2/12 × 25 × 0.97 = 4.04	
Total	14.75		8.21
Working Capital Needed			
26.84 − 14.75 =	12.09	14.75 − 8.21 =	6.54
Profit Produced			
100(0.97 − 0.70) =	27.00	50(0.97 − 0.88) =	4.50

D Sells Two Units Each Time S Sells One. Both Carry A 60 Day Inventory And 60 Days Receivables. Each Doubles The Number Of Units Sold Annually. Sales Are Priced At $0.97 Per Unit.

FIGURE 24-3 Calculation of the Dominant Competitor's Working Capital Advantage.

The dominant competitor can provide for growth in inventory and accounts receivable and still make the necessary contributions to scale, investment, and redesign, and there may be some profit left over to reward the investors. The subordinate competitor cannot even support the growth in inventory and accounts receivable.

Entrepreneurs, being curious and realistic, look at these numbers and say, "Ah yes, but what happens the following year?" Figures 24-4 and 24-5 apply the same logic to the same competitors on the same curve one year later. Price is established by S. Both have increased

155

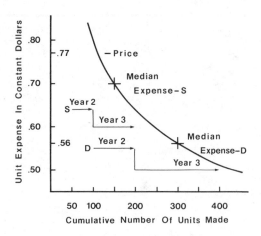

FIGURE 24-4 *S* and *D* Continue to Compete in a Successive Year.

profits by 55.6 percent while doubling the number of units sold. Both have maintained sixty-day receivables and held inventories to a sixty-day supply. *D* is still adequately financed from internally generated resources; *S* is still unable to cover growth in inventory and receivables.[6]

For the reader with some background in finance and accounting we wish to recognize that the inventory we have calculated here is 100 percent finished goods and the actual inventory may be less than that. On the other hand, the combination of raw materials inventory, the work in process inventory, and the finished goods inventory will be nearly as represented here, and the overall comparison of the two competitors is not changed materially.

We also recognize that the accounts payable will grow as the business grows, and that item represents a financial resource comparable to borrowed money. You may wish to assume what portion of the inventory is represented by materials and supplies that may be purchased on credit and calculate the growth in accounts payable. That growth figure may be added to the profit as a contribution to working capital to support inventory and accounts receivable. You will note from Figure 24-3 that, if the entire growth in inventory were covered by growth in accounts payable, *S* would still need $4.04 to support growth in accounts receivable while generating $4.50 in profits. There is still inadequate internally generated financing to support the additional investment needed to double sales again next year.

Some readers may view the growth in accounts receivable as an asset on which to borrow short-term monies from the bank. If the receivables are "good" the bank may very well provide short-term financing using them as collateral, but, of course, the bank will not lend 100 percent of the face value of the accounts receivable. That kind of borrowing by *S* is tying up assets and reducing management maneuverability in the event of adversity. *D* doesn't have that problem.

These two competitors represent large market share compared to small market share, both undergoing rapid growth. To maintain their

Competitor D		Competitor S	
End Of Year (3)			
Inventory			
2/12×200×0.51= $17.00		2/12×100×0.64=$ 10.67	
Receivables			
2/12×200×0.77= 25.67		2/12×100×0.77= 12.83	
Total	$42.67		$23.50
Beginning Of Year (3)			
Inventory			
2/12×100×C.64= 10.67		2/12×50×0.80= 6.67	
Receivables			
2/12×100×∪.77= 12.83		2/12×50×0.77= 6.42	
Total	23.50		13.09
Working Capital Needed			
42.67−23.50=	19.17	23.50−13.09=	10.41
Profit Produced			
200(0.77−0.56)=	42.00	100(0.77−0.70)=	7.00

D Sells Two Units Each Time S Sells One. Both Carry A 60 Day Inventory And 60 Days Receivables. Each Doubles The Number Of Units Sold Annually. Sales Are Priced At $0.77 Per Unit.

FIGURE 24-5 Calculation of the Dominant Competitor's Working Capital Advantage One Year Later.

current market shares they must grow at the same rate the market grows. Should the growth rate of the market decrease our two competitors would represent large and small market shares undergoing little or no growth.

Growth in inventory and accounts receivable resulted from growth in sales. If growth in sales becomes small, then the additional working capital needed to support these two items will be small. This does not, however, decrease sales and profit margins. Both competitors would be producing profits but not needing them to support growth. The subordinate competitor may then breathe a little easier and sleep a little more soundly. The dominant competitor may be laughing all the way to the bank.

The figures in this chapter provide a further insight into the implications of the economic experience curve. In a rapidly growing market the competitors must grow equally rapidly or lose their current market shares. To gain a desirable position on the curve and maintain it requires rapid growth, which imposes great demands for financing, skillful and professional management, and a relentless effort to force expenses to decline in conformance with the curve.

Comparing the sales of D for the two successive years in the tables we find that while doubling sales in terms of units shipped, the reported revenues increased from $97 in the first year to $154 in the second, an increase of 59 percent. While management had to worry about physically handling twice as many units, the investors grant credit for only a 59 percent improvement in sales. Had the curve used in the examples declined at 25 percent or 30 percent with each doubling of experience, the improvement in sales and plaudits from the investors would have been even less.

In Chapter 19 we mentioned creative spending. The examples in this section illustrate one way in which it arises. D was able to maintain superior profit margins because S needed a sales price considerably above what D could justify in the absence of S. So long as the dominant competitor could find consumers for all the goods it produced and maintain a market share, it could enjoy the benefits of the larger margins. On the other hand, the dominant competitor would likely be reluctant to report margins of 27¢ on sales of 97¢, 28 percent, while S is reporting 9 percent as shown in Figure 24-3. This situation demands some creative spending to achieve reasonable reported profit margins.

An experienced management will recognize that a good thing can't last forever. The competitors may ride down that economic experience curve only until something changes either in the marketplace or in the technology of the product or its production. To ensure the continued viability of the business, never mind its continued growth, new curves must be identified. A product has a life cycle just as any living organism. And like a living organism the species is maintained by the birth of new organisms with new strength and vitality.

The dominant competitor can allocate a considerable sum to looking at new ideas, new products or services, new markets. There is ample support for people and equipment to experiment and to test market. There is money available to buy or acquire another business that needs management, equipment, marketing, and working capital. The resources are available to expand the existing product line and find new uses for it. While the subordinate competitor is struggling to look good, the dominant competitor is looking for new ball games to play.

For a business there may be some truth to the cliché the rich get richer and the poor get poorer, not because the rich fall into it, but because they apply their resources wisely and in a timely fashion. Dominant competitors can afford to buy acorns and nurture them into forests.

The Entrepreneur's Odyssey

A manager is all too often aware of how little freedom of choice is available when guiding the destiny of the business. Despite title, position, and the appearance of power the manager is constrained by forces far more powerful and unforgiving. One facet of these constraints emerges from another examination of the analysis of Chapter 24. The examples of that chapter compared the performance of two competitors, each appearing to be doing well. Both were doubling the number of units shipped annually. For the competitors to maintain their market shares while doubling annually, the market they served had to be doubling in size annually. If the market had been growing less rapidly, then each of the competitors would have been increasing its market share, although their shares when compared with each other would have remained the same.

CALCULATING MARKET SHARE

Market share is the ratio of the competitor's annual sales to the total annual sales of competitive products in the market being served by the competitors. It is usually measured by dividing the competitor's sales in dollars by the total sales volume in dollars for the industry. Dollars are used in the calculation because monetary value is usually easy to obtain.

As may be seen from the dimensions describing the horizontal axis of the economic experience curve, it would make more sense to measure the market share in units sold during the year. Dollar volume does not double when volume in units shipped doubles if price decreases with experience.[1] In an example in Chapter 24 sales revenue increased from $97 to $154 while D doubled the number of units shipped. If we are interested in measuring things with fundamental value, we must count in units that have a fundamental relationship.

The dimensions of the experience curve are fully allocated unit expense in constant dollars and cumulative number of units produced. In the examples of the previous chapter the reference to doubling sales was measured in units shipped. Because this kind of measure could be counted off on the horizontal axis of the curve, it was possible to relate the growth in shipments to fully allocated expense in constant dollars, a reasonable profit margin, and the resulting dollar volume of sales. When relating the dominant competitor's market share to that of the subordinate competitor in the examples, the assumption was stated as, *D* sells two units each time *S* sells one.

The difficulty in obtaining the information needed to calculate market shares in terms of units shipped is often resolved by trade association data, which reports in both units and dollars. Still, the associations may not include every possible competitor among their membership. In almost all cases, however, the nonmembers are not big enough to be significant. Even without the nonmember data, the trade association information is a good approximation to the actual figures.

There is no dearth of trade association data. Most businesses are members of some association. The *Encyclopedia of Associations,* published annually, lists thousands of such organizations.[2] Even industries that appear small and obscure are usually listed.

Given that sufficient data is available, it is not entirely necessary to know a competitor's exact market share. The information most meaningful to a manager is market share compared to that of the nearest competitor. This gives rise to the concept of a *market share ratio.*

The Boston Consulting Group proposed a ratio that has special meaning when used in conjunction with the economic experience curve.[3] The ratio may be best understood as

$$\text{Market Share Ratio} = \frac{\text{Your Market Share}}{\text{Market Share of Your Biggest Competitor}}$$

The interesting result of defining the ratio this way is that only one competitor has a ratio greater than one. All the others have fractional ratios, less than one. For instance, if you hold the largest market share your biggest competitor will have a smaller share than you, and your ratio will be a number greater than one. If your biggest competitor has a market share larger than yours, your ratio will be less than one.

Because only one competitor has a market share ratio greater than unity, the dominant competitor is identified by a number greater than one. Also, the degree of the biggest competitor's dominance is indicated by the size of the number. In the examples of Chapters 18 and 24 the dominant competitor sold two units each time the subordinate competitor sold one. The market share ratio of the *D* competitor was 2.0, for the *S* competitor it was 0.5, a clear indication of dominance.

Typically, when a new business concept arises that can be represented by an economic experience curve, several competitors enter the marketplace within a very short span of time. There is an initial market penetration in which market shares are established. Managers have learned how difficult it is to change the market share of the competitors once they have been established. Market shares among suppliers who are competing forcefully tend to remain reasonably constant. Cumulative experience relative to other competitors tends to be aligned with the market share ratios.

But this is not always exactly true. Remember the comments about dominance and market share in Chapter 18. The examples associated with Figure 18-3 describe competitors with equal market shares, but the competitor who started first is dominant because dominance is held by the one with the most total accumulated experience.

MARKET GROWTH

In Chapter 24 the examples examined competitors who maintained their market ratios and also doubled the number of units shipped each year. To do this the marketplace would have to be doubling in size annually to absorb the additional number of units shipped by the competitors. Or any change in current market share by one of them would have to be matched by a proportional change in the current market share of the other. If market shares of established competitors tended to remain stable, then the total market must have been doubling.

The rate of growth of the market is important to the manager because it indicates the rate of growth in capacity required. When the rate falls to zero there is no need for further increase in capacity to produce. There is still the need to invest in cost reduction through scale and redesign, but new plant, equipment, employee recruiting, and training become problems of the past. On the other hand, a high growth rate in the market demands that the manager obtain the investment needed for both expansion and cost reduction.

Chapter 24 demonstrated how high growth rate and differing market shares influence some major sources and uses of financial resources. The competitors in the examples of that chapter could be located on a graph showing the two variables, growth rate and market share ratio, as the axes of the graph as in Figure 25-1.

A market growth rate of interest would be the minimum rate where an investment in further growth is worth making. For instance, investing in a market that will grow 50 percent annually can be very attractive. Investing in a market that will grow 10 percent annually is only marginal. A market that is predicted to grow 10 percent next year, but that has been trending toward smaller growth rates, would probably not be of interest to investors. A market showing no growth or actually shrinking will not likely attract any investment.

161

A NEW CLASSIFICATION
OF COMPETITORS

The cutoff growth rate of interest will vary from one business to another, but it will probably lie in the range of 10 percent to 25 percent per year with the trend growing, holding at that level, or changing very little in the near future. It takes several years to obtain return of the investment plus a reasonable reward.

This being the case, Figure 25-1 might be more meaningful if the horizontal axis were drawn at the cutoff growth rate of interest. We might arbitrarily choose 15 percent market growth rate for the horizontal axis and then extend the vertical axis to zero and beyond.

The significance of this change in the graph is that growth consumes financial resources. Above the horizontal axis the business will choose to invest its resources to continue growth. Below that axis, the business will not be much interested in investing for further growth. There will be no need to consume the resources it produces by its operations to support growth of the existing products.

We would like to propose one more change in the graph. For reasons that should make more sense before the end of this chapter, we propose to rotate the axes of the graph 45° counterclockwise. Then growth in market share ratio would be toward the upper right. Increasing market growth rate will be in the direction of the upper left, as in Figure 25-2. The four quadrants are identified with numbers.

Recalling now the examples of Chapter 24, the dominant competitor had large market share and high growth rate. It was clearly located in Quadrant 2. It required considerable financing to support its growth in inventory and accounts receivable plus investment in growth of capacity and continued cost reduction. On the other hand, it produced attractive profit margins, which contributed to financing these needs. In the examples this competitor produced financial resources in excess of

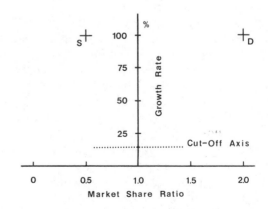

FIGURE 25-1 Competitors *D* and *S* Identified by Their Market Share Ratio and Growth Rate.

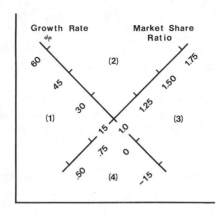

FIGURE 25-2 The Growth Rate–Market Share Ratio Matrix.

those needed for growth in inventory and accounts receivable. This competitor is everything an investor would like it to be. The investment community would call this kind of competitor a *star*.[4]

The other competitor had rapid growth in sales, but small market share. This subordinate competitor would be found in Quadrant 1. Its growth demanded financing to support greater inventory and accounts receivable, cost reduction, and increased capacity. Its restricted profit margins did not permit it to generate the financing internally to support these. The manager of this competitor is found each year reporting that "sales are up, profits are up, and all we need, sir, is a little more capital."

This kind of competitor is called a *question mark*. Each year the news is good, but the company needs additional help. There is always the question of whether next year will be better and whether the company can obtain the financing needed to continue operations for another year. The future of that business is not yet assured.

Quadrant 3 would represent a competitor with large market share and little or no growth rate. It might even have a negative growth rate. The financial resources needed to support growth in inventory and accounts receivable would be nominal at best. As the growth in sales shrinks to zero there is no need for financial resources to support growth in inventory or accounts receivable. With negative growth the business will begin to receive cash resources from its shrinking inventory and accounts receivable. Meanwhile, because of its dominant market share, it maintains its favorable profit margins. The competitor in Quadrant 3 produces cash, but doesn't need it. This kind of competitor is called a *cash cow*.

The competitor in Quadrant 4 has small market share and small growth. This competitor doesn't produce much profit because of the constricted margins available to a subordinate competitor. On the other hand, it doesn't need much financial help because it isn't growing. It just isn't going anywhere. It won't find much interest among investors. Who is going to get excited about a business that isn't doing much or going anywhere? This kind of competitor is called a *dog*.

163

Recalling the dimensions of Figure 25-2, there is only one competitor in the star–cash cow half of the figure. All the subordinate competitors are in the question mark–dog half. Growth rate determines whether they are stars or cash cows, or for the subordinate competitors, question marks or dogs.

Consider now the entry into the field displayed by Figure 25-2 of several competitors before the market is well established. Where do they enter? On day one of business, does a competitor have a big market share or a small one? On day one, having sold none, the new competitor has zero market share and zero market share ratio.

On the first day of business, does a competitor have a large growth rate or a small one? When a new competitor sells the first unit, having sold none before, the growth rate is one divided by zero, which equals infinity. When the second unit is sold, having sold one before, the growth rate is one divided by one, which equals one. When the third unit is sold, having sold two before, the growth rate is one divided by two, or one-half.

The growth rate of a new competitor starts at infinity and decreases very rapidly into the field of the figure. Because it also starts from no market share at all, the entry is from the upper left, in the question-mark quadrant.

As the new competitors penetrate the market and establish their market shares, one will move across into the star quadrant. All the others will remain as question marks. Because established market shares typically remain fairly constant, the competitors will be strung out above the market share ratio axis. How far above that axis depends on the growth rate of the marketplace. If the competitors are to maintain their respective market shares, their growth rate must be that of the marketplace.

Suppose we consider a competitor who enters the field as a question mark and manages to cross over the line and become a star before the market shares among the competitors are established. If that competitor is to hold market share ratio, then the only place it can move on the graph is perpendicular to the market share ratio axis. In a market with an increasing growth rate that competitor becomes a *rising star*.

Everyone loves a rising star. It has success and expects more of the same. It needs investment, but it generates much cash internally. Investors see a small investment in a rising star growing and multiplying to become a large return. Although investors want to join a rising star, the star can be indifferent to unattractive investment offers. If there were ever any thought of selling some of the original investment to reap the rewards, this is the time for that action.

If for any reason the growth rate of the market, not necessarily the growth itself, should turn around and begin to decrease, the competitor becomes a *falling star*. Unfortunately, investors become fickle lovers of a falling star. They see its promise of a grand future as having peaked out. Now the star is fortunate that it is able to generate enough

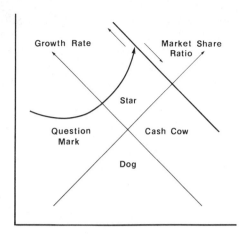

FIGURE 25-3 The Entrepreneur's Odyssey among Stars, Dogs, Cash Cows, and Question Marks.

resources internally to satisfy its investment needs. Few investors seem interested in a falling star.

If the owners and manager will just be patient, however, the decreasing growth rate of the market will fall below the market share ratio axis and the star will become a cash cow. Once again, there will be investors who want to join the business, and it may be indifferent to unattractive investment offers. The cash cow shown in Figure 25-3 is making investment offers, not accepting them.

During the ride from first establishing market shares through being a rising star and a falling star until becoming a cash cow, the competitor must maintain market share ratio. A rising star that is losing market share moves in the direction of becoming a question mark. A falling star that is losing market share moves toward becoming a dog. Management must maintain vigilance and pursue vigorous marketing with declining expense to maintain that market share ratio.

The aspiring entrepreneur may have already noted that during the periods of entry into the field, the rising star and the falling star, the business needs all its financial resources to provide for its own demands. An indulgent manager may mistake the clamour of investors while the star is rising for a signal to reward management and the owners more generously with cash and perquisites. But the shrewd manager will keep a tight reign on the purse strings and provide for the needs of an embryonic cash cow. With patience and perseverance the needs of the business will diminish sufficiently that cash begins to build up in the bank. Then, and only then, can the manager become magnanimous.

Actually, the cash that then accumulates belongs to the investors, and management is only a fiduciary to the benefit of their interests. Perhaps management should give the cash to the investors. But that seldom happens. Somehow managers always perceive themselves to be

165

better able to choose the best investment with that cash, on behalf of the investors, of course. They come up with new business concepts and invest the money generated by the cash cow. Like every new business, their investment enters the field as a question mark. They make question marks out of cash cows and hope they can repeat the perilous journey portrayed in this entrepreneur's odyssey.

26

The Business Concept's Time Line

The entrepreneur is much like a ship's officer who has just received that most desirable piece of paper, a license to command a vessel as its captain. But the captain needs a ship to go anywhere. And the kind of ship determines where the captain may go. A leaky rowboat would not seem very desirable. A coastal freighter would not venture far out to sea. On the other hand, an enormous supertanker would not venture too close to shore, even in the world's great seaports. The captain would need a submarine to sail beneath the polar ice caps. And the aircraft carrier Nimitz with its flotilla of escort ships won't maneuver in narrow expanses of water like the Persian Gulf, even though it is 150 miles wide and 600 miles long.

The captain's license confirms that the individual who has it is experienced at sea, is conversant with the problems of navigation, and is skilled at using navigational tools and aids. That person knows the rules and can guide a ship safely across open oceans and through perilous straits. Help is available from charts, lights, radio, radar, orbiting satellites, and heavenly bodies. But despite this array of assistance, the captain must still exercise superior judgment, because sandbars move, storms shroud the bridge pilings, and wind and currents carry the ship off course.

BUSINESS NAVIGATION

For a business, the need to exercise superior judgment is even greater. The business is always sailing in uncharted seas. Not only is it operating in an accounting period not yet accounted for, but the environment in which it navigates is multidimensional and ever-changing. There is no radio, radar, or orbiting satellite for assistance. And the heavenly bodies provide little more help than the brief astrological statements in the morning paper listed by the signs of the zodiac.

167

A ship sails on a two-dimensional surface. It uses the time dimension to relate its changing position on that surface. Airplanes fly in a three-dimensional space above a two-dimensional surface. They, too, use the time dimension to relate their changing position within that space. Spaceships roam in a four-dimensional time-space in which the two-dimensional surface has faded to a distant sphere. Destinations and points of departure are moving spheres traveling in elliptical paths. Only the distant stars at the far reaches of the visible universe seem fixed. To intercept another spaceship or a planet destination requires an orbital path about the sun meeting another orbital path at precisely the right time.

A business navigates through an even greater sea of complexity, in which there is a veritable alphabet of dimensions needed to describe its position, its direction, and its velocity. A business is a group of people—employees, managers, owners, suppliers, customers, and the family members related to them. Each of these individuals behaves according to his or her personal dimensions. Their emotions and their passions play as large a role in determining their behavior as the more mundane needs to find food, shelter, and clothing.

Greed, power, love, fad, and self-perception, to mention only a few of the driving forces in human nature, govern the behavior of people. People cannot be reduced to a simple model, such as the so-called economic man. Business consists of transactions in which individuals exchange things they consider of value; the price is determined by what a willing buyer will pay a willing seller. That alone is certain to involve emotions. Objectivity is notably absent from the transaction, although most parties to the interaction pay lip service to it. Beyond subsistence, the most likely motivator for a sale is "want," not need, a visible manifestation of the emotions.

The business concept is the entrepreneur's vessel. It constrains where the entrepreneur may go, how long the journey will be, and how bumpy the ride. It needs sufficient opportunity in an economic environment to survive and thrive despite its manager's restricted vision, occasional vertigo, and unanticipated wrong turns. It needs the opportunity to survive in the face of the adversity and uncertainty it will certainly encounter from time to time. Business concepts are not born equal. Nor do they have the benefit of equal opportunity under the law. Business concepts are more like seeds strewn on an open field. Which ones thrive and grow depends on sun, rain, and the other seeds. The weeds are ever-present and discouragingly aggressive.

Many business concepts are available (see Chapter 21). But how does an entrepreneur recognize a good one? Or, at least, how can you recognize one that may reach a desired destination? With ships and airplanes there are reasonable indications of size, horsepower, range, and navigational equipment. With business these measures are less objective and far greater in number. On the customer side the measures include whim, fancy, and the ability to accumulate the money needed to purchase. On the supplier side the measures include availability, financing, transportation, labor-management tranquillity, and continuity. In between lies the entrepreneur's ability to assemble and manage all the distinctive business functions.

MATHEMATICAL EXPRESSION
OF THE ECONOMIC
EXPERIENCE CURVE

How is the entrepreneur to find guidance? Where are the charts to plot strategy, tactics, and action? We have found a hypothesis based on more than a hundred years of observation of repetitive tasks. The aspect of help to the entrepreneur, however, is a recent development.

Within the world of work, where achievement ranks above credentials, the hypothesis has been tested and approved in a most dramatic fashion. It was first recognized in the aircraft industry in the mid-1920s, when it could be studied in a new and burgeoning field, unrestrained by tradition and preconceived knowledge. It has come into clear understanding in the newer and even less restrained electronics industry. And it has been applied and confirmed in yet another new industry, that of the microprocessor.

No doubt we have much yet to learn about the consistent and persistent decline in fully allocated expense of produced units measured in a currency free of the effects of inflation. We have yet to agree on a name for the phenomenon. But our present knowledge is sufficient to provide qualitative guidance supported with some quantitative mileposts. And our present understanding clearly suggests that one of the most fruitful arenas in which to apply the hypothesis is entrepreneurship.

This is the phenomenon we refer to as the economic experience curve. It provides a means to identify the entrepreneur's vessel, a chart and navigational aids, and what intelligence information is needed to plot a reasonable course in the multidimensional milieu in which a business must sail.

Unlike the descriptions of the characteristics of the entrepreneur and the successful entrepreneur's career path, in which words alone must be used, the basis for examining a business concept has at least one aspect that may be reduced to numbers. A fundamental expression, as simple as Newton's Law of Gravitation, has been identified. It is based on the observation that in stable industries the fully allocated unit expense, in constant dollars, decreases by an equal percentage each time total accumulated experience doubles in the production of an identifiable unit. That statement may be reduced to mathematics with the expression

$$Y = AX^b$$

169

where Y is the fully allocated expense of a unit in constant dollars, A is a constant identifying the magnitude of Y for some particular number of units produced, X is the cumulative number of units produced, and b is determined by the fraction of the initial unit expense found to exist after a doubling of cumulative total number of units made.

Five examples of the term b frequently observed in production are listed below.

FRACTIONAL EXPENSE PER DOUBLING (%)	VALUE OF THE TERM b
90	−0.152
85	−0.234
80	−0.322
75	−0.415
70	−0.515

The implication of a fractional expense per doubling of 80 percent is that the expense to produce a unit at the end of the doubling of experience is only 80 percent of the expense per unit at the beginning. The expense per unit has been reduced 20 percent by doubling total cumulative experience. In the case of a 70 percent fractional expense, the expense per unit has been reduced 30 percent by doubling total cumulative experience.

This relationship reveals an additional unexpected dimension to our understanding. It suggests a fundamental unit or dimension—the cumulative number of units made, the horizontal axis of the graph representing this relationship. It also permits identifying position on that axis relative to a fixed and invariant reference point, the completion of the first unit produced, regardless of how long ago that was or what might have transpired since.

The significance of this fundamental unit is apparent when considering the abundant measures of business and economic activity provided by trade associations, business research organizations, the many agencies of the U.S. Department of Commerce, economists, and analysts of the financial community. Their data compares one period of time against another. One of the best examples of the weakness in this kind of reporting is the quarterly reports of public corporations and the news media response they evoke.

Corporations feel obliged to report increases and decreases in their earnings as a percentage change from the prior year. When earnings increase from $1 million to $2 million, the report to stockholders hails the 100 percent increase in profits. When, in a subsequent period, the earnings drop from $2 million to $1 million, the same report to stockholders "explains" the 50 percent decrease in profits. If you assume the perspective of management trying to look good in the eyes of the stockholders, the reason for this kind of reporting is not obscure. But the news media gets an entirely different meaning from the description. They see the corporation increasing profits by $1 million, and in bad years they see that profits are off by only 50 percent of that.

An unchanging standard of comparison is essential to knowing the condition of what is being measured. The economic experience curve provides that standard for a business's operations over extended periods in relation to its total cumulative units produced.

The vertical axis of the graph displaying the curve is not nearly so precise. It portrays fully allocated expense per unit in constant dollars. The determination of "fully allocated expense" may vary greatly within "generally accepted accounting principles," and the index chosen to remove the effects of inflation may be selected from an array provided by the government or private sources. Fortunately, the selection of accounting principles and the deflator are not so important as is their consistent application.

Chapter 16 introduced the economic experience curve. Chapter 17 demonstrated how it may be used to portray an economic productivity curve. Whether the relationship is viewed as an experience curve or a productivity curve, that is, in terms of expense declines or productivity gains, the business's goals and strategy may be tied to measurable events with consistency and a stable, unchanging reference point.

Portraying the relationship in its productivity form may be more attractive psychologically when dealing with employees, investors, and government interventionists. In a sense, it is a more positive portrayal. Productivity is accepted as desirable. Portraying the relationship in its economic experience form is more descriptive of what management can work on to bring about the productivity gains.

The full breadth of the effort to attain goals is revealed in these curves. They encompass all the distinctive business functions and provide a pictorial focal point for common team objectives and achievement. They break down the scorekeeping to earthy levels, like letters typed or invoices prepared.

The curves display in a most dramatic fashion the critical need for superior accounting data from day one of the business's operations. "Check-stub accounting" is inadequate to provide the manager the strategic weapons available from the curves. Even the normal financial record keeping in full double-entry accounting is inadequate to provide experience curve data. Detailed unit cost accounting is needed. Typically, managers do not install a full cost accounting system until their businesses become large. Knowledge of the economic experience curve may provide entrepreneurs with an appreciation for the desirability of full cost accounting from the beginning. The added expense of bookkeepers and clerks is small compared with the potential benefit available.

Application of the hypothesis and the implications of the curve are not without their difficulties. Identification of the pertinent unit, the cumulative number of units made, the fully allocated expense, and a reasonable deflator to remove the effects of inflation all involve judgment with some experimentation. Within these limits, however, even imprecise and qualitative measurements provide navigational aids not available just a generation ago.

IDENTIFYING AND CHANGING A BUSINESS'S CURVE

One of the greatest difficulties in applying this new knowledge lies in identifying your curve. Chapter 14 described ways to find and describe a curve, but in this aspect we are back to using words instead of precise numbers. Chapter 14 showed why the list of words describing an experience curve cannot be closed; it must be changing continually. A manager must be attuned to the culture of the moment throughout the geographic area in which the business provides its products and services. A manager who seeks seclusion from the everyday fight in the marketplace quickly becomes vulnerable to challenge from the venturesome entrepreneur out on the street.

The concept of the economic experience curve points out with elegant emphasis the importance of experience—relevant experience. It also displays with superb clarity the imperative need for dedication and commitment to declining price in constant dollars. This price competition provides the motivation for ever greater efficiency imposed by the free, open market system. The dream of building the business to the point where the owner-manager can relax and enjoy the fruits of having created and built a business is just that, a dream. The manager must be eternally vigilant, striving, and achieving. The number of aspiring entrepreneurs actively seeking the opportunity to build their own economic freedom is larger than the number who have already achieved that station.

The curve provides illumination in the often hidden recesses of constraints on the manager's ability and opportunity to keep the ship afloat even in a warm, balmy breeze. Growth of the business is constrained by growth of the market, external financing, training of personnel, acquisition of personnel with pertinent experience, and new technology. The manager's success in bringing price down makes more difficult the task of achieving increased production volume, which will bring accolades from the investors. Accepting reasonable profit margins in the near term to obtain long-term gains may be difficult to explain to uninformed investors.

Timing and an adequate time span in which to build a track record are prerequisites for successfully applying the strategies imposed by the curve. An entrepreneur wants to catch a new curve at the beginning of its life cycle. Like the surfer, the entrepreneur wants to catch a big wave, preferably far from the beach.

Submitting to the dictates of the curve implies another constraint. Figure 26-1, from the *Harvard Business Review*, demonstrates beautifully the persistence and consistency of the price decline for the Ford Motor Company's Model T automobile.[1] That the declining price extended over so long a period is impressive evidence that the economic experience curve is profound and fundamental.

The figure was published in connection with another observation, however. Having specialized in the production of the Model T for so long, the Ford Motor Company had created a mechanism so dedicated to manufacturing one product that it was almost unable to produce anything else. When General Motors introduced the heavier, closed-body design in 1921, Ford was faced with the dilemma of changing its entire production plant and equipment to produce a competitive automobile. In 1927 Ford faced up to that fact and the great River Rouge plant was closed for nearly a year to retool and make the transition.

Once again we see a demonstration that management must stay attuned to the current culture in which it operates. Henry Ford, having created a market for automobiles, failed to recognize the next wave of distinctive perceived consumer values. It cost him his dominance as the major competitor in the industry. The entire United States automobile industry repeated that mistake in the late 1970s and lost a major portion of the market to foreign manufacturers.

The business concept, described by distinctive perceived consumer values and portrayed as an experience curve, is dynamic and changing. Like a fine racehorse, a business concept has its day at the derby and then retires to the farm.

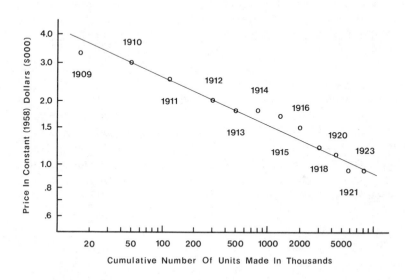

FIGURE 26-1 The Ford Model T Automobile's Economic Experience Curve from 1909 to 1923.

27

What Is
Venture Capital?

In starting a business you can use the help of family, friends, and children. You can use the garage and the basement for quarters. You can borrow furniture and equipment. But after all the resources of family and friends have been obtained, there is still the need for some hard cold cash. It takes a little money to pay for things like raw materials, telephone, postage, letterhead stationery, and possibly some salaries and wages. This start-up money is sometimes referred to as *seed money*. It may be the most venturesome kind of venture capital.

To improve the probability of success in starting a new business, it takes the right kind of person with the right kind of business concept. More than that, the person should be at a particular point along the career path and the business concept should be timely in the context of perceived consumer values as well as current technology. Even with the right person at the right time, and the right business concept at the right time, there is still the need for venture capital to give the new business a chance to win in the marketplace competition.

Venture capital is liquid assets invested in an unproven business. Money placed with a proven business enterprise for its prudent use can be thought of as *invested capital*. Money placed with any other business enterprise is at risk to a greater or lesser degree and can be thought of as venture capital. There are few enough proven businesses, and it is easier to identify and describe one of them than it is to try and describe one of the many, many unproven businesses.

RECOGNIZING PROVEN ENTERPRISES

A proven enterprise has several characteristics. The following list provides some help to recognize an investment quality proven business:

1. *Track Record.* A proven enterprise has a long and consistent record of desirable performance.

2. *Conservative Management.* A proven enterprise does not alter its past behavior dramatically. It may change, but its rate of change is small.

3. *Stable Assets.* A proven enterprise has assets with a long life expectancy and stable value in sufficient quantity to support and document its worth.

4. *Momentum.* A proven enterprise has strong momentum, evidenced by established channels of supply and distribution that are well stocked, committed, and obligated to future deliveries. It has well-functioning, highly organized operations to convert what is supplied into what is distributed. The operations are not subject to large changes in performance in the face of adversity, such as poor economic conditions, changing technology, the sudden loss of key management people, or weakness in the financial markets.

5. *Foreseeable Continuity.* A proven enterprise is not facing strong new external forces in the near future. It is not in a position to require immediate implementation of major strategic decisions because of changes in control of its raw materials, new government regulations, new political philosophy, new technological innovations, or new consumer perceptions resulting from social or cultural change.

6. *Diverse Sources of Capital.* A proven enterprise is not restricted to only one source of financing, such as bank loans, but rather has access to debt and equity through a variety of channels. A proven enterprise is in a position to choose the source of its capital best suited to its needs and objectives.

NEWTON'S LAWS APPLIED TO BUSINESS

It may come as a surprise that a number of the characteristics of a proven enterprise are described by Newton's Laws of Motion. Issac Newton is probably best known for his recognition of the Law of Gravity. Most of us have seen the cartoon reference to Newton lying under an apple tree with one of the fruits falling on his head. This law was, in fact, an extremely fundamental contribution to science and technology and has been verified and substantiated in astronomy.

Newton also propounded three fundamental Laws of Motion. These are familiar to high-school and college students who have had any course in physics. They are usually described with reference to something like billiard balls. They are absolutely true for billiard balls, baseballs, and bullets. They also provide insight for a much broader spectrum of bodies, including people, groups of people, and their behavior.

Newton's first law says that a body at rest will remain at rest until acted on by some external force. Nothing is going to change unless something changes it. The law also says that a body in motion will remain in motion at the same speed and in the same direction until forced to change speed, direction, or both by some external force. This is called *inertia*.

If a business enterprise has a lot of inertia you can feel reasonably assured that things are not going to change. The track record of a business suggests its speed and direction. A conservative management will keep it moving at that speed and in that direction. Stable assets in sufficient quantity provide mass to the enterprise and support its inertia.

Newton's second law says that the rate of change depends on the mass. The more massive the body, the more external force it takes to make it change its speed and direction. New forces in the marketplace, like new technology, changing conditions in the economy, and constraints on supplies, materials, and able employees, have less effect on massive business enterprises. Their rate of change is small unless faced with massive external forces. You will recall that it took the combination of long lines at the gas pumps, record high interest rates, government-imposed environmental regulation, a sluggish economy, and aggressive competition from foreign carmakers to make the United States auto industry alter its speed and direction.

This law also says, if you want to bring about a significant change in your enterprise, you are going to have to exert a significant effort to make it happen. Your business will continue drifting along as is until something comes along to make it change. You can be sure something will come along. Sooner or later adversity will strike. And having struck it will strike again. You, as the owner-manager, must exert enough force to keep your business going where you want it to.

Momentum is like the obstinacy of bodies having mass and motion. The more massive they are or the more velocity they have, the more momentum they have. A big strong business with a big market identity and market share has both mass and velocity. Momentum is the product of the two. It takes a lot of force to change the speed and direction of a business with a lot of momentum.

Foreseeable continuity is assured if a business has plenty of momentum and there are no new external forces on the horizon. The vacuum tube business had plenty of momentum. A new force emerged in the marketplace, however, in the form of transistors which resulted in solid state electronics replacing the tubes. A dwindling supply of petroleum can alter the momentum of the petrochemical businesses. A shortage of petroleum might also have a strong influence on the momentum of motels, hotels, and restaurants.

Newton's third law says that to every action there is an equal and opposite reaction. That means that when you exert a force to bring about change you can expect resistance to your effort, and the resistance will not be incidental.

A business may not look like a billiard ball or a bowling ball, but in fundamental ways their behavior is the same. A new or small business does not have much mass or motion. Its speed and direction is determined more by the external forces it meets in the marketplace than by its own motion. Its path of flight is like that of a leaf blown from a tree by strong, gusty winds. A proven enterprise is more like the pine needle of an old fir tree. Despite violent summer thunderstorms and howling winter blizzards, the pine needle is still on the old tree.

If a proven enterprise is viewed as one end of a spectrum of investment opportunities, the other end of the spectrum would be the new venture. It has no track record, no past behavior to emulate, no assets; it is highly volatile in its response to adversity, faces an uncertain future fraught with strategic decisions, and has little if any access to external capital.[1] The new venture may offer hope and promise, but very little assurance and no certainty.

Among the things an entrepreneur must contend with are suppliers who want to be paid cash in advance, customers who ask if you will be around the next time they want to order, landlords who want your personal guarantee on the lease, prospective employees who ask about the security of their position if they join you, and bankers who want your deposits but are unable to lend you money. Without depth of management and qualified personnel in reserve to fill any function, the entrepreneur and what little staff there is must be responsible for multiple functions in the business.

The implications of the word *venture* are venturesome, risky, uncertain, uneasy, or scary. Other implications are dangerous, thrilling, exciting, and daring. All these words arouse an emotional response. They make the heart beat faster and increase the flow of adrenaline. A venture investor shares the feelings of a skydiver.

The return, or reward, expected on an investment is related to the position of the enterprise on the spectrum between proven enterprise and new venture. Many investors will compete to invest in a proven enterprise, thus lowerng the cost to the investee, few investors will compete to invest in a new venture. In fact, so few will compete that the cost to the entrepreneur to induce any investment at all may be more than the new venture can afford to pay.

Think of it this way—when there are many people with plenty of money available for investment there are many competitors for the available investments. The bidding for investment in proven enterprises will drive the price down. Some investors will then find the reward too low to be of interest, and they will bid on investments further out on the spectrum toward new ventures. Some investors will find the other end of the spectrum interesting for some small portion of their total investment. If there are very many people with very much money available for investment, as in the 1960s, the flow of venture capital, that is investment in unproven enterprises, may become significant enough that the cost of venture capital is affordable.

Money is hard enough to accumulate that only the foolhardy squander it. Everyone would like more money, but not at the risk of losing what they have. Preserving what you have is more important than making a lot more, hence return on investment is measured in small percentage numbers.

177

CALCULATING RETURN ON INVESTMENT

It is interesting to consider what might be a reasonable return on investment in a proven enterprise. A person's productive lifetime is about forty-five years, that is from about age 20 to about age 65. If you were so fortunate as to have been given a pool of assets at age 20, you could feel very proud and satisfied at age 65 if you doubled the value of that pool three to five times. Doubling three times means $1,000 going to $2,000 to $4,000 and then to $8,000. Doubling five times would carry the $8,000 to $16,000 and then to $32,000.

A thumbnail rule used in the investment community relates interest, or return on investment, to the time it takes to double your money. It is known as the "Rule of 72." It says that the number of years it takes to double your money is approximately seventy-two divided by the annual interest or return.

$$\text{Principal Doubles in } \frac{72}{\text{Annual Interest Rate}} \text{ Years}$$

To double your assets three times in a productive lifetime of forty-five years you would have to double your assets about once every fifteen years.

The algebraic expression may be stated as

$$\text{Years to Double Principal} = \frac{72}{\text{Interest Rate}}$$

or

$$\text{Interest Rate} = \frac{72}{\text{Years}}$$

To double three times requires an interest or return of $72/15$ which is about 5 percent. To double five times requires an interest or return of $72/9$, about 8 percent. It is interesting to note that the interest rates paid by safe investments like savings accounts or the common stock of blue-chip companies of the New York Stock Exchange have averaged in the range of 5 percent to 8 percent when the economy was reasonably stable and inflation was not significant.

AVAILABILITY OF VENTURE CAPITAL

When the number of people investing or the amount of money available for investment decreases, the bidding for investment in proven enterprises decreases. The result, predictably, is an offer of greater return by the investee. When there are few investors with money to invest, the investees become the bidders and compete for the limited investment available. At such times there are few investors interested in any part of the spectrum beyond the proven enterprises. The cost to the new venture entrepreneur can and does become astronomical, and venture capital may virtually disappear, as it did in 1974–1975.

It is clear, then, that the cost of capital depends not only on the position of the enterprise on the spectrum of investments, but also on the number of investors and the amount of money available for investment. This implies that the condition of the economy has as much to do with the availability of venture capital as the condition of the enterprise. Both change with time. And there is no reason to expect the economy to be up when the enterprise is up or vice versa. But both have to be in an up condition at the same time to provide the possibility for a venture capital investment.

We might inquire into the return on investment expected by the people who invest. The lower range of return exists when there are many investors with much money to invest. This is almost invariably associated with economic conditions of high employment, good growth in the gross national product, high and rising stock market index figures, and a euphoric attitude among investors. In their search for good investments the investors turn to intermediaries, such as banks, trust funds, brokers, underwriters, and finders.

The upper range of expected return exists when there are few investors with little money available to invest in proven enterprises. The proven enterprises themselves become the bidders for the few investment dollars available and intermediaries are often not needed. The few available investors deal directly with the proven enterprises.

When the lower range of return is available on proven enterprises, some small portion of the money available for investment will be placed in less proven enterprises, but at a higher price or return on investment. The expected return on a new venture seldom drops to the 40 percent compounded annual rate shown in Figure 27-1, but it can and sometimes does.

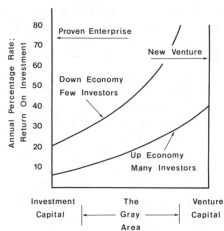

FIGURE 27-1 Expected Return on Investment from Proven Enterprise to New Ventures.

Needless to say, with many opportunities available in proven enterprises, nobody wants to invest in unproven enterprises except with a very small fraction of available money and then only if the return is very high. In times of extremely difficult economic conditions there is practically no return high enough to induce investors to provide money to a new venture. As economic conditions turn down the money available to new ventures disappears very rapidly.

Investors who are active in the venture capital market have a rule of thumb to determine the return they find interesting. It sets a bottom limit on the return that will attract their attention. During the early 1970s they were saying they like to get three times their money in three years or five times their money in five years. If you calculate the compound annual interest rates comparable to these rules you will find that three times in three years is 44 percent and five times in five years is 38 percent. In 1980 these same investors were saying they would like to get four times their money in three years or ten times in five years. This is approximaely a 59 percent compound rate of return, or doubling your money approximately every 15 months.

A cliché used by some venture capital investors sets the tone for the realm in which you deal when you try to raise capital for a new venture: "Only bet on aces, straights, and cinches." An example of such an investment is exercising a firm option to purchase a piece of raw land after you have already obtained a firm commitment from a developer to buy it from you at a profit.

Entrepreneurs often feel that the bank is or should be a source of capital for a new venture. It is worth mentioning that banks are fiduciaries. Further, they have been entrusted with your dear mother's savings. You don't want them using her savings to play the venture capital game. Their objective must necessarily be preservation of the assets entrusted to them. They, more than anyone else, must restrict their investments to proven enterprises.

One way banks can ensure that they are investing in a proven enterprise is to gain control of some property worth as much as their investment even when sold at auction or under fire sale conditions. They do this by requiring collateral or by having someone co-sign the note who has assets that could be sold to satisfy any outstanding investment should you be unable or unwilling to repay in a timely manner. As long as you and your relatives entrust hard earned money to the bank for safekeeping you wouldn't want them to invest in any other way.

To be liquid, assets need to be in the form of cash or something that can be converted to cash easily. If an investor's assets consist of pecan trees in northern Louisiana, it would be of little help to the entrepreneur to be given 10,000 trees. On the other hand, if the potential investor had just sold the pecan orchard for a million dollars, the entrepreneur could use some of those dollars. Another possibility might be available if the potential investor could, and was willing to, put the orchard up as collateral and borrow some cash. In any case, the business needs the kind of assets the bank will accept as deposits and dispense as disbursements. That is what is meant by liquid assets.

From time to time liquid assets are available to totally unproven enterprises. At those times the entrepreneur can aspire to obtain financing for a new venture. Within those times, however, many factors affect the possibility and the probability of obtaining financing. These factors can be influenced by the entrepreneur. They may be viewed as the entrepreneur's and the business concept's accessibility to venture capital. Both are constrained by the regulatory agencies of the state and federal governments. These constraints and the influence the entrepreneur may bring to bear will be examined in more detail in the following chapters.

28

The Entrepreneur's Access to Venture Capital

Almost every bank loan officer and venture capital investor will tell you that they invest in the person. They don't mean to imply that they invest in the person to the exclusion of everything else, but if often sounds that way. If you yourself have ever made an investment in a new venture you will have a better idea what they mean. In a new venture there is no past record of performance, and the only assets are those you and your coinvestors have given to the entrepreneur. At least some, if not all, of your assets are going to be consumed by the new venture, leaving you with little, if any, collateral. This is a situation sure to arouse your emotions, especially if the money you are investing is more than you would gladly lay down on a lottery ticket.

The investors truly are investing in the entrepreneur in a new venture, because the entrepreneur gains control of the invested money and spends it. After the investment has been made it is commonplace to hear the investors say, "That woman is going to get someplace," or "I like that young fella." These are the kind of things you say when you have nothing concrete to say. They make you feel less foolish about what you have just done.

THE INVESTMENT DECISION

A new venture investment is the result of an emotional decision. The natural instinct to preserve what you already have runs far deeper than the intellectual experience of making a reasonable investment decision. All the questions of logic and fact asked by investors are used to increase their confidence in the entrepreneur and the business concept. In the end, however, when all the questions have been asked and answered, the investment decision is based on the investors' attachment to their liquid assets and their emotional reaction to the entrepreneur and the business

182

proposition. At times an investor's emotional attachment to the concept precipitates an investment decision. But most of the time the emotional response of the investor is to the person or persons who will control the investor's money.

The entrepreneur needs to know people with money to invest in new ventures. Those people must, in turn, know the entrepreneur well enough to make a favorable emotional investment decision. When you are young and have little business experience the only people who know you well enough are those who love you—your parents, your grandparents, your aunts, uncles, brothers, sisters, and perhaps a close friend of the family. In time, with work experience, you expand the circle of friends who like you enough to part with their hard-earned cash to help. At this time you can add friends and business associates to relatives as sources of venture capital.[1]

Among these friends and business associates the potential sources of venture capital are those people who have enough income that they already have most of the things they would like to have—a home, car, vacations far from home, some savings, and some investments. They also probably have very good income from salary, commissions, ownership of a small business, or a partnership interest. They are people like vice-presidents, manufacturers' representatives, doctors, lawyers, accountants, and professionals with good present income.

Many of these people come to realize, at some time in their careers, the limitations on their ability to build an estate. At that time they begin to wonder if a small investment in an unproven enterprise, which will provide very high return on investment, wouldn't give them the chance to break out of the limitations on their aspirations. They are thinking about gambling.

Gambling arouses the emotions. For some people the emotional involvement is addictive. For most it is a momentary thrill, like riding the roller coaster. For most high-income individuals it is a risky encounter, uncomfortable and intimidating. These people obtain and maintain their high income by avoiding risk. Facing up to a venture capital investment for them is frightening and unfamiliar, something they can't explain to their family and friends. Facing family and friends with explanations again arouses strong emotional feelings.

Bankers are among the entrepreneur's friends and business associates. They too have an emotional response to the proposition. Their constraints are somewhat different from those of the people we have just been talking about. In the first place the banker is not dealing with cash earned through personal effort. Bankers are fiduciaries, trustees, the guardians of other people's savings.

On the other hand, bankers are people, and they too have emotional feelings about their friends and business associates. Also, they get a raise and a promotion by making good loans for the bank. Good loans are paid on schedule and make a better than normal return on investment. The bank examiners will not allow bankers to move very far out on

183

the spectrum from proven enterprise. But the banker has a little freedom. Within that, he or she will make investments in proven enterprises based on logic and reason and an occasional investment in unproven enterprises based on emotional reactions to the entrepreneur. Sometimes a United States Small Business Administration guarantee behind 90 percent of a loan can help a banker have a favorable emotional response by making the enterprise appear less unproven.

When the entrepreneur has some track record and experience, another class of investors become available. These are the venture capital organizations. Again, despite pronouncements to the contrary, the investment decision is emotional. The review of facts, data, conclusions; the penetrating questions about marketing, administration, production; and the depth of the interviews and examination of references is much greater. But in the end the decision is emotional.

We have studied venture capital firms including large private groups, small private groups, and the SBICs (Small Business Investment Companies, which are supported and regulated by the Small Business Administration). They almost invariably have a written, public description of their investment policy and their interests. We have talked at length to the managers of such firms about what kind of proposition they would like to review, in what form they would like to receive it, and to what review process it would be subjected. We have then come in the front door as strangers with business plans tailored to their desires.

Surprisingly, our propositions have seldom received more than a cursory review and rejection. Of course, it is possible that our perception of a plan worth reading is different from that of a professional venture capital firm staff member. But we have then interviewed the staff of the same firms whose managers we spoke to at length. We found that the staff perception of the firm's policy and investment interests did not coincide with the written pronouncements or the manager's description. Instead, we found that the staff people attempt to minimize the chance of making a mistake without having an unquestionable excuse to explain their reason for choosing to invest.

The best way to avoid making a wrong investment decision is to avoid making an investment decision. There is nothing wrong with being thorough in your investigation of the facts surrounding a potential investment. What we found, however, is that venture capital staff people often seek to discover the flaw in investment proposals. Their behavior seemed to be aimed at protecting the boss from making a bad decision. In that effort the staff devotes itself to dreaming up all the things that could possibly be wrong with the investment. In this behavioral posture, you don't examine the pros of an investment opportunity, you concentrate on the cons.

On the other hand, it is necessary to make some investments if you are in the investment business. Venture capital staff people behave as if a positive investment decision is tolerable if in case it doesn't work out they can justify their decision. For instance, if the entrepreneur has a long and successful track record, who could have guessed that this endeavor would not have worked? Or if it can be said that all research departments of all the underwriting houses predicted high growth in the market, who could have guessed that the market would not materialize?

SEEKING VENTURE CAPITAL

Seeking venture capital may be the most difficult task an entrepreneur has to face. It involves knocking on many doors and having few if any open. It is also a frustrating task of explaining and reexplaining what to the entrepreneur may seem obvious. During our distinguished speaker series the entrepreneurs repeatedly made the statement, "I knocked on every door until there was only one door left." Sometimes they were talking about a few weeks and sometimes a few months. In each case they eventually found a door that would open, and they raised the capital they needed. Their perception was that they had exhausted all their possible avenues to capital. The facts suggest that they were persistent enough that they could always have found another door if the one that opened hadn't.

It helps to talk to potential investors who already know something about the industry or the business being discussed. We were assisting an entrepreneur who needed capital for a drylot dairy with 1,000 cows. We soon learned that being in the cattle business doesn't contribute anything to understanding the dairy business. We had better luck with people experienced in real estate, who saw the acreage needed as the investment and the dairy operation as an intermediate land use. But, again, we found that a wealthy friend who made a fortune in urban rental property could see nothing in the acreage needed for a dairy farm.

The experience curve is at work again when considering an investment. People who have been successful at investing in fast-food restaurants have a lot of self-confidence in making such investments. They also have a lot of experience in sensing a combination that will work and one that won't. They may not be able to state their reasons for feeling good about an investment, but they feel it. They almost smell it or taste it. People who have made successful investments in any segment of commerce will have a similar sense about their area of experience.

It is difficult to imagine what the venture investor feels until you make such an investment yourself. For most entrepreneurs that is nearly impossible, because they don't have the money. We had an experience with a group of graduate students that provided the opportunity to know what it is like to invest in an entrepreneur.

When the Caruth Institute of Owner-Managed Business was started at the Edwin L. Cox School of Business at Southern Methodist University, its founding director, an entrepreneur, possessed a small line of products for the medical trade. It was the director's intention to start a business and market these products. He described this product

185

line and its potential to the MBA students, and they were invited to join in the new venture. Forty-five accepted the invitation.

These students studied the market and the product, came up with three channels of distribution, designed the packaging, even developed a patentable improvement to the product line. They tested the product; made trial shipments by air, rail, and truck; obtained copyright and trademark protection; and performed all the rituals to convince themselves of the prospects for their new business. At a general meeting they decided to invest their own money in the enterprise.

It was decided that each student who wished might invest any amount up to $1,000 in the form of a convertible note. A date was set for the checks to be delivered. In time $8,000 was contributed to the business.

Each student had been party to everything that had transpired in the study and development of the business concept. Each had cast a vote for every action of the corporation. All meetings had been taped so that people could go back over who said what. Copies of all written material had been distributed to everyone in the group. But as each of the eighteen students who became investors approached the director with check in hand, each drew back, holding the check between thumb and forefinger, and said, "Sir, there are just a couple of questions I would like to ask you."

Therein lay the moment of truth, the parting with their own hard-earned cash. No question remained unexamined. No information had been withheld. The decision to invest was unanimous and enthusiastic. But parting with that check revealed a new and different sensation. This was an emotional experience shared with no other person in the group, nor with anyone else. At that moment their judgment of their own judgment came under question. The penalty for being wrong was tangible and visible between their thumbs and forefingers. There was no question who was at fault or who should reap the reward if they released their grip on that little piece of paper.

When seeking venture capital it might help to recognize this controlling constraint on the investor's decision. It takes a lot of faith, trust, confidence, even affection, for the investor to make a favorable investment decision on your behalf. This kind of feeling toward you is difficult to arouse from strangers. It is hard enough to obtain from people who know you very well and think highly of you. It should not be hard to understand that when you are young the only people who know you that well are your parents.

DEVELOPING RELATIONSHIPS
WITH POTENTIAL INVESTORS

An entrepreneur is developing the relationships necessary to obtain venture capital all the time, beginning with the early school years. Entrepreneurs are usually stand-out individuals, achievers. Although they often suppress their realistic assessments and curtail their achievements to conform to what seems to be the expected norm of their environment, they usually display their identity at a very early age. Teenagers seem to have a great need to conform to a norm established by their peer group. Often the norm is closer to mediocrity than superiority, to getting by rather than achieving. But reliable people with an achievement orientation are few enough in number that they never go unnoticed. And the achievers never completely suppress the real person within themselves.

The entrepreneur develops relationships with teachers, classmates, and the relatives of classmates through elementary school, high school, and college. Work experience enlarges the circle of relationships and produces some that might be more fruitful in seeking venture capital. Although some souls may decry the advantages that fall to students of exclusive and expensive private schools, a realistic observer will accept the fact that the old-school-chum relationships that develop in those settings are substantial advantages. The schools themselves enhance the bonds by discipline, tradition, and the continuing active involvement of alumni.

Have you noticed the things said about a speaker during an introduction? The master of ceremonies always tells you where the speaker went to school. You always learn where the speaker has worked in the past as well as how the speaker is presently employed. This recital of the speakers' credentials gains the audience's acceptance of the speaker and draws the mantle of the speaker's credentials around the organization able to induce him or her to share this moment with its membership.

Subconsciously the audience attributes power and wisdom to the speaker because of his or her presumed circle of friends and associates. There may be no factual substance to the presumption, but it exists and is pervasive. It exists because so often it is true. It is pretty hard to go through years of school and work without making many friends.

The number of opportunities for fruitful relationships with school and work friends may be more bountiful in Ivy League colleges and employment on Wall Street, but they exist in every school and every job. Being realistic, the entrepreneur makes the most out of what is available.

Between school and work the entrepreneur develops skills that grow with experience. With skill the entrepreneur begins to display achievement. A series of achievements over time produces a track record. You may be able to observe that this series of achievements is like a

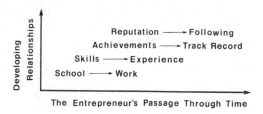

The Entrepreneur's Passage Through Time

resume. A good resume shows growth, achievement, and consistency. In time a person develops a reputation for achievement and in still more time may even develop a following of people based on that reputation.

Achievements are noted by the members of service clubs—Lions, Rotary—the representatives of the business community. They are noted by bosses and other employers seeking good help. They are noted by college professors who delight in introducing their "good" students to their consulting clients and research grantors. Often one individual having some influence in the business community will take a particular interest in a promising young person and assume the role of a mentor.

A mentor fills two roles in relationship to an entrepreneur. One is the much needed role of confidant, someone to talk to. Everyone needs the opportunity to share feelings of uncertainty and doubt with someone they know will not take advantage of them during that moment. The other role is that of providing an introduction or a reputable reference. It is always easier to accept the word of a trusted friend. A mentor often serves as the trusted friend to the potential investor you want to meet.

The entrepreneur does not first decide to start a business and then seek investors. Entrepreneurs are building the ability to obtain venture capital throughout their lives and particularly throughout their work careers. They develop in friends, relatives, and business associates the faith, trust, confidence, and affection needed by those people to make a favorable emotional decision to support the entrepreneur. Normally it takes considerable time to develop these relationships.

But what of the entrepreneur who has moved far from home and wishes to start a business? The old school ties and the family members may be geographically remote. But bonds are not limited by geography. Only the communication is constrained by distance. Introductions and references are still as readily available, even if somewhat delayed by the time required for the round trip of telephone and postal messages.

Another phenomenon appears to emerge in this instance. Those with the characteristics described in Chapter 8 who are far from home and alone are in control of a major portion of their lives. This enhances their self-confidence. It also puts them in a position comparable to being challenged with adversity, a situation in which their normal reaction is to rise to the occasion, to be cool, decisive, and active. And this behavior is precisely the kind that gains the trust and confidence of friends and business associates.

The entrepreneur should recognize the need for both a personal track record and the trust and confidence of friends who may be in a position to help when venture capital is needed. The needed record and interpersonal bonds then can be cultivated and nurtured while progressing from Step 1 to Step 4 on the career path of the successful entrepreneur.

29

The Business Concept's Access to Venture Capital

It is almost impossible to find anyone who knows which business concept is the best for investment at any given time. But there are many people *claiming* to know a good one if not the best. The most interesting concepts for venture capital investors will be those that are new, different, and exciting. Being exciting, they arouse the emotions.

THE ATTRACTION OF FAMILIARITY

When emotions are aroused the excited investors tell their friends, who tell their friends. Before long there is a common body of words circulating among the available investors, and some concept will become "hot." Stories will then emerge purporting to be research studies, and these will be followed by magazine and newspaper articles. The stories may, in fact, be based on solid research. On the other hand, many concepts that catch the imagination of the talkers and writers are merely exciting speculation, great cocktail party conversation. But if your business concept is one of those considered "hot" and you seek venture capital when these emotions are aroused, you have a higher probability of obtaining financial support.

When double-knit fabrics were first introduced there was quite a bit of venture capital available for knitting mills with the ability to make them. That opportunity has now passed. At a later date some good examples of "hot" concepts were solar heating, home insulation, smoke or fire detectors for the home, security systems for the home, and, for the more technology oriented, microprocessor applications, gene splicing, mining the sea floor, or manufacturing in space.

The concept need not be as sophisticated as these to be hot. There are always some groups or organizations around the country promoting ideas for new businesses of the kind that take very little

189

capital and a minimum of entrepreneurial characteristics. Some monthly magazines publish dozens of suggestions for businesses that seem to be working at the moment. They range from foolish things like pet rocks to good solid business concepts like specialized services for automobile owners.

Associations promote franchise opportunities. They often set up booths at conventions displaying the variety of products and services available and demonstrate how their equipment works. You won't likely find McDonald's or Kentucky Fried Chicken at these shows. Conventions attract the less well known franchisors who have to promote their businesses. And they attract new franchisors who have not yet developed a track record of their own. Nonetheless, the ideas displayed at these meetings usually represent business concepts that are reasonably timely and might attract venture capital. A word of caution is in order about these sources of business ideas. Some old, worn-out concepts keep reappearing. The realistic entrepreneur will be quick to recognize such an old saw.

The thing those ideas have in common, both the sophisticated and the unsophisticated, is a degree of familiarity. They don't sound strange and unknown to potential investors. Frequently your friends, relatives, and business associates react to these ideas with something akin to, "Why didn't I think of that?" Describing the concept to them provides reinforcement for a thought they have had only fuzzily. The clarity of your description and accompanying enthusiasm provide a confidence in the listeners that they would not have had on their own.

Trying to sell an idea that is truly unique and different is a most difficult task. The concept of the office copy machine, so common today, nearly failed to find financing. Because it hadn't been done, because nobody had seen such a thing, because its success depended on people doing their normal routine tasks in an entirely new way, it was difficult for potential investors to develop the enthusiasm and confidence needed to make an investment decision.

Technology plays a large role in the ability of a concept to find financing. New technological advances begin in the laboratory where scientists recognize fundamental physical or chemical relationships. Scientists can satisfy their doubts and produce conclusive evidence for their new effects with inferential experiments on a molecular level. Few but the scientists can grasp the significance of such experiments.

The application of a new scientific effect requires a demonstration on a more practical scale. What goes in and what goes out needs to be explained in lay terms. The usual first step to this demonstration is a pilot model. The first pilot is frequently a monstrosity of jumbled pipes and wires with little apparent order. And the pilot produces so little product that it is still hard for the nonscientist to see its practical application.

This is followed by a bigger and more sophisticated pilot plant. At this point the cost becomes burdensome while the result is still in question. Finding financing for this step can be extremely difficult. This is a stage when the developers cannot afford all the technical expertise required to solve the remaining technical problems properly. This is also the stage when developers frequently become paranoid about losing control of their invention.

If this pilot plant can be built and tuned to work well, the developers feel great confidence that, at last, investors will see the virtue of the business concept and flock to support its development. Unfortunately, the result is usually disappointing. Even when investors see the pilot in operation they are great skeptics about its promise. They want to talk about return on investment and how immediate it will be. Their questions about the market, marketing, distribution, management, and production capability can seem interminable.

Most investors sense how long the road between operating a pilot plant and seeing production quantities emerging from a factory like pastries from a cookie cutter. The technology needed to produce a pilot plant or pilot model is far less than the technology needed to reproduce the pilot in quantity. One wit has commented that the pilot plant runs on tender loving care, while in production it has to run despite the inattention provided by untrained and unskilled laborers wearing fingerless mittens.

The analogy may not be apparent between the pilot and its counterpart breadboard model in a new electronic device or electrical relay or mechanical pump. But they are analogous. Producing silicon wafers in the laboratory for use by scientists and producing them in the factory for use by production workers are two entirely different things. If the technology of production has not yet been developed, the potential investors will find it hard to make a favorable investment decision.

One step beyond production is an equally large obstacle. Even if production technology is available, is the market ready to use the new product or device? Investors have already seen or read about great ideas launched into the marketplace too soon. It takes time for consumers to learn about new things available and still more time to try them. Then more time passes while the demand grows sufficient to support the relentless ongoing cost to operate the production facilities with their associated marketing, administration, and overhead expenses.

People who have the kind of money to make a venture capital investment already have some knowledge and experience about possibilities for success and failure of new businesses. They usually have a circle of acquaintances familiar with the current climate in business. They probably read at least some literature of a business nature, such as the *Wall Street Journal, Business Week,* or *Fortune.* They no doubt read the financial pages of the daily newspaper.

These people will be aware of some of the current commentary on businesses and business opportunities. Knowing this, the entrepreneur might want to read similar publications. Conversations about familiar things lead to a more receptive ear when you bring up your own business concept. If the business pages of the newspaper are talking about a decline in new construction, you may want to avoid the subject of a new landscape contracting business.

On the other hand, if the news is reporting on the growth in new housing starts, you may find a more receptive ear for a proposed business that serves new houses. New houses need lawns, shrubs, carpets, furniture, appliances, curtains and drapes, lamps, bedroom and bathroom accessories, automatic garage door openers, door locks, telephones, smoke alarms, and a host of other things. New housing starts also imply new retail outlets providing for the needs and amenities of a community.

Potential investors are likely to be, as has been said before, high-income individuals found among friends and business associates. They keep themselves current on the news. They already have some investments. They probably have a broker, banker, lawyer, and accountant providing services to them. All these professionals will be reading the same kind of professional and business news. Things familiar to them from this current news will stimulate a more receptive response when their clients ask for advice about whatever you are proposing.

One result of this response to familiarity is that it is often easier to get venture capital for an emerging new industry. If you recall the initial data of the economic experience curve, price versus experience shown in Figure 16-3, the first phase of the price history represents the entry into the marketplace by many competitors. Before the shakeout it seems that everybody wants to get into the act. In fact, that is what is happening. Should you be seeking venture capital at a time when everybody wants to get into the competition, you may find it easier to raise the money. But you cannot overlook the implications of the experience curve. If you join such a competition you must be prepared to follow the strategy imposed by the curve, even if the competitors don't, or face the inevitable shakeout.

ALTERNATIVE SOURCES
OF ASSETS AND FINANCING

Many potential investors will look at a new business proposition in terms of the assets they are buying. If 90 percent of the desired capital is to purchase land, buildings, or equipment with a ready resale value close to their cost, the investors feel reasonably secure in their investment, at least to the extent of that 90 percent. The part of the investment that bothers them is the salaries, rent, advertising, and similar expenses, which do not result in something tangible and valuable to support their investment.

Sam Wyly turned this kind of situation to his advantage by buying a used computer for less than its current market value.[1] The investors then viewed the computer as more than sufficient collateral to support their investment. Sometimes tangible assets can be acquired on a very attractive basis. For instance, one large electronics firm wanted to close a semiconductor production facility. Its objective was to get rid of that small and unexciting division in such a way that it would make its income statement and balance sheet look good to its investors. It was prepared to sell the division's equipment on extremely reasonable terms, like 15¢ on the dollar and payment in four equal installments over a three-year period. The write-down on the equipment from its depreciated value was so small it wouldn't be significant on the financial report. And the company was sufficiently solvent that it could carry the financing. A skilled technician in the use of that equipment turned it to good use.

Entrepreneurs very often overlook the value of used assets when placed in the right hands. Used machinery and equipment of every kind is available in the huge used industrial equipment industry. Often excellent equipment is available at bargain prices because of the misfortune or ineptness of other entrepreneurs. Even when the exact equipment desired is hard to find, it is not unusual to find superior quality equipment that can do the job after minor modifications. The business concept that may be precluded from obtaining financing because of the cost of capital equipment might, and often does, find financing when used equipment makes the investment more attractive.

An entrepreneur who is clear about the business concept can often be flexible about how it is initiated and patient in finding the right assets. Entrepreneurs put themselves in a position to be lucky with their achievement orientation, their realistic view of the world, and their superior conceptual ability. They find investment comes in many forms. Cash is usually going to be spent. What it will buy is as good as the cash when it comes to the venture capital they need.

Bill Clements, who founded SEDCO, the offshore drilling equipment company, began with first one and then two very old drilling rigs held together with bolts and bailing wire. His big opportunity came along when an oil well supply firm found itself with canceled orders on five big drilling rigs. Clements obtained the rigs on very favorable terms and turned a struggling little drilling contractor into one of the world's biggest.[2]

When an entrepreneur is willing to build on old but functional equipment circumstances often make it possible to get several dollars' worth of assets for a dollar. Often the price is not as important as the payment terms. As one entrepreneur said, "It isn't the price that matters, it's how they want to be paid. I'll pay virtually any price if I can pay a dollar down and a dollar a week."

Periodically manufacturers of equipment find themselves overstocked for various reasons. To keep their production plants running they can be very flexible and creative in making it possible for an entrepreneur to gain control of the equipment. They may use their good credit rating to supplement the entrepreneur's lack of one. When Southwest Airlines was being started, Lamar Muse, its entrepreneur,

The Business Concept's Access to Venture Capital

193

was looking for three DC-9 aircraft.[3] As it turned out, however, Boeing had five unsold 737s on its hands at that time. Needless to say, Southwest started flying 737s financed on very favorable terms.

Many communities seeking to induce industry to locate in their towns will provide land and buildings on very favorable terms. If the business concept lends itself to their location, a major part of the financing may not be necessary. Sometimes these communities also provide money for equipment and working capital through development corporations funded by the taxpayers.

John Welsh created a new business in Great Britain. The principal reason for the location was access to the markets of Great Britain and Europe by air. The local development authority provided the reason for locating in the city of Irvine, near Prestwick Airport in Scotland rather than in Manchester or London. Through a combination of incentives it provided a highly specialized building with equally specialized equipment and salary subsidies for technicians brought into the area from Glasgow's depressed labor market. Through further incentives to exporters by the national government they made Prestwick a more desirable location than Frankfurt or Paris. The investment in that company, Flow Laboratories, Ltd., was almost entirely in people and raw materials. Five years earlier those incentives were not available, and five years later would have been too late. That concept and that place met in a timely fashion.

A business concept will often find that its principal customers are an excellent source of financing. When there is a shortage of foundry capacity, the users of castings find it in their best interest to encourage an entrepreneur wanting to start a foundry. They need not put up cash to be encouraging. If they are substantial businesses with good standing at the banks, their firm, irrevocable orders for future deliveries can induce suppliers, including bankers, to provide equipment and working capital. And investors always feel more comfortable with firm orders in hand before the business starts. They sound like aces, straights, and cinches.

Perhaps you can begin to see that a business concept might be matched with suppliers who have the needed assets and are trying to move them and with customers who need the product or service and are dissatisfied with their existing sources. The amount of actual cash investment required can sometimes be reduced to a level that the entrepreneur can obtain without looking beyond friends, relatives, and business associates.

Of course, timing plays a large role in obtaining control of assets without going through direct venture capital investment. Used equipment of the right kind may not be available when it is needed. Available land and buildings may not lie near the market or near an adequate pool of workers. But the cash wanted from investors may not be available to the potential investors when it is needed either. A group of airline pilots wanted to own a piece of a pipe and tobacco shop only to find that all their liquid assets had just been pledged against a real estate syndication when the pipe store became available.

But therein lies another suggestion. Pipe-smoking vice-presidents, physicians, and airline pilots might like to hear about a pipe store investment. Physicians who send out dozens of specimens to the local laboratory for testing might like to hear of an investment opportunity in a diagnostic or blood testing lab. Accountants might be interested in an investment opportunity in a computer service company serving the accounting profession. One inventor who came to us for guidance had devised a minnow bucket that kept the minnows alive and frisky even in the hot sun out on the lake. He found a group of physicians, all fishermen, who liked his design and provided him with seed money.

There are, of course, times when a business concept seems too foreign to get the attention of anyone. Most of the time, however, there are potential investors somewhere who have at least a passing familiarity with the concept. Almost always there are potential investors with knowledge and interest in the concept. If the business concept is discussed with individuals who have some interest in the idea and some knowledge or experience in its area of commerce, the door is opened for that more crucial determination, the emotional contentment with the entrepreneur.

30

Coping with the Blue-Sky Laws

Government regulation and intervention is very pervasive in our daily lives, especially in business activities. That intervention is both supportive and restrictive. Also, it is constantly changing. The intent of government is generally to provide justice, orderliness, and fairness. A realistic observer may also perceive a governmental desire to play Robin Hood. Some entrepreneurs will find themselves the objects of Robin's beneficence. Most owner-managers see too much of his ever-present Merry Men.

Entrepreneurs usually don't concern themselves much with the creation and enforcement of government regulations. Being realistic, they just want to know the rules. They ask how it works and then go on about the business of building their enterprise. Because entrepreneurs need all the help they can get, they will use the rules and regulations that can in any way help the business. If the rules are not helpful they will avoid getting into a position where the rules interfere with the progress of the business. The problem for entrepreneurs is that the regulatory bureaucracy is so massive and complex that they have trouble understanding the rules.

The specialists who devote their professional lives to understanding the rules and providing guidance to the rest of us must concentrate on a small segment of the rules to be able to keep up with the changes and the latest nuances in interpretation. This results in the need for many specialists. Despite the burden on time and financial resources, however, it is most prudent to obtain sufficient advice and guidance at least to avoid the wrath and interference of the regulators.

SECURITIES ACTS

Attempting to obtain venture capital is one area in which the entrepreneur places body and soul in the hands of a very active and aggressive group of regulators, the ones concerned with money. That is an area

certain to be charged with emotional involvement. It is also one in which
indiscretions can be painful.

The Securities Act of 1933 and its many amendments were the
result of government's desire to protect inexperienced and unsophisticated investors. Although protection was needed by an innocent portion
of the public from some unscrupulous promoters, the regulations have
resulted in the opportunity for the less than innocent, but disgruntled,
investor to be very troublesome. Unless the entrepreneur is very much
within the law when raising venture capital, it is possible for disgruntled
investors to invoke the recision provisions of the rules and demand to
have their investments returned. Recision never occurs when the business is doing well. Investors become discontented when things are going
poorly. The demand for return of their money usually comes at a time
when the business can least afford it.

We hope this introduction will serve notice to the entrepreneur
that this is not a subject to be taken lightly. There is a wealth of assistance
available from the government on the process of obtaining the money
needed to start a business. The aid ranges from data, education, and
management consulting to guaranteeing bank loans and even direct
loans to individuals. But the bureaucracy is big and complicated. Its
sword cuts both ways. This is one area in which the expense of competent and experienced lawyers may be well worthwhile.

During the early part of this century the federal government and
the various states created legislation to protect innocent and naive
people from being seduced into investing their life savings in dubious
business ventures. The state of Kansas passed the first such law in 1911.
The landmark legislation was the federal Securities Act of 1933.[1] What it
says, in effect, is that no "security" may be sold without first having been
registered with the Securities and Exchange Commission (SEC). A *security* is defined by the federal securities act as

> any note, stock, treasury stock, bond, debenture, evidence of indebted-
> ness, certificate of interest or participation in any profit-sharing agree-
> ment, collateral-trust certificate, preorganization certificate or sub-
> scription, transferable share, investment contract, voting-trust certifi-
> cate, certificate of deposit for a security, fractional undivided interest in
> oil, gas, or other mineral rights, or, in general, any interest or instrument
> commonly known as a "security," or any certificate of interest or par-
> ticipation in, temporary or interim certificate for, receipt for, guarantee
> of, or warrant or right to subscribe to or purchase, any of the foregoing.

The act said all securities must be registered. Congress recognized,
however, that in some instances the protection of the act is not needed.
They had no desire to impede the orderly accumulation of capital for
legitimate business needs, so they inserted statements intended to
clarify the act's intent. Specifically, they listed in Section 3 the exempted
securities and in Section 4 the exempted transactions. Since 1933 the
courts and the Congress have been trying further to clarify the intent of
the act. Usually in this process a body of precedent emerges over time so

that lawyers can obtain guidance for the opinions they express to or for their clients. Unfortunately, the precedents in this instance have not converged on a body of guidelines. Fifty years later it is still difficult for a lawyer to tell you for sure that you are not in violation of the act unless you register the transaction in which you raise money.

There are two significant points about registration. One, it is the *transaction* that is registered, *not the stock* of the company. The entrepreneur having an opportunity to sell company stock to the public for the first time is often dismayed to discover this principle. Founder stock and stock sold to investors to provide the seed money may be included in the transaction being registered if it is in fact going to be sold in the transaction. If the founders intend to hold on to their stock it is not a part of the transaction being registered and therefore does not become "public stock" that may be freely traded.

The second point is that registration is a very expensive process. The expense is in the fees to lawyers, accountants, prospectus printers, and underwriters' commissions. Registration requires a detailed and certified audit of the company's financial records all the way back to the day of founding. It also requires a detailed legal study of the circumstances surrounding each and every transaction involving the securities of the company back to ground zero. All closets have to cough up their skeletons.

Therein lies one of the cautions to entrepreneurs. A business just being created seldom has access to the public market for capital. It does not yet have sufficient characteristics of a proven venture to be a freely traded security. But the circumstances surrounding each and every transaction will someday be examined in great detail if the business ever achieves the degree of success that it can to want to go public. Many businesses with sufficient success to want to go public cannot hope to obtain registration because of incautious, indiscrete, or naive behavior when raising their venture capital.

The problem is further compounded because the founders and seed money investors cannot freely trade their securities. In recent years the Congress and the SEC have promulgated some rules to make it less onerous to be the holder of founder stock or unregistered stock. Still, the rules do not remove the basic premise of the Securities Act of 1933. In general, the sale of unregistered founder and investor stock is dependent on some stock of the company having passed through registration to ensure that any indiscretions of the past are revealed to potential new investors.

Each state has its own securities act. Each is at least a little different from the federal act and from every other state's act. When selling securities you must satisfy the requirements of the state in which they are sold. If sold in two states, the transaction must satisfy the acts of the two states and the federal act simultaneously. Companies that sell stock nationwide must satisfy the acts of all fifty states and the federal act simultaneously. That kind of registration is very expensive and time consuming.

The acts, state and federal, are of two general kinds. Some, like the federal act, are based on the philosophy of *full disclosure,* assuming that an informed buyer can make a prudent investment decision. The others are based on the criteria of *fair, just, and equitable.* The decision as to what is fair, just, and equitable rests, ultimately, with the state's commissioner of securities. The exact title and name of the office varies from state to state.

All the acts have included, either specifically or by inference, circumstances under which securities may be sold without prior registration. This has given lawyers the opportunity to try to guide their clients through the acquisition of venture capital without violating the law. The acts were created to protect the unwary. They were not intended to protect investors who don't need that protection, generally referred to as sophisticated investors. But the acts, state and federal, have not specifically defined such individuals. Guidelines may be provided to identify a sophisticated investor, but the decision is left to the courts.

One of the guidelines for entrepreneurs evolves from this aspect of the laws. Don't raise money from orphans or elderly widows. Do deal with sophisticated people who are accustomed to making such investments. These people know that the odds for its success are not attractive, and they have enough money and assets that if they lose their investments in the venture it won't hurt them.

Another guideline follows from the same aspect of the rules. The acts were designed to protect the public. Under the federal act, if the stock is not offered to "the public" it doesn't have to be registered. The full disclosure provisions apply under any circumstances. Lawyers have tried to define a "public" through many court cases, and although the results have not been clear or decisive, some guidance is provided by these cases.

One lawyer in a very large New York firm with considerable experience in the financing area stated that he could not describe a course of action in raising capital that would assure no future problems with the SEC. He could, however, provide some guidelines. He suggested a spectrum of circumstances surrounding the sale of securities. At one end of the spectrum is the entrepreneur standing on the sidewalk at the intersection of Wall Street and Broadway in lower Manhattan. One arm is raised high holding stock certificates while the entrepreneur barks loudly the merits of the stock to passing pedestrians. This is clearly a public offering.

The other end of the spectrum was described as follows. Two people enter a smoke-filled bistro with lighting so low they must grope to find their table. Once they have been served, their conversation turns to the new business venture of one of them. It sounds very promising, and the other asks if an investment is available. After a brief discussion it

199

is agreed that one will sell the other a specified number of shares at a stated price. Their eyes having become accustomed to the light, they glance around the room finding no familiar faces or acquaintances. They talk further about the things of interest to them. Then, in time, they rise, leave the bistro, and go their separate ways.

The transaction in the smoke-filled room was not a public offering. It could be called a *private placement*. The lawyer suggested that, in money-raising activities, you should stay as far away from the busy street corner and get as close to the smoke-filled room as possible. And under any circumstances provide full disclosure along with a fair, just, and equitable proposition and deal only with sophisticated investors.

Certain clichés have gained credence over the years regarding how many investors constitute a public. It is often said that if you don't have more than twenty-five investors you are on safe ground with the SEC. But the act does not mention any number; there have been court cases in which a single investor was considered to constitute a public.

In some state acts numbers are mentioned under specific exemption provisions. A common one is that if there are fewer than thirty-five investors it is not necessary to register under certain conditions, but in the conversation down at the club you never hear about these other conditions. For instance, one of them is, "provided there is no solicitation or advertising." The terms *solicitation* and *advertising* are not defined. The questions immediately arise, how can you sell the security if you don't let folks know about it—advertise—and how can you expect them to give you money if you don't ask for it—solicitation? It should be clear that it takes more than a couple of introductory courses in business law to keep you out of trouble with the securities rules and regulations.

INTERNAL REVENUE SERVICE REGULATIONS

The Internal Revenue Service rules also have influence on when, and if, you can get venture capital. Investors in new ventures hope to obtain a large return that will be permitted favorable capital gains treatment by the IRS. From time to time Congress and the IRS change the rules about what is to be treated as capital gains and how favorable the treatment will be. When capital gains treatment is available to any investment held for one year or more and the gain is taxed at half the ordinary income rate, investors find this a good incentive to invest.

This was the rule in effect for quite a long period, including the years from 1950 to 1970 of great growth in the economy and in the number of new high technology companies. In time, however, some portion of the population felt that the creators of these new enterprises, both investors and entrepreneurs, were doing too well financially. The rules were changed so that these achievers couldn't be so well rewarded. Consequently, investors found less reason to support entrepreneurs.

During the late 1950s and early 1960s the IRS permitted businesses to provide to their founders and key employees stock options that were very attractive. An *option* is an agreement under which key contributors to the business receive the right to buy stock at some future time at today's price provided they contribute their time and effort to the building of the enterprise during the intervening period. Options could be exercised to purchase stock several years later and held until the need or desire arose to sell some. At the time of sale the key people would have a taxable income. With only a little patience their tax rate could be that for capital gains.

As you might expect, many hard-working achievers made that opportunity pay off handsomely. In 1964 and again in 1969 Congress changed the rules and severely restricted that kind of reward. It was restricted to the point that it really was not attractive anymore. When those options were available they were like noncash capital to the new business. The latest trend in Congress, however, has been to reverse these changes and once again these kinds of incentives are available to entrepreneurs and their investors.

OTHER GOVERNMENT REGULATIONS

The SEC and the IRS have primary influence on the constraints to obtaining venture capital. Many regulatory agencies have a secondary influence, usually with respect to how much capital is needed. For instance, the Department of Labor of the federal government and its counterparts in each state determine the number of hours employees may work and the minimum pay they must receive. Flow Laboratories, Inc., was twenty-two months old and had about thirty employees when the Department of Labor inspector showed up, unannounced.

The inspector was very polite, but firm. He wished to see the time cards and payroll records and to interview all the employees. The inspector was provided with an office and whatever he wanted. Two weeks later he announced that the audit was complete and he wanted to conduct the exit interview with the company's officers. At the meeting he praised the management and told of the high morale and good employee rapport in the company. There was just one thing of importance he had to discuss. It seemed that there were eighteen employees to whom overtime pay was owed, and if the company refused to pay them the government would take the case to court on their behalf.

Management was surprised and shocked. There was no intention to underpay those good people. Management would gladly rectify the situation. They then asked how this condition arose. As it turned out all the situations were similar to Albert's. Albert was the janitor. He told the inspector that he enjoyed working for this company so much that he clocked out at eleven every night and then worked until one in the morning to make the floors shine. Hence, according to the government inspector, the company owed him two hours overtime for every day for the past year, unless the company could prove that he didn't work those hours.

201

The Occupational Safety and Health Act, or OSHA, has much to say about what equipment a business may use. Used equipment, which the entrepreneur might afford, could very well not meet the latest OSHA requirements. And so it goes with the long list of agencies of government.

Because the regulations are in a constant state of flux, there is a continual change in their influence on how much capital is needed and how readily available it might be. This is good reason for the entrepreneur to dig into the subject and treat it seriously. Take the time to become personally aware of the constraints, and don't dismiss responsibility for the problem to advisers. Professional advisers can only provide their best opinion. The entrepreneur must live with the consequences.

REGULATIONS CONCERNING
THE BUSINESS PLAN

One of the most troublesome facets of raising venture capital without violating the law lies in the written business plan. Starting a business without a plan is almost universally assailed as unwise to say the least. Writing the plan in a neat, orderly fashion enhances both the writer's clarity and the reader's comprehension.

The problem arises in what is done with the plan in connection with raising venture capital. Having prepared a carefully thought out course of action and described it concisely in writing, what better way to convey the story to a prospective investor than to share the written plan? But the plan now may take on the attributes of an advertisement or promotional brochure. It portrays an exciting return on investment. The plan is inherently promotional in nature.

Although the various securities laws and regulations require that the potential investor be provided with all the information needed to make an informed, prudent investment decision, they also require that the written description of the proposed transaction be registered with the governmental authorities. The available exemptions from registration revolve around the concept of a transaction not involving the "public."

Attempts to convey the intent of the acts have used various words and phrases to explain what was meant. For instance, one state's exemptions include the following typical language: "The sale of securities is exempt provided such sale is made without the use of advertisements, circulars, agents, salesmen, solicitors, or any form of public solicitation." When a dispute is brought before a judge, the question of whether any advertisement or circular was used to induce the investor to part with hard-earned cash is prominent in the arguments put forth by the attorneys. And the question arises whether anything in writing describing the future operations of the business can be excluded from the description of advertisements and circulars.

If the written business plan, or excerpts from it, can be construed to be an advertisement or circular, can it not then be argued that an advertisement or circular was shown to a group of people as an aid in soliciting their investment? And is this not a form of public solicitation?

If you are confused by this recitation perhaps you will feel better knowing that the attorneys who deal with the problem every day are also unable to explain it fully or resolve the problem. The question is always decided case by case in the courts. But with care and caution before seeking capital most entrepreneurs never have to present themselves to a judge.

One useful suggestion is to insert a disclaimer statement at the front of any written material presented to potential investors. The statement might read something like

> This memorandum is not an offering for sale of any securities of the Company. It is for your confidential use only and may not be reproduced, sold, or redistributed without prior written approval of the Company. Any action contrary to these restrictions may place you and the issuer hereof in violation of state and federal Securities Acts.

HOW TO INFORM YOURSELF

A problem entrepreneurs and owner-managers cause for themselves often arises from the way they seek professional assistance. So often the first hour or several hours of discussion with an attorney consists of educating the attorney about the client's background and then posing a very general question. All the while the attorney's time meter is running. Clients and lawyers would both be better off, and the service would cost less, if the client first learned something about the problem for which professional assistance is needed.

The government publishes many pamphlets and booklets that are free or almost free on virtually every aspect of its services and its regulations. You may find the language of the SEC and IRS pamphlets awkward, but with a little effort you can discern it and begin to grasp the problems and possible solutions. You are then in a much better position to formulate a specific question for the attorney. And you can assemble the background data the attorney needs.

Without this preparation for an encounter with the lawyer entrepreneurs reveal one common weakness. They behave as if dismissing their problem to some other person. If ever a day of reckoning arises it will be clear that relying on others to solve your problems for you is like a free lunch. There is no such thing as a *free* lunch.

Some relatively easy to read books are available that should be part of the entrepreneur's library.[2] It isn't necessary to digest their contents. Reading through them once will move you significantly up the expert curve.

The Legal Entity

There are few restraints preventing a citizen from starting a business. You can simply begin buying and selling. Or, if you have the talent or ability to provide a service, you can just start selling that. When there are limitations, they are usually reasonable. Demonstrating a minimum level of competence through licensing or certification is often the only constraint.

While there may be few restraints on starting a business, there are often many rules of behavior imposed by local, state, and federal governments. Zoning laws may restrict where you can locate the business. Environmental protection laws may restrict your business affairs. Taxing authorities may require you to assist them in collecting sales taxes, employee withholding taxes, and social security taxes.

Businesses are subject to the law just as each citizen is. Government authorities want to know exactly *who* in the business is responsible when businesses don't abide by the law. More precisely, they want to know who they take to court in the event the business does something wrong. State law defines the forms of business entities that will be legally recognized and who, exactly, will be responsible parties.

The kinds of legal entities a business may become are, for the most part, not complicated. The complexity arises through how the taxing authorities, notably the federal Internal Revenue Service, will treat the entity for tax purposes. And then the state and federal securities laws add their blanket of complexity.

The forms the business legal entity may assume are primarily of three kinds: proprietorship, partnership, or corporation. There are several variations on these which influence who is liable, to what extent and how they shall be treated for tax purposes. There are also other forms of business entities, such as trust companies, investment companies, or financial entities. Proprietorships, partnerships, and corporations are the ones of principal interest to entrepreneurs.

An individual may go into business alone—buying, selling, borrowing, contracting, hiring and firing—without sharing ownership or liability with anyone else. That individual's business is a proprietorship, the most prevalent form of business entity. Seventy-eight percent of all businesses in the United States are proprietorships. Ninety-six percent of these proprietorships have annual sales of less than $100,000. At the other end of the size scale, 18,000 proprietorships, or 0.16 percent of all proprietorships, have annual sales of more than one million dollars.[1]

Proprietorships are usually small because the proprietors have limited financial resources. Opportunities to grow almost invariably require additional capital to finance equipment, inventory, and accounts receivable. Individuals can seldom borrow enough to finance these opportunities.

One alternative to borrowing capital for growth is selling a portion of the business to investors. These investors, however, do not want to share in the potential liabilities of the business. They will usually limit their liability by requiring that the proprietor incorporate the business. Due to outside investors, this incorporation is a continual process among proprietorships.

From the tax collectors' perspective, a proprietorship and its proprietor are one and the same. A schedule reflecting the operation of the proprietorship is a required attachment to the proprietor's individual tax return. The proprietorship's profit or loss is added to the proprietor's other sources of income and deductions. The tax rate for individuals applies to the total.

Proprietors have considerable freedom. They don't have to get partners or a board of directors to agree and approve. On the other hand, proprietors carry all of the liability. They make contracts in their own name. They sign the note when borrowing money. They assume personal liability when they buy materials, equipment, or supplies and they are personally liable when they lease or rent anything. Worst of all, if their business is sued, the proprietor is the defendant. Everything the proprietor owns may be lost in such a legal action, including property which has nothing to do with the business. By incorporating, proprietors can limit their personal liability to what they have invested in their business.

Proprietorships are often identified with their proprietor, but they need not be. Proprietors may do business under any name so long as that name does not cause the public to be misled. Exxon would probably sue an individual doing business under the name Exxon Enterprises.

When doing business under a name other than your own, that name may have to be registered with the state and local authorities, usually the county clerk and the Secretary of State. You may be required to sign legal documents in your own name followed by the initials, d.b.a., which stands for "doing business as."

The proprietorship terminates when the proprietor dies. The business and its assets and liabilities become part of the proprietor's estate. For a relative, friend, or anyone else to continue the business, they must obtain the assets and liabilities from the estate and create a new proprietorship in their own name or d.b.a. name.

PARTNERSHIP

Two or more people going into business for themselves is like a multi-person proprietorship. It is called a partnership. The partnership generally terminates upon death of any one of the partners. However, some states permit continuation of the partnership by the survivor under a partnership agreement.

There is no legal requirement that the partners prepare an agreement, nor that they register with a government agency to be in business. They may need to register the name under which they are doing business if it is different from their own names. They may need certification or licensing to conduct their kind of business. Each state has a law governing partnerships which is usually called the Unified Partnership Act.

About eight percent of all businesses in the United States are partnerships. Of these, 76 percent have sales of less than $100,000 per year while 1.8 percent have sales in excess of $1 million per year.[2] This suggests that two or more individuals can carry the burden of more sales and muster more capital to support growth than proprietorships.

Many professional people choose to operate as partners. Although there is a trend away from professional partnerships toward professional corporations, there are still many lawyers, doctors, accountants, brokers and consultants who choose the partnership form.

Taxing authorities treat a partnership as a collection of individuals, each of whom is liable for their share of the partnership's profits. Each of the partners is required to add the pro-rata share of the partnership's profits to their income on their tax return. Likewise, but subject to certain restrictions, each of the partners may show their pro-rata share of a partnership's loss on their tax return as a deduction from their other income up to the total the partner has invested in the partnership.

Over the years, the practice evolved of drawing up a contract among the partners, usually called the partnership agreement. It spelled out who should have what share of the profits, losses, liabilities, and the obligation for investment and management responsibility. The resulting partnership agreement provides for great flexibility in structuring a partnership to suit the needs and desires of the partners.

Generally the partners are liable jointly and severally for partnership debts and obligations. The partnership, as a whole, bears the total liability even if only one of the partners is at fault, but the individual partner's pro-rata portion of that liability may be specified in the partnership agreement. With the continued formation of new and different partnerships to meet the needs of an ever-changing marketplace, there evolved another kind of partnership, the limited partnership.

LIMITED PARTNERSHIP

Some prospective investors want to be passive partners. They are willing to put up money and share in the gains or losses, but they do not want to devote any time to the management of the partnership's business nor do they want to be held liable for the actions of the active partners.

State laws now provide for a partnership in which certain partners bear the liability—the general partners. The other partners, the limited partners, are liable only to the extent of their investment in the partnership. Limited partnership means that the liability within the partnership is limited. This results in the opportunity to finance a partnership by selling partnership interests to investors who don't want to be involved in managing the business of the partnership.

The taxing authorities treat the limited partnerships the same as an ordinary partnership. This opens the door to financing partnerships which contemplate losing money in their early years. The passive investors may take their share of the partnership's losses as a deduction against their other income when filing their tax returns. For people who are in high tax brackets, this becomes an attractive investment vehicle.

Limited partnerships have become very popular for businesses which have the potential for showing losses for tax purposes while generating positive cash flows during the early years of operation. Oil and gas well exploration is one example. So is the production of a new motion picture or broadway show. This kind of partnership is also a popular vehicle for highly leveraged real estate investments. It permits the partners to invest only their share of the down payment on a property and subsequently their share of the quarterly or annual mortgage payments. Meanwhile, the partnership has the possibility of showing losses on an accrual basis as a result of maintenance, interest and depreciation expense.

THE R&D PARTNERSHIP

The variety of investment vehicles and the legal form of these vehicles is limited only by the creative imagination of entrepreneurs. One interesting form is called the R&D partnership. Basically, it is a limited partnership, given its uniqueness by the IRS. Under some rules of the IRS, research and development expense may be treated, for tax purposes, much like oil and gas exploration.

While the R&D partnership is easy to describe, the partnership agreement and the prospectus are complex and their preparation re-

207

quires the assistance of experienced lawyers. One recent R&D partnership prospectus offered to the public ran to 117 pages.

The R&D partnership is a vehicle for financing the start-up of a business requiring heavy research and development expenditures before the business has a salable product in hand. For example, a group of technical people form a company to develop and market a complex new product. Their business plan includes spending $1 million for research and development in the first year or two and then marketing the resulting product.

When the technical people present this idea to investors, they get a cool reception. From the investor's perspective, there is no assurance that a product will ever emerge from the research. But suppose the investors could write-off the $1 million on their personal income tax return for the coming year. For investors who are in the highest tax bracket, the net cost, whether a salable product evolves from the research or not, is reduced to approximately one half of their investment. This makes the risky investment less onerous.

The R&D partnership vehicle provides just such an opportunity with an additional interesting prospect for the investors. The partnership raises the $1 million and contracts with the company formed by the technical people to perform the research. The partnership then owns the resulting product. Next the partnership gives the technical company an exclusive license to the product in return for a continuing stream of future payments which may be related to sales. The interesting prospect for the investors is in that the future stream of income may be given capital gains instead of ordinary income treatment for tax purposes.

An entrepreneur contemplating the use of an R&D partnership to fund research would be prudent to seek assistance from lawyers with recent experience in this area of the law.

CORPORATION

Corporations are a creation of the government. They are like a legal person. Their life span is not related to the birth and death of any owner. Corporations may live forever, although they usually don't.

Corporations are defined by the states. Each state has its Business Corporations Act or a law with a similar name. Although they differ from state to state, and from country to country, they are the same in their essentials. A group of people, which may be as few in number as one, may file a simple form with the state, usually an office called the Secretary of State, asking for a charter. Typically, the state wants to know the name of the corporation, the name and address of its registered agent, that is, the person to contact on legal matters, the business the corporation intends to conduct, the number of shares of common stock the corporation wishes the state to authorize for subsequent sale or distribution, and the par value of those shares.

The corporation doesn't have to sell all the shares authorized. In fact, corporations almost always obtain authorization for more shares than they will need in the forseeable future. Also, the corporation may sell its shares for more than par value. The corporation may even assign no par value to its authorized shares, and when the par value is zero, the corporation must assign a value to its stated capital, probably what it received when selling its shares.

Par value shows up on the balance sheet of corporations and sometimes leads to misunderstanding by uninformed readers of balance sheets. Under the Capital section of the balance sheet, corporations list the number of shares authorized, their par value, the number of such shares actually sold, and the total par value of those shares. Immediately following, they list the capital paid in excess of par value, if any, which is the difference between what the corporation actually received for its shares and what it would have received had the shares been sold at par value.

The structure of the corporation is very democratic. The founders of the corporation sell shares to investors and others who contribute to the capital of the company. These may include the founders who contribute expertise, time, money, prototypes, business plans, or anything else of value. The shareholders then become the owners and have the right to vote on the control and operation of the corporation. To accomplish this, they elect a Board of Directors to govern the affairs of the corporation. The directors need not be shareholders. Then the directors, in turn, elect officers to carry out the affairs of the corporation under the direction of the board. This clear chain of authority and responsibility is one of the advantages of the corporate form, especially when there are very many shareholders.

At the time the corporation is formed, its founders are required to adopt a set of by-laws. These by-laws become the governing law within the corporation. They describe the duties and responsibilities of the officers and directors and how each shall be elected. So long as the officers, directors, and stockholders behave in accordance with the by-laws, including holding and recording minutes of meetings, the corporation shields its shareholders from any liability in excess of what they paid for their shares. If they don't observe the formalities of the by-laws, they may "pierce the corporate veil" and lose this limited liability.

In the event the corporation goes broke while still owing large sums of money to creditors, the owners are still limited in their liability only to what they have already put into the corporation. This provides passive investors the same limited liability which was provided by the limited partnership.

Corporations are taxed on their profits. The tax rate is the corporate rate, which is different from the individual taxpayer's rate. If corporations have losses, they may deduct the losses from the profit of prior years or succeeding years so that, for the most part, they are taxed on their net additions to capital generated by the operations of the business.

As you might expect, there are limitations to how many years forward or backward you can go when offsetting losses against gains.

Corporations may distribute money from earnings to their shareholders or they may keep the money and reinvest it in the corporation or they can do some of both. They may not, however, just keep the money and do nothing with it. The IRS views the retained earnings as belonging to the shareholders. When the corporation passes them on to the shareholders as dividends, they become income to the individual stockholders and are taxed at the individual income tax rates. This is referred to as double taxation because first the corporation pays taxes on earnings and then the shareholders pay taxes on the dividends.

The IRS does not object to the corporation keeping the money and reinvesting it in anticipation of greater profits later. But, if the corporation is not going to invest in greater earnings, which means more taxes to the IRS, then the IRS wants the money given to shareholders so it can be taxed as dividends. Undistributed retained earnings greater than what the corporation needs for its continued good health and growth is viewed as Excess Retained Earnings and the IRS imposes a very heavy penalty tax on this excess.

THE SUBCHAPTER S CORPORATION

There are about two million corporations in the United States. Of these, 44 percent have sales of less than $100,000 per year and 13 percent have sales in excess of $1 million per year.[3] Less than one percent are big enough to be recognized among the big publicly held corporations whose stock is traded in the stock markets.

Many of the new technologies and their resulting new industries emerge from small corporations. But it takes capital to grow. In order to induce some people in high tax brackets to invest in these promising small businesses, congress agreed to give them the favorable tax treatment available to a partnership.

With the approval of congress, the IRS inserted a new paragraph into the tax code at a point in the code identified as Subchapter S. This paragraph says that for small corporations which meet certain criteria, the shareholders may elect to be taxed at the shareholder level on the corporation's income. The corporation does not pay taxes, but its owners pay for their share of the corporation's profits or losses on their own individual income tax return. This is similar to the way partners are taxed.

As long as all of the shareholders agree, Subchapter S tax treatment may be elected or dropped at the beginning of any fiscal year of the corporation. Typically, the owners elect Subchapter S treatment while there are losses so they can include them as deductions on their individual tax returns. When the corporation becomes profitable, they may choose to be taxed as a corporation and avoid adding the profits of the business to their individual tax returns.

Congress has a history of approving changes in the tax laws which will help small corporations to solicit high tax bracket investors. One is found in section 1244 of the tax code. Under this section, the board of directors of small corporations is given the right to issue stock under section 1244. There are certain requirements, including a limitation of passive income and the need to be largely an operating company.

A shareholder's losses on stock issued under section 1244 is treated as an ordinary loss for tax purposes while gains on the exchange, sale or transfer of the stock may qualify for capital gains tax treatment. This may sound similar to the Subchapter S tax treatment. But the difference is that under 1244, the gains or losses are those the shareholder sustains on the subsequent sale of the shares. Under Subchapter S, the gains or losses are the operating profits or losses of the corporation. When a corporation is small and also has a small number of shareholders, it may issue 1244 stock and elect Subchapter S tax treatment.

There is sufficient confusion in the minds of the general public that it seems desirable to mention once again that Subchapter S and 1244 stock come from the IRS tax code. They do not change the legal characteristics of the corporation or the steps required to form and maintain a corporation. A Subchapter S corporation is a corporation whose shareholders have elected to be treated in a particular way for tax purposes. A 1244 corporation, a terminology which is a misnomer, is a corporation whose directors have chosen to issue certain shares of stock which have a right to a particular tax treatment when they are sold.

NON-PROFIT CORPORATION

There have always been good Samaritans—individuals and organizations who come to the aid of others. Many organizations whose sole purpose is to do good have assumed the corporate legal form.

Congress has recognized the desirability of such corporations and taken steps to encourage them. One major step has been to allow them to be exempted from paying corporate income taxes. Somehow the name "non-profit corporations," has emerged to identify these legal entities. They may be very profitable. No business entity can survive for long if it doesn't have more revenue than expense.

These corporations are formed by applying to the state for a regular corporate charter. That the entity is a non-profit corporation has to do with its intended operating purpose. Legally, the entity is just a corporation.

After forming the corporation, its founders may apply to the IRS for tax-exempt status. The IRS code provides for several kinds of activities which may qualify for exemption from the income tax liability. They are primarily religious, charitable, or educational, and include such things as churches, charities, private schools, and universities, labor unions, trade associations, research organizations, and museums and art galleries.

The essential difference between an ordinary corporation and a tax-exempt corporation is that the investors in a tax-exempt corporation cannot derive any benefit from the operations of the business. Investors may put money into a tax-exempt corporation, but they can never get it back nor can they receive any dividends. All of the profit of a tax-exempt corporation must be used by the corporation to further its religious, charitable, or educational objectives.

You may often hear the remark, by the uninformed, that you can start a non-profit business and pay yourself an exhorbitant salary. As you may guess after reflecting on that comment, it is just not true. Even a non-profit organization must file an income tax return with its attached financial statements. If the IRS review of the financial statement suggests that anyone is unreasonably benefiting from the operations of the business, you can be sure they will start proceedings to revoke the tax-exempt status.

CHOOSING AMONG THE FORMS OF LEGAL ENTITY

An entrepreneur considering the question, "which legal form should I choose?" is faced with essentially three choices. They are proprietorship, partnership, or corporation. The logic which leads to their choice is influenced primarily by two considerations—liability and taxation.

The liability may be important because of the potential that the firm's product or service might cause harm to individuals or because of a need to raise capital from individuals who do not want to share in any potential liability. If potential liability is not perceived to be important, proprietorship for an individual or partnership for two or more individuals provides a convenient legal form with maximum freedom to the entrepreneur and minimum burden from the formalities of being a corporation.

Tax considerations may be important if passive investors must be brought into the ownership. Limited partnerships and corporations are more likely to meet the objectives of passive investors. If it is contemplated that there will be very many investors, a corporation is probably the only reasonable choice.

If a business is going to require enough capital that investors who are not active in the affairs of the business will be needed, it may be important to consider the status of those investors from the tax perspective. The legal form chosen can provide them with the most advantageous tax treatment and thus help to induce them to invest. Limited partnerships, Subchapter S, and section 1244 stock are the tools available to accomplish this.

A word of caution is in order at this point. It is possible to deal directly with government authorities. One popular phrase in the market place says you can form a corporation for $50.00 without a lawyer. We don't recommend that. We do recommend that you obtain a copy of your state's Business Corporations Act, Unified Partnership Act, or whatever law is applicable to your enterprise. Become as knowledgeable as you have time to before visiting your attorney. But, a prudent entrepreneur will ask a knowledgeable and experienced lawyer to conduct the interaction with government authorities.

32

The Venture Capital Time-Line

The stories told by those who have obtained venture capital are many, varied, and long, and they often sound like Alfred Hitchcock scripts. Often the tale is only a mystery until the money seems assured. Then it becomes one of suspense, thrill, and drama. But the experience is hard to avoid if the business is to get off the ground. In Chapter 6 we described the launch window by three dimensions, one of which is the entrepreneur's access to venture capital when the business concept is in hand. Venture capital, in the three-dimensional cube, provides the east and west walls on the box.

Capital comes in many forms. Your own labor is capital. So is that of your friends and relatives. The things the capital will buy or rent are capital as much as is the money needed to acquire them. Obtaining control over the property needed by the business by whatever means—borrowing, renting, leasing, buying secondhand, obtaining on credit or consignment—is venture capital. Many things needed by the new business can be obtained in these ways. When all of these things have been done, however, there is almost invariably a need for some hard, cold cash for things like the payroll, deposits, stationery, telephone, and purchases from unsympathetic suppliers.

There are many books, magazine stories, journal articles, seminar presentations, and guides of various sorts listing sources of venture capital.[1] Libraries have directories of venture capital.[2] The local office of the U.S. Small Business Administration can be helpful. Bankers, lawyers, and accountants have contacts and suggestions. The Yellow Pages in any major city will list venture capital under "See Financing Consultants," and a number of possibilities are listed under "Investments." The SBA has a directory of Small Business Investment Corporations and their cousins, the Minority Enterprise Small Business Investment Corporations. With very little digging you can locate the formal sources of venture capital in your community.

There is a much larger pool of venture capital available from informal sources.[3] Unfortunately they are not to be found listed in any directory. Almost every community has a few citizens with more than average wealth. Sometimes they are conspicuous by their homes, cars, club memberships, and community activities. Just as often they are very inconspicuous. They have more solicitations for contributions and investments than they can handle without advertising the fact that they might be a hot prospect for such things. This group of people can only be found through introductions by the few friends and advisers they trust.

Finding these informal sources of capital may not be as difficult as it first appears. They frequently know one another and invest together. They form informal loops and chains. A good investment opportunity brought to the attention of any member of the loop will find its way around his or her chain of contacts. The way they find out about good investment opportunities is by hearing of them from their professional advisers, their bankers, lawyers, accountants, and investment brokers. There is no easy way to make the initial contact. You just keep talking, following leads, and knocking on doors.

THE INVESTOR'S DECISION-MAKING PROCESS

A bigger problem, by far, is presenting the investment opportunity to the prospective investor or the personal representative of an investor. The investor's interaction with an entrepreneur-supplicant seeking a blessing of hard, cold cash transpires on more than one level. The levels may be viewed as two general types—those of the head and those of the heart. Level one might be considered the intellect and level two would be the emotions. Within each of these levels are three major areas of concern. They may be thought of, from the perspective of the investor, as the business concept, the entrepreneur, and me.

Level one is more easily expressed in words and supported by reference to authority. It is easier to carry on a discussion on this level, and it is easier to pass along information of this intellectual nature. So many of us have been through the same schooling and read the same books and journals that we have a body of familiar terminology to lean on. Large chunks of understanding can be conveyed with a few words. For instance, to say, "They are way down their learning curve," has broad and very positive implications and carries with it an aura of authority to those familiar with the terminology.

Level two is far more difficult to describe in words. Often the emotional response is clear and can be expressed with common terms, but the reasons for it are elusive to our native tongue. For instance, most

215

people viewing an oil painting will have feelings that lead them to say, "I like it," or "I don't like it," but when pressed to explain why, they are at a loss for rational or logical rhetoric. This level of interaction provides conclusions based on subjective rather than objective data. It is often illogical. Decisions can be based on hearsay and feeling rather than fact.

Most of the discussion surrounding the presentation of a business investment and the investigation of its merits is carried on at level one. Most of the decision making is at level two. It is fruitless to discuss whether this is fair, just, equitable, realistic, smart, or anything else. When you ask people to part with their money you reach into a part of their innermost being. You deal with greed, love, ego, hate, anger, and prejudice. The entrepreneur, being realistic, will appreciate this perspective before going after the venture capital. What the investor is looking for is what we commonly describe with the phrase, "The chemistry is right." The investor is looking for a comfort level that can be lived with.

Examine the following array of considerations from the perspective of the potential investor. The setting is beyond the introductions and into the beginnings of the discussion about a potential investment. The conversation begins with the subject of the business concept and proceeds to questions about the entrepreneur. While these are carried on the investor is consciously or subconsciously relating the entire interaction to personal, though unspoken, thoughts, feelings, and financial relationships.

To organize these considerations let us look at the discussions about the business concept first. We can examine them on the intellectual level and then on the emotional level. Then let's examine the discussions about the entrepreneur. Finally, let's examine what the potential investor might be thinking and feeling about him- or herself on those same two levels. And let's keep the examination in terms of what the potential investor thinks and feels rather than says.

Consideration of the Business Concept, on the Intellectual Level. Does this concept make sense? Do I understand it? Is it familiar? Is this idea "far out"? It may not be wild to those young dudes who frequent disco bars, but how can I understand this? Is it like something I have seen before? Has anybody else done this? Did it work out well? If it's so good why isn't someone already doing it?

How will the consumer view this? Are there very many consumers who might be interested? Have you checked the trade association data on things like this? Can you profile the consumers so we can find them in statistical data like the census or the media markets? How are you going to reach those consumers? Can you reach them with advertising? Will this be a hard sell? Can the consumers afford this? Can they finance it?

Can you make this thing? Can you sell it? Is there a better way to make it? Is there a better way to sell it? Who else can make this? Who else can sell it? How many are already making it? Are they making something like this? How does this compare with theirs? How many others are thinking about making this? Will every Tom and Jane be out in the marketplace with this? Do you have some special talent, experience, patents, or trade secrets that give you an edge? How hard would it be for others to get into this business?

Have you priced out everything? Have you overlooked anything? Are you sure you can get the supplies at that price? Can you get the quantities you need? What alternatives do you have if your supplier goes out of business? Suppose your competitor buys the supplier? Can your supplier finance the growth needed to take care of your orders? Will the market change in the near future? Is there anything in the business climate that might affect your suppliers? Is there anything out there that might affect your customers? How about anything that might affect their ability to finance the purchase?

Can this thing survive the next business downturn in the economy? Can you find the kind of help you will need? Do you need skilled labor? What is happening to labor rates in this business? Can you keep the labor down with new technology? Will you require union labor? What are unions demanding these days? What about government intervention? Is this business regulated? Which agencies regulate it? What kind of legal fees will that incur?

How big could this business become? Does it have any possibility of going public? If it did would it carry a high price-to-earnings (P/E) ratio? Is it what the investment community would consider glamorous? Would this be an attractive acquisition for somebody? I wonder what the research department of my broker's firm would say about this business. Will this thing generate the assets it needs to collateralize its future financing?

And so the questions will continue. You can probably fantasize another page or two of questions that will come to the mind of the potential investor. This list should be enough for our purposes at the moment. While these questions are being asked, let's look at the emotional side of the potential investor.

Consideration of the Business Concept, on the Emotional Level. How sure is this thing? Is this one of those aces, straights, and cinches? What is the certainty of winning? Is this thing interesting to me? Is it aesthetic? (From my own perspective, of course.) It is interesting. It kind of captures your imagination. Actually, it's fascinating. I wonder if this is just the tip of an iceberg, the beginning of something big? Can we try this without getting in too deep until we know it will work? If it doesn't work, how can I get myself out of this?

Does this thing deserve to happen? Is it right? Is it good? Is it worth doing? Should it happen for our city? For our people?

In the cross-currents of human emotions there are often seemingly conflicting interests, desires, and actions. Even investors who

appear rich often display strong feelings of what they consider to be right
and good. They can be proud of their community, whether that is a town,
a church, a school, a profession, or a club, to the point of being aggressive
and tough in backing a business venture they consider good or worthy.

Will this business help my friends? Will it help my peers? Will it
hurt them? Can I explain this thing to my colleagues? I wonder if my
colleagues would join me in this. What will my peers think of me for
backing this venture? Will I look foolish in their eyes? Will this help me
look smart to my peers? Will I appear shrewd to my superiors?

The investor may have ample opportunities to make safe and
profitable investments. Sometimes these are terribly lacking in psychic
rewards. Investors want and need good strokes as much as anyone. In
Maslow's hierachy we would see this as esteem. Esteem among beggars
may come from the ability to tell a good story, among investors it more
likely comes from making a shrewd and profitable business deal, that is,
telling a different kind of good story.

Could this deal help me get even with my old adversary? If we
build this they will never get that zoning they have been after.

The power of money is not in the money itself. It is in what can be
brought about with the backing of money. Although cash may sometimes be used successfully to buy favor and position, more often power is
purchased by making an investment in something that becomes big and
highly visible.

Consideration of the Entrepreneur, on the Intellectual Level:
What credentials do you have? What kind of a track record have you
built? How much experience do you have in this kind of business?
Where did you get it? In what positions? Can I talk to some of your former
coworkers? Have you ever managed people before? Have you ever managed a business? The whole business? Have you ever managed money
before?

Have you accumulated any assets of your own? Do you pay your
bills on time? Do you understand the fundamentals of business? Do you
know how to exercise financial control? Do you know how to handle the
administration? What do you know about marketing? Who is going to be
your production manager? What kind of management team do you have?
What kind do you propose? Who will be on the team?

Do you have the health, energy, and stamina needed for this job?
Do you have a police record? Are you married? Do you have a stable
home? Do you have children? Will your spouse support you in this
venture?

Consideration of the Entrepreneur, on the Emotional Level. Do I
know your daddy? Were you on the varsity team at school? Which
school? Which sport? What bankers do you know whom I might know?
Why do you wear your hair that way? Why do you dress like that? Why
do you keep rubbing your nose? What kind of car do you drive? How did
you finance it? What part of town are you from?

How would you come across to my friends, the bankers, lawyers, brokers, the people at the club? What will I do if you botch the job? How do I know I can trust you? Can you handle your booze? Can I live with your religious convictions? Can I live with your social attitudes? Can I tolerate your political affiliations?

Are you going to behave yourself with the opposite sex? Will you need a big fancy office? What kind of an expense account are you going to run up?

Will you keep me informed? Will you listen to advice [meaning my advice, of course]? Do you know how to negotiate a hard business deal? How are you going to handle those employees? I don't know how I can expect a young one like you to do the job right.

Consideration of the Investor's Self-Interest, on the Intellectual Level. Do I have the money to get into this? Is this investment small enough that I can afford to take the chance? Is the potential gain substantial? Are there any tax advantages to me? Will I see some return fairly soon? What is my downside risk? Am I sharing the risk?

Is there another way to finance this? Is it much different from my other investments? Will this need a lot of my time to watch over it? Is that the way I would put it together? Can I come up with a more reasonable financial package?

Consideration of the Investor's Self-Interest, on the Emotional Level. What would they think of me if I backed this? Is the potential gain fantastic? How much control will I have? How can I get a bigger piece of this action? How can I leverage myself into this? Maybe this one will make up for the last three disasters I got myself into.

If I get into this I won't have the cash to get into that thing I saw yesterday. I do [or do not] need the tax loss. Can I use this as a tax shelter? If my colleague backed this I would join the group. I might give this a little money and see how it works out.

If I do this I can show those big mouths a really shrewd investment. This will keep my old adversary from having a free hand. How will this look in my estate? How would my colleagues feel about this? I wonder if they would join me? Maybe I could merge this with my other investment. This could provide a good spot for my kid later on. This business would be a good tenant for my real estate. I wonder if I could buy and lease back to them?

We hope this discourse doesn't paint a dismal picture of all investors. Actually, they are more than willing to back a good entrepreneur with a good business concept, provided the financial arrangement makes their reward commensurate with the risk, the misgivings, and the patience they must endure.

This array of considerations could be redone from the perspective of the entrepreneur. An objective observer would probably find as much self-interest and prejudice circulating in the entrepreneur's inner musings, both conscious and subconscious. It might help the entrepreneur to go through this exercise before attempting to raise venture capital. You could learn much about the parties on both sides of the table and the subsequent discussion might more quickly converge on that ethereal thing we allude to as "the chemistry."

It is interesting to look at the preeminent emotional considerations for the potential investor. When considering the business concept the concern for winning is very important. This may not be so much the desire to win as the need to avoid losing what you already have. As has been said, it is far more important to investors to preserve their property than it is to increase its quantity, hence investments are preferred in proven ventures at lower potential return on investment. Venture capital investments are made with only a small portion of a person's total assets.

The thought that something is right or good is a very powerful motivator for everyone. Potential investors often have the means to support what they perceive to be right and good to a far greater extent than most of us. Again, they don't want to lose what they already have, so they may support what they wish only to the extent that the cost of support is not large compared with their total worth. In other words, those with the means to make a venture capital investment would choose to do so in ways that support their personal convictions.

The perception that the business opportunity is interesting, even fascinating, to a willing investor leads us back to the thought that a venture capital investment is somewhat like gambling. The investor finds in the business concept something akin to what the tourists at Las Vegas find in the flashing lights, ringing bells, and clanking coins of the endless rows of slot machines. There is thrill and excitement in the relationship with a new venture. In the staid world of proven ventures there is little fun, no frivolity, and no possibility for an outrageous gain. A new business might put some life into what at times could be construed to be a routine existence.

The concern for feeling foolish or looking silly in the eyes of peers is not a province only for investors—we all share it from the time we are small children through old age. It is no less a concern for the investor because of wealth or position. It may be even a greater load to carry for those who are expected to know better when it comes to investing. The entrepreneur may carry a much smaller burden in this regard, having little to lose but much to gain and venturing into a realm not previously tested.

The need for extensive preparation is not to be diminished by these considerations of the emotional influences on a favorable venture capital investment decision. The emotional decision and conclusions are heavily influenced by a meaningful interaction on the intellectual level. There is, first and foremost, the need for a timely business concept in the hands of an entrepreneur whose time has come if a meaningful intellectual discussion is to prompt a favorable emotional reaction. There is also a need for the intellectual discussion to occur at a propitious time. The prospective investor must have access to liquid assets in sufficient quantity that a small portion might be available to bring some thrill into a serious vocation, with small downside risk and the possibility of leverage to make the investor appear shrewd.

OTHER FACTORS

It takes time to cultivate relationships with potential investors. It takes time to build a track record and a reputation to be admired by investors. It may take a few false starts by the entrepreneur to learn what really pleases potential investors. Clearly an eager youngster who wants to raise venture capital will have to be very lucky.

Having built the track record and the trusting relationships that might lead to a venture capital investment, the entrepreneur must face the world in which investments are made. Sometimes the economy is up and sometimes it is down. Even when it is up the particular individuals the entrepreneur knows may not have liquid assets available for an investment.

And then there is the climate of the regulatory agencies of the states and the nation. Sometimes the regulations are more favorable and sometimes they are not. Within these constraints some entrepreneurs do prevail and venture capital is obtained. The entrepreneur's access to venture capital, like the entrepreneur and the business concept, may be thought of as a missile traveling on a trajectory. If it is on target there will be a small stretch along the trajectory when the time is right for a meeting with a ripe entrepreneur and a timely business concept.

This venture capital trajectory provides for the third dimension of the cube described in Chapter 6. Launching a new business from within the cube portends excellent probabilities for success. Knowing yourself and creating a promising business concept put you in the region of the cube. Long before you get there, however, you will have had to generate the relationships of trust and admiration among potential investors. After all, a cube with the east and west walls missing is but a hollow tunnel.

33

You Can Only
Manage the Future

Clearly we can't manage the past. It is water under the bridge. It is less clear that we can't manage the present. After all, when driving a car we manage its speed and direction as it proceeds along the road. Actually, we manage its future speed and direction by anticipating where it will be a few seconds from now. We can't change where it is now. When you see the police car behind you and notice that the speedometer is reading more than the speed limit, it is already too late to manage the present.

Electromechanical feedback systems, like the automatic pilot in an airplane, are managers. They are given a predetermined objective, which may be as simple as "hold it straight and level." The feedback system compares the actual altitude and direction with that desired. Whenever they differ the system makes a correction to bring them back to what is desired. To operate, the system needs three things: an objective, a standard to compare with, and constant measurements of the actual situation. It acts immediately when it detects an error between desired and actual, but were there no detectable error it would not act.

Owner-managers are in the same position as the auto pilot. They need the same information—a goal or objective, a picture of where they should be at any particular point in time, and continual reporting of where they actually are compared with where they want to be. Unfortunately, owner-managers seldom have the resources of time and money needed to obtain sophisticated analysis and perpetual reporting of the business's condition. They frequently must make decisions of great importance to their business with little data or analysis. Their decisions must frequently be based on "feel."

To improve their decisions entrepreneurs need a simple picture of the condition of the business and the future results to be expected from present actions. The picture might be better described as simplistic, although it has to be fundamental and accurate. It needs to be sufficiently simple that already overburdened entrepreneurs can understand it, internalize it, carry it in the circuits of their gray matter, and use it as a standard for comparison when making decisions minute by minute throughout their working day.

Studies report that the tragically high number of small business failures is the result of undercapitalization, insufficient sales, and lack of management skill. When small businesses are examined in more detail we find that owner-managers don't know how much capital they need or how to find out how much will be needed. Although insufficient sales when measured in the number of units shipped is a fatal disease in business, the problem more often is that the owner-manager doesn't know how to price the units to cover the cost of making and selling them. Price is reduced to make the sale. Cost, in many owner-managed businesses having trouble, is unknown.

Management skill, or the lack of that skill, is the cause of the first two reasons given for business failures. Unless the business is offering for sale an item that is not wanted, not needed, or nor affordable, all reasons for business failure are the result of inadequacy of the owner-manager. Much of the time spent by these managers is misdirected, focusing on the wrong problem or allocating too much time to a single area of the operations to the neglect of other areas at least as critical to survival.

Problems outside the scope of the manager's knowledge or interest are often neglected or referred to expert counselors, advisers, specialists, consultants, or employees. But managers cannot allow themselves to become dependent on experts for advice. It takes too long and it costs too much.

It would be helpful if managers could be knowledgeable about every aspect of their job. Unfortunately, there is so much knowledge needed in so many areas of management that few people can acquire what they would like to know and have any time left for doing something with it. Successful managers overcome this dilemma by assembling a collection of people, each of whom has some portion of the total knowledge needed. Managers can then guide their business using an overall picture of the total operations.

FINANCIAL REPORTS—AND THEIR DELAYS

An entire business is described beautifully, succinctly, and precisely by its financial reports. The description is in terms of money, but the money is merely measuring the value of the actions and interactions of all the boxes, machinery, people, and so on that compose the enterprise. Those pages of numbers represent people and things doing something. Experts, presumably, can read those hieroglyphics and make recommendations based on them. Unfortunately, the problems must be solved long before the financial reports are available. The reports, presented after the fact, document history.

Every manager who has tried to bring about a change in operations has felt at least a little anguish over the time required to make it

223

happen. Nothing happens instantaneously. It is often painful to experience the time and energy expended in bringing about change. And then the results don't show up when the change is completed. It is necessary to operate under the changed conditions for enough time that the results will appear in the historical documentation prepared by the bookkeepers.

Suppose the manager is concerned about the performance of the business last month, June. As soon as the financial reports are delivered the picture will be apparent. The only trouble is that it takes time to prepare the reports. If the business has in-house bookkeeping, a management sympathetic to the magnitude of the bookkeeping task, and the desire to get the reports out quickly, they might be delivered by the tenth of the following month—July.

When the description of the operations for June is obtained, we hope the manager will look at it on its way to the files. Looking at it you can't help but get some feelings, like, you'd like it to be better, or you'd like to keep it from getting worse. The manager can study the reports and choose a course of action designed to improve the picture. This may take a day or two to decide. Then management can begin the action. But it may take anywhere from a few days to a few weeks to complete the change. Nonetheless, management can initiate the change and eagerly await the next financial report to see how it worked out.

With management dedicated to getting the report out quickly, the next report should be available on, or about, August 10, but alas, it describes the operations of July. The change wasn't begun until July was nearly half over, and during the remainder of July the operations were in transition while the change was being implemented.

To learn whether the actions taken in July to improve the reported performance in June were effective, it is necessary to wait still another month. It will be September 10 before that information appears in the historical documentation.

On the morning of the tenth of July the manager was blind to the operations from June 1, forty days. By September 10 the manager was blind to the improvement in reported operations from July 10, sixty days. As regards the comparison of the results of management changes and the performance that precipitated the changes, the manager was blind from June 1 to September 10, one hundred days. And it could be even longer.

Frequently, managers conclude that they can correct this situation and remove their blind spot by installing a computer. But what we are talking about is independent of whether your "computer" is an electronic wizard or a clerk with a high-school education. Both must wait until the period to be reported has ended, collect all the documentation, manipulate the numerical information, and prepare the summary reports. The electronic wizard may do its arithmetic faster than the clerk. It may type the summary report at a higher rate of speed, but the best you can hope for from the electronic wizard is that the reports might be out by the first day or two of the month instead of the tenth. You will then have decreased the blind spots mentioned above from forty, sixty, or one hundred days all the way down to thirty, fifty, or ninety days.

A business is always operating in an accounting period not yet accounted for. Even with timely financial reports the manager has a two- to three-month blind spot. Imagine the manager who only gets quarterly reports. That blind spot can be six months long. The business can die during that long a period and the manager won't even witness its passing. In practice, it is not unusual to find that the reports are prepared thirty to ninety days after the close of the month being reported. In that case the manager in our example was preparing the Father's Day picture for a Christmas gift.

You can only manage the future. You fantasize what you would like next month, and the months that follow, to look like. Then you take action now to make the future come out the way you would like it to be. The financial reports will eventually confirm or deny your success, but meanwhile you *must* take action *now*.

Managers sometimes find themselves willing to offer their businesses for acquisition. This rarely happens when the businesses are doing well; it almost always results from the businesses doing so poorly that the managers want to withdraw from the unpleasant situation. Two reasons for this have to do with knowing the condition of the business. We identify them as (1) not understanding the language of business, the numbers; and (2) not having frequent and timely financial reports.[1] It may now be easier to understand the importance of these two management shortcomings.

In Chapter 8 we described the characteristics common among entrepreneurs who have succeeded. One of these was a superior conceptual ability, the ability to see relationships among functions and things in the midst of confusion and clutter. Successful entrepreneurs are able to see the problems faster than those around them, and they are good at solving problems. They are adept at scheming a deal. When they know what they want they are good achievers.

What owner-managers need is a picture of what kind of deal is good for the business. They need a road map that will indicate the future results of today's actions and contractual relationships. They may or may not be able to negotiate all the best deals, but they can move in that direction. At least they can avoid those that are obviously bad for the business.

A useful road map would be a forecast of what the financial reports will look like in the future as a result of management actions taken now. It would be even more useful if portrayed from the perspective of the owner-manager. What the manager sees is what comes in and what goes out. You conduct transactions with the objective of having at least as much come in as goes out—preferably, more coming in than goes out.

One of the standard financial reports, the income statement, profit and loss statement, or operating statement, is such a summary.

Those titles all refer to the same report, which describes what came in, the revenues, and what went out, the expenses, during a period such as a month.

ACCRUAL ACCOUNTING AND CASH FLOW

Before the end of World War I most managers kept track of cash out and cash in. Many senior-citizen owner-managers still do today. There is an inherent problem in keeping the records that way, however, if the business offers and receives much credit. Doing business on credit displaces the time of the exchange of cash from the exchange of goods and services. Sometimes very little cash comes in during a particular month and very much cash comes in during other months. The same is true of cash out.

Keeping track of what you pay or get paid for credit transactions causes the monthly reports describing the operations to fluctuate from month to month even though the goods and services flowing in and out of the business may be very much the same. About 1920 the accounting profession began placing emphasis on the accrual method of accounting to overcome this difficulty.

The accrual method portrays the smoothed-out profit as if all the transactions had been for cash *and* as if the business had purchased only exactly what was needed to make the sale. It is not an accurate portrayal of everything going on in the business, but it is a good approximation of the *net effect of those things that affect profit*. The problem is that so much emphasis has been placed on the accrual method income statement and balance sheet that the importance of cash has been relegated to virtual obscurity.

Even this result is satisfactory when the reports are describing large businesses with access to external financing through the stock market, commercial paper, and bank loans at the prime interest rate. But companies that do not have access to these external sources of financing have a different problem. For them, the flow of cash through the business means life or death, whether the accrual based profit is great or terrible. When new or small businesses need cash they must turn to the bank or to the personal savings of the owner-manager. And if they turn to the bank, the banker will look to the personal savings and assets of the owner-manager for collateral.

Accountants have not forgotten nor overlooked the importance of cash. They recognize the need for cash in sufficient quantity to keep the business operating. For their purposes, however, they often *infer* the cash available to the business from the income statements and describe future cash availability with the balance sheets. They, and others, frequently describe it as: cash flow equals net profit after taxes plus depreciation and other noncash expenses, such as amortization.

This statement is incorrect except under some very stringent preconditions that rarely exist in practice for a small business.[2] This statement is an approximation that is valid for large and stable businesses in which changes from year to year are small and the statements from which the cash flow is inferred are annual reports. For a small or new business looking at monthly financial reports this approximation is inadequate. In a small, growing business the net cash flow to the firm's bank account does not equal the net profit plus depreciation. Profit is not cash nor is it cash flow.

Although this pronouncement may be unconventional, entrepreneurs are realistic. Successful entrepreneurs ask how it really works and then get on with building their business. In the conventional approach the analysts, having inferred cash flow from profit, depreciation, and amortization, stop there, allowing their readers to assume that the resulting cash is in the bank waiting to be spent. The next five chapters of this book will demonstrate that this is far from the fact. You will see why we refer to this subject as the critical skill for success in building your own business and acquiring your own economic freedom.

Owner-managers are dealing with a stark, primitive kind of money—cash. For the most part it is internally generated cash from operations and their own savings. Their picture of the condition of their businesses must be portrayed in this same stark currency. On the other hand, their simplistic picture needs to accommodate the problems of communicating with the sophisticated practitioners with whom the entrepreneurs must deal in the course of business: bankers, accountants, investors, lawyers, insurance agents, customers, suppliers, employees, and agencies of the federal, state, and local governments. Failure to comprehend the language of these groups and to be able to communicate meaningfully with them seriously reduces the probabilities for the business to survive and thrive.

Fortunately for the entrepreneur starting a business and the owner-manager operating a business, a simple picture of the condition of the business and the future results of present actions is available. And it doesn't require a college education to understand. But painting the picture is a skill that must be learned. Talent and aptitude help, but knowing how to paint this picture is not a gift. Mozart had a gift. We all acquire skills—by drill and practice.

The methodology to be presented in the following chapters is a manager's skill. It is not a service to be provided by others. As in the other facets of management, you can and may have help. But the help is the kind provided by calculators and computers. These devices accept the information provided to them and manipulate it according to rules given them previously. They don't think or make independent judgments. They don't know what deals the manager might be able to close. The skill is not in the manipulation of numbers. It is in grasping and using the interrelationships among the many transactions in the business to achieve the overall end objective of creating a thriving economic entity.

Among the many successful entrepreneurs we know some outstanding examples apparently never learned the critical skill. Some seemingly jumped off the bridge and fell into a warm, bubbly bath of economic success. This part of this book is not for them. When dealing with people there is a fabulous spectrum of talent, aptitude, and just plain blind luck. If you have that blind luck, which is comparable to Mozart's gift, you can read on for fun and forget the skill. But consider the record of failure among those who have tried it. To improve the probabilities of winning your economic freedom, try acquiring the skill.

34

Forecasting Profit

Seeing the future may sound like the work of mystics, but judging what is most likely to happen in the near future is a reasonable analytical exercise. Forecasting is a skill. You get better at it with practice. To manage is to bring about a desired course of events. Once that has been accomplished, to manage means to maintain that situation despite changing conditions which can be anticipated for the near future.

Some things are already determined, but in large measure we can influence what the future holds for us. The objective of this discussion is to convey the skill of forecasting profits within the limits of what is known about the future right now. The following exercise illustrates a convenient way to relate the things that happen in a business's day-to-day activities. It is a description in simple language of what results from the decisions and the deals the manager makes in the normal course of work.

The format is a general one. It is the basic list of items describing what is bought and what is sold in any business. You will want to change the individual items listed to make them describe your business more precisely, but the main headings apply to all businesses. The total number of items that should be listed will depend on the business. The important thing is, don't leave anything out. Profit forecasting is the starting point for planning, budgeting and decision making in business. It is step one in managing a business.

This discussion is basic in approach. That is intentional. One thing we learn with experience is how often we have forgotten, or overlooked, or failed to understand fully the fundamentals of our trade. The discussion is from the perspective of the owner-manager, the decision maker. It is not accounting, nor is the exercise trying to teach accounting. The financial record-keeping system tells where the business has been. Forecasting talks about where the business is going. This is a manager's skill.

Profit is the most common measure of the health of a business. Without profit a business will surely die. Profit is not the only measure of winning or losing, but it is the starting point for determining whether the business has the opportunity to survive and thrive. To manage a business, it would be well to understand profit as well as you understand your own personal needs for food and sleep.

In the course of its day to day operations a business conducts a series of transactions. Few businesses conduct a series of identical transactions. Usually it takes many different interactions to complete the overall transaction that characterizes the business. For instance, you buy materials in one transaction, hire people to work on the materials in another transaction, rent the space where the people work in still another, and so on. These transactions come in many forms and have different values. What is measured is their value.

The business is a legal entity separate and apart from its owners and managers. The counting must always record what the business gave up and what it received in return. Even in a proprietorship, where the owner and the business may be taxed as one, transactions attributable to the business should be separated from those attributable to the proprietor's private life.

It is easy to see a transaction when a store clerk hands you a magazine and you hand him or her a dollar. Many transactions, however, involve something more. Drive into a service station, fill the gas tank, and give the service station attendant a credit card. Much later, there will be more money in their bank account and less in yours. If transactions are counted when product, service, or cash is actually given up, then their beginning and ending are separated in time. The generally accepted practice when measuring profit is to ignore when things are paid for and make the count when someone becomes obligated to pay or to be paid. We save or collect or, in the professional language, we *accrue liability*. We count at the time liability is accrued.

By recording when we accrue liability to pay and when others accrue liability to pay us, we can relate the counting to our actions. When we ship some product to a customer, we have obligated the customer to pay us. On the accrual basis, we have made a transaction. We count the promises to pay.

A business gives up one thing of value for which it receives another thing of value. If the business were continually to give more than it received, it would soon run out of whatever is given up. To survive a business must receive at least as much as it gives. To thrive it must receive more than that. In the normal course of operations a business receives compensation for the goods and services it sells to customers. This compensation is referred to as *revenue*.

Expense is the price paid for all the things the business had to buy to generate the revenue being recorded for a particular period.

Expense is the counterpart of revenue. Expense for a period is what was used up to bring in the revenue for that period. It doesn't matter how much material was actually purchased. It doesn't matter that a whole year's insurance was paid in advance. It doesn't matter that the advertising hasn't been paid yet. What counts is the cost of the portion of these things used up to generate the revenue of that particular period.

To illustrate this "used up" concept, consider the business that has to buy a one-year insurance policy for $6,000. The policy covers twelve months. Each month, one-twelfth of the annual policy is consumed or used up. We had to buy a $6,000 policy, but the expense each month is one-twelfth of that, or $500. Or consider the goods sold. A shop may purchase thirty suits at $100 each and sell twenty. The expense is 20 × $100 or $2,000 for the suits that were sold.

The format for determining profit can be described very simply. Prepare orderly lists of the revenue and the expense for a given period of time. Then, *profit* equals the *total revenue* minus the *total expense*.

Profit is the answer to an arithmetic problem. *Revenue* is the sum of the obligations to pay the business for goods and services delivered during a period. It is the promises made by customers to pay, whether they have actually paid or not. *Expense* is the total of some of the obligations to pay others, the portion *used up* to generate the revenue of the period, whether actually paid or not.

The forecast begins with an educated guess about how many *units* will be sold each month. Both revenue and expense depend on the number of units actually sold. If we make and sell widgets, we can recognize the widget as the unit. We may make several kinds of widgets. Then we have several kinds of units, and each should be listed separately. Some businesses, such as service businesses, may not make anything. Even in a service business, however, there is a unit.

Residential real estate agents facilitate the sale of homes. They don't make the homes. They are not the seller of the homes. They gather information about a house available for sale, put that information in a form convenient for use when talking to a buyer, and then seek potential buyers. When a customer agrees to buy a house, the agent gets the seller and the buyer to agree on a price. Then the agent, normally, provides the services needed to close the transaction legally.

When the buyer, the seller, the mortgage institution, the title service, and all the parties to the transaction sign their names to the documents at the closing and the money involved in the transaction changes hands, then the real estate agent gets paid. There is the clue to the unit in the residential real estate agency. Nobody owes the agent until the transaction has gone through all the steps up to and including the closing. You may choose any word you prefer to identify the unit in this business, but it has to be related to closings.

Units may be thought of as the items sold or, for a service business, the shortest list of activities that when completed obligates a customer to pay.

231

The most frequent statements made by owner-managers when discussing forecasts are, "My business is different. You can't forecast in my kind of business." People who operate a business know a tremendous amount about their business and its prospects for the future. They know what they sell and who they sell to. They know why the customers are willing to buy and a host of other details about the customers and the product or service. Managers also know in considerable detail what is needed, where to get it, how to get it, and how much it is likely to cost.

The first encounter with putting this wealth of information down in a neat and orderly form using numbers instead of words seems an insurmountable challenge. It is not, of course. It takes time and effort, which in themselves may seem insurmountable obstacles. But, like learning to walk and learning to talk, it becomes easy with practice.

The first step in giving the forecast a try is describing what the business does. The more clearly that description can be stated the less difficulty there will be with the forecast. The heart of that description is a definition of what we call the units. What does the business do that obligates customers to part with money?

You cannot write the numbers describing the transactions until you know about the "deal" the business has made with someone. Each deal is described by a little story. Each story is like a footnote to the numbers, a brief description of the deal made for the item described. The deal includes who we buy from, in what quantities, at what price, how units are delivered, and so on. Writing a footnote helps to clarify the deal in your own mind and remember where the numbers came from.

Once the story is told you can write all the numbers. Before that you can't write any numbers. This is an important clue to management. You change the future results by negotiating differently before the transaction takes place.

Some people manage by guessing which deals should be made. They then wait to see how things work out for the business. But they can go broke if their guess is wrong. They may never have the benefit of learning what happened. Writing all the numbers in the forecast and looking at the result allows the manager to see how to change the deals to make the final outcome more desirable. Fantasizing the future with paper and pencil doesn't cost very much, and your fantasy can be changed.

The best way to explain this forecasting process is to lead you through an example. The following pages consist of the footnotes to a forecast. There is a blank form on which to do the forecast in Figure 34-1 at the end of this chapter. The footnotes will serve as a step-by-step guide through the exercise. The footnotes are numbered to identify the line each describes in Figure 34-1. You may prefer to do this exercise on a full-size sheet of paper from your ruled tablet. Figure 34-1 will provide the format to be followed.

example, Intercity Assembly Company, is used in a more advanced book
on management by the authors.[1] The particular example in this chapter
is the subject of a popular educational film.[2]

FOOTNOTES TO PROFIT FORECASTING

1. *Units Shipped.* Intercity Assembly Company is about three years old.
In the past year sales have grown rapidly, but it appears to the owner-
manager that they will settle down to more reasonable growth in the
coming year. It is believed that the company will ship 40,000 units next
month. Next month is labeled as month number 1. The following month,
month 2, 42,000 units will be shipped. This is about 5 percent growth
between months 1 and 2. The company is very confident that it can
maintain this growth rate and will ship 44,000 units in month 3, 47,000
in month 4, 50,000 in month 5, 53,000 in month 6, and 55,000 in month
7.

2. *Sales.* Intercity sells the units for a very competitive $2 each.
In month 7, 55,000 units shipped make $110,000 in sales. On an an-
nualized basis the sales that month will be running at the rate of about
$1,300,000 per year (twelve months times $110,000).

3. *Materials.* The materials expense is the cost of the materials
in units actually shipped. They cost Intercity $1 per unit delivered.

4. *Labor.* Historically, the company has used a subcontract assembly firm down the street to put the product together. Now Intercity
has grown to the point where it seems desirable to bring the process in-
house. This will require some skilled workers and some expensive
equipment. On the other hand, it will cut the labor cost in half. With the
new equipment the estimated labor cost to assemble the units will be 10¢
per unit sold.

5. *Overhead.* This item includes the expenses related to where
the labor people do their work on the materials. It usually includes some
rent, heat, electricity, insurance, fringe benefits to labor employees, and
similar things needed to keep the production people and the manufacturing plant working.

In this particular example only two expenses are significant.
One is the depreciation on the new manufacturing equipment; the other
is the salary for the supervisor of the laborers. Any other expenses, like
insurance, are so small they will not be charged to overhead but left in
the administrative expenses of doing business. For instance, rent for the
production space will be included under Item 9 and insurance for
laborers and production equipment will be in Item 10.

The new equipment will cost $162,000. It is estimated that it can
be used for five years. The equipment will be assumed to have no salvage
value after those five years. To calculate *depreciation* divide the *cost* by

the *estimated useful life*. To calculate the depreciation per month, the useful life has to be in months.[3]

The other significant overhead cost is the supervisor's salary. Intercity employs a supervisor for $1,300 per month. This salary plus the monthly depreciation will be the total overhead.

6. *Cost of Goods Sold*. Materials, labor, and overhead are added to get the total *cost of goods sold*. This is shortened from the full title, *cost of the goods that were sold* (from which comes the concept of "used up"). This sum is also called the *total direct expense*. Materials is sometimes called *direct material* and labor is sometimes called *direct labor* to make clear that these are the costs of materials and labor used in making the product sold. Overhead is the indirect expense specifically related to the direct material and the direct labor.

In a retail or wholesale business the company buys the products already in a condition ready to be sold. The retailer doesn't care how much of the cost of goods sold went to labor, materials, or overhead. For businesses that buy their products in a condition ready to be sold the list of expenses starts with cost of goods sold and omits our Lines 3, 4, and 5.

In a service business that doesn't sell anything tangible there are no goods sold, hence no cost of goods sold. A service business may begin its list of expenses with our Line 8, salaries. Contractors may or may not begin with cost of goods sold depending on what kind of contractors they are. Those who build things or rebuild things will probably have materials, labor, and overhead expenses. Those who only repair things may not have these expense items. As you can see, the numbers paint a picture of the business. To decide what numbers are needed you have to look at the business and how it works.

In a retail or wholesale business that stocks hundreds or thousands of items it becomes awkward to keep track of what was paid for each and every item sold. One way people make it easy is to calculate or estimate the cost of the goods sold. The usual method is to count the inventory at the beginning of the reporting period and estimate its cost. Then add to that sum the cost of additional inventory purchased during the reporting period. At the end of the period you can count the inventory again and estimate its cost. The inventory at the beginning of the period plus what was purchased during the period minus what is left at the end of the period must be the total of what was removed and sold during the period, as follows:

Beginning Inventory	xxx
Purchases	+ yy
Ending Inventory	−zzz
Cost of Goods Sold	ABC

7. *Gross Profit*. Gross Profit is the difference between *revenue* and *cost of goods sold*. Gross profit is the amount left over to pay for selling, administration, income taxes, new product development,

financing equipment and facilities, and paying the owners for the use of the money they invested in the business. Managers usually monitor gross profit to know that there will be enough money available to cover all those other expenses.

8. *Salaries*. These salaries are for the nonproduction workers. They include the president, the administrators, and the clerical employees. Intercity decided to lump together the total cost to the company for these people, including the employees' salaries plus the employer's contributions to Social Security, workers' compensation, group health insurance, and any sums required by the state and federal governments. Salaries for month 1 will be $6,900. Of course, the take-home pay by the employees will be smaller than that because of payroll deductions, contributions to Social Security, and fringe benefits.

This expense item is for salaries paid to people whose work cannot be directly related to getting the goods ready to be shipped. The total company payroll would include this item plus the direct labor and the salary for the supervisor included in overhead.

Estimates for salaries in month 2 are $7,450 and for month 3, $7,500. It looks like somebody got a $50-a-month raise in month 3. Then salaries will be $8,350 in months 4 and 5 and $9,000 in months 6 and 7. It looks like additional employees were hired in months 4 and 6. The company must have hired one person in month 2, also.

9. *Rent*. Intercity Assembly Company is moving to new and more adequate facilities. Starting with next month, month 1, the rent will be $2,000 per month.

10. *Insurance*. The company has a friendly insurance agent. Is there any other kind? The agent looks like a part-time employee, judging from the cost. The annual policy will run $6,000. Each month the company uses up one-twelfth of that annual amount, or $500.

11. *Depreciation*. This is the depreciation expense for equipment the business owns other than the manufacturing equipment. It is mostly office furniture and equipment which, it is expected, will last for five years and have a salvage value of zero. Up until this point in time, that is during the past three years, the company has bought $7,200 worth of furniture and equipment. Now, because Intercity is moving to a new facility, it will have to buy another $3,000 worth in month 1. You can calculate the monthly depreciation expense using the method described in the footnote for the equipment under *Overhead*.

12. *Interest*. Intercity doesn't have any loans, so it doesn't have any interest expense. This figure will be zero every month. How fortunate can you be?

13. *Other General & Administrative*. The business has grown to the point where it has a number of small and other miscellaneous items that have to be paid, such as legal and auditing expenses, travel, and entertainment. Rather than make a long list of these, it was decided to lump them all together and call them *other G & A*, or other general and administrative expenses. In month 1 this is estimated to total $3,000. In

month 2 it will be $4,100. In the months that follow it will be $4,550 in month 3, $5,500 in month 4, $6,600 in month 5, $7,050 in month 6, and in month 7, $7,850.

14. *Advertising.* Eon, the free-lance graphic designer, provides Intercity with an estimated cost for advertising to achieve the sales the company has forecast. For this seven-month period, Eon forecasts the advertising will cost $9,750 in month 1, $9,800 in month 2, $10,200 in month 3, and $11,000 in month 4. Then he forecasts $11,600 in month 5, $12,500 in month 6, and $13,000 in month 7.

15. *Brochures.* Intercity Assembly Company uses an inexpensive brochure to respond to inquiries about its product. You have to buy in large quantities from a printer to obtain a reasonable per unit price. The company decided to buy a one-year supply for $5,400 and use them up all along, one-twelfth of the supply each month.

16. *Total Expense.* The total expense shown here is for everything: materials, labor, overhead, salaries, and all the other expenses. Sometimes managers or accountants prefer to add up the expenses listed below the cost of goods sold and call that *operating expense.* Use whatever makes the most sense to you in your business. In this presentation it seemed more logical to add all the expenses. That would be Lines 3, 4, and 5 plus Lines 8 through 15.

17. *Pretax Profit.* Pretax profit is the difference between the *revenues* and all the *expenses* incurred to make the sales. If the pretax profit is negative, that is, if it is a loss, we usually show that by putting brackets around the number. This is not yet the net profit. Many managers forget that income taxes are an expense of doing business. The reason for calculating pretax profit is that you can't tell how much the tax expense is without it. Uncle Sam wants a percentage of this number. Income tax is such a large percentage of this item, even in a very small business, that it cannot be treated lightly. Worse yet, Uncle Sam is not a sympathetic creditor.

18. *Income Tax.* The income tax rates are changed from time to time by Congress. The best way to find out what you must pay is to get a copy of the IRS publication "Tax Guide for Small Business." It's free at your nearest office of the Internal Revenue Service. You pay taxes on the pretax profit for the taxable year. You may have losses in some months and profits in others. To calculate the taxable profit add the profits for the taxable year to date and subtract the losses for the same taxable year. If the result is a loss for the taxable year to date, no income tax is due. If the result is a profit for the year to date, you pay a percentage of that profit. Once the profits to date exceed the losses to date, the taxes incurred in a month are a percentage of the new pretax profit earned in that month. In the example, month 1 is the beginning of the taxable year. Intercity estimates that its tax rate will be 30 percent for each month of the coming year.

19. *Net Profit.* Net profit is what is left after paying the income tax. Subtract the *income tax* due each month from the *pretax* profit for each month to find the bottom line *net profit* for the month.

If you have been filling in the numbers on Figure 34-1 as you read through the footnotes, you have just forecast the profit for Intercity Assembly Co., Inc., for the next seven months. Congratulations.

INTERCITY ASSEMBLY COMPANY, INC.
INCOME STATEMENT FORECAST

Month	1	2	3	4	5	6	7
REVENUES							
(1) Units Shipped							
(2) Sales							
EXPENSES							
(3) Materials............							
(4) Labor							
(5) Overhead							
(6) Cost of Goods Sold.....							
(7) Gross Profit...........							
(8) Salaries							
(9) Rent							
(10) Insurance.............							
(11) Depreciation							
(12) Interest...............							
(13) Other G&A							
(14) Advertising							
(15) Brochures							
(16) Total Expense							
(17) Pre-Tax Profit							
(18) Income Taxes							
(19) **Net Profit**							

FIGURE 34-1 The Form on Which to Forecast Sales, Expenses, and Profits.

35

Forecasting Cash Flow

Cash flow is different from profit. Profit is the difference between revenues and expenses. Cash flow is the difference between receipts and disbursements of cash. Profit may flow whether or not anybody has paid for anything. Cash flows *only* when somebody pays for something. Time after time, businesses with good sales and good profits go broke. It is surprisingly commonplace. The problem is that the *cash* doesn't flow when the *profit* flows.

The well-publicized explanations for the large number of new business failures in the United States, undercapitalization, inadequate management, and poor marketing, may be valid, but in our experience the overwhelming reason is that the managers did not understand cash flow. They behaved as if profit were cash, which it is not. They acted as if all that is needed to win the business game is to make a profit, which is not true. Cash is different from profit. You need both to win the business game.

A business can survive and thrive only if it has both positive profit (not losses) and positive cash flow (more flowing into the bank than out of it). To win you must produce more than you consume, and you must do it in such a way that you can meet critical payments as they come due.

Profit may be the most common measure of whether a business is winning or losing, but cash flow is the most critical measure. Businesses can survive a surprisingly long time without profit. They die on the first payday there is no cash.

Your company's bank is like a reservoir for the business's cash. The concept is familiar. The cookie jar is a reservoir, so is the gas tank. And what is in the reservoir is easy to measure. The amount in the reservoir is what was put in minus what was taken out. A convenient way to measure whether the supply is increasing or decreasing is to measure whether more was entering or leaving during the most recent period of time. Cash flow into the bank account is such a measure. How much is in the reservoir is of interest, of course, but it is changed by changing the cash flow.

SOME TERMS DEFINED

Cash coming into the business is anything that can be deposited in the company's bank account. To identify this kind of cash, near-cash or like-cash, we use the word *receipts*. Cash leaving the business is almost always the result of writing a check. We identify this kind of instruction to the bank with the word *disbursements*. Cash flow equals *receipts* minus *disbursements*.

One of the most important reasons for using the word *receipts* and understanding its meaning is to separate the two words: *revenues* and *receipts*. Revenue is the sum of obligations to pay the business as a result of goods and services provided. Receipts appear when those obligations are fulfilled. There are other receipts. When the owners buy common stock in the business, there is a receipt of the cash paid for it. When the business borrows from the bank, it receives cash.

The name *disbursements* is associated with instructing the bank to disburse some cash. Disbursements are no more a counterpart to expenses than receipts are a counterpart to revenues. Disbursement means the movement of real cash from the business. Expense only implies an obligation to move cash. The size and timing of disbursements can be and usually are very different from those of expenses. Disbursements are related to cash flow. With the definition of cash flow clearly in mind, it is important to use the word *disbursements* and to mean just that.

If disbursements are bigger than receipts, the cash flow is a negative number. That means the cash balance is decreasing at the bank. When cash flow is a positive number, the cash balance is increasing at the bank. If you are not familiar with adding negative numbers, it may be wise to ask someone for help. Cash flow ebbs and flows. You will almost certainly have some negative cash flow. The brief explanation at the end of this chapter may be helpful.

For the sake of clarity we prefer to name the form on which we forecast cash flow the *checkbook*. The checkbook always provides a place to record deposits, checks withdrawn, and a current balance. Usually deposits and checks withdrawn are recorded for a whole month. Then the current balance can be found at the end of the month.

It is helpful to have the income statement conveniently nearby. The income statement is a partial checklist to remind us what checks have to be written. Sometimes the check is the same size as the expense, as for salaries. Sometimes the size of the check is not that of the expense, as for insurance. Sometimes the check to be written and the expense seem totally unrelated, as for materials. But an expense always provokes a disbursement of some size at some time.

The cash flow forecast is like the income statement in that it is a list of what comes in and what goes out. The difference is in what is being listed. For cash flow, the list is receipts and disbursements. This array of numbers is often called the *statement of receipts and disbursements,* a better name for it than *cash flow statement.* It focuses your thinking on what is in the statement rather than on the result and keeps your attention on the things the manager can do something about.

The list of receipts and disbursements includes *all* the cash coming in or going out. If there is one admonition you would want to make to someone preparing this forecast it is, "Don't leave out anything."

Some receipts and disbursements do not appear on the income statement. For instance, cash received for the issurance of common stock is a receipt, but it does not appear on the income statement. If the business has borrowed money, the loan shows up as a deposit. The interest on the loan will show up as an expense on the income statement, and there will be a corresponding disbursement to pay the interest. But the repayment of principal does not appear on the income statement. You have to jog your memory about when to write that check. The interest is "used up." The principal is not.

One of the biggest problems in forecasting disbursements is predicting when to buy goods and materials. A service business may not have this problem; if it does, the problem is usually minor. All other businesses seem to have the problem. A retail store has to stock its shelves with goods to sell. A manufacturer has to have the raw materials to make products. A contractor needs the raw materials of the trade. The problem arises because you don't normally buy precisely the quantities that will be consumed to make the sale. You buy a supply to work from.

The quantities of materials bought are usually different from the quantities used. The time when materials are purchased is almost always different from when they are used. The time materials are paid for is almost always later than when they were received. All these are related to when the materials are used up, that is, when the sale is made, but the relationship is not in any way a simple one.

In most nonservice businesses, materials alone make up 20 percent to 60 percent of all disbursements. The size and the timing of the disbursements for materials are important enough that you must make the effort to determine these numbers in some detail. This is done by making a separate listing or schedule.

An *inventory schedule* can list when units come in and go out. The important information to be obtained from this listing has to do with when you will have to write checks. There may already be some materials in inventory, and you have to add some periodically to make certain enough are on hand at the time they are needed. What you write checks for are the items you have to buy to have enough on hand to complete sales.

In the example that follows the materials have to be purchased in multiples of 5,000 units. This has nothing to do with how they are used up. This minimum order quantity allows us to demonstrate how the check to be written for materials could be much different from the expense for these materials. It is much like saying you can only buy in six-packs or in boxes of one hundred.

A good format for this inventory schedule lists *beginning inventory* minus *units shipped* plus *units received* equals *ending inventory*. This is a convenient way to decide how many units will have to be brought in each month. Then, knowing how many will be received and when the supplier expects to be paid, you can decide when a check should be written and how big it will be.

If two major units are needed in the business instead of one, then you should go through the exercise twice. There will be Unit A and Unit B. If you have ten major units, then list Unit A through Unit J. Don't cringe at the work. It may be painful but it is not fatal.

BEGINNING THE CASH FLOW FORECAST

The footnotes to the cash flow forecast resulting from the activities described in the profit forecast of Chapter 34 are presented on the following pages. There is a blank form in Figure 35-2, where you can

INTERCITY ASSEMBLY COMPANY, INC.
INCOME STATEMENT FORECAST

Month	1	2	3	4	5	6	7
REVENUES							
Units Sold	40,000	42,000	44,000	47,000	50,000	53,000	55,000
Sales	$80,000	84,000	88,000	94,000	100,000	106,000	110,000
EXPENSES							
Direct Materials	40,000	42,000	44,000	47,000	50,000	53,000	55,000
Direct Labor.............	4,000	4,200	4,400	4,700	5,000	5,300	5,500
Overhead	4,000	4,000	4,000	4,000	4,000	4,000	4,000
Cost of Goods Sold	48,000	50,200	52,400	55,700	59,000	62,300	64,500
Gross Profit	32,000	33,800	35,600	38,300	41,000	43,700	45,500
General & Administrative							
Salaries	6,900	7,450	7,500	8,350	8,350	9,000	9,000
Rent	2,000	2,000	2,000	2,000	2,000	2,000	2,000
Insurance..............	500	500	500	500	500	500	500
Depreciation	170	170	170	170	170	170	170
Interest................	0	0	0	0	0	0	0
Other G&A	3,000	4,100	4,550	5,500	6,600	7,050	7,850
Marketing							
Advertising.............	9,750	9,800	10,200	11,000	11,600	12,500	13,000
Brochures	450	450	450	450	450	450	450
Total Expense	70,770	74,670	77,770	83,670	88,670	93,970	97,470
Taxable Income	9,230	9,330	10,230	10,330	11,330	12,030	12,530
Income Taxes	2,769	2,799	3,069	3,099	3,399	3,609	3,759
Net Profit	$ 6,461	6,531	7,161	7,231	7,931	8,421	8,771

FIGURE 35-1 The Completed Income Statement Forecast.

create the forecast. There is also a blank form of the subsidiary excursion into what quantities of materials to buy and when in Figure 35-3. This is the inventory calculations.

The income statement forecast from Chapter 34 is in Figure 35-1. You will find this a helpful guide along with the footnotes. The income statement forecast is the necessary Step 1 in the process. The cash flow forecast is Step 2. Therein lies another clue to management.

Using the footnotes and what you remember from preparing the profit forecast, you should be able to prepare the cash flow forecast and determine the future bank balances for Intercity Assembly Company. We would like you to give it a try.

Intercity Assembly Company is the subject of a more advanced book on management.[1] The particular example in this chapter is the subject of one of their educational films.[2]

FOOTNOTES TO CASH FLOW FORECASTING

1. *Sales Receipts.* Sales receipts is the money received in payment for products shipped and billed, or for services rendered and billed. All checks and cash should be deposited immediately, first to be sure the cash isn't lost or stolen, and second to be sure the checks are good. If they are going to bounce, you would like to know right away. Third, this is the

INTERCITY ASSEMBLY COMPANY, INC.
CASH FLOW FORECAST

Month	1	2	3	4	5	6	7
RECEIPTS							
(1) Sales Receipts							
(2) Other Receipts							
DISBURSEMENTS							
(3) Materials.............							
(4) Labor							
(5) Overhead							
(6) Manufacturing Equip. ...							
(7) Salaries							
(8) Rent							
(9) Insurance.............							
(10) Office Equipment.......							
(11) Principal & Interest							
(12) Other G&A							
(13) Advertising							
(14) Brochures							
(15) Income Taxes							
(16) Total Disbursed							
(17) **Cash Flow**							
(18) Beginning Balance							
(19) **Ending Balance**							

FIGURE 35-2 The Form on Which to Forecast Cash Flow and Bank Balances.

surest way to have a good record of what came in and when. The owner-manager said the terms of sale are the industry terms, net thirty days. We would expect that sales in month 1 would result in receipts in month 2. But the manager also said, "Our customers pay us promptly in sixty days." Sales made on the income statement show up on the cash flow forecast two months later, when the payment is received and deposited at the bank. Sales made in prior months result in deposits in months 1 and 2. Sales this month, the month before month 1 on the forecast, look like they will be $77,000. Last month, two months before month 1, sales were $74,000. This $74,000 will be deposited next month, month 1 of the forecast.

2. *Other Receipts*. In addition to sales receipts, the company expects to receive money from investors. The new manufacturing equipment will cost $162,000. Intercity found some investors who are anxious to buy $157,000 worth of Intercity common stock. Their subscription agreements say they will deliver the money in month 2. After considering bank loans and leases this seemed to be the best deal for the company.

3. *Materials*. Disbursements for materials are checks written to the materials supplier. The materials supplier was emphatic in saying the checks are due in "thirty days and not thirty-one days." That means one month after Intercity receives the materials. The only problem is that Intercity has to buy the materials in multiples of 5,000 units. For instance, it can't buy 42,000 units, the way they are used up in month 2. That means we need a little side schedule or subsidiary schedule to figure out when to receive how many units. Then we can tell when to write checks to the materials supplier. The form in Figure 35-3 is called the inventory schedule; this form can be used to find out when checks are written for materials.

FOOTNOTES TO THE INVENTORY SCHEDULE

a. *Units*. This schedule is worked out in the number of units, not dollars, involved. It is units sold and shipped, not dollars. Because sometimes the price goes up or down, it is easier to count in units and later attach a price to them.

MATERIALS INVENTORY SCHEDULE

Month	1	2	3	4	5	6	7
(a) **UNITS**							
(b) Beginning Inventory....							
(c) – Shipments (Out)							
(d) + Purchases (Rec'd)							
(e) Ending Inventory.......							
(f) Cash Disbursements ...							

FIGURE 35-3 The Form on Which to Forecast Materials Purchases.

b. *Beginning Inventory.* At the beginning of month 1, Intercity expects to have 43,500 units on hand. Therefore, the beginning inventory is 43,500. In month 2 the beginning inventory will be what was left over from month 1 after shipping the units sold and receiving the ones delivered by the supplier. In month 3 the beginning inventory will be what was left over from month 2.

c. *Units Shipped.* This is the number of units shipped out each month and is the same as the number of units shipped on the income statement forecast in the corresponding month.

d. *Units Received.* From time to time Intercity will have to order additional materials. The company has made it a policy to receive the units in advance so that there are always enough on hand at the end of the month to take care of next month's anticipated sales. In the example, ending inventory should always be equal to or bigger than the next month's sales. The supplier will only ship quantities that are multiples of 5,000 units. There is no need to receive any more multiples of 5,000 units than will make the ending inventory just big enough to handle next month's anticipated sales.

e. *Ending Inventory.* Ending inventory describes how many units are on hand at the end of the month. This number is equal to the *beginning inventory* minus the *units shipped* and plus the *units received.* You start with some in the warehouse. Then you subtract those shipped out to customers and add those bought from the supplier. The ending inventory at five o'clock on the last day of the month will still be there the next morning, at eight o'clock on the first day of the next month.

f. *Checks Written.* After you have calculated the number of units Intercity needs to receive each month, you can fill in the size of the check to be written and when. The units cost $1 each, and the check is written one month after the materials are received.

CONTINUING THE CASH FLOW FOOTNOTES

Now, back to the cash flow forecast of Figure 35-2. Line 3 in the checkbook and Line f on the inventory schedule are identical. The company brought in 40,000 units in the month preceding month 1 and will have to write a check for $40,000 in month 1, thirty days later.

4. *Labor.* Employees want to be paid in the month they do the work. A labor expense on the income statement will show up as a check disbursed in the same month on the cash flow forecast.

5. *Overhead.* The overhead expense was composed of two parts, the depreciation expense on the new manufacturing equipment and the salary for the supervisor of the laborers. The supervisor cost the company $1,300 per month, including the company's contributions to Social Security and other fringe benefits. The equipment costs $162,000, and

when depreciated over five years to a salvage value equal to zero, the depreciation is $2,700 per month. But you don't write a check for depreciation. Who would you write it to? The check you write is to the equipment supplier, and that is for the full cost of the equipment. So the only check to be written under overhead is to the supervisor.

6. *Manufacturing Equipment.* It is time to think about that $162,000 check to the equipment supplier. The company expects to bring in $157,000 in month 2 by selling common stock. The equipment check will be $162,000 in month 2. Some of the investors may have to guarantee the payment to obtain delivery of the equipment in month 1.

7. *Salaries.* Salaries on the income statement show up as checks the same month.

8. *Rent.* Intercity had to expand to more adequate facilities. The company will move in by the first of month 1. The rent on the new space is $2,000 per month. It is normal to pay the rent for the entire month during the first couple of days of the month.

9. *Insurance.* Insurance companies have several payment plans for coverage. Normally, they like to be paid for the year in advance. They will finance the premium and let you pay monthly or quarterly, but they charge a fee for that service. Intercity decided to pay for the annual policy in advance, in month 1, and avoid paying the interest or carrying fee. The income statement shows how the company "used up" the insurance at $500 per month, but in the checkbook the whole year is paid for in month 1.

10. *Office Equipment.* Intercity will buy $3,000 worth of office equipment for the new facility in month 1. The company has thirty-day terms with this supplier, so the check won't have to be written until one month after the equipment arrives in month 1.

11. *Principal & Interest.* Intercity doesn't have any loans, so it doesn't have to write checks to pay principal and interest. It is interesting to observe that only the interest showed up on the income statement. Both principal and interest have to be paid when you write the check. Principal is not "used up"; it is only borrowed for a while and then given back. Interest, on the other hand, is like rent on the principal. Principal repayments are not part of the profit calculation, but they are part of the cash flow.

12. *Other General & Administrative.* This group of miscellaneous items tends to be the kinds of things paid for in thirty days, one month after the expense is incurred. The month before month 1 the forecast was $2,800, which will be paid for in month 1.

13. *Advertising.* Eon, the free-lance graphic designer who handles the promotion program, likes to be paid in thirty days, one month after the expense is incurred. The month before month 1, Eon billed $9,000 for promotion services.

14. *Brochures.* The printer will deliver $5,400 worth of brochures in month 1. Intercity has thirty days to pay for them.

15. *Income Tax.* From most businesses, the government wants to receive a check each quarter covering the estimated taxes due for the prior three months. There are some choices on how you estimate the amount, and the payments are usually due in months four, six, nine, and twelve of your fiscal year. The details of how much and when can be found in the IRS publication "Tax Guide for Small Business." Intercity's policy is to make the tax deposit in the month following the end of the quarter and to deposit the amount actually accrued during the quarter. The last quarter, which ended in the month before month 1, was a good one. The company owes $11,000 tax for it. This payment will be made in month 1.

16. *Total Disbursed.* Total disbursed is the sum of all the checks written that month. Some owner-managers call this their "total thrill."

17. *Cash Flow.* The cash flow is the *deposits* put into the bank minus the *checks* written. It is the net cash flowing into the bank for any given month. *Negative cash flow* is shown by placing brackets around the numbers. Negative cash flow should be expected occasionally in the normal course of business.

18. *Beginning Balance.* Beginning balance means the cash in the bank at the beginning of the month. Intercity will begin month 1 with a "low four-figure balance" of $1,100.

19. *Ending Balance.* The ending balance is what is in the bank account at the end of the month. If you add the *cash flow* into the bank to the bank *balance at the beginning of the month* you get the *ending balance.* The ending balance of this month becomes the beginning balance for the next month. You have to keep track of the negative numbers. If you have trouble adding negative numbers, see the brief description at the end of this chapter.

The ending bank balance is a crucial piece of information available from all this forecasting. While portraying the future with pencil and paper, we can allow the bank balance to be negative, that is, overdraft. Of course, we can't do that in actual practice. If we propose to initiate the actions and the contractual terms described by the forecasts, then we must also make arrangements in advance to obtain financing. The size of the overdrafts tells us the size of the financing needed and when we have to have it. The financing is the cash the owner-manager must have to continue operations according to plan.

Most owner-managers can find some way to obtain the needed financing so long as they know how much is needed and when. Presenting the forecasts to prospective sources of financing, like the banker, in the format used in Chapter 34 and here will help to obtain the financing. These forecasts show the banker precisely why the money is needed, for how long it will be needed, and where the money is coming from to repay any loans. That is exactly the information the banker needs to understand the request for a loan and to justify making it.

ADDING POSITIVE AND NEGATIVE NUMBERS

When adding positive and negative numbers you can run into six different situations. The following examples will be useful if you are not already familiar with negative numbers. Negative numbers are the ones in brackets, for instance: [300].

Example

1. *Positive plus Positive.* Adding two positive numbers gives a larger positive number. This is the solution we learned in school.

$$\begin{array}{r} 400 \\ +\ \ 300 \\ \hline 700 \end{array}$$

2. *Large Positive plus Small Negative.* When adding a positive number plus a negative number, first ask if the negative number is bigger or smaller than the positive number. If the negative number is smaller than the positive number, subtract the negative number from the positive number; the answer is a smaller positive number.

$$\begin{array}{r} 400 \\ +[\ 300] \\ \hline 100 \end{array}$$

3. *Small Positive plus Large Negative.* When adding a positive number plus a negative number and the negative number is bigger than the positive number, you subtract the positive number from the negative number; the answer is a smaller negative number.

$$\begin{array}{r} 400 \\ +[500] \\ \hline [100] \end{array}$$

4. *Negative plus Negative.* When adding a negative number plus a negative number, you add them as if they were positive numbers; the answer is a bigger negative number.

$$\begin{array}{r} [400] \\ +[300] \\ \hline [700] \end{array}$$

5. *Large Negative plus Small Positive.* When adding a negative number plus a positive number and the positive number is smaller than the negative number, you subtract the positive number from the negative number; the answer is a smaller negative number.

$$\begin{array}{r} [400] \\ +\ \ 300 \\ \hline [100] \end{array}$$

6. *Small Negative plus Large Positive.* When adding a negative number plus a positive number and the positive number is bigger than the negative number, subtract the negative number from the positive number; the answer is a smaller positive number.

$$\begin{array}{r} [400] \\ +\ \ 500 \\ \hline 100 \end{array}$$

As you can see from these examples, two positive numbers add to make a bigger positive number, and two negative numbers add to make a bigger negative number. When adding one positive and one negative number, you subtract the smaller number from the bigger one, and the answer bears the plus or minus sign of the bigger number you started with.

An example of this kind may be helpful. Working with positive and negative numbers may be thought of as adding a series of numbers where the plus or minus sign indicates the direction. Suppose plus means in the direction of the North Pole and minus means in the direction of the South Pole. If the numbers mean distance in yards and the plus or minus sign means in which direction, then after adding the numbers the answer means how many yards from the starting point.

In Example 1, measure from a starting point. First measure 400 yards north. Then, starting from there, measure 300 yards north. Now how far are you from the starting point? You are 700 yards north.

In Example 2, measure 400 yards north from the starting point. Then measure 300 yards south from there. Now how far are you from the starting point? You are 100 yards north.

In Example 3, measure 400 yards north from the starting point. Then measure 500 yards south from there. Now how far are you from the starting point? You are 100 yards south.

If these numbers were referring to the progress of a football team, you might think of Example 2 as a gain of four yards followed by a loss of three yards. The call would then be third down and nine to go.

36
Growth
Consumes Cash

The American dream is to carve out of the forest-wilderness a clearing you can call your own. It is to enter today's economic jumble of trees and underbrush and plant your own furrow of grain or fruits and vegetables. It is to find a niche in the world of commerce and stake a claim to some small share of the gross national product.

The pioneer who cleared a small patch of the forest for a house and garden soon cleared an acre for corn and another acre to graze the cow. In time many acres were cleared and a farm emerged with fences to divide the pastures and the fields. A barn was built to store the summer's crop for winter feeding. And the house grew to accommodate the increasing number of progeny.

This growth from forest clearing to fully integrated farm is as much a part of the American dream as was the first clearing. A furrow of your own in the economic forest is to be followed by a field of furrows. A fully functioning business with its edifice and its outlying fields clearly visible and identifiable is embedded in the embryo of starting a business. In all living organisms, birth implies growth. And a business is no less a living organism than an acorn.

When a business is started where none existed before it has a very rapid rate of growth from zero to something. We hope that something is sufficient to make it economically viable. Then we anticipate that it will grow further to provide more money coming in than is needed to cover what is going out. The dream includes providing the owner-manager with freedom from concerns about the cost of things needed and wanted.

But you may have noticed that as people's needs are satisfied, they grow. And when the new and greater needs are satisfied, they grow again. As the business inflows exceed the outflows, the demand on the excess continually exerts pressure for an ever-greater excess. The phenomenon is hardly new. It is evident in the artifacts of all ancient civilizations.

Growth Consumes Cash

A business must grow. For a new business growth to a viable size is essential for survival. For a viable business growth is essential to provide adequate rewards to its owners and key employees. Growth provides opportunities for advancement in position and compensation. It provides the need for managers. And with opportunities for promotion to management come self-satisfaction, esteem, and the possibility for self-actualization. Everyone knows that with growth you have bigger sales and bigger profits.

The dilemma for the owner-manager is that growth seems so obvious and desirable, but the rate of growth that can be supported without external financing is severely constrained. And worse still, growth with earnings bears all the signs of success and imposes demands on the resources of the business to demonstrate its success with the symbols of affluence, such as dividends, raises, bonuses, and buildings.

RECALCULATING INTERCITY'S FORECASTS

The last two chapters described the next seven months' operations for Intercity Assembly Company. We chose to leave the exercise forms blank in hopes that you would try to perform the exercise. The completed

INTERCITY ASSEMBLY COMPANY, INC.
INCOME STATEMENT FORECAST

Month	1	2	3	4	5	6	7
REVENUES							
Units Sold	40,000	42,000	44,000	47,000	50,000	53,000	55,000
Sales	$80,000	84,000	88,000	94,000	100,000	106,000	110,000
EXPENSES							
Direct Materials	40,000	42,000	44,000	47,000	50,000	53,000	55,000
Direct Labor	4,000	4,200	4,400	4,700	5,000	5,300	5,500
Overhead	4,000	4,000	4,000	4,000	4,000	4,000	4,000
Cost of Goods Sold	48,000	50,200	52,400	55,700	59,000	62,300	64,500
Gross Profit	32,000	33,800	35,600	38,300	41,000	43,700	45,500
General & Administrative							
Salaries	6,900	7,450	7,500	8,350	8,350	9,000	9,000
Rent	2,000	2,000	2,000	2,000	2,000	2,000	2,000
Insurance	500	500	500	500	500	500	500
Depreciation	170	170	170	170	170	170	170
Interest	0	0	0	0	0	0	0
Other G&A	3,000	4,100	4,550	5,500	6,600	7,050	7,850
Marketing							
Advertising	9,750	9,800	10,200	11,000	11,600	12,500	13,000
Brochures	450	450	450	450	450	450	450
Total Expense	70,770	74,670	77,770	83,670	88,670	93,970	97,470
Taxable Income	9,230	9,330	10,230	10,330	11,330	12,030	12,530
Income Taxes	2,769	2,799	3,069	3,099	3,399	3,609	3,759
Net Profit	$ 6,461	6,531	7,161	7,231	7,931	8,421	8,771

FIGURE 36-1 The Completed Income Statement Forecast.

INTERCITY ASSEMBLY COMPANY, INC.
CASH FLOW FORECAST

Month	1	2	3	4	5	6	7
RECEIPTS							
Sales Receipts	74,000*	77,000*	80,000	84,000	88,000	94,000	100,000
Common Stock	—	157,000	—	—	—	—	—
Total Received	$74,000	234,000	80,000	84,000	88,000	94,000	100,000
DISBURSEMENTS							
Direct Materials	40,000*	40,000	45,000	45,000	50,000	55,000	55,000
Direct Labor.	4,000	4,200	4,400	4,700	5,000	5,300	5,500
Overhead	1,300	1,300	1,300	1,300	1,300	1,300	1,300
Manufacturing Equipment . . .	—	162,000	—	—	—	—	—
Salaries	6,900	7,450	7,500	8,350	8,350	9,000	9,000
Rent	2,000	2,000	2,000	2,000	2,000	2,000	2,000
Insurance	6,000	—	—	—	—	—	—
Office Equipment	—	3,000	—	—	—	—	—
Principal & Interest	—	—	—	—	—	—	—
Other G&A	2,800*	3,000	4,100	4,550	5,500	6,600	7,050
Advertising	9,000*	9,750	9,800	10,200	11,000	11,600	12,500
Brochures	—	5,400	—	—	—	—	—
Taxes	11,000*	—	—	8,637	—	—	10,107
Total Disbursed	83,000	238,100	74,100	84,737	83,150	90,800	102,457
Total Cash Flow	(9,000)	(4,100)	5,900	(737)	4,850	3,200	(2,457)
Beginning Balance	1,100	(7,900)	(12,000)	(6,100)	(6,837)	(1,987)	1,213
Ending Balance	$(7,900)	(12,000)	(6,100)	(6,837)	(1,987)	1,213	(1,244)

*From operations during prior periods.

FIGURE 36-2 The Completed Cash Flow Forecast.

MATERIALS INVENTORY SCHEDULE (IN UNITS)

Month	1	2	3	4	5	6	7
Beginning Inventory	43,500	43,500	46,500	47,500	50,500	55,500	57,500
– Shipments (Out)	40,000	42,000	44,000	47,000	50,000	53,000	55,000
+ Purchases (Received)	40,000	45,000	45,000	50,000	55,000	55,000	55,000
Ending Inventory	43,500	46,500	47,500	50,500	55,500	57,500	57,500
Cash Disbursements	$40,000*	40,000	45,000	45,000	50,000	55,000	55,000

*Due to a transaction of a prior period.

FIGURE 36-3 The Completed Materials Inventory Schedule.

forms are presented here in Figures 36-1 through 36-3.[1] As you can see from Figure 36-1, the income statement forecast, Intercity is growing nicely and profitably. Sales in month 1 are $80,000, in month 7 they are $110,000. Profits for the seven-month period are $52,507.

Figure 36-2 is the cash flow forecast. Intercity shows $1,100 in the bank at the beginning of month 1. At the end of month 7, after all those highly profitable sales, the bank balance will be *overdrawn* $1,244. During this seven-month period the cash flow was negative (out of the bank) by $2,344. Profitable growth consumed cash.

251

That wasn't the worst of it. The company's bank balance was overdrawn in six out of the seven months. The worst overdraft was in month 2, when the company had a deficit of $12,000. We hope Intercity has a friendly banker who will make short-term loans to the company to cover these overdrafts. Otherwise some of those checks the company plans to write will bounce.

You may find it interesting to compare the net profit after tax plus depreciation with the cash flow in these two exhibits. In month 1, on the income statement, depreciation was $2,700 of the overhead and $170 for office furniture and equipment, while the profit was $6,461. That is a total of $9,331. In the checkbook the cash flow was $9,000, and it was negative. That method of inferring the cash flow from the income statement didn't work that month, did it? In month 2 profiit plus depreciation was $9,401, but the cash flow was negative $4,100. Didn't work there either! Enough said?

Some owner-managers feel that the answer to a negative cash position as portrayed in Figure 36-2 is to increase sales. More profits, it seems, would eliminate the problem through internally generated cash. The manager in our example discussed the possibility of increasing sales with the company's advertising professional. This resulted in a decision to concentrate all the promotion budget on a small target market.

The advertising professional identified such a target market. It will take a little time to see the effect of a new promotion program, but by month 4 the company expects to ship 50,000 units instead of the 47,000 in the forecast. After that shipments will grow by 5,000 per month through month 7. That's 55,000 units in month 5, 60,000 units in month 6, and 65,000 units in month 7.

Changing the number of units shipped in Figure 36-1 will change the sales. That will change the expense for materials. In month 4 we will "use up" 50,000 units at $1 each instead of the 47,000 we had projected. And the labor will change. We will use up 50,000 units at 10¢ each. The supervisor's salary won't change. And the depreciation on the production equipment won't change, so the overhead stays the same.

Cost of goods sold will change because it is the sum of materials, labor, and overhead. That will change the gross profit. Administrative salaries shouldn't change, nor should rent. We moved into new and more adequate facilities in month 1. That should handle the bigger sales. None of the remainder of the expenses should change. The big item is advertising, and Eon said that budget won't change. It will just be focused on a smaller, but more defined, target market.

Total expense will change. So will the pretax profit. That means the accrued taxes will change, and there will be a new bottom line net profit. Well, that's more than a couple of numbers, but we should be able to recalculate the forecast for the last four months in just a few minutes. Figure 36-4 is the original income statement with the numbers that change blocked out.

As long as we are at it, we might be wise to look at what happens to the checkbook, Figure 36-2, as a result of these bigger sales. The sales receipts will change if the sales are different. Intercity's customers pay in sixty days. That means the new sales figure in month 4 will show up as a sales receipt in month 6. Month 7 sales receipts will change too.

How about the check for materials? Will that change? We found the size and timing of checks to the materials supplier on that side calculation, the inventory schedule. The units shipped numbers will change on that schedule. That will change some other numbers. Figure 36-6 shows the inventory forecast with the numbers that change blocked out. It appears the check to the materials supplier will change in months 4 through 7.

Of course, the labor checks will change. Those people expect to be paid in the month they do the work. If the labor changed on the income statement it will change in the cash flow forecast. That would be months 4 through 7.

That would seem to be all the checks that change. Oh, there is one more. The accrued income tax for the second quarter, months 4, 5, and 6, has changed. Total disbursed will also change for the last four months. So will the cash flow. That means there will be new ending bank balances. Figure 36-5 shows the cash flow forecast with all the numbers that change blocked out.

The newly calculated numbers are shown in Figures 36-7 through 36-9.[2] Don't turn away from all those numbers. That's money. Bigger sales and bigger profits. Just as we expected, the sales for the seven-month period are up from $662,000 to $712,000, and the seven months' net profit is up from $52,507 to $68,257, a gain of nearly $16,000.

Down at the bank, the balance at the end of month 7 is now overdraft $16,794 instead of only $1,244. Because we had $1,100 in the bank at the beginning of this period, the net cash flow must have been $17,894 negative.

We said it before, now we'll say it again—growth consumes cash. Figure 36-10 dispays the normal situation in business; rapid growth in sales, even though accompanied by growth in profit, results in negative cash flow. And as you can see from this example, faster growth consumes cash faster. To quote many owner-managers, "You see all that profit I'm making? Where is it? It's not down at the bank."

COVERING ANTICIPATED OVERDRAFTS

This phenomenon is related to growth. Intercity grew by shipping more units. So often a restaurant that is doing well will open a second restaurant. The results are the same. Opening an additional dress shop or furniture store will do it. Adding a new product line will do it. So will launching a new department or a branch sales office or building an additional production or warehouse facility or adding to the fleet of

INTERCITY ASSEMBLY COMPANY, INC.
INCOME STATEMENT FORECAST
ANTICIPATING GROWTH IN SALES

Month	1	2	3	4	5	6	7
REVENUES							
Units Sold	40,000	42,000	44,000				
Sales	$80,000	84,000	88,000				
EXPENSES							
Direct Materials	40,000	42,000	44,000				
Direct Labor	4,000	4,200	4,400				
Overhead	4,000	4,000	4,000	4,000	4,000	4,000	4,000
Cost of Goods Sold	48,000	50,200	52,400				
Gross Profit	32,000	33,800	35,600				
General & Administrative							
Salaries	6,900	7,450	7,500	8,350	8,350	9,000	9,000
Rent	2,000	2,000	2,000	2,000	2,000	2,000	2,000
Insurance	500	500	500	500	500	500	500
Depreciation	170	170	170	170	170	170	170
Interest	0	0	0	0	0	0	0
Other G&A	3,000	4,100	4,550	5,500	6,600	7,050	7,850
Marketing							
Advertising	9,750	9,800	10,200	11,000	11,600	12,500	13,000
Brochures	450	450	450	450	450	450	450
Total Expense	70,770	74,670	77,770				
Taxable Income	9,230	9,330	10,230				
Income Taxes	2,769	2,799	3,069				
Net Profit	$ 6,461	6,531	7,161				

FIGURE 36-4 Income Statement Forecast Showing Which Numbers Change When Anticipating Rapid Growth.

delivery vans. It even happens to service businesses and contracting businesses.

There are rare exceptions to this rule. The emphasis must be on the word *rare*. Don't kid yourself into thinking you are so lucky. If it turns out that way, just be grateful—and humble. Even for the rare exceptions the world keeps changing.

In the forecasts we have been making in this chapter and in Chapter 35 we have repeatedly come up with overdrafts at the bank. The banker won't let us do that in practice. Somehow we have to arrange financing in advance to cover those anticipated overdrafts. The last thing your friendly banker wants is surprises. If you go rushing in one morning saying, "I need $20,000 to meet the payroll this afternoon," you are likely to feel as if you were talking to the statue in the Lincoln Memorial in Washington, D.C.

The overdrafts in the forecasts are probably the most important bit of information from this exercise. They indicate how much financing must be obtained and when you have to have it. Without that financing

INTERCITY ASSEMBLY COMPANY, INC.
CASH FLOW FORECAST
ANTICIPATING GROWTH IN SALES

Month	1	2	3	4	5	6	7
RECEIPTS							
Sales Receipts	74,000*	77,000*	80,000	84,000	88,000		
Common Stock	—	157,000	—	—	—	—	—
Total Received	$74,000	234,000	80,000	84,000	88,000		
DISBURSEMENTS							
Direct Materials	40,000*	40,000	45,000				
Direct Labor...............	4,000	4,200	4,400				
Overhead	1,300	1,300	1,300	1,300	1,300	1,300	1,300
Manufacturing Equipment ...	—	162,000	—	—	—	—	—
Salaries	6,900	7,450	7,500	8,350	8,350	9,000	9,000
Rent	2,000	2,000	2,000	2,000	2,000	2,000	2,000
Insurance................	6,000	—	—	—	—	—	—
Office Equipment	—	3,000	—	—	—	—	—
Principal & Interest	—	—	—	—	—	—	—
Other G&A	2,800*	3,000	4,100	4,550	5,500	6,600	7,050
Advertising	9,000*	9,750	9,800	10,200	11,000	11,600	12,500
Brochures	—	5,400	—	—	—	—	—
Taxes	11,000*	—	—	8,637	—	—	
Total Disbursed	83,000	238,100	74,100				
Total Cash Flow	(9,000)	(4,100)	5,900				
Beginning Balance	1,100	(7,900)	(12,000)	(6,100)			
Ending Balance	$ (7,900)	(12,000)	(6,100)				

*From operations during prior periods.

FIGURE 36-5 Cash Flow Forecast Showing Which Numbers Change When Anticipating Rapid Growth.

MATERIALS INVENTORY SCHEDULE (IN UNITS)
ANTICIPATING GROWTH IN SALES

Month	1	2	3	4	5	6	7
Beginning Inventory	43,500	43,500	46,500				
– Shipments (Out)	40,000	42,000	44,000				
+ Purchases (Received)	40,000	45,000					
Ending Inventory	43,500	46,500					
Cash Disbursements	$40,000*	40,000	45,000				

*Due to a transaction of a prior period.

FIGURE 36-6 Materials Inventory Schedule Showing Which Numbers Change When Anticipating Rapid Growth.

INTERCITY ASSEMBLY COMPANY, INC.
INCOME STATEMENT FORECAST
WITH GROWTH IN SALES

Month	1	2	3	4	5	6	7
REVENUES							
Units Sold	40,000	42,000	44,000	50,000	55,000	60,000	65,000
Sales	$80,000	84,000	88,000	100,000	110,000	120,000	130,000
EXPENSES							
Direct Materials	40,000	42,000	44,000	50,000	55,000	60,000	65,000
Direct Labor..............	4,000	4,200	4,400	5,000	5,500	6,000	6,500
Overhead	4,000	4,000	4,000	4,000	4,000	4,000	4,000
Cost of Goods Sold	48,000	50,200	52,400	59,000	64,500	70,000	75,500
Gross Profit	32,000	33,800	35,600	41,000	45,500	50,000	54,500
General & Administrative							
Salaries	6,900	7,450	7,500	8,350	8,350	9,000	9,000
Rent	2,000	2,000	2,000	2,000	2,000	2,000	2,000
Insurance	500	500	500	500	500	500	500
Depreciation	170	170	170	170	170	170	170
Interest.................	0	0	0	0	0	0	0
Other G&A	3,000	4,100	4,550	5,500	6,600	7,050	7,850
Marketing							
Advertising.............	9,750	9,800	10,200	11,000	11,600	12,500	13,000
Brochures	450	450	450	450	450	450	450
Total Expense	70,770	74,670	77,770	86,970	94,170	101,670	108,470
Taxable Income	9,230	9,330	10,230	13,030	15,830	18,330	21,530
Income Taxes	2,769	2,799	3,069	3,909	4,749	5,499	6,459
Net Profit	$ 6,461	6,531	7,161	9,121	11,081	12,831	15,071

FIGURE 36-7 The Completed Income Statement Forecast Resulting from More Rapid Growth in Sales.

the course of action portrayed in the forecasts cannot be initiated. To take action that will lead you to a position where you can't cover the payroll check, or the rent check, or the payment due at the bank, is tantamount to corporate suicide.

In the original example, Intercity had to find short-term loans at the bank, sell some additional stock, or make arrangements to pay somebody later. A $12,000 loan in month 1 could have been paid off in month 6. Of course, a new loan of at least $1,244 would be needed in month 7. In the changed forecast with those greater profits, that $12,000 loan would not have been enough in month 4. An additional loan of $5,000 would have been needed to get through month 7.

All too many owner-managers "charge up the hill" building sales and profits without understanding this phenomenon. Time after time the authors have met people who tell the story, "I've had three businesses, and in each one the month I went broke I had record sales." What usually happens in practice is that the company writes the checks when it receives checks. Looking at Figure 36-8, the company would be

INTERCITY ASSEMBLY COMPANY, INC.
CASH FLOW FORECAST
WITH GROWTH IN SALES

Month	1	2	3	4	5	6	7
RECEIPTS							
Sales Receipts	74,000*	77,000*	80,000	84,000	88,000	100,000	110,000
Common Stock	—	157,000	—	—	—	—	—
Total Received	$74,000	234,000	80,000	84,000	88,000	100,000	110,000
DISBURSEMENTS							
Direct Materials	40,000*	40,000	45,000	50,000	55,000	60,000	65,000
Direct Labor	4,000	4,200	4,400	5,000	5,500	6,000	6,500
Overhead	1,300	1,300	1,300	1,300	1,300	1,300	1,300
Manufacturing Equipment . . .	—	162,000	—	—	—	—	—
Salaries	6,900	7,450	7,500	8,350	8,350	9,000	9,000
Rent	2,000	2,000	2,000	2,000	2,000	2,000	2,000
Insurance	6,000	—	—	—	—	—	—
Office Equipment	—	3,000	—	—	—	—	—
Principal & Interest	—	—	—	—	—	—	—
Other G&A	2,800*	3,000	4,100	4,550	5,500	6,600	7,050
Advertising	9,000*	9,750	9,800	10,200	11,000	11,600	12,500
Brochures	—	5,400	—	—	—	—	—
Taxes	11,000*	—	—	8,637	—	—	14,157
Total Disbursed	83,000	238,100	74,100	90,037	88,650	96,500	117,507
Total Cash Flow	(9,000)	(4,100)	5,900	(6,037)	(650)	3,500	(7,507)
Beginning Balance	1,100	(7,900)	(12,000)	(6,100)	(12,137)	(12,787)	(9,287)
Ending Balance	$ (7,900)	(12,000)	(6,100)	(12,137)	(12,787)	(9,287)	(16,794)

*From operations during prior periods

FIGURE 36-8 The Completed Cash Flow Forecast Resulting from More Rapid Growth in Sales.

MATERIALS INVENTORY SCHEDULE (IN UNITS)
WITH GROWTH IN SALES

Month	1	2	3	4	5	6	7
Beginning Inventory	43,500	43,500	46,500	52,500	57,500	62,500	67,500
- Shipments (Out)	40,000	42,000	44,000	50,000	55,000	60,000	65,000
+ Purchases (Received)	40,000	45,000	50,000	55,000	60,000	65,000	70,000
Ending Inventory	43,500	46,500	52,500	57,500	62,500	67,500	72,500
Cash Disbursements	$40,000*	40,000	45,000	50,000	55,000	60,000	65,000

*Due to a transaction of a prior period

FIGURE 36-9 The Completed Materials Inventory Schedule Resulting from More Rapid Growth in Sales.

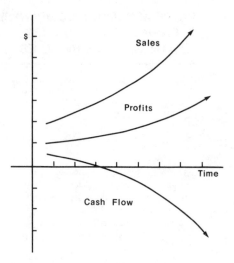

FIGURE 36-10 Typical Relationships Among Sales, Profits, and Cash Flow
Resulting from Rapid Growth.

late in paying $7,900 of its bills in month 1 and $12,000 of its bills in
month 2. In this example the late payments may be manageable, but
month 7 may be a problem.

In month 7, $32,957 is needed for payroll, income taxes, and
rent. That materials supplier said the terms are "thirty days and not
thirty-one days." The materials check is for $65,000. If Intercity can't
delay any of those checks, it has two line items left to work with—Eon,
the free-lance advertising agent, and that group of things called Other
G&A. They total $19,550.

You might observe that if the company just stretches the payments a little it will be late paying $16,794 of the bills in month 7. Maybe
you can live with that, at least for a little while. But look at the trend! In
both examples the net cash flow for the seven months is negative—out of
the bank. In the second example it is happening faster. If this growth
trend continues, the late payments will get later and bigger. In time some
of the suppliers will begin to complain. Later they will get forceful.
Eventually they will stop supplying.

Meanwhile Intercity has all the signs of success, and the local
Daimler-Benz dealer will be tempting the owner-manager with an SL-
450, the yacht shop has an irresistible deal on a thirty-two foot sloop, and
the trade association is holding its annual meeting in Honolulu. The
owner-manager is being courted by the Chamber of Commerce and the
Lions Club as an active participant in their current fund-raising events.
The company is asked to buy a table for ten at the political party's honors
banquet. And the church needs an able businessperson to be its treasurer. What is an entrepreneur to do?

If Intercity is going to be around next year its owner-manager

258

must face the facts. Growth consumes cash. If the car is going to be purchased, then the company can't grow that fast.

Have you ever thought about all those public companies that trade their stock on the American Stock Exchange or in the over-the-counter market? How many give their stockholders dividends? They didn't list their stock to be traded publicly to distribute cash. They registered and listed their stock so they would have access to the public for financing. They are publicly traded to obtain cash, not distribute it.

Growth has to be financed. The owner-manager can obtain financing from several sources—bank loans, investment in the business by investors, or the owner-manager's personal savings. In each case the cash comes from *somebody's* savings. Over a long period you can repay these sources for the use of their cash, but, in general, not while the business is growing, because growth consumes cash.

We all have an instinctive wish that we could find some formula or recipe to tell us how fast we can grow without having a problem at the bank. Unfortunately, there is no simple guideline. Each business has its own distinctive characteristics, which alter its ability to grow using only internally generated cash. If there were a rule that worked for one business, it would not work for another. There is also the problem of changing conditions in the marketplace and the economy. A rule, if there were one, for any particular business would have to change with these changing conditions.

There is only one way to calculate how fast you can grow with the financing available to you. That is, make the kind of forecasts we have just completed. The whole process begins with a best guess of what the sales will be. If the end result shows trouble down at the bank, reforecast using a different best guess of what the sales will be. It won't take·more than two or three tries to come up with the best strategy to fit your means.

This process of assuming some starting point, calculating the result, assuming another starting point, and recalculating the result is called an *iteration process*. It may seem like a lot of work, but as you can see from the example in this chapter, changing the numbers is not the big problem. Creating the array of numbers in the first place is what consumes the time. But that is the only way you can know where you are going, how you are going to get there, and how you will like it when you arrive.

37

The Record-Keeping Process

An owner-manager who cannot read and interpret the financial reports describing the condition of the business is like a football coach who is unable to watch the game. The coach can call plays and change players, but the outcome of the game depends on chance.

There is no need for an owner-manager to study accounting—that is a separate and distinct profession. You don't need to know how to change the oil to drive a car. On the other hand, you do need to know that the oil should be changed and when it should be changed. To maintain a car in running condition the owner-driver needs to know some auto mechanic language. Likewise, the business owner-manager needs to know some accountant language. For both the driver and the manager it helps to know more rather than less, although in neither case is it necessary to know more than enough to communicate intelligently.

Unfortunately, entrepreneurs and owner-managers do not come from any particular slice of the population that might be exposed to the language of business either through educational or vocational interest. Entrepreneurs may have the full spectrum of backgrounds and experiences. Only some will have the aptitudes that provide a facility with numbers or even a tolerance for discussions involving numbers. But numbers are the language of business. They are fourth-grade arithmetic numbers, not calculus, but numbers nonetheless.

The result of this broad array of aptitudes is that all too many owner-managers don't want even to try to understand the record-keeping system in business. Worse yet, the people who do understand the system have developed a very insular language of their own, unintelligible to most novitiates without serious study and prolonged effort. That is most unfortunate, because the record-keeping system in business is really quite simple. Keeping the record is tedious and can be very involved, but understanding how it works is within the grasp of everyone who has learned to add and subtract.

A corporation is a legal person. A proprietorship or partnership is like that legal person. It can buy, sell, borrow, lend, or own property. But the legal person is not a real person. It buys from, sells to, borrows from, and lends to people. In the end, however, it represents the people who own it. One of the major problems for small-business owner-managers is that they all too often neglect to separate their legal person from themselves.

THREE STEPS TO THE ACCOUNTING PROCESS

Step one is to bring all the information about changes in the property owned by the business to one central location.[1] That information is almost always on a little piece of paper. To ensure that it is included in the records it should *always* be on paper. Examples of the pieces of paper are invoices, bills, checks, payroll time cards, and contracts.

Step two is to put the information into a form that makes it easy to get to. It is hard to use the information when it is in a pile of paper. The little pieces of paper come in many sizes and shapes. It is not unusual to find that you have the fourth carbon copy and can hardly read it. This step is the process of taking the information from those little pieces of paper and making a readable, chronological list of the things that have happened to change the property owned by the business.

Step three is to rearrange the chronological list into clusters of information that give management answers to its questions. For instance, management would like to separate out all the things that affected the equipment owned by the business. Or the owner-manager might like to know what things have happened that affect the cash in the bank.

DOUBLE-ENTRY ACCOUNTING

To record this information in an orderly system the record keepers go back to the reservoir concept of the gas tank and the cookie jar. What the business owns is what was put in minus what was taken out. In ancient civilizations they kept this record on a tablet with a line drawn down the middle. Increases in the property were recorded on the left side and decreases on the right side of the vertical line. We use the same system today, and at any time we can add up the increases and subtract the decreases to find the balance left in the business.

This kind of record would be sufficient if everything the business owned belonged to one owner, like the king or the tribal chief or the head of the family. It is even sufficient if there are several owners, as in today's corporation. But a problem arose when some enterprising entrepreneur introduced the concept of credit. And that concept was not uncommon even in biblical times. The problem is that lenders want to retain a claim against the borrower until they are paid back.

261

Credit introduced the need to record how much of the business's property is subject to claims by creditors and how much belongs to the owners free and clear. Obviously, the sum total of the property to which the creditors have a claim and the property to which the owners have a claim is everything the business owns. This concept can be stated as an equation.

The total property owned by the business
equals
The portion of the property to which creditors have a right
plus
The portion of the property to which the owners have a right

An equation with that many words is awkward. It can be simplified if we give short names to its three parts. The generally accepted name for the property of the business is *assets*. The name given the portion of the property to which the creditors have a right is *liabilities*. For the portion of the property to which the owners have a right, the name is *capital*. Using these names we can write the fundamental relationship in the accounting process

Assets = Liabilities + Capital

Languages often use the same word to mean several things. For instance, in the English language, *bear* may be a large and ferocious animal, a small cuddly animal or toy, a stock market that is decreasing in value, or the act of carrying something. Likewise, the words in this fundamental relationship sometimes have several meanings. A troublesome one is the many uses of the word *capital*. Economists and political theoreticians have attached quite different meanings to the word. In the record-keeping system in business it is rather important to remember the meaning of the word as used in the context of the accounting process—*capital* is the portion of a business's property that the owners can claim as their own, free and clear.

About 700 years ago the record keepers in northern Italy recognized a very clever possibility for putting these records into one unified system. They observed that every time there is an increase in the assets there is an equal increase in either the liabilities or the capital or some combination of increases in both liabilities and capital. Likewise, a decrease in assets results in an equal decrease in the liabilities plus capital.

Those tablets with the vertical line provided the clue to such a system. By reversing the increase-decrease sides of the liabilities and capital tablets they could establish the rule that, for every left-side entry there has to be an equal right-side entry.

The result of this system is that it made it easy to check the work. If for every left-side entry there is an equal right-side entry, then at any time you can stop the process, add all the left sides, then add all the right sides, and, if the work has been done correctly, the sums will be equal. Notice that the only arithmetic you need to know to keep the records by this system is addition. Any youngster bright enough to learn how to read and write could handle addition.

The convention that evolved is shown in Figure 37-1. This system of record keeping was first described in a book by Luca Paciolo, published in Venice in 1494; he said, this is the way records have been kept by successful businesses for the past 200 years.[2] You may be surprised to hear that this is exactly the way the records are kept today.

To understand how this system is used it helps to recognize, first of all, that everything that happens in a business that might affect its property consists of a transaction, the giving up of one thing to get another. There are two parts to every transaction. This fits in exactly with the concept of left-side and right-side entries. Every transaction is recorded with a left-side and a right-side entry.

Because every transaction has two parts, one on the left and one on the right side of a vertical line, it is customary to make the chronological listing of transactions, Step 2 in the process, on a form that has a vertical line. The form might also contain a date and description of the transaction. Such a form is shown in Figure 37-2. A name frequently used to identify this form is *the book of original entry*. It may be only a page in a book or it may be just a sheet of paper, but through the centuries it has been treated with the respect of a book.

Having the information in this form permits a manager to ask how many transactions have occurred, but that isn't the kind of question usually asked. The owner-manager wants to know what happened to cash, equipment, sales, and other specific categories of transactions. To answer these questions the chronological listing can be reorganized into clusters of pertinent information. For instance, all the entries in the book of original entry that involve cash may be listed together. Some will be on the left side and some on the right side of the vertical line.

Because management might like to ask about each kind of entry it would be well to cluster each in the reorganized form. Some of the clusters might be *cash, accounts receivable* (what others owe us), *accounts payable* (what we owe others), and *notes payable* (what we owe

FIGURE 37-1 Key Relationships in the Accounting Process.

ASSETS		=	LIABILITIES		+	CAPITAL	
(Increase)	(Decrease)		(Decrease)	(Increase)		(Decrease)	(Increase)
+	–		–	+		–	+
L	R		L	R		L	R

Sum of L's = Sum of R's

the bank). We observe that some of these items are property of the business, assets, and others are claims against the business by creditors, liabilities. It the clusters were arranged in columns under those headings, the display would look like the fundamental relationship in Figure 37-1 in its detailed form.

We would have to add capital, of course. Under capital there are two major categories. First is the property contributed by the owners for use by the business. This is usually in the form of cash paid in return for stock or other evidence of ownership. In a corporation it is usually called *common stock*. In a proprietorship or partnership is it usually called *paid-in-capital*. Second under capital, are the owners' rights generated by the successful operations of the business. They are the cumulative profit minus any dividends or other withdrawals by the owners. A generally accepted name for them is *retained earnings*, a summary of what the business has earned and contributed to its own support.

Revenue increases retained earnings. Expense decreases retained earnings. Because increases in capital are recorded on the right side of the vertical line, revenues should be recorded on the right side under retained earnings. Expenses should then be recorded on the left side of that line.

If such a form were used to display the clusters of information of interest to management it would look like that in Figure 37-3. The categories of assets shown are cash, accounts receivable, and equipment. Your business will have many more categories. The same is true for the clusters under liabilities. The categories under capital are sufficient for many businesses, although you may want to see even more detail than shown on this form.

With the information in this form, it is possible to stop the process at any time and ask what is the status. You might ask, for any category, how much has it increased, how much has it decreased, what is the balance in the category, the total increases minus the total decreases. You might ask for the balance in every category. In the accounting process the categories are called *accounts*. If you found the balance in every account and then made an orderly listing of the balances on a clean sheet of paper, what would you call that sheet? The balance sheet, of course.

The *balance sheet* is the summary report of the accounting process. The form in Figure 37-4 is the result of making an orderly list of the balances from Figure 37-3. The actions of management resulting in little pieces of paper find their way into the book of original entry, into the reorganized clusters of information, and finally onto the balance sheet.

Managers are creating the story to be reported. Their actions in the everyday course of business determine what the record will say. The record keepers will report it after the fact, so long as they are made aware of what happened. The owner-manager who is aware of how daily activity ends up on the financial reports can visualize the result and choose actions to paint the desired picture.[3] That manager will recognize that a record of every action is required if it is to be in the final picture. The tedium of documenting everything that happens becomes less a chore imposed by the accounting people and more a brush stroke by the master painter, the manager.

SAMPLE TRANSACTIONS

The best way to understand this record-keeping system is to work through a few transactions.[4] The following five transactions illustrate a variety of the things that happen in business. They are: exchanging something for cash, selling on credit, buying for cash, buying on credit and, finally, using up something that requires neither cash nor credit. These transactions may be entered in the book of original entry in Figure 37-2.

BOOK OF ORIGINAL ENTRY

DATE	DESCRIPTION	LEFT SIDE	RIGHT SIDE
(1) a	Cash	$5,000	
(1) b	Common Stock		$5,000
(2) a			
(2) b			
(3) a			
(3) b			
(4) a			
(4) b			
(5) a			
(5) b			

FIGURE 37-2 Form of the Book of Original Entry, The Starting Point of the Record-Keeping Process.

ASSETS	LIABILITIES	CAPITAL	
CASH	ACCOUNTS	COMMON	
	PAYABLE	STOCK	
5,000		(PAID-IN	
		CAPITAL)	
ACCOUNTS	NOTES		5,000
RECEIVABLE	PAYABLE		
		RETAINED	
		EARNINGS	
EQUIPMENT		EXPENSE	REVENUE
ACCUMULATED			
DEPRECIATION			

FIGURE 37-3 Form for Organizing Original Entries into Clusters of Interest to Management.

1. Issuing Common Stock for Cash. The business issues $5,000 worth of its common stock in exchange for cash. Cash is property of the business, an asset. Receiving cash means the cash of the business increases.

Cash is an asset. According to the rule shown in Figure 37-1, increases in an asset are recorded on the left side of the vertical line. The record should show that cash, recorded on the left side of the vertical line, increases by $5,000, (1)a.

The other half of the transaction was the business issuing common stock for $5,000. Common stock represents owners' rights to a portion of the property of the business, capital. Do the owners' rights increase or decrease as a result of this transaction? They increase. Common stock is capital. Increases in capital are recorded on the right side of the vertical line. The record should show that common stock, recorded on the right side of the vertical line, increased by $5,000, (1)b.

It took two entries to record this transaction. This is true for all transactions. They require a double entry; hence the name double-entry accounting to describe this record-keeping system.

THE BALANCE SHEET

ASSETS	
CASH	
ACCOUNTS RECEIVABLE	
EQUIPMENT, LESS	
ACCUMULATED DEPRECIATION	
TOTAL ASSETS	
LIABILITIES	
ACCOUNTS PAYABLE	
NOTES PAYABLE	
TOTAL LIABILITIES	
CAPITAL	
COMMON STOCK	
RETAINED EARNINGS	
TOTAL CAPITAL	
TOTAL LIABILITIES PLUS CAPITAL	

FIGURE 37-4 Form of a Balance Sheet.

2. Making a Sale on Credit. The business sells some of its products or service to a customer and mails an invoice to that customer for $400. What are the two parts of this transaction? A sale was made. That is one part. What did the business receive in return? Not cash. The business mailed an invoice. What the business received was a promise by the customer to pay later, an account receivable. It is property of the business. It is not quite as good as cash, but almost. Being property of the business, it is an asset.

In this transaction, did the accounts receivable increase or decrease? It would appear that we added something to the accounts receivable held by the business. Accounts receivable is an asset. Increases in assets are recorded on the left. The record should show that accounts receivable, recorded on the left side of the vertical line, increased by $400, (2)a.

The other half of the transaction was the sale. Sales are revenues. If you examine the various accounts in Figure 37-3, revenues show up as a right-side entry under retained earnings. The other half of this transaction should then show that retained earnings, recorded on the right side of the vertical line, increased by $400, (2)b. That completes another double entry.

3. Making a Cash Purchase. Suppose the business needs something to decorate the reception area, like flowers. Someone is given a company check to go to the flower shop and purchase $30 worth of flowers. One side of the transaction is clearly the business giving up some of its cash. The other side is receiving something that is used up in the daily operations of the business. Things "used up" in the operation of the business are called expenses.

Figure 37-3 indicates that expenses are recorded on the left side of retained earnings, a capital account. Thus, the record should show that retained earnings, recorded on the left side, decreased by $30, (3)a.

Since cash was used, it was taken from the property of the business. The cash owned by the business decreased. Cash is an asset. A decrease in an asset is recorded on the right side of the vertical line. The record should show that cash, recorded on the right side, decreased by $30, (3)b. Another double entry is thus completed.

4. Acquiring Equipment on Credit. The business purchased $2,400 worth of new equipment. The supplier sent an invoice. The business will pay later.

The new equipment is property. Because the business purchased it, the total property of the business increased, that is, the assets increased. Increases in assets are recorded on the left side of the vertical line. The record should show the equipment, recorded on the left side, increased by $2,400, (4)a.

The other half of the transaction is an obligation on the part of the business to pay out $2,400. It is a promise to pay, an account payable. It represents the creditor's claim against some of the property of the business, in this case the new equipment, until it is paid for. This is precisely what is meant by liabilities.

Does the accounts payable account increase or decrease as a result of this transaction? Hasn't the business just added to its promises to pay? Accounts payable is a liability. Increases in liabilities are recorded on the right side of the vertical line. The record should show the accounts payable increased by $2,400, (4)b. That completes still another double entry.

5. Depreciation. As time passes, the new equipment will be used up, a little at a time. The business manager estimates that in normal usage this will amount to $100 per month. We would like to record the using up of this equipment, depreciation, for the first month.

So far we have not mentioned an account called depreciation in Figure 37-3. But clearly additions to equipment are recorded on the left side of the equipment account. Why not show subtractions from the equipment by recording on the right side of the equipment account? That would be reasonable, but there is another question managers would like answered. That is, "How old is the equipment?" They might phrase it, "How much of the equipment has been used up, depreciated?" Answering that management question suggests keeping track of depreciation separately from the equipment account.

To keep track of depreciation separately, it would make sense to establish a separate account beneath the equipment account to keep up with the accumulation of depreciation. The account could be called accumulated depreciation. Increases from the purchase of new equipment could be recorded on the left side of the equipment account, and decreases in the equipment from depreciation could be recorded on the right side of the accumulated depreciation account.

Adding this account to Figure 37-3 will provide an additional balance each time we calculate balances. The orderly list of balances in Figure 37-4 will have an additional item called *less Accumulated Depreciation*. The net value of the equipment as recorded in the books of the business will be listed as the difference between these. It is normal to find equipment (at cost) less accumulated depreciation on a balance sheet.

The record should show the accumulated depreciation, listed on the right side, increased by $100, (5)b. That takes care of one-half of the transaction. The other half of this transaction is the "using up" of something in the operation of the business, an expense, recorded on the left side of retained earnings. The other half of this transaction would be shown as a decrease in retained earnings or $100, (5)a. And that completes the double entry.

Step 3 in the accounting process is to take the information from the book of original entry and recast it in clusters of interest to management. Having completed Figure 37-2 and having the form of Figure 37-3, it is relatively easy to transfer the information from the chronological listing to the small clusters that provide answers to management questions.

Because there are so many items to be transferred, it is wise to check off each number as it is recorded. Going down the list, we can transfer the items. Cash, $5,000 on the left, may be recorded under the cash account in Figure 37-3. It should be recorded on the left side of the vertical line. Having completed this recording you can place a check mark next to the item in Figure 37-2. Then common stock, $5,000 on the right, may be recorded under the common stock account. It should be placed on the right side of the vertical line. When this recording is made you can check off that item in Figure 37-2. This process of transferring the numbers can be continued right on down the list.

PROFESSIONAL TERMINOLOGY

As you transfer these numbers, you will notice something the record keepers noticed a long time ago. If there were very many of these transactions, this could become quite a job. It is so much of a job, in fact, that they have given it a special name. Moving the numbers from Figure 37-2 to Figure 37-3 is what they call *posting*. They post from a page in one book to a page in another book.

Because record keepers have to refer to these books frequently, they have given them names. The book represented by Figure 37-2 is called the *Journal*. The book represented by Figure 37-3 is called the *ledger*. They post from the journal to the ledger.

The journal and the ledger shown are very simplified to help you understand how they fit together. When you see the actual accounting books, it may take some effort to relate the real books to these examples. This is not because they are different, it is because the record keepers expand and reorganize the books to make their work easier.

For instance, the journal might be broken into two or more journals. It is not uncommon to find that there are so many cash transactions that a separate book is kept for cash transactions. This book would be referred to as the *cash journal*. The same is true for sales. There may be so many entries under sales that they keep a separate *sales journal*. They may also have an *expense journal* and one they call the *General Journal*.

As you can see from this exercise, maintaining the journals can be quite time consuming. One way people reduce the work is to keep separate journals for accounts that involve many transactions, obtain totals for each account in the various journals, and only post the total. When they transfer from the journals to the ledger and find the balances, they recombine the records just as you have seen them in this example.

When all of the numbers in the journal have been posted to the ledger, you can stop recording for the moment. The balance in each account can be determined by subtracting the decreases from the increases. It would be normal to find that the balance is on the side of the account where increases are recorded. That being the case, you would expect to find the balance in asset accounts to be on the left side and the balance in the liabilities and capital accounts to be on the right. There is nothing wrong with a balance on the side where decreases are recorded. It is a negative balance.

The Retained Earnings account contains three numbers: $400 on the right and both $30 and $100 on the left. This is the same as a $400 increase minus $130 decrease, for a net increase of $270. This is shown in a balance of $270 on the right. You can perform this arithmetic for each of the accounts in the ledger, Figure 37-3.

There is something else to be noted at this point. In the example there was no balance from previous transactions. This was done to simplify the illustration. Normally, there would have been a balance from a prior period, from the last time balances were taken. Then, when adding and subtracting, the previous balances would be included.

For instance, in the Retained Earnings account example, there might have been a previous balance of $1,000 on the right side. Then in taking a new balance, there would have been $1,000 and $400 on the right, and $30 and $100 on the left. That would be $1,400 on the right and

$130 on the left, or a balance of $1,270 on the right. Thus the balance is the position of the account as of a point in time, taking into consideration every transaction that has ever been recorded in the account since the formation of the business, even if the business is a hundred years old.

If you will complete the balances, you can make an orderly listing in Figure 37-4. The balance in the cash account will be placed opposite the title *cash*. The balance in the accounts receivable account will be placed opposite the title *accounts receivable*. All the balances can be transferred in this fashion.

Don't forget that when $2,400 is recorded next to the word *equipment* and $100 next to *accumulated depreciation*, leave room to record the difference, equipment minus accumulated depreciation, at the right side of the balance sheet in a column under the numbers opposite cash and accounts receivable.

It is customary to record the total assets, total liabilities, total capital, and total liabilities plus capital. If you have filled in the numbers following the discussion this far you have created a balance sheet. Having done this, total assets should equal total liabilities plus capital. Your balance sheet should look like Figure 37-7. Figures 37-5 and 37-6 show the completed journal and ledger for this example.

THE COMPLETED JOURNAL

DATE	DESCRIPTION	LEFT SIDE	RIGHT SIDE
(1) a	Cash	$5,000	
(1) b	Common Stock		$5,000
(2) a	Accounts Receivable	400	
(2) b	Retained Earnings		400
(3) a	Retained Earnings	30	
(3) b	Cash		30
(4) a	Equipment	2,400	
(4) b	Accounts Payable		2,400
(5) a	Retained Earnings	100	
(5) b	Accumulated Depreciation		100

FIGURE 37-5 The Completed Book of Original Entry, or Journal.

ASSETS		LIABILITIES		CAPITAL	
CASH		ACCOUNTS PAYABLE		COMMON STOCK (PAID-IN CAPITAL)	
5,000	30				
			2,400		
ACCOUNTS RECEIVABLE		NOTES PAYABLE			5,000
				RETAINED EARNINGS	
400					
EQUIPMENT				EXPENSE	REVENUE
2,400				30	400
				100	
ACCUMULATED DEPRECIATION					
	100				

FIGURE 37-6 The Completed Ledger.

There are other presentations of financial information available from these records. One question managers may ask regards how things changed in any individual account during a given period of time. For instance, a manager might ask how the cash account changed during the period of the transaction recorded in the example. What flowed into and what flowed out of the cash account during this period?

If you were to make an orderly listing on a separate sheet of paper of what flowed into and what flowed out of the cash account during this period, what would you be likely to call that report? It doesn't take much imagination to come up with the title, the *cash flow report* or the *cash flow statement*. This would, of course, portray cash flow for a time period already completed and reported. A cash flow forecast would portray what this report might look like for a future period.

Similar reports could be prepared for each of the accounts. One of considerable interest to managers and owners, as well as bankers and analysts, is the retained earnings account. If you were to make an orderly listing on a separate sheet of paper of what flowed into and what flowed out of the retained earnings account during a given period of time, what might you call that report? To be consistent with the cash flow example,

THE COMPLETED BALANCE SHEET

ASSETS		
CASH		$4,970
ACCOUNTS RECEIVABLE		400
EQUIPMENT, LESS	2,400	
ACCUMULATED DEPRECIATION	100	2,300
TOTAL ASSETS		7,670
LIABILITIES		
ACCOUNTS PAYABLE		2,400
NOTES PAYABLE		0
TOTAL LIABILITIES		2,400
CAPITAL		
COMMON STOCK		5,000
RETAINED EARNINGS		270
TOTAL CAPITAL		5,270
TOTAL LIABILITIES PLUS CAPITAL		$7,670

FIGURE 37-7 The Completed Balance Sheet.

this might be called the *retained earnings flow statement*. The names usually given to it are *income statement, profit and loss statement,* or *operating statement.*

The balance in the cash account does not equal the balance in the retained earnings account. Also, the cash flow does not equal the retained earnings flow, or what is usually called profit. The flow into or out of the retained earnings account is the result of double entries, only one of which is in the retained earnings account. The other of these entries may be recorded in almost any asset , liability or capital account.

The flow into or out of the cash account is also the result of double entries, only one of which is in the cash account. The other one of these entries may be recorded in almost any account except accumulated depreciation. These two observations make it evident that cash flow is not likely to equal retained earnings flow, the profit, except by some unusual coincidence. In the normal course of business, profit does not equal cash flow.

Throughout this example we have avoided the use of technical words from the accounting profession. It has been our intent to lead you through the process without these technical terms and from the man-

273

ager's perspective. As you now know, you can prepare a balance sheet, a cash flow statement, and an income statement, even though you may have known almost nothing about the subject at the outset.

Having done this exercise and completed the forms, take a moment to reflect on some words you understand precisely as they are used in the accounting process. For instance, words like *assets*, *liabilities*, *capital*, *journal*, *ledger*, *accounts receivable*, *accounts payable*, *paid-in capital*, *retained earnings*, and *accumulated depreciation*. And there is still more.

DEBITS AND CREDITS

The method of recording increases and decreases always involves the left side or the right side of a vertical line. Sometimes increases are on the left and sometimes they are on the right. The words, *left* and *right*, denote position. But sometimes these two parts of the accounts may be physically separated in the books for convenience and to reduce the work. Right side and left side have very specific meanings when used in the accounting process. Having such specific meanings, they deserve special names. The origin of the names given them dates back to the Middle Ages. They are *debit* and *credit*.

Debit refers to the left side of the vertical line in the record-keeping system in business. *Credit* refers to the right side of the vertical line. Debit does not mean increase or decrease. It could mean either one, depending on whether it is a debit in assets, or a debit in the liabilities or capital. To debit is to increase in the assets. In the liabilities or in capital, to debit is to decrease.

A source of confusion for those who are not versed in accounting is the use of these two words when referring to a transaction between two businesses or between a business and an individual. To say that an account has been debited without also saying in whose records it has been debited does not describe what has taken place. For instance, between a customer and a supplier, what is owed *by* one is owed *to* the other. What is an account payable to one is an account receivable to the other. Debit in accounts payable means decrease, in accounts receivable it means increase.

There is one more thing to be said. We have named the left sides *debits* and the right sides *credits*. Instead of saying that the left sides equal the right sides, we can make the statement concisely, precisely, and simply: the debits equal the credits.

Reading
the Financial Report

Reading financial statements can be very enjoyable once you know how they are put together. Having completed the exercise in Chapter 37 you are in a position to experience that pleasure. Financial reports are not read like a book; rather they are like a crossword puzzle. They provide information that permits you to deduce other information. The fun in reading them is in looking for logical and consistent relationships.

The more you know about how a business conducts its affairs, about what its facilities look like, about how its suppliers and customers behave, and so on, the more you can read from the business's financial statements. We now know quite a bit about Intercity Assembly Company, Inc., and its business operations. We should be able to deduce a large amount about that company from its audited financial statements.

INTERCITY'S AUDITED FINANCIAL REPORT

Intercity Assembly Company decided to obtain an audited financial report at the end of the year we examined in previous chapters. In the example, month 1 was the month of January, the first month of the company's fourth year of operations. The audit was for the last six months of the fourth year, the six months ended December 31.

The company engaged a well known and reputable firm of accountants to prepare its year-end audit. The certified financial reports prepared by this firm, Swearbyit Company, are presented at the end of the chapter.[1] The first page, Figure 38-1, is the cover page identifying the report. The second page, Figure 38-2, is the first one containing information about the audit. It is the "opinion" page.

The opinion page contains a letter showing to whom the report is addressed. The letter says that the financial statements report fairly the position of Intercity in accordance with generally accepted accounting principles applied on a consistent basis. If the auditors had any doubt about the company, its record, or its financial condition, they would say so in this letter.

This letter, which is often overlooked by owner-managers but seldom by bankers, lenders, or sophisticated investors and creditors, can be very damaging if it is not a "clean" opinion. The example shown is a clean opinion from a very large and reputable accounting firm. Any deviation from this brief and concise statement can raise suspicions about the company.

A participant in one of our seminars showed us his financial statements and asked a question about his business. We, in our inevitable manner, looked first at the opinion letter. To our dismay it included statements like, "this information is incomplete," "we are unable to substantiate the accuracy of . . ." and, even worse, "this information should not be used by anyone other than the President." This participant, the president of a company, had never read the opinion. He was proudly passing out copies of his statements to bankers and creditors.

The first page of numbers in the report is the balance sheet shown in Figure 38-3. This one says, as of December 31, 19XX. As you can see, it lists assets, liabilities, and capital. Under *assets*, the first item is, as usual, the *cash*. The sum appears to be comfortable. At least there is some. Next is *accounts receivable*. We are familiar enough with this company to have some feeling about how long Intercity waits to collect for sales. If the company is still collecting its receipts from sales in sixty days, how big are the sales in the last couple of months? Is this consistent with what we know about the first seven months of this year? If $294,000 represents two months' sales, the monthly sales for the last two months must average about $147,000. In month 1 they were $80,000. In month 7, they were $110,000. It appears that sales continued to grow at a consistent rate throughout the year.

The next item is *inventory*. So far as we know Intercity has been paying $1 per unit received and operating under a policy of having enough on hand at the end of the month to satisfy next month's anticipated sales. Also, the company buys materials for $1 and sells the finished product for $2. If this inventory represents what will be shipped next month, plus some number less than 5,000 because the company buys in multiples of 5,000, can you deduce the anticipated sales for next month? Is that consistent with the sales deduced from the amount of accounts receivable? The purchases were probably 75,000 units at a dollar each. Sales next month look like at least 75,000 units, but not more than 78,500 units. That would put next month's sales at $150,000 to $157,000.

The next item is *supplies* (brochures). When did the company buy its supply of brochures? How did Intercity expect to use them up? Perhaps you will want to review the footnote on brochures in the profit forecasting example in Chapter 34. Would there be any brochures on hand on December 31, 19XX? When will the company buy the next supply?

Next is an item called *prepaid insurance*. What was Intercity's attitude about paying for insurance? Maybe you will want to review the footnote on insurance in the cash flow forecasting example in Chapter 35. When does Intercity pay for the insurance policy? Is it reasonable to assume that the insurance purchased in January is all used up on December 31, 19XX?

The next item is *equipment less accumulated depreciation*. If the bulk of the equipment has a useful life of five years and the company uses the straight-line method of depreciation, how old is it? Is the bulk of the equipment relatively new or relatively old?

Next come the *liabilities*. Under these the first item is *accounts payable (materials)*. What are the terms of payment likely to be for materials? What have they been in the example? What are the most common terms? If the accounts payable (materials) represents payments for materials on net thirty-day terms and we compare this to the inventory shown under assets, how much inventory is the company carrying in terms of months? What are next month's sales likely to be? It looks as though 75,000 units were received at $1 each in December. Knowing the policy on inventory, next month's sales should total about $150,000, and the company is carrying about one month's inventory.

The next item is *accounts payable (other)*. There is also an item called *accounts payable (advertising)*. How has Intercity been paying for advertising? What kind of terms does the company have with Eon? What percentage of sales have been spent on advertising? Does this accounts payable (advertising) seem reasonable? How many months' advertising does the company owe?

The accounts payable (other) must represent something besides materials and advertising. What else was purchased on credit? Look at example of the cash flow forecast, Figure 36-2. What is the name of the expense item to which this liability refers? It is an item that is obtained on credit. There is only one left unaccounted for on the cash flow forecast, the *other G&A*.

Next is *accrued taxes payable*. Would you say the company has been doing well during the last three months of the audited year? How does this liability compare with that of one year ago? (It is in the cash flow forecast.) What were the pretax profits, approximately, for the last quarter?

Now we come to *capital*. The first item is *common stock*. We know where $157,000 of that came from. Do you think any of the remainder came in more than a year ago? Did at least some of it have to come in more than a year ago? Could some of it have come in during the past five months? We don't know at this point whether any came in within the last five months.

Next is *retained earnings*. This is the cumulative profits less any dividends paid to the owners. How does that number compare with the number contributed by the sale of common stock? Does that number represent reasonable earnings from the four years the company has been operating?

Before moving on we might check the *current ratio*. It is sometimes called the *working capital ratio*. It is *current assets* divided by *current liabilities*. In this report it appears that the total liabilities are all current, that is, they are all due within the next twelve months. Is the ratio greater than one? Is it much greater than one? Does it look like a comfortable ratio? The *working capital* is *current assets* minus *current liabilities*: $381,299 − $121,007, or $260,292. The working capital ratio (or current ratio) is 3.15.

Just from this report alone, how do you feel about the condition of this company? Do you see any problems? Has the business continued operating in the same way it did in the examples in Chapters 34 and 35? Would you like to own this company?

The next page of numbers reports on the operations of the business during the six months ended December 31, 19XX, Figure 38-4. It is unusual to receive such a statement for six months. Usually it would be for the past twelve months. Apparently Swearbyit has prepared this special report for our analysis.

The first thing we observe is that the report is very abbreviated. Why would that be? Who gets this report? The opinion letter names some recipients. Who else might see it? Since the invention of the office copying machine, it is hard to know how many people will see this report.

The next thing that catches our eye is the bottom line, the *net profit*. How does that compare to the first line, the *sales*? What is the net profit as a percent of sales? What was the *net profit margin* for month 7 of the example in Chapter 34 (see Figure 36-1). Has it changed? No, in both cases it is just below 8 percent.

What are the average monthly sales during this period? How do they compare with the first seven months of the year? How do they compare with the sales for month 12 as deduced from the balance sheet? Is this consistent? Reasonable? Average sales would be $788,000 divided by six, or $131,333 per month. Because we know they were $110,000 in the first of these six months, is our estimate of about $150,000 in December–January reasonable?

Can you obtain the *gross profit margin*? How does that compare with the first seven months? Would you say that general and administrative and marketing expenses have been kept in line? *Gross profit* is *sales* minus *cost of goods sold*, $330,600, which is 41.9 percent of sales. What was it in month 7?

Do you see any problems in this report? Has the company continued to perform as in the example we examined earlier? Would you like to buy some of this company's stock?

These two statements, the balance sheet and the income statement, are the standard reports prepared by auditors. There will be additional information, such as footnotes and changes in financial resources, but the balance sheet and the income statement are the heart of the audited report.

To prepare the audited reports the auditors had access to the detailed records of the company. We might examine some of these. Figures 38-5 through 38-8 are internal financial reports from the company. Perhaps by examining these we can learn more about Intercity's operations and its financial condition.

The first report is a balance sheet as of June 30, 19XX. That is six months before the audited report. We can compare the two balance sheets. We see that cash improved. That's comforting. Accounts receivable grew a little, but the increase looks like the kind you would expect to support a higher level of sales. The same might be said of the inventory. These numbers come from the figures in the profit forecast and the cash flow forecast. You can check them yourself in Figures 36-1 and 36-2. Sales in months 5 and 6 total $206,000. All of that money is still uncollected. Ending inventory in month 6 is on the inventory schedule, Figure 36-3.

Prepaid insurance is $3,000 on June 30 and zero on December 31. How much did the annual policy cost? When did Intercity purchase it? Did the company pay cash in advance for the one-year policy?

The next item is equipment less accumulated depreciation. It appears that the company acquired $6,000 in new equipment during the six-month period.

Accounts payable (materials) is $55,000. We can find that number on the inventory schedule, Figure 36-3. The units received in month 6 are to be paid for in month 7. Accounts payable (other general and administrative) is $7,050. That number is shown as an expense in month 6 on the income statement forecast and as a check written in month 7 on the cash flow forecast. The advertising payables may be found in the same places. The tax payable is the sum of the monthly taxes accrued in months 4, 5, and 6. It shows up as a check in month 7 on the cash flow forecast.

Common stock has not increased. We know of one stock sale for $157,000. When was the other $19,000 worth of stock sold? Could it have been at any time during the twelve months covered by the audited report and the example in Chapters 34 and 35?

How much have the retained earnings increased in these six months? Retained earnings increase by the net profit minus any dividends or owner's withdrawals. Look at the income statement the auditors prepared for this six months' period and compare it with the change in retained earnings on the two balance sheets. Did Intercity pay out any dividends? Couldn't have, could it?

The next report, Figure 38-6, is a series of income statements, month by month, for the six months covered by the audited report. Does the performance appear to be different from the first seven months depicted in the exercise in Chapters 34 and 35? Are the trends in

279

revenues and the expenses reasonably smooth and consistent? Does anything show up in these reports that would change the conclusions drawn from the audited reports? No, nothing seems unusual or unexpected. The company appears to be consistently growing profitably in a nice, uniform, and conservative manner. The owner-manager seems to have resisted the temptation to make any expenditures on things like company cars, boats, and airplanes.

INTERCITY'S MISSING REPORTS

How many reports have we looked at? The auditors provided two. We had one balance sheet from the company. Now we have six income statements, one for each month, months 7 through 12. That is nine detailed, timely reports covering one six months' period of operations. And what is the message? Solid. Good. Reliable. Conservative. Growing profitably. No problems.

Before spending some time working on the examples in this book you might be content to stop right here. Having gotten this far into the subject matter, however, you might want to ask one more question.

The last report from the company records is the cash flow shown in Figure 38-7. The inventory schedule in Figure 38-8 was needed to prepare the cash flow statement. What do you find on the bottom line of the cash flow statement? Are there any months in which the company has overdrafts at the bank? What percentage of the six months show overdrafts? Are any of the overdrafts severe? Where could we have deduced this information from any of the nine detailed, timely reports that the company and auditors provided? This information slipped right through those other reports. Monthly balance sheets would have to be added to the list of reports to obtain this information. That is five more reports.

You might find it interesting to consider what the cash position would have been on quarterly reports. That would be months 3, 6, 9, and 12, as portrayed below. Would that have been frequent enough to portray this picture?

CASH BALANCES FROM QUARTERLY REPORTS

End of Month	3	6	9	12
Cash Balance	[$6,100]	$1,213	$4,556	$8,799

Quarterly balance sheets would have reported good cash balances in the last three quarters, with an apparent trend away from overdrafts. Because we have access to the monthly balances in the cash flow reports, we know that during the first six months of this year month 6 was the only month when there was cash in the bank. We also know that the worst overdraft was $12,000 in month 2. That is $6,000 worse than shown in the quarterly reports. During the last six months Intercity had overdrafts in three. The quarterly balance sheets would have reported the bank balances for three of the four months when there was cash in the bank during the whole year.

Clearly a business needs detailed, timely, and *frequent* financial reports. Annual, semiannual, and quarterly reports are not sufficient to provide an owner-manager with the critical information needed to keep the ship from drifting onto the shoals.

INTERCITY ASSEMBLY COMPANY, INC.

Audited Financial Statements

December 31, 19XX

SWEARBYIT COMPANY

CERTIFIED PUBLIC ACCOUNTANTS

FIGURE 38-1 Cover Page of an Audited Report for Intercity Assembly Company, Inc.

SWEARBYIT COMPANY [1]
CERTIFIED PUBLIC ACCOUNTANTS
DALLAS, TEXAS

To The Shareholders and Board of Directors
INTERCITY ASSEMBLY CO., INC.:

We have examined the balance sheet of INTERCITY ASSEMBLY CO.,
INC. (a Texas Corporation), as of December 31, 19XX, and the related
statements of income and financial position. Our examination was made
in accordance with generally accepted auditing standards, and accord-
ingly included such tests of the accounting records and such other
auditing procedures as we considered necessary in the circumstances.

In our opinion, the accompanying balance sheet and statements
of income and changes in financial position present fairly the financial
position of INTERCITY ASSEMBLY CO., INC. as of December 31, 19XX, in
conformity with generally accepted accounting principles applied on a
consistent basis during the periods.

SWEARBYIT COMPANY

Dallas, Texas
January 21, 19XX

FIGURE 38-2 Opinion Page, The First Page of an Audited Report.

INTERCITY ASSEMBLY CO., INC.
Balance Sheet as of
December 31, 19XX

_____

ASSETS

CURRENT:
Cash		$ 8,799
Accounts Receivable		294,000
Inventory (Materials)		78,500
Supplies (Brochures)		-
Prepaid Insurance		-
Total Current Assets		381,299

FIXED:
Capital Equipment	178,200	
Less Accumulated Depr.	37,560	140,640
Total Assets		521,939

LIABILITIES

CURRENT:
Accounts Payable (Materials)	75,000
Accounts Payable (Other)	13,000
Accounts Payable (Advertising)	18,100
Accrued Taxes Payable	14,907
Total Liabilities	121,007

CAPITAL

Common Stock	176,000
Retained Earnings	224,932
Total Capital	400,932
TOTAL LIABILITIES + CAPITAL	$ 521,939

_____

SWEARBYIT CO. CERTIFIED PUBLIC ACCOUNTANTS

FIGURE 38-3 Intercity Assembly Company, Inc., Audited Balance Sheet as of December 31, 19XX.

INTERCITY ASSEMBLY CO., INC.
Statement of Income
for the Six Months Ended December 31, 19XX

REVENUE $ 788,000

EXPENSE
    Cost of Goods Sold   457,400
    General & Administrative   140,720
    Marketing   100,000

        Total Expense   698,120

Income before Federal
    Income Tax   89,880

Federal Income Tax   26,964

NET PROFIT $ 62,916
                                            =========

SWEARBYIT CO. CERTIFIED PUBLIC ACCOUNTANTS

FIGURE 38-4 Intercity Assembly Company, Inc., Audited Statement of Income
for the Six Months Ended December 31, 19XX.

INTERCITY ASSEMBLY CO., INC.
Balance Sheet as of
June 30, 19XX

ASSETS

CURRENT:

Cash	$ 1,213
Accounts Receivable	206,000
Inventory (Materials)	57,500
Supplies (Brochures)	2,700
Prepaid Insurance	3,000
Total Current Assets	270,413

FIXED:

Capital Equipment	172,200	
Less Accumulated Depr.	19,940	152,260
Total Assets		422,673

LIABILITIES

CURRENT:

Accounts Payable (Materials)	55,000
Accounts Payable (Other)	7,050
Accounts Payable (Advertising)	12,500
Accrued Taxes Payable	10,107
Total Liabilities	84,657

CAPITAL

Common Stock	176,000
Retained Earnings	162,016
Total Capital	338,016
TOTAL LIABILITIES + CAPITAL	$ 422,673

UNAUDITED

FIGURE 38-5 Internal Report, Intercity Assembly Company, Inc., Balance Sheet as of June 30, 19XX.

Month	7	8	9	10	11	12
REVENUE						
(1) Units Shipped	55,000	59,000	64,000	69,000	72,000	75,000
(2) Sales	110,000	118,000	128,000	138,000	144,000	150,000
EXPENSE						
(3) Materials	55,000	59,000	64,000	69,000	72,000	75,000
(4) Labor	5,500	5,900	6,400	6,900	7,200	7,500
(5) Overhead	4,000	4,000	4,000	4,000	4,000	4,000
(6) Cost of Goods	64,500	68,900	74,400	79,900	83,200	86,500
(7) Gross Profit	45,500	49,100	53,600	58,100	60,800	63,500
(8) Salaries	9,000	9,700	9,700	10,400	10,400	11,300
(9) Rent	2,000	2,000	2,000	2,000	2,000	2,000
(10) Insurance	500	500	500	500	500	500
(11) Depreciation	170	220	220	270	270	270
(12) Other G&A	7,850	8,450	10,150	11,850	12,500	13,000
(13) Advertising	13,000	14,600	16,100	17,700	17,800	18,100
(14) Brochures	450	450	450	450	450	450
(15) Interest	–	–	–	–	–	–
(16) Total Expense	97,470	104,820	113,520	123,070	127,120	132,120
(17) Pre-Tax Profit	12,530	13,180	14,480	14,930	16,880	17,880
(18) Income Tax	3,759	3,954	4,344	4,479	5,064	5,364
(19) NET PROFIT	8,771	9,226	10,136	10,451	11,816	12,516

UNAUDITED

FIGURE 38-6 Internal Report, Intercity Assembly Company, Inc., Income
Statements for the Six Months Ending December 31, 19XX.

INTERNAL REPORT
INTERCITY ASSEMBLY CO., INC.
CASH FLOW STATEMENT

Month	7	8	9	10	11	12
RECEIPTS						
(1) Sales Receipts	100,000*	106,000*	110,000	118,000	128,000	138,000
(2) Other Receipts	–	–	–	–	–	–
DISBURSEMENTS						
(3) Materials	55,000*	60,000	65,000	65,000	75,000	75,000
(4) Labor	5,500	5,900	6,400	6,900	7,200	7,500
(5) Overhead	1,300	1,300	1,300	1,300	1,300	1,300
(6) Mfg. Equip.	–	–	–	–	–	–
(7) Salaries	9,000	9,700	9,700	10,400	10,400	11,300
(8) Rent	2,000	2,000	2,000	2,000	2,000	2,000
(9) Insurance	–	–	–	–	–	–
(10) Office Equip.	–	–	3,000	–	3,000	–
(11) Other G&A	7,050*	7,850	8,450	10,150	11,850	12,500
(12) Advertising	12,500*	13,000	14,600	16,100	17,700	17,800
(13) Brochures	–	–	–	–	–	–
(14) Prin. & Int.	–	–	–	–	–	–
(15) Income Tax	10,107	–	–	12,057	–	–
(16) Total Disbursed	102,457	99,750	110,450	123,907	128,450	127,400
(17) CASH FLOW	(2,457)	6,250	(450)	(5,907)	(450)	10,600
(18) Beginning Bal.	1,213	(1,244)	5,006	4,556	(1,351)	(1,801)
(19) ENDING BAL.	(1,244)	5,006	4,556	(1,351)	(1,801)	8,799

UNAUDITED

FIGURE 38-7 Internal Report, Intercity Assembly Company, Inc., Cash Flow
Statements for the Six Months Ending December 31, 19XX.

Month	7	8	9	10	11	12
(a) UNITS						
(b) Beginning Inv.	57,500	62,500	68,500	69,500	75,500	78,500
(c) - Ship	55,000	59,000	64,000	69,000	72,000	75,000
(d) + Receive	60,000	65,000	65,000	75,000	75,000	75,000
(e) Ending Inv.	62,500	68,500	69,500	75,500	78,500	78,500
(f) Write Check	$ 55,000*	60,000	65,000	65,000	75,000	75,000

_____

*Transaction of a prior period.

FIGURE 38-8 Internal Report, Intercity Assembly Company, Inc., Inventory
Schedule for the Six Months Ending December 31, 19XX.

39

Forecasting
Sales

In the preceding chapters the forecasts began with a best guess of how many units would be sold each month. *Price* times *units sold* is *sales*. Forecasting the number of units to be sold is *sales forecasting*. The plan begins with a sales forecast. This is the most uncertain part of business planning and is usually the most uncertain part of managing or operating a business. There is really no way to know what the sales will be. We have to wait until they have occurred and then find out what they were. But in the meantime all the planning and forecasting, budgeting and projecting are dependent on the rate at which sales materialize. It is essential that a "best estimate" be prepared.

The best estimate can be hedged by making several estimates. It is prudent at least to consider forecasting three levels of sales, that is, based on (1) the sales most likely to emerge, (2) the worst sales level imaginable, and (3) the most optimistic sales level. Then you can be prepared for any foreseeable contingency while working to achieve the most likely level of sales. Having chosen the sales most likely to emerge, that level becomes the *objective sales quota*.

A sales quota has some seemingly magical properties. They are the same properties that accompany crystal clear goals described in down-to-earth but precise terms. When the goals are clear and ever-present, the mind has a way of scheming continuously toward their achievement. The person with the characteristics described in Chapter 8 enjoys relating functions and things toward the achievement of goals. Almost everyone enjoys that experience when emotionally involved in the process. Successful entrepreneurs are a little better at it than most.

Once you have chosen a sales quota, the rest of the forecasting depends on digging up the data describing what will be needed to achieve the quota, what it will cost, and when it will have to be paid for. All this can be determined in great detail and with considerable accuracy in the near-term future. If only we knew what the sales were going to be, there would be small risk in business.

The sales forecast, then, is a crucial element in the planning

process and one that deserves a major portion of the time and energy
expended in forecasting. This may explain why the section of a business
plan describing the anticipated sales is usually more extensive than a
footnote. It reviews, in some depth, the market, the marketing, the
competition, and the potential for success in achieving the predicted
level of sales. It states clearly what the product is, who the customer is,
and what the channel of distribution conveying the product from the
business to the customer will be.

With the level of sales chosen for each month, it is possible to
describe what comes in and what goes out to achieve those sales. The
forecast of how the business will operate and what will be needed is
again a best estimate, although in the near term the value of these things
can be determined with some confidence. How it will operate depends
on the entrepreneur's fantasy of who will be employed, where they will
work, what tools and facilities they will need, and how this entrepreneur
will manage all the activities. Behind this fantasy and this best guess is
likely to be some logic, some reason to believe, some cause for confidence in the estimate. This reassuring background may be described in
footnotes supporting each number in the forecasts.

There is no "right way" to derive a sales forecast. There are many
ways and each entrepreneur may see, or be more comfortable with, a
different approach. The right approach for you is the method that gives
you the most confidence in your forecast. Your experience, when combined with the data available to you and subjected to your logic, produces your forecast. The result is a level of anticipated sales month by
month in the future. The actual level of sales may differ from the forecast,
but the activities and the resources needed to support any particular
level of sales will not.

If you look back at the example of Chapter 36, the income
statement forecast, Figure 36-1, shows levels of sales ranging from
$80,000 to $110,000 per month. If the $110,000 level is achieved in
month 5 instead of month 7 as projected, then what is needed to support
the actual sales in month 5 is described by the expenses listed under
month 7 of the forecast. It is more important to determine realistically the
activities (described in terms of money) that support each level of sales
than to predict exactly when that level of sales will be achieved. Of
course, the timing has a dominant influence on the cash forecast, but the
cash needs are derived from the income statement. The underlying
source of management information is a detailed income statement forecast.

IDENTIFYING THE UNIT

To build a sales forecast it helps to begin with identifying the "unit" that
will be sold. If you manufature motor homes the unit is easy to identify. It
is motor homes. If you build bridges the unit is bridges. A manufacturer's
representative will probably have several units. Reps normally sell a
product or product line from several manufacturers. For them, the first

guess at the units would be Product Line A, Product Line B, and so on. Reps usually carry four to six lines, so they would have Product Lines A through D or F.

Distributors usually carry many products. They may think of them in categories of who makes the products or alternatively in terms of who buys them. When there are many products the manager is usually more concerned with the ones that generate the most revenue. From the management standpoint the important units are probably the ones that move in greatest volume. The ancillary products may be handled more as a service to customers or to provide the appearance to the customers of being the place to call when you need a particular class of products that includes the volume items. The units chosen, then, may be Volume Item A, Volume Item B, and so on, with Volume Item Z being all the slower moving items lumped together.

Retailers range across a spectrum from the single unit lemonade stand to the multiunit department store. Most, however, carry a short list of items among which are volume items and slower moving items. For instance, a dress shop may sell buttons and tape, but its volume items are the dresses. Units for a retailer are like those for the distributor.

Service businesses may have more difficulty in recognizing their units, but they can be identified. You may remember the description in Chapter 34 of the units for a real estate agency. In a professional service business the unit is usually billable hours. That is how lawyers, accountants, and consultants view their sales. In personal service the unit is usually associated with the service provided, for instance, shoes shined, suits pressed, hands manicured, or customers massaged. In contract services the unit is also associated with the service performed. For instance, lawns cut, television sets repaired, air conditioning units worked on, or kitchen cabinets installed.

A magazine publisher has two major units. They are advertising pages sold and new subscriptions obtained. The same is true for a newspaper publisher. Some restaurants also have two major units. They are meals and drinks served. Restaurant managers think in terms of the average ticket for meals, which means the average size of the bill to a customer. Then by counting heads, or customers, and multiplying by the average bill, the sales can be observed or forecast. Drinks to a restaurant manager means alcoholic beverages. The fraction of each dollar paid for drinks that stays with the restaurants is usually more than that same fraction of a meal ticket. In many restaurants the meals bring in the customers and the drinks bring in the owner's recompense for the effort.

KNOWING THE NATURE
OF YOUR BUSINESS

Each kind of business has its own subtleties and peculiarities. These subtleties can only be learned by experience, but they can be crucial to understanding how a business works. It is one thing to know about a business from the perspective of the customer. It is quite another to have the perspective of the stock clerk, the bookkeeper, or the owner.

Some of the important peculiarities may be illustrated by considering just two or three examples. Construction contractors make many bids to obtain a few contracts. In some sense they have two major efforts. One is the bidding business and the other is satisfying the contracts obtained.

The form of construction bids is usually cost plus overhead plus profit. An airplane manufacturer, on the other hand, would bid materials, labor, overhead, general and administrative expense, and a fee. The bids that a construction contractor can make are constrained by the company's bonding capacity, a resource provided by insurance carriers.

The management operations of a construction firm are characterized by temporary and transient labor and owned, rented, or leased equipment, which is very expensive and cannot be allowed to remain idle. Usually the weather plays havoc with scheduling. Pilferage of supplies on a construction site can be devastating. And just think of how many sidewalks you have seen with some kid's initials cast in concrete.

A company providing biological supplies may find that its products require licensing by the U.S. Food and Drug Administration. Its product may also be regulated by the Department of Agriculture. Shipping will be regulated by at least the Interstate Commerce Commission, the Department of Agriculture, and the U.S. Postal Service. Biological products come from living organisms, and in some cases the products are still alive. Living organisms get sick and often can, in turn, make other living things get sick. Therein lies a whole barn full of problems peculiar to the biologicals business.

The garment industry is characterized by long lead times. This requires managers to have good intuition and feel for the fashions to become popular next year. The retail store buyers must choose their products months in advance of their sale in the store. The designers and manufacturers must be ready with their product before the buyers show up, and the fabric manufacturers must anticipate what the designers will want. The fabric for the dress on sale today may have been chosen by the manufacturers about a year ago.

TARGETING BUYERS PRECISELY

Having considered the subtleties and peculiarities, a reasonable next question to consider is, who will buy your product or service? The word *who* is the important one in that question. The *who* is somebody—a person, an individual, someone with likes and dislikes, good days and bad days, headaches, sneezes, and occasional sore feet. It is not some faceless, mindless stone edifice. Let us tell you of a personal experience to illustrate the point.

In 1966 Flow Laboratories, Inc., acquired a small firm that raised rabbits for sale to biological laboratories. The president of the acquired company told us of the great need for a laboratory-grade rabbit raised under strict and uniform conditions. It seems that most rabbits used by laboratories were raised by backyard operators, usually retired people living in the country who just happen to like raising rabbits. Dealers would purchase the rabbits from these producers at 30¢ per pound and deliver them to the laboratories for 60¢ per pound.

Several problems arose out of this arrangement. First of all, the users could never be sure of the genealogy of the animals, and they did not know whether different breeds would react differently under laboratory tests. Second, rabbits are extremely sensitive to the trauma of travel. When the rabbits arrived at the laboratory they had to be isolated and pampered for two weeks to permit them to regain their normal good health. Frequently, 50 percent of the rabbits died during this period. The result was that the users were paying more than $1.20 per pound for the usable animals that finally arrived in the laboratory technicians' hands.

Our newly acquired president presented a plan for raising rabbits under laboratory conditions with careful control of food, bedding, and medication so that the customer could use the rabbits with confidence immediately upon their delivery. He said that the laboratories would be happy to pay $1.50 per pound for such rabbits. He took us on a tour of customer facilities where we had the opportunity to confirm for ourselves that these laboratory people would indeed be happy to pay $1.50 per pound for such rabbits.

Thereupon, we set out to produce the best rabbit possible for our good customers. First we had to design and build facilities. We would have no more than 200 breeding females in any one location to reduce the possibility of spreading infection. To be sure of uniform genealogy we would begin our breeding stock with only 10 males and 200 females from a carefully tested and certified pedigree. From the offspring of these we would select only the best stock to expand our breeding population to 2,000 females and 200 males.

As you know, rabbits have a reputation for multiplying rapidly. The plan called for the original stock to produce the full breeding colony and salable product in one year. Unfortunately, our rabbits were unaware of this reputation. Somehow, the litters were smaller than expected, our veterinarian was far more selective in choosing breeders than anticipated, and the rabbits were far less interested in postpartum copulation than we had been led to believe. Nonetheless, in due time the colony began to grow, and we were able to confirm our original estimates that we could raise these laboratory quality rabbits for 90¢ per pound.

Once the colony settled down and began producing, we discovered where that reputation for reproductivity among rabbits came from. To our delight we were abundantly stocked with young, five-pound rabbits available for sale. Needless to say, we proudly toured those customer facilities again, this time with a cage of our progeny in hand. And the results were most gratifying. Everybody in the laboratories said

this was just what they wanted, and they worried about our ability to *Forecasting Sales*
supply the number of rabbits they would be ordering immediately.

On returning to our office we altered our forecasts upward to reflect this newfound data from the marketplace. And then we waited for the orders to arrive. And we waited, and we waited. Then we called the customers only to be reassured that the order was coming.

While we were waiting, the population of rabbits was growing. When we made that tour we had 3,000 pounds of live rabbits for sale. When we called for reassurance the number was up to 6,000 pounds. When the stock reached 9,000 pounds we went back to visit the customer facilities. During this visit we were again reassured of their desire to buy our rabbits at $1.50 per pound and told that they had placed their purchase requisition with their purchasing department. We could visit the purchasing agents to verify that the order was on its way. This seemed prudent and we did, indeed, visit the purchasing agents. After identifying ourselves and describing our dilemma, each of the purchasing agents said, "Oh yes, I have that requisition, but I can purchase rabbits for 60¢ per pound."

By the time we had completed a number of futile phone calls to our good customers, the rabbit stock was up to 12,000 pounds of little bunnies, who overflowed the holding facilities and were now using the warehouse. And that was the day the butcher called from New York City to inquire about a supply of rabbits. We sold the butcher 12,000 pounds of live rabbits for 30¢ per pound.

You see, we had identified who would *use* the rabbits. We forgot that we should have been looking for who would *buy* the rabbits. The purchasing agent's job is to buy at the best price. It would take enormous pressure from the users to provide the agent with sufficient justification to face a critical management. The agent would rather buy at 59¢ per pound and let the users talk to the controller.

The task to be faced is to identify the exact person who exercises the authority to spend money. Then try to characterize that person so similar people can be recognized and identified. With this information it may be possible to locate that kind of person by characteristics available in statistical data. It is prudent to get to know as much as possible about that person as an individual and as a class of individuals. Know who, exactly, you sell to, how you find them, and what you say to get them to part with their hard-earned cash.

It takes substantial time and resources just to talk to potential customers. First you have to find them. Then you have to take the time, your time, to talk to them. With the passing of time and some increase in your resources you may increase your efficiency in talking to potential customers through advertising, direct mail, manufacturer's reps, and a sales force. Depending on the kind of business, you may increase the effort through distributors, wholesalers, and retailers. Even then, however, the task can never be dismissed to someone else. You have to continue talking to the customers, directly or indirectly.

295

CHARACTERISTIC SALES GROWTH PATTERNS

In considering how sales will develop for your new business it is helpful to consider the characteristic growth for similar businesses. Retail outlets typically reach a significant level of sales soon after they open the doors. Thereafter their sales grow slowly. Sales may decline if the store does not provide a pleasant experience to the first customers. If the people who visit the store are pleased with the experience they will tell others about it, and that good news plus additional promotion in the media will cause sales to rise slowly. The level of sales reached on opening is so important that retailers have adopted the grand opening scheme for starting sales. If the initial level of sales obtained by a retailer is less than that needed to break even, the store may find itself in trouble. It could take a long time for the sales to grow slowly to break even.

Service businesses tend to grow gradually. In personal services, like a beauty shop, and professional services, like bookkeeping, the proprietor usually starts with a few clients from prior business relationships. Then the business grows gradually until it reaches a level that consumes the proprietor's capacity to provide the service. Technician service businesses, like plumbers, tend to grow gradually from day one and level out at the proprietor's capacity.

These characteristic sales growth patterns may be portrayed graphically. The retail pattern rises rapidly and levels off to slow growth. The service business growth accelerates from some starting point and then looks like the retail pattern. Technician service may grow from zero; personal and professional service businesses usually grow from some initial volume. Personal service sales growth depends on reputation. Technician service growth depends on reputation and the need for the service in the midst of the existing competition. Professional service usually has a greater lag between start-up and the needed level of sales to support the business. It frequently involves providing time-consuming service to be paid for at some later date, as in a real estate agency.

Construction contracting and similar businesses, which bid on many jobs to obtain a few contracts, typically have a stepwise growth in sales. Manufacturers, on the other hand, have to build their production capacity gradually in most cases. Their growth accelerates, as for the technician service business but it takes longer to get going and grows to greater levels over more time.

Manufacturers' representatives and distributors who do not stock inventory tend to have a little accelerated growth following the acquisition of each new manufacturer's product line. Most of the time they start out with some product line and some in-house accounts.

Wholesalers and distributors who stock some inventory tend to have a reasonably rapid initial growth followed by slow growth. They too usually begin with some in-house accounts.

In each of these examples the most desirable growth is that

which is limited by capacity to produce. When sales are equal to everything you can deliver, it is probable that you don't have to carry any expenses for nonproductive assets.

There is another important characteristic of sales patterns to be considered. That is the seasonal variation or the variation with economic conditions. Expanding a chain of home furnishing retail stores in the face of a decline in the number of houses being built can give an owner-manager some sleepless nights. Opening a new ski resort motel in April might do the same thing.

Many retail businesses break even eleven months of the year and make their earnings during December. Lawn- and garden-related businesses don't often have attractive sales in December. For businesses with strong seasonal variations in their sales patterns it is worth considering which month is most propitious for their birth.

One of the most common approaches to sales forecasting should be avoided. We knew an entrepreneur who made a widget to fit into the socket of light bulbs. It prolonged the life of the bulb to two or three times the normal life. This individual began the sales forecast by reporting that there are 14 billion incandescent light sockets in the United States. By reaching only 0.1 percent of them in three years, sales would be 14 million units, which, at 65¢ each, would be $9.1 million in sales. Imagine finding and then talking to the decision makers representing 14 billion light bulbs. It's possible, but not probable. The individual did not provide any justification for selecting the 0.1 percent factor.

If your ability to deliver limits the units available to a very small number compared with the total market *available to you*, then your sales forecast is the same as your "growth in capacity" forecast. This is the best! For instance, we met a water well driller on the West Coast. He buys new equipment to reduce his backlog from twelve to three weeks, then lets the backlog grow to twelve weeks again.

In summary, decide on a sales forecast on which you are willing to bet a significant piece of your lifetime and all your wealth. This is your sales quota, your achievable goal.

40

The Launch Vehicle

The record of failure among new businesses is unnecessary. Entrepreneurs leap after their dream with little, if any, conception of the responsibility they are about to assume and without adequate preparation. What is needed is a Plan. It should look far enough into the future to demonstrate a level of performance representing the stable operation of the business. A Plan prepared for them is not adequate. It must be the entrepreneur's Plan. The entrepreneur must know it, understand it, feel it and be able to defend it without reference to the printed material.

Perhaps the greatest virtue of a Plan properly prepared by the entrepreneur is the experience in preparing the Income Statements, Cash Flow forecasts and Balance Sheets. Having prepared them once, the entrepreneur can relate the actual activity of the business to those pages of hieroglyphics prepared monthly by the accountant. No other exercise can engage the learning circuits of their grey matter so consistently, or demonstrate so succinctly, the necessity for timely, accurate and detailed financial reports and the profound importance of the Cash Flow forecast.*

A plan does not create the future. It lights the way into the dimly perceived future. The downhill racer has memorized the course and fantasized skiing every bump and turn many times over before leaving the starting gate. But wind and sun change the condition of the course. A glazed high-speed turn may become like soft powder. A small bump may have grown and moved like the shifting sands of the desert. At the moment of the race the course is like the one memorized, but it is not the same. The skiers display an opportunistic reaction to the circumstances in which they find themselves.

One virtue of a business plan is in the similarities between the course memorized beforehand and the actual course at the time of the

*Paraphrased from John A. Welsh, "Heed the Achilles Heel," *Financial Trend*, Dec. 15, 1972.

race. Like the downhill skier who discovers something changed while traveling at seventy miles per hour, the owner-manager is constantly confronted with the absolute need to react instantaneously while events stream by at a pace that blurs the vision. It is much easier to cope with an aberration when it is found in a familiar landscape. Even a steady stream of aberrations are manageable in the setting of familiar terrain. The more formal and detailed the plan, the more familiar the scene will appear as the owner-manager travels the course.

In truth, many owner-managers who have started their own businesses and survived began without a business plan. We surveyed 873 owner-managers who had businesses with sales in the $1 to $10 million range. Of these, 551 founded their businesses. And 140 of the 551 said they had never prepared a business plan. Our distinguished entrepreneur speakers typically had little or no formal plans in the beginning other than those needed to raise venture capital. Because some of them did not seek venture capital to start their businesses, they did not feel a need for a formal business plan.

Successful owner-managers describing how they built their businesses almost always tell a story of opportunistic reaction to the circumstances in which they found themselves. A recurrent observation is, "The harder I work the luckier I get." Dominant themes are a dedication to providing their customers a product or service that is better than what is available from existing sources and a never-ending sense of urgency to find and provide it. It is not unusual to hear that the initial concept of what the consumer would buy did not work, but a modification of the original concept or a newly perceived opportunity did. Flexibility, as opposed to rigidity, seems necessary and desirable to provide for the discovery of what will induce consumers to part with their hard-earned money.

Things may not work out according to the plan. It might even be said that things almost never work out exactly as planned. This being true, it might be said that there is little reason for preparing a formal detailed plan. That reason may also be an excuse for avoiding the discomfort, the expenditure of time and energy, and the psychic burden of digging for data and making decisions. At a time when the entrepreneurial personality wants to get on with the action, it isn't difficult to treat the planning process with disdain.

Most owner-managers who have built a business that survives, thrives, and grows have somewhere along the road made a plan. It is not unusual to find that the plan came after the business was started. With the passing of time, however, they have had the experience of preparing a plan and observing its contribution to their success. When these owner-managers are queried about the virtues of a plan their response is an almost universal admonition to *start with a plan.*

Self-confident entrepreneurs with the never-ending sense of urgency may perceive the preparation of a formal plan to be a bore, an impediment to action and achievement, and an infringement on the

299

freedom to control and direct whatever action is to be taken. Having rafted down the river of white waters, however, successful entrepreneurs are then willing to concede that they would have been better off had they fantasized their way down the river beforehand. And their advice to those who would emulate them is *prepare a plan*.

The plan for a new business is the description, in precise and concise language, of the activities that will take place and the net result of the exchanges of value in the transactions that will occur during the early months and years in the life of a new enterprise. A well-prepared plan will demonstrate that the entrepreneur, the business concept, and the entrepreneur's access to venture capital with this business concept are positioned clearly inside the launch window described in Chapter 6. The entrepreneur's plan confirms his or her mastery of the critical skill. The plan is a script for a significant piece of the entrepreneur's lifetime and the birth of living economic entity. It should be treated with the gravity and the solemnity of bringing a new life into this world.

We cannot show you how to prepare *your* business plan. What we can do is provide you with some guidance and a few examples. In what follows we will try to raise questions and illustrate answers for the preparation of a business plan. We refer you to the appendices for samples of the basic plan. These samples show that the plan is in numbers, with words used to embellish the numbers. The words chosen and their quantity depend on who is expected to read the plan and who is writing it.

There is one thing to be remembered about the prose associated with the plan. Many people write in a language that assumes that the reader has the same background knowledge and experience as the writer. Most of the time this is not so. This leads to the reader only partially understanding what is being said. The reader does not question the writer, however, for fear of appearing dumb. It is safer, emotionally and intellectually, for the reader to smile knowingly and go away. That way the reader can avoid any embarrassment. But if this occurs, the writer has failed to convey a message or make a point, and the writer's work may be an exercise in futility. If the reader is a potential investor, the cost of neglecting this consideration may be very painful.

Three samples of business plans are provided in the appendix. One of them is for a retail/service business that sells not only personal services but also items from inventory. One is for a substantial new contracting business in the petroleum industry. The third is for a manufacturer of a specialty consumer product marketed through truckstops. All of them are real. Specific names, dates, and places have been changed at the entrepreneurs' requests. The numbers and logic are genuine.

These example plans are not offered as ideal. They represent the thinking of the individuals who wrote them at the time they were prepared. They are good plans, however, and we feel they represent the kind of preparation that will improve the entrepreneur's probability of success. We hope that you enjoy reading them and that they will help you to see your own business described in the planning format.

As mentioned earlier, each business has its peculiarities and its subtleties. They come from a rainbow of influences, some of which result from tradition, some from the uniqueness of the product or service, some from the manager's personality, and some from the behavior of employees, customers, and suppliers in the current economic and social conditions. As the social, economic, ethnic, political, geographic, and technological environments change, all the people involved with the business will change, producing a veritable kaleidoscope of business plans.

These subtleties and peculiarities are what make experience, timely and relevant experience, so important to the entrepreneur. The experience curves of Chapter 16 demonstrated quantitatively the benefit of experience and the advantage that falls to the person who has it. All the training, guidance, learning, and knowledge provided by writers of books is still only superficial when compared with what will be learned from experience.

Nobody can plan your business for you. Others can prepare *their* plans. If it is to be your business, only you can decide how you will behave in response to the opportunities and the adversity that are uniquely yours and perceived only by your own mind's eye.

There are many right and wrong ways to run your business. It is hard to say that there is *the* way to run it. Like the downhill racer, you can read all the books on theory and watch all the films of the racing greats, you can ski the slopes, familiarize yourself with the terrain, and fantasize how you will run the race, but when you leave the starting gate your feet are bound to those skis. You will discover what's new and different while traveling at your best speed. And you are out there all alone to make the most of what you find.

That, really, is the American Dream—to be your own boss, to face your own adversity, and to overcome it with your wits, your energy, and your stamina. It is to win when you know you could have lost and to savor your own full authority, responsibility, and accountability. That is the freedom that has attracted so many to the shores of North America and made the United States such a sparkling example of what the venturesome spirit of competitive free enterprise can and does produce.

Appendices

The following appendices illustrate how three different businesses presented their concepts for building an independent enterprise. Each is modeled after a real business opportunity and attempts to capture the flavor and style of three different entrepreneurs.

Names and places in these sample plans, including letterhead and signatures, are fictitious. Any similarity to real people or places is purely coincidental.

RETAIL/SERVICE BUSINESS

The first business plan is for Chimney Services, Inc., a retail/service business. This plan is an example of a business capitalizing on the personal experience and training of its entrepreneur. It requires a low investment and is geographically limited. In addition to identifying a niche for a particular technician service, the plan also incorporates the retail functions of selling "off the shelf" merchandise and maintaining and accounting for inventory.

This plan does a particularly good job of mapping out a promotion campaign to support the sales effort. It also illustrates projected price increases and demonstrates the first-in-first-out (FIFO) method of costing items in inventory.

CONTRACTING BUSINESS

The second business plan is for Bahnhof-X, Inc., a contracting business. In contrast to the small retail/service business presented in the first business plan, Bahnhof -X requires a substantial amount of capital and grows very rapidly. More than $2 million in equipment financing and $800,000 in equity is required in the first year of operations. The business becomes profitable after six months of start-up losses and grows to more than $5 million in sales the second year in business.

As in the other business plans, it is interesting to note the personal background and experience of the entrepreneur. High credibility results from a substantial and relevant track record.

There is an additional section in this business plan not found in the other examples. The effort is sufficiently involved that the entrepreneur felt a need to communicate the different major phases of execution of the plan.

MANUFACTURING BUSINESS

The third business plan is for Thermos-Tote, Inc., a manufacturing business. This plan is interesting in that it includes a wide spectrum of business functions. There are expenses for patenting the "widget," attending trade shows, developing brochures, leasing a large truck, sales commissions, consulting fees, and other items.

One of the main areas in which this business plan differs from the previous two is the need to keep up with raw materials and finished goods inventory. This difference is particularly evident when observing the income statement treatment of direct expenses and the cash flow consideration of when materials are ordered and paid for.

This is a good example of a company engaged in all the functions of business, from basic fabrication of the product to payment collection from the customer.

BUSINESS PLAN STYLE AND FORMAT

These business plans are reproduced in a manner that permits you to observe differing but acceptable writing styles and typing formats. An effort was made to preserve the different personalities of three separate entrepreneurs. Most business plans are typed on only one side of each sheet of paper. Printing here is on both sides to streamline the publishing process. For the same reason, major topics are run together rather than each beginning at the top of its own page.

APPENDIX I: CHIMNEY SERVICES, INC.

Business Plan for a
Retail/Service Business

CHIMNEY SERVICES, INC.

Proposal for a Chimney Cleaning Service

Prepared by

Tom F. Johnson
2062 Lexington Street
Metro City, Missouri   46211
(223) 641-8226

SECURITIES NOTICE

TABLE OF CONTENTS

BUSINESS CONCEPT

This business plan describes a market opportunity and a game plan for operating a quality chimney-cleaning service in the Metro City, Missouri, area.

Background

The oil embargo of 1973, escalating heating costs, an apparent trend toward colder winters, and energy consciousness have caused millions of Americans to return to solid fuels. Consequently, chimneys in this geographic region are doing a lot more work.

Increased interest in energy conservation has resulted in an upsurge in the use of wood-burning fireplaces and stoves as a supplemental heating source. In Metro City more than 90% of all new homes have fireplaces.

Coupled with this trend is the alarming statistic that there were over 40,000 chimney fires in the United States last year, causing more than $25 million in damages. Chimney fires have tripled in the last three years and are among the top ten fire hazards at home. In Metro City, where there are a large number of homes with wood shingles, the dangers from a chimney fire are more imminent.

The need for chimney cleaning results from creosote, the thick residue that cakes the flue lining. Creosote is formed when the hot volatile gases released by burning solid fuels enter the cooler flue chamber and condense into a flaky, tarlike substance.

It is reported that every year one million Americans buy a wood-burning stove. In 1971 there were only one million in the entire country. These wood-burning stoves typically have higher heat efficiency and a lower smoke temperature. This results in a cooler flue and a higher condensation of creosote.

This buildup of creosote is very flammable. If ignited, it burns with volcanic force, cremating the flue's lining and weakening the chimney. The first fire in a chimney is a terrifying experience; the second fire is often a total disaster.

Chimneys used three times a week or more during a burning season should be inspected and cleaned annually. Others used less often can be cleaned every couple of years. Wood-burning stoves and their chimneys should always be cleaned at least once a year.

The Concept

Chimney sweeping is a simple concept. The initial investment is low and attractive profits are possible.
The appeal of this service will be to the

higher-income households, which frequently live in homes with wood shingles. They are also the customers who can best afford this service. Further, our target customers tend to be geographically concentrated, thereby affording opportunities for operating efficiencies.

The profit potential depends on the number of chimneys cleaned each day and the number of customers maintained during the year. The typical charge in Metro City is $50 per chimney or flue.

A cleaning job will take a maximum of an hour and a half. With efficient equipment six jobs are possible a day. Furthermore, other services can be rendered by a chimney sweep on the job, such as brick repair, ash resistor installations, and safety inspections. Later, the business can be expanded into fire coating of wood shingle roofs, sale of fireplace accessory items, and contract firewood delivery.

This proposed business concept has the additional characteristic of low start-up costs. Contributing to low start-up costs is the fact that no office is needed. Paperwork and billing can be done from a small office in the home. A van will serve as a mobile office and as storage for the equipment, which should be protected from the weather.

Equipment

To handle a greater volume of business and minimize labor costs, a high-pressure dust collection system is necessary. High-powered vacuums of the type Chimney Services, Inc., will acquire move 700 cubic feet of air a minute. Air is moved from the room into the fireplace, keeping the enormous dust clouds inside the chimney. Rods and brushes for scrubbing the inside of a flue to remove the caked-in creosote, an assortment of brushes of various sizes and shapes to fit a flue's diameter exactly, a respiratory fire extinguisher, ladder (Class II), toolbox, and miscellaneous small tools will also be needed.

MARKETING OVERVIEW

Chimney Services, Inc., has selected a prime target market. This target market will be approached with a well-planned promotion campaign, which should be effective against the existing, largely unaggressive, competitors.

Target Market

Chimney Services, Inc., will serve the more affluent communities, where households can afford the Company's service and where almost 100% of the homes have chimneys

and wood shingle roofs. The map shown below was derived from
U.S. Dept. of Commerce Census Block Statistics, the
Commercial and Residential Building Survey by the Metro City
Chamber of Commerce, and the city Development Commission's
report, Recent and Future Trends in Housing Development.
These reports identified the cross-hatched area as having a
high concentration of homes with 2000-4000 sq. ft. of living
space and medium to high income. These reports confirm this
as the prime target market.

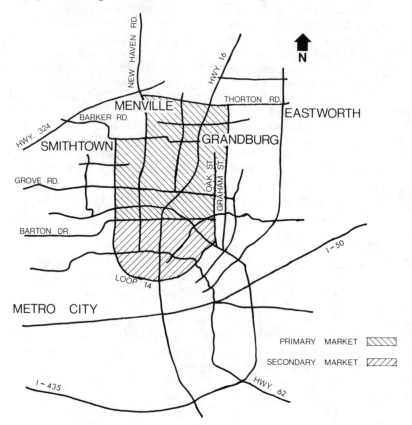

Promotion Campaign

Silhouettes and sketches of top hats and tails, brooms
and chimney tops, are all natural for ads. These symbols
will soon be identified with the business and help to
catch the consumer's eye. This image, copy message, and
community endorsement will sell the main idea--Safety.
Making individuals aware of the potentially serious fire
problem in their homes is the key. A sample of the type of
advertisement envisioned is shown here.
   Yellow Pages, classified ads in selected local
newspapers, direct mail campaigns, door-to-door fliers,
and personal contacts are the most effective promotion.
In addition, a professionally painted sign on the van

will act as an excellent billboard. A detailed
advertising schedule specifying media, frequency, and
costs is presented in Appendices M and N.

Getting out in full costume and canvassing the target
area should also be effective. Virgin territory is a two-
or three-year-old housing development where the people
have not yet had their chimneys swept—a significant
percentage of the target area population.

As a special promotion, a 10% discount can be
extended to customers who give referrals that lead to a
job.

A chimney sweep by the very nature of the costume has
built-in public relations value. By getting to know the
editor of local newspapers, some front page publicity can
be gained. Also, the business will be promoted through
talks and lectures on fire prevention as well as
demonstrations regarding the proper use of wood stoves
and fireplaces at community group or organization
functions. In addition, it is desired that one of these
groups be encouraged to endorse the business. Such an
endorsement will make it easier to arrange publicity
coverage and the support of local officials, business
owners, and community leaders.

Because many people call a fireplace store first when
looking for someone to clean their chimney, one of the
prominent objectives is to become well known by local
dealers selling wood-burning stoves and fireplaces. An
adequate supply of attractive business cards will be made
available for them to hand out to their customers.

Competition

The chimney-sweeping service business is a highly
personal one, which grows by developing a steady customer
base. Referrals and a strong repeat business are
essential to successful long-term growth.

Two area fireplace supply businesses aided in the
conduct of an informal survey of their customers. A total
of 375 individuals were asked if they had ever bought
chimney-sweeping services. Of the 182 who had, only 23
were satisfied with the service they received. The
competitors have been taking the customers for granted
and have been delivering shoddy and impersonal service.
The market is ripe for Chimney Services, Inc.

The direct competitors and their standard charges
are listed in Appendix B. None conducts itself in a very
professional manner, and they never advertise. They
should be very vulnerable to the company's well-planned
promotion campaign.

MANAGEMENT

The owner-manager of Chimney Services, Inc., is Tom F.
Johnson. Mr. Johnson is 28 years old. He graduated from
Metro City Community College, where his emphasis was on
vocational technology and small business management. Mr.
Johnson then worked for two years with Cecil Jones
Builders, Inc., as an assistant foreman helping to build
middle-class and upper-middle-class homes, most of which
were built in north Metro City and most of which had
fireplaces.

Mr. Johnson worked with Galaxy Stove Manufacturing
Co. for three years, first in their fabrication area as a
lead man and then as a staff support person in the sales
area. Galaxy Stove Manufacturing Co. is, of course, the
regionally prominent producer and marketer of
high-efficiency wood-burning stoves.

After his employment with Galaxy he became assistant
manager of The Fireplace Center, an established fireplace
supply retail store. While in this position, Mr. Johnson
observed the need for a quality, reliable
chimney-cleaning service.

FINANCIAL PERFORMANCE

Chimney Services, Inc., is a business with many financially attractive features. With an initial investment of only $6,000, the company is solidly profitable at the end of its first year in operation. Owner's Equity more than doubles the second year of operation.

Detailed income statements, cash flow statements, and balance sheets have been produced on a pro forma basis for the next two years of operations. A summary of these projections follows.

Pro Forma Income Statements

Monthly income statement projections have been prepared for 24 months. The basic operating results are portrayed in the following table.

	Year 1	Year 2
Sales	$26,982	$48,025
Gross Profit	21,741	38,768
Net Income	9,592	19,165

The detailed projections with descriptive footnotes are presented in Appendix A.

Pro Forma Cash Flow Statements

Month-by-month cash flow projections have been prepared for 24 months. An overview of the results is shown in the following table.

	Year 1	Year 2
Receipts	$26,982	$48,025
Disbursements	21,160	30,949
Cash Flow	5,822	17,076

Detailed projections and explanatory footnotes are presented in Appendix C.

Pro Forma Balance Sheets

Balance sheets are produced as of the end of Year 1 and Year 2; a summary is presented in the following table.

	Year 1	Year 2
Total Assets	$7,517	$14,995
Total Liabilities	2,925	238
Owner's Equity	4,592	14,757

Detailed balance sheets are presented in Appendix D.

APPENDIX A

Pro Forma Income Statements
and
Explanatory Footnotes

CHIMNEY SERVICES, INC.
PRO FORMA INCOME STATEMENT
Fiscal Year 1

		Nov	Dec	Jan	Feb	Mar
(1)	REVENUES					
	Service	$ 2,000	2,000	1,600	1,400	1,200
	Specialty Products	413	1,086	1,004	828	719
	Total Revenues	2,413	3,086	2,604	2,228	1,919
(2)	Beginning Inventory	-	226	329	359	232
	Purchases	484	711	587	334	371
	Cost of Goods Avail. for Sale	484	937	916	693	603
	Ending Inventory	226	329	359	232	203
	Cost of Goods Sold	258	608	557	461	400
	Gross Profit Margin	2,155	2,478	2,047	1,767	1,519
	OPERATING EXPENSES					
(3)	Advertising	200	200	160	140	120
(4)	Depreciation	109	109	109	109	109
(5)	Subscriptions	5	5	5	5	5
(6)	Bank Charges	20	5	5	5	5
(7)	Legal Expense	8	8	9	8	8
(8)	Insurance	192	192	192	192	192
(9)	License, Insp., Title-Van	11	11	11	12	11
(10)	Telephone	96	47	47	47	47
(11)	Artwork & Layout	11	11	11	11	11
(12)	Office Expense	10	10	10	10	10
(13)	Gasoline, Oil, Main.-Van	125	125	125	125	125
(14)	Audit Cost	15	15	15	15	15
(15)	Equipment Main.	-	-	-	-	-
(16)	Rent	-	-	-	-	-
(17)	Postage	5	5	5	5	5
(18)	Business Cards	4	4	4	4	4
(19)	Supplies & Small Tools	75	75	75	76	75
(20)	Utilities	-	-	-	-	-
(21)	Brochures	10	-	-	-	10
(22)	Samples (Specialty Products)	15	-	-	-	-
(23)	Miscellaneous	25	25	25	25	25
	Total Oper. Expenses	936	847	808	789	777
	Net Operating Income	1,219	1,631	1,239	978	742
(25)	Financial Expense	-	75	72	70	67
	Net Income Before Taxes	1,219	1,556	1,167	908	675
(26)	Estimated Income Taxes	56*	265	198	154	115
	Net Income	1,163	1,291	969	754	560

*Reduced by $151 reflecting the investment tax credit
from fiscal year 1 purchase of the van and vacuum system.

312

Apr	May	Jun	Jul	Aug	Sep	Oct	Fiscal Year Total
1,200	1,000	1,000	1,000	1,300	1,800	2,500	18,000
652	610	543	543	612	843	1,129	8,982
1,852	1,610	1,543	1,543	1,912	2,643	3,629	26,982
203	209	182	208	180	102	121	
389	336	354	301	301	524	595	
592	545	536	509	481	626	716	
209	182	208	180	102	121	46	
383	363	328	329	379	505	670	5,241
1,469	1,247	1,215	1,214	1,533	2,138	2,959	21,741
120	100	100	100	130	180	250	1,800
109	109	109	109	109	109	109	1,308
5	5	5	5	5	5	5	60
5	5	5	5	5	5	5	75
9	8	8	9	8	8	9	100
192	192	191	191	191	191	191	2,299
11	11	12	11	11	11	12	135
47	47	47	47	47	47	47	613
10	11	11	11	11	11	10	130
10	10	10	10	10	10	10	120
125	125	125	125	125	125	125	1,500
15	15	15	15	15	15	15	180
-	-	-	-	-	-	-	-
-	-	-	-	-	-	-	-
5	5	5	5	5	5	5	60
5	4	4	4	4	4	5	50
75	75	76	75	75	75	76	903
-	-	-	-	-	-	-	-
-	-	-	10	-	-	-	30
-	-	-	-	15	-	-	30
25	25	25	25	25	25	25	300
768	747	748	757	791	826	899	9,693
701	500	467	457	742	1,312	2,060	12,048
64	62	59	56	53	50	47	675
637	438	408	401	689	1,262	2,013	11,373
108	74	69	68	117	215	342	1,781
529	364	339	333	572	1,047	1,671	9,592

CHIMNEY SERVICES, INC.
PRO FORMA INCOME STATEMENT
Fiscal Year 2

		Nov	Dec	Jan	Feb	Mar
(1)	REVENUES					
	Service	$ 3,375	3,510	3,015	3,015	2,700
	Specialty Products	1,557	1,822	1,791	1,569	1,508
	Total Revenues	4,932	5,332	4,806	4,584	4,208
(2)	Beginning Inventory	46	1,053	1,043	946	965
	Purchases	1,931	1,013	898	898	521
	Cost of Goods Avail. for Sale	1,977	2,066	1,941	1,844	1,486
	Ending Inventory	1,053	1,043	946	965	645
	Cost of Goods Sold	924	1,023	995	879	841
	Gross Profit Margin	4,008	4,309	3,811	3,705	3,367
	OPERATING EXPENSES					
(3)	Advertising	450	450	300	400	400
(4)	Depreciation	59	58	59	58	59
(5)	Subscriptions	7	7	7	7	7
(6)	Bank Charges	8	8	8	8	8
(8)	Insurance	192	192	192	192	192
(10)	Telephone	50	50	50	50	50
(12)	Office Expense	10	10	10	10	10
(13)	Gas, Oil, Main.-Van	140	140	140	140	140
(14)	Audit Costs	20	20	20	20	20
(15)	Equipment Maintenance	10	10	10	10	10
(17)	Postage	6	6	6	6	6
(18)	Business Cards	6	6	6	7	6
(19)	Supplies & Small Tools	25	25	25	25	25
(21)	Brochures	10	10	10	10	10
(23)	Miscellaneous	25	25	25	25	25
(24)	Contract Labor	617	667	601	573	526
	Total Oper. Expenses	1,635	1,684	1,469	1,541	1,494
	Net Operating Income	2,373	2,625	2,342	2,164	1,873
(25)	Financial Expense	44	41	38	35	31
	Net Income Before Taxes	2,329	2,584	2,304	2,129	1,842
(26)	Estimated Income Taxes	396	439	392	362	313
	Net Income	1,933	2,145	1,912	1,767	1,529

314

Apr	May	Jun	Jul	Aug	Sep	Oct	Fiscal Year Total
2,520	2,025	1,800	1,800	1,800	2,520	3,510	31,590
1,396	1,224	1,030	956	956	1,100	1,526	16,435
3,916	3,249	2,830	2,756	2,756	3,620	5,036	48,025
645	628	692	485	596	428	682	
762	743	367	646	367	879	338	
1,407	1,371	1,059	1,131	963	1,307	1,020	
628	692	485	596	428	682	152	
779	679	574	535	535	625	868	9,257
3,137	2,570	2,256	2,221	2,221	2,995	4,168	38,768
350	300	300	300	300	400	500	4,450
58	59	58	59	59	59	59	704
7	7	7	7	7	7	7	84
8	8	8	8	8	8	8	96
192	192	191	191	191	191	191	2,299
50	50	50	50	50	50	50	600
10	10	10	10	10	10	10	120
140	140	140	140	140	140	140	1,680
20	20	20	20	20	20	20	240
10	10	10	10	10	10	10	120
6	6	6	6	6	6	6	72
6	6	7	6	6	6	7	75
25	25	25	25	25	25	25	300
10	10	10	10	10	10	10	120
25	25	25	25	25	25	25	300
490	-	-	-	-	-	630	4,104
1,407	868	867	867	867	967	1,698	15,364
1,730	1,702	1,389	1,354	1,354	2,028	2,470	23,404
28	25	21	18	14	11	7	313
1,702	1,677	1,368	1,336	1,340	2,017	2,463	23,091
289	285	233	227	228	343	419	3,926
1,413	1,392	1,135	1,109	1,112	1,674	2,044	19,165

CHIMNEY SERVICES, INC.

Budgeted Monthly Income Statement Notes

1. Sales
    a. Service. Represents the number of jobs (chimneys cleaned) at $40 per chimney during Year 1 and $45 during Year 2 and considers the time available for servicing as a part-time endeavor and the seasonality (see Appendix B).

    b. Specialty Products & Installation. Represents sales of
        i. Chimney caps and screens: Based on the average selling price of $67.35 during Year 1 and $74.09 during Year 2 for various sizes and a sales ratio of one cap every five cleaning jobs (20%). Orders are booked at time of cleaning and installed the following month. This is to keep the inventory of caps at a minimum until experience will show the most common sizes to have in stock.
        ii. Chimfex (flare type fire extinguisher for chimney fires): Based on two flares per customer at $6.95/flare during Year 1 and $7.65 during Year 2 and a sales ratio of two flares for every second cleaning (50%).
        iii. Thurmalox 270 (stove paint): $6.50 per 13 oz. can during Year 1 and $7.15 during Year 2; at a sales ratio of one can for every fifth customer (20%).

    A detailed cost analysis and selling price for each inventory item is portrayed in Appendices E and F and a detailed breakdown of sales by product by month is presented in Appendices G and H.

2. Inventory. Initial inventory is a 30-day supply of Chimfex and Thurmalox 270 with an allowance for lead time to fill beginning of next month's demand. Also includes two chimney caps for demonstrations. Experience will show the proper amount of inventory and stock sizes after several months. Costing is on a first-in-first-out (FIFO) basis. Inventory usage in units is portrayed in Appendices I and J. Inventory usage in dollars (cost of goods sold) is computed in the tables of Appendices L and K.

3. Advertising. Advertising expenditures are based on 10% of gross service income. This is the average for a beginning chimney sweep business. Recommendations are from Chimney Sweeps Research Institute and the Walls and Mather Agency. See Appendices M and N for detailed advertising schedule.

4. Depreciation. The vacuum sweeper that cost $782 is depreciated over seven years using double-declining balance method, and the used van is depreciated over three years using 150% declining balance.

5. Subscriptions. Cost of industry magazine publications and reading material in the wood-burning field. Customers must perceive that I am knowledgeable in the areas of wood, wood burning, fireplace construction and repair, fire

316

prevention, energy conservation, and not just chimney cleaning. The budget for Year 1 is $60, and for Year 2 it is $84.

6. Bank Charges. Cost of bank service charge for checking account at Metro City National Bank, Metro City, Missouri.

7. Legal Expenses. A budget of $100 is allocated for Month 1 relative to start-up matters.

8. Insurance. Insurance for the van is quoted by Farmers Insurance Co. at $416/yr. for full coverage. Liability insurance of $300,000 quoted by USGAF at $1,790, and 20% down. An interest add-on of $93 on the unpaid balance of the annual premium will be incurred and amortized over the period of coverage.

9. Van License, Inspection, Title Transfer. This item includes an allowance of $30, $5, and $100, respectively, for the three listed expense categories.

10. Telephone. Telephone answering service, including call forwarding, includes monthly charge of $47/mo. for FY1 and $50/mo. for FY2, and an additional $49 charge for installation. The installation charge is expensed in Month 1 of FY1. Limited to 75 calls monthly and 35¢ per overcall. Service is Monday–Saturday, 8:00 A.M.–8:00 P.M.

11. Artwork & Layout. Includes cost for artist to structure and sketch my copy for the Grandburg Daily News. Artwork becomes my property and not that of the newspaper. Charges of $30 in November and $100 in August were amortized over the first year on a monthly basis.

12. Office Expense. Covers such items as envelopes, paper, etc., based on my experience of running a business from the home. Ten dollars per month is budgeted.

13. Gasoline, Oil, Maintenance—Van. Covers the van-associated expenses costed at 20¢ per mile. This is the experience of other chimney sweeps per the National Entrepreneurship Association. Costs are expected to increase $15/mo. in FY2.

14. Audit Costs. Covers cost of monthly summary, operating statement, and year-end tax determination by a local bookkeeper.

15. Equipment Maintenance. The only piece of equipment requiring maintenance besides the van is the vacuum system. Manufacturer of the system warrants all parts for one year. Typically, the only maintenance required is new brushes after 2,000 hours of operation. The vacuum system is relatively maintenance free, up to 5,000 hours of operation, when a new motor is usually required. A charge of $10/mo. is allocated for this item in FY2.

16. Rent. The business can be run from a telephone in my home. Furthermore, because I have another business being run from the same home office, no charge is being allocated for this item during the first two years and until the business is well established.

17. Postage. A minimal amount is allocated to cover normal correspondence.

317

18. Business Cards. Based on an average layout, design, and lots of 500 cards. The budget for FY1 is $50 and for FY2 is $75.

19. Supplies and Small Tools. This covers the supplies, small tools, and accessories needed to perform the service. The budget for FY1 is $903 and for FY2 it is $300. See Appendix O for details regarding exact items to be purchased.

20. Utilities. Because the business is run from a telephone in my home and the utility charges are written off for the office I already have in my home, none is allocated to this business during the first two years of operations.

21. Brochures. This item covers handouts describing the various specialty products for sale at $10 for a 250 count. They are expensed over the year in equal amounts each month.

22. Samples (Specialty Products). Covers cost of Chimfex (fire extinguisher), stove paint, and miscellaneous items for display and illustrations to customers. These items are utilized in FY1 only and are expensed as acquired.

23. Miscellaneous. For unforeseen contingencies that normally arise but which cannot be specifically predicted, $25 per month is budgeted.

24. Contract Labor. Covers cost of part-time college student working as independent contractor in FY2. Student receives 25% of revenues that he or she is responsible for.

25. Financial Expense. Based on a loan value of $5,000 for 24 months at 18% interest. (See Appendix P.)

26. Estimated Income Taxes. Income taxes are estimated at the 17% level and are reduced by the amount of the FY1 Investment Tax Credit, in the amount of $151, resulting from the purchase of the van and the vacuum system.

318

APPENDIX B

Chimney Services, Inc.

List of Competitors, Services, and Charges

1. ACE Chimney Cleaning $55.00
   2504 Main St.
   611–1247

2. ACME Chimney Sweeps of Missouri   50.00
   518 Harmon St.
   524–8107
   gives tips on how to burn wood most efficiently
   cleans firebox, grate, rod irons
   gives free chimney safety inspection
   equipment cost $1,000

3. The Chimney Sweeper   50.00
   4441 Loop 14
   234–4302
   complete fireplace service; cleaning, repairs,
   caps, screens

4. The Fireplace Doctor   55.00
   7656 Barton Dr.
   666–3232

5. Mercury Power Cleaning of Metro City   75.00
   2133 Thornton Rd.
   772–3319
   screen (spark arrester) $20 extra

APPENDIX C

Pro Forma Cash Flow Statements
and
Explanatory Footnotes

CHIMNEY SERVICES, INC.
PRO FORMA CASH FLOW STATEMENT
Fiscal Year 1

		Nov	Dec	Jan	Feb	Mar
	RECEIPTS					
(1)	Sales (total)	$ 2,413	3,086	2,604	2,228	1,919
	DISBURSEMENTS					
(2)	Purchases	484	711	587	334	371
(3)	Advertising	200	200	160	140	120
(4)	Subscriptions	-	60	-	-	-
(5)	Bank Charges	20	5	5	5	5
(6)	Legal Expenses	-	100	-	-	-
(7)	Insurance	427	222	222	222	222
(8)	License, Insp., Title-Van	135	-	-	-	-
(9)	Telephone	96	47	47	47	47
(10)	Art Work & Layout	30	-	-	-	-
(11)	Office Expense	10	10	10	10	10
(12)	Gasoline, Oil, Main.-Van	125	125	125	125	125
(13)	Audit Costs	-	-	-	45	-
(15)	Postage	5	5	5	5	5
(16)	Business Cards	25	-	-	-	-
(17)	Supplies & Small Tools	653	-	50	-	50
(18)	Brochures	10	-	-	-	10
(19)	Samples(Specialty Prod.)	15	-	-	-	-
(20)	Miscellaneous	25	25	25	25	25
(21)	Vacuum System	782	-	-	-	-
(22)	1977 Van	2,175	-	-	-	-
(24)	Bank Loan Payments	-	250	250	250	250
(25)	Income Tax Due	-	-	519	-	-
	Total Disbursements	5,217	1,760	2,005	1,208	1,240
	Cash Flow	(2,804)	1,326	599	1,020	679
(26)	Beginning Balance	6,000	2,696	3,522	3,621	4,141
	Net Cash Change	(2,804)	1,326	599	1,020	679
	Balance	3,196	4,022	4,121	4,641	4,820
(27)	Owner's Withdrawals(option.)	(500)	(500)	(500)	(500)	(500)
	Ending Balance	2,696	3,522	3,621	4,141	4,320

320

Apr	May	Jun	Jul	Aug	Sep	Oct	Fiscal Year Total
1,852	1,610	1,543	1,543	1,912	2,643	3,629	26,982
389	336	354	301	301	524	595	5,287
120	100	100	100	130	180	250	1,800
-	-	-	-	-	-	-	60
5	5	5	5	5	5	5	75
-	-	-	-	-	-	-	100
222	222	222	222	32	32	32	2,299
-	-	-	-	-	-	-	135
47	47	47	47	47	47	47	613
-	-	-	-	100	-	-	130
10	10	10	10	10	10	10	120
125	125	125	125	125	125	125	1,500
-	45	-	45	-	-	45	180
5	5	5	5	5	5	5	60
-	25	-	-	-	-	-	50
-	50	-	50	-	50	-	903
-	-	-	10	-	-	-	30
-	-	-	-	15	-	-	30
25	25	25	25	25	25	25	300
-	-	-	-	-	-	-	782
-	-	-	-	-	-	-	2,175
250	250	250	250	250	250	250	2,750
377	-	-	211	-	-	674	1,781
1,575	1,245	1,143	1,406	1,045	1,253	2,063	21,160
277	365	400	137	867	1,390	1,566	5,822
4,320	4,097	3,962	3,862	3,499	3,866	4,756	6,000
277	365	400	137	867	1,390	1,566	5,822
4,597	4,462	4,362	3,999	4,366	5,256	6,322	11,822
(500)	(500)	(500)	(500)	(500)	(500)	(500)	(6,000)
4,097	3,962	3,862	3,499	3,866	4,756	5,822	5,822

CHIMNEY SERVICES, INC.
PRO FORMA CASH FLOW STATEMENT
Fiscal Year 2

		Nov	Dec	Jan	Feb	Mar
	RECEIPTS					
(1)	Sales (total)	$ 4,932	5,332	4,806	4,584	4,208
	DISBURSEMENTS					
(2)	Purchases	1,931	1,013	898	898	521
(3)	Advertising	450	450	300	400	400
(4)	Subscriptions	84	-	-	-	-
(5)	Bank Charges	8	8	8	8	8
(7)	Insurance	427	222	222	222	222
(9)	Telephone	50	50	50	50	50
(11)	Office Expense	10	10	10	10	10
(12)	Gasoline, Oil, Main.-Van	140	140	140	140	140
(13)	Audit Costs	-	-	-	60	-
(14)	Equipment Maintenance	10	10	10	10	10
(15)	Postage	6	6	6	6	6
(16)	Business Cards	25	-	-	-	25
(17)	Small Tools	50	-	50	-	50
(18)	Brochures	30	-	-	30	-
(20)	Miscellaneous	25	25	25	25	25
(23)	Contract Labor	617	667	601	573	526
(24)	Bank Loan Payments	250	250	250	250	250
(25)	Income Tax Due	-	-	1,227	-	-
	Total Disbursements	4,113	2,851	3,797	2,682	2,243
	Cash Flow	819	2,481	1,009	1,902	1,965
(26)	Beginning Balance	5,822	5,891	7,622	7,881	9,033
	Net Cash Change	819	2,481	1,009	1,902	1,965
	Balance	6,641	8,372	8,631	9,783	10,998
(27)	Owner's Withdrawals(option.)	(750)	(750)	(750)	(750)	(750)
	Ending Balance	5,891	7,622	7,881	9,033	10,248

Apr	May	Jun	Jul	Aug	Sep	Oct	Fiscal Year Total
3,916	3,249	2,830	2,756	2,756	3,620	5,036	48,025
762	743	367	646	367	879	338	9,363
350	300	300	300	300	400	500	4,450
-	-	-	-	-	-	-	84
8	8	8	8	8	8	8	96
222	222	222	222	32	32	32	2,299
50	50	50	50	50	50	50	600
10	10	10	10	10	10	10	120
140	140	140	140	140	140	140	1,680
-	60	-	60	-	-	60	240
10	10	10	10	10	10	10	120
6	6	6	6	6	6	6	72
-	-	-	-	25	-	-	75
-	50	-	50	-	50	-	300
-	30	-	-	30	-	-	120
25	25	25	25	25	25	25	300
490	-	-	-	-	-	630	4,104
250	250	250	250	250	250	250	3,000
964	-	-	745	-	-	990	3,926
3,287	1,904	1,388	2,522	1,253	1,860	3,049	30,949
629	1,345	1,442	234	1,503	1,760	1,987	17,076
10,248	10,127	10,722	11,414	10,898	11,651	12,661	5,822
629	1,345	1,442	234	1,503	1,760	1,987	17,076
10,877	11,472	12,164	11,648	12,401	13,411	14,648	22,898
(750)	(750)	(750)	(750)	(750)	(750)	(750)	(9,000)
10,127	10,722	11,414	10,898	11,651	12,661	13,898	13,898

CHIMNEY SERVICES, INC.

Pro Forma Cash Flow Statement Notes

1. Sales Receipts. All sales are cash and collected at time service is performed and merchandise sold.

2. Purchases. This item includes merchandise for inventory and booked orders, which are paid for by cashier's check when orders are placed.

3. Advertising. All advertising expenses are paid in the month incurred.

4. Subscriptions. Paid immediately when ordered.

5. Bank Charges. The $20 shown in Month 1 of FY1 is for checks and is paid immediately. The other charges represent a monthly service charge for a checking account.

6. Legal Expenses. Paid the second month of FY1 for services rendered in start—up, name search, title searches, etc.

7. Insurance. Includes an initial down payment of 20% on annual premium of $1,790 for liability insurance and first and last months' premiums on insurance for van ($416/yr.). Liability insurance balance interest is paid in equal installments over next 8 months. Balance of van insurance paid over remaining 11 months.

8. Van License, Inspection, Title Transfer. These items are required to be paid in cash immediately. Cost of these items is

License	$ 30.00
State Inspection	5.00
Title Transfer	100.00

9. Telephone. This item covers first and last months' answering service charges and call forwarding on my home phone. Thereafter, payment for next month's services is made at beginning of the month.

10. Artwork & Layout. Includes initial artwork done by staff artist at Grandburg Daily News. August 1981 expense is for more elaborate work in various advertisements to kick off the busy season.

11. Office Expense. To be paid as incurred.

12. Gasoline, Oil, Maintenance——Van. To be paid as incurred.

13. Audit Costs. Paid quarterly.

14. Equipment Maintenance. Paid as incurred.

15. Postage. Paid as incurred.

16. Business Cards. Payment required by printer when cards received.

17. Supplies & Small Tools. Paid when acquired.

18. Brochures. Covers local printing and paid when received.

19. Samples. Paid for when ordered with inventory items.

20. Miscellaneous. Paid as incurred.

21. Vacuum System. Paid when delivered per policy of Dallas Distribution on merchandise sold to new businesses.

22. 1977 Van. Acquired from an individual and paid when acquired with proceeds from bank loan.

23. Contract Labor. Paid daily for work performed.

24. Bank Loan Payments. Paid beginning of each month. See Loan Amortization Schedule in Appendix P.

25. Income Tax Due. Income tax deposits are projected to be made on a quarterly basis in the last month of each quarter in the amount accrued on the income statement.

26. Beginning Balance. Includes $1,000 personal contribution and two-year, 18%, $5,000 bank loan.

27. Owner's Withdrawal. Optional resource available to me personally. Compensation for my time and work not needed to meet any minimum living standards. Funds could be left to accumulate in the business. If this amount were necessary compensation for work performed, it would be shown as a salary on both the Income and Cash Flow Statements.

APPENDIX D

Chimney Services, Inc.
Pro Forma Balance Sheets

	Fiscal Year 1		Fiscal Year 2	
Current Assets				
Cash	$5,822		$13,898	
Merchandise Inventory	46		152	
Total		$5,868		$14,050
Fixed Assets				
Equipment (Vacuum System)	782		782	
Less Accumulated Depreciation	220	562	380	402
Van	2,175		2,175	
Less Accumulated Depreciation	1,088	1,087	1,632	543
Total Assets		7,517		14,995
Liabilities				
Notes Payable*	2,925		238	
Total Liabilities		2,925		238
Owner's Equity				
Contributed Capital	1,000		1,000	
Retained Earnings Beginning of Year	-0-		9,592	
Add: Net Income (current year)	9,592		19,165	
Less: Owner's Withdrawal (current year)	(6,000)		(9,000)	
Less: Owner's Withdrawal (prior year)	–		(6,000)	
Total Owner's Equity		4,592		14,757
Total Liabilities and Owner's Equity		7,517		14,995

*Slight differences from Amortization Table, Appendix O, from rounding on the cash flow forecast.

APPENDIX E

Inventory Cost Analysis
Year 1

	Wholesale Cost[1]	Unit Cost	Unit Markup	Suggested Selling Price
Chimney Caps	$ 35.05[2]	$35.05	$32.30	$67.35[3]
Chimfex:				
1 case lot (24/cs)	125.50	5.23	1.72	6.95
2 case lots	225.72	4.70	2.25	6.95
3 case lots	306.90	4.26	2.69	6.95
Thurmalox 270				
1 case lot (12/cs)	53.33	4.44	2.06	6.50
2 case lots	106.66	4.44	2.06	6.50

[1]Includes all freight at 41¢ per pound for shipping charges.
[2]Based on average cost of ten different sizes in three different styles.
[3]Based on average suggested selling price including installation.

APPENDIX F

Inventory Cost Analysis*
Year 2

	Wholesale Cost[1]	Unit Cost	Unit Markup	Suggested Selling Price
Chimney Caps	$ 38.56	$38.56[2]	$35.53	$74.09[3]
Chimfex:				
1 case lot (24/cs)	138.00	5.75	1.90	7.65
2 case lots	248.16	5.17	2.48	7.65
3 case lots	337.68	4.69	2.96	7.65
Thurmalox 270				
1 case lot (12/cs)	58.66	4.89	2.26	7.15
2 case lots	117.33	4.89	2.26	7.15

*All costs adjusted up for anticipated price increases.
[1]Includes all freight.
[2]Based on average cost of ten different sizes in three different styles.
[3]Based on average selling price including installation.

APPENDIX G

Sales Projections (Specialty Products)*
Year 1

Month	Chimfex	Caps	Thurmalox 270	Total
November	$ 347.50	$ -0-	$ 65.00	$ 412.50
December	347.50	673.50	65.00	1,086.00
January	278.00	673.50	52.00	1,003.50
February	243.25	538.80	45.50	827.55
March	208.50	471.45	39.00	718.95
April	208.50	404.10	39.00	651.60
May	173.75	404.10	32.50	610.35

Month	Chimfex	Caps	Thurmalox 270	Total
June	173.75	336.75	32.50	543.00
July	173.75	336.75	32.50	543.00
August	229.35	336.75	45.50	611.60
September	312.75	471.45	58.50	842.70
October	437.85	606.15	84.50	1,128.50
Total	3,134.45	5,253.30	591.50	8,979.25

*See Notes to Income Statement for forecast method.

APPENDIX H

Sales Projections (Specialty Products)*
Year 2

Month	Chimfex	Caps	Thurmalox 270	Total
November	$ 573.75	$ 875.55	$ 107.25	$ 1,556.55
December	596.70	1,111.35	114.40	1,822.45
January	512.55	1,185.44	92.95	1,790.94
February	512.55	963.17	92.95	1,568.67
March	459.00	963.17	85.80	1,507.97
April	428.40	889.08	78.65	1,396.13
May	344.25	814.99	64.35	1,223.59
June	306.00	666.81	57.20	1,030.01
July	306.00	592.72	57.20	955.92
August	306.00	592.72	57.20	955.92
September	428.40	592.72	78.65	1,099.77
October	596.70	814.99	114.40	1,526.09
Total	5,370.30	10,062.71	1,001.00	16,434.01

*See Notes to Income Statement for forecast method.

APPENDIX I

Inventory Usage (Units)
Year 1

Month	Item	Beginning	Buy	Sell	Ending
November	(a) Chimfex	0	72	50	22
	(b) Caps	0	2	0	2
	(c) Paint	0	24	10	14
December	(a) Chimfex	22	72	50	44
	(b) Caps	2	10	10	2
	(c) Paint	14	12	10	16
January	(a) Chimfex	44	72	40	76
	(b) Caps	2	8	10	0
	(c) Paint	16	0	8	8
February	(a) Chimfex	76	0	35	41
	(b) Caps	0	8	8	0
	(c) Paint	8	12	7	13
March	(a) Chimfex	41	24	30	35
	(b) Caps	0	7	7	0
	(c) Paint	13	0	6	7

Month	Item	Beginning	Buy	Sell	Ending
April	(a) Chimfex	35	24	30	29
	(b) Caps	0	6	6	0
	(c) Paint	7	12	6	13
May	(a) Chimfex	29	24	25	28
	(b) Caps	0	6	6	0
	(c) Paint	13	0	5	8
June	(a) Chimfex	28	24	25	27
	(b) Caps	0	5	5	0
	(c) Paint	8	12	5	15
July	(a) Chimfex	27	24	25	26
	(b) Caps	0	5	5	0
	(c) Paint	15	0	5	10
August	(a) Chimfex	26	24	33	17
	(b) Caps	0	5	5	0
	(c) Paint	10	0	7	3
September	(a) Chimfex	17	48	45	20
	(b) Caps	0	7	7	0
	(c) Paint	3	12	9	6
October	(a) Chimfex	20	48	63	5
	(b) Caps	0	9	9	0
	(c) Paint	6	12	13	5

APPENDIX J

Inventory Usage (Units)
Year 2

Month	Item	Beginning	Buy	Sell	Ending
November	(a) Chimfex	5	144	75	74
	(b) Caps	0	28	13	15
	(c) Paint	5	36	15	26
December	(a) Chimfex	74	72	78	68
	(b) Caps	15	16	15	16
	(c) Paint	26	12	16	22
January	(a) Chimfex	68	72	67	73
	(b) Caps	16	13	16	13
	(c) Paint	22	12	13	21
February	(a) Chimfex	73	72	67	78
	(b) Caps	13	13	13	13
	(c) Paint	21	12	13	20
March	(a) Chimfex	78	0	60	18
	(b) Caps	13	12	13	12
	(c) Paint	20	12	12	20
April	(a) Chimfex	18	72	56	34
	(b) Caps	12	11	12	11
	(c) Paint	20	0	11	9
May	(a) Chimfex	34	72	45	61
	(b) Caps	11	9	11	9
	(c) Paint	9	12	9	12
June	(a) Chimfex	61	0	40	21
	(b) Caps	9	8	9	8
	(c) Paint	12	12	8	16
July	(a) Chimfex	21	72	40	53
	(b) Caps	8	8	8	8
	(c) Paint	16	0	8	8
August	(a) Chimfex	53	0	40	13
	(b) Caps	8	8	8	8
	(c) Paint	8	12	8	12

Month	Item	Beginning	Buy	Sell	Ending
September	(a) Chimfex	13	72	56	29
	(b) Caps	8	11	8	11
	(c) Paint	12	24	11	25
October	(a) Chimfex	29	72	78	23
	(b) Caps	11	0	11	0
	(c) Paint	25	0	16	9

APPENDIX K

Inventory Usage (Dollars)
Year 1

Month	Item	Beginning	Purchases[1]	Sales[2]	Ending[3]
November	(a) Chimfex	$ 0	$ 306.90	$213.00	$ 93.72
	(b) Caps	0	70.10	0	70.10
	(c) Paint	0	106.66	44.40	62.26
December	(a) Chimfex	93.72	306.90	213.00	187.44
	(b) Caps	70.10	350.50	350.50	70.10
	(c) Paint	62.26	53.33	44.40	71.19
January	(a) Chimfex	187.44	306.90	170.40	323.76
	(b) Caps	70.10	280.40	350.50	0
	(c) Paint	71.19	0	35.52	35.67
February	(a) Chimfex	323.76	0	149.10	174.66
	(b) Caps	0	280.40	280.40	0
	(c) Paint	35.67	53.33	31.08	57.92
March	(a) Chimfex	174.66	125.50	127.80	172.36
	(b) Caps	0	245.35	245.35	0
	(c) Paint	57.92	0	26.64	31.28
April	(a) Chimfex	172.36	125.50	146.23	151.67
	(b) Caps	0	210.30	210.30	0
	(c) Paint	31.28	53.33	26.64	57.97
May	(a) Chimfex	151.67	125.50	130.75	146.44
	(b) Caps	0	210.30	210.30	0
	(c) Paint	57.97	0	22.20	35.77
June	(a) Chimfex	146.44	125.50	130.75	141.21
	(b) Caps	0	175.25	175.25	0
	(c) Paint	35.77	53.33	22.20	66.60
July	(a) Chimfex	141.21	125.50	130.75	135.98
	(b) Caps	0	175.25	175.25	0
	(c) Paint	66.60	0	22.20	44.40
August	(a) Chimfex	135.98	125.50	172.59	88.91
	(b) Caps	0	175.25	175.25	0
	(c) Paint	44.40	0	31.08	13.32
September	(a) Chimfex	88.91	225.72	220.51	94.00
	(b) Caps	0	245.35	245.35	0
	(c) Paint	13.32	53.33	39.96	26.64
October	(a) Chimfex	94.00	225.72	296.10	23.50
	(b) Caps	0	315.45	315.45	0
	(c) Paint	26.64	53.33	57.72	22.20

[1]Based on the most favorable price per case lot per month.
[2]At cost (i.e. cost of goods sold). Also, Chimfex and paint cost of units sold are calculated using the FIFO method.
[3]Taken from ending inventory units in Appendix I. Will differ from beginning + purchase − sales here because of rounding of cents per unit.

Inventory Usage (Dollars)
Year 2

Month	Item	Beginning	Purchases[1]	Sales[2]	Ending[3]
November	(a) Chimfex	23.50	675.36	351.80	347.06
	(b) Caps	0	1,079.68	501.28	578.40
	(c) Paint	22.20	176.04	71.10	127.14
December	(a) Chimfex	347.06	337.68	365.82	318.92
	(b) Caps	578.40	616.96	578.40	616.96
	(c) Paint	127.14	58.68	78.24	107.58
January	(a) Chimfex	318.92	337.68	314.23	342.37
	(b) Caps	616.96	501.28	616.96	501.29
	(c) Paint	107.58	58.68	63.57	102.69
February	(a) Chimfex	342.37	337.68	314.23	365.82
	(b) Caps	501.28	501.28	501.28	501.28
	(c) Paint	102.69	68.58	63.57	97.80
March	(a) Chimfex	365.82	0	281.40	84.42
	(b) Caps	501.28	462.72	501.28	462.72
	(c) Paint	97.80	58.68	58.68	97.80
April	(a) Chimfex	84.42	337.68	262.64	159.46
	(b) Caps	462.72	424.16	462.72	424.16
	(c) Paint	97.80	0	53.79	44.01
May	(a) Chimfex	159.46	337.68	211.05	286.09
	(b) Caps	424.16	347.04	424.16	347.04
	(c) Paint	44.01	58.68	44.01	58.68
June	(a) Chimfex	286.09	0	187.60	98.49
	(b) Caps	347.04	308.48	347.04	308.48
	(c) Paint	58.68	58.68	39.12	78.24
July	(a) Chimfex	98.49	337.68	187.60	248.57
	(b) Caps	308.48	308.48	308.48	308.48
	(c) Paint	78.24	0	39.12	39.12
August	(a) Chimfex	248.57	0	187.60	60.97
	(b) Caps	308.48	308.48	308.48	308.48
	(c) Paint	39.12	58.68	39.12	58.68
September	(a) Chimfex	60.97	337.68	262.64	136.01
	(b) Caps	308.48	424.16	308.48	424.16
	(c) Paint	58.68	117.36	53.79	122.25
October	(a) Chimfex	136.01	337.68	365.82	107.87
	(b) Caps	424.16	0	424.16	0
	(c) Paint	122.25	0	78.24	44.01

[1] Based on the most favorable price per case lot per month.
[2] At cost (i.e. cost of goods sold). Also, Chimfex and paint cost of units sold are calculated using the FIFO method.
[3] Taken from ending inventory units in Appendix J. Will differ from beginning + purchase – sales here because of rounding of cents per unit.

APPENDIX M

Advertising Schedule
Year 1

Month	Advertisement	Cost
November	Business & Professional Gazette	$ –0–
	Grandburg Daily News	61.60 (1)
	Manville Daily Star	36.00 (2)
	Suburban News	22.08 (3)
	Eastworth Daily News	26.88 (4)
	Hand Circulations	53.44 (5)
		200.00

Month	Advertisement	Cost
December	Same as above	200.00
January	Business & Professional Gazette	61.60
	Manville Daily Star	43.20
	Suburban News	35.80
	Hand Circulations	19.40
		160.00
February	Metro City Penny Power	100.00 (6)
	Hand Circulations	40.00
		140.00
March	Metro City Penny Power	100.00
	Hand Circulations	20.00
		120.00
April	Yellow Pages, Boldface (Manville, Eastworth, Smithtown, Metro City, Grandburg)	35.20 (7)
	Hand Circulations	84.80
		120.00
May	Yellow Pages	35.20
	Hand Circulations	64.80
		100.00
June	Same as above	100.00
July	Same as above	100.00
August	Yellow Pages	35.20
	Metro City Penny Power	50.00
	Hand Circulations	44.80
		130.00
September	Yellow Pages	35.20
	Metro City Penny Power	100.00
	Hand Circulations	44.80
		180.00
October	Yellow Pages	35.20
	Business & Professional Gazette	65.90 (8)
	Manville Daily Star	35.50 (9)
	Suburban News	23.60 (10)
	Eastworth Daily News	28.80 (11)
	Hand Circulations	68.00
		250.00

GENERAL: Layout of ad is based on 2" x 2" (See Exhibit 2) copy for hand circulations, boldface lettering in Yellow Pages and Metro City Penny Power (2½" x 3 5/8").

1. Each Tuesday in Industrial Section of Grandburg Daily News. Includes 13 weeks of advertising and two stories with photos within 13-week period.
2. Based on open rate of $3.00 per column inch.
3. Based on open rate of $3.68 per column inch (Wednesday edition).
4. Based on open rate of $4.48 per column inch (Wednesday edition).
5. Covers xeroxing and payment to neighbor's son for distribution.
6. 1/8 page. $25.00 per week in one zone per week.
7. Manville ($4.20), Eastworth ($0.80), Smithtown ($4.10), Metro City ($14.10), Grandburg ($7.00).
8. Adjusted upward 7% for rate increases.
9. Adjusted upward 7% for rate increases.
10. Adjusted upward 7% for rate increases.
11. Adjusted upward 7% for rate increases.

APPENDIX N

Advertising Schedule
Year 2

Month	Advertisement	Cost
November	Business & Professional Gazette	$ –0–
	Grandburg Daily News	67.76 (1)
	Manville Daily Star	39.60 (2)
	Suburban News	24.29 (3)
	Eastworth Daily News	29.57 (4)
	Metro City Penny Power	47.30 (6)
	Yellow Pages	35.20 (7)
	Greensheet Weekly	194.40
	Hand Circulations	11.88 (5)
		450.00
December	Same as above	450.00
January	Business & Professional Gazette	67.76
	Yellow Pages	35.20
	Greensheet Weekly	194.40 (8)
	Hand Circulations	2.60
		300.00
February	Yellow Pages	35.20
	Greensheet Weekly	97.20
	Metro City Penny Power	110.00
	Grandburg Daily News	23.80
	Manville Daily Star	39.60
	Suburban News	24.29
	Eastworth Daily News	29.47
	Hand Circulations	40.34
		400.00
March	Same as above	400.00
April	Yellow Pages	35.20
	Greensheet Weekly	194.40
	Metro City Penny Power	82.50
	Hand Circulations	37.90
		350.00
May	Yellow Pages	35.20
	Greensheet Weekly	97.20
	Metro City Penny Power	110.00
	Hand Circulations	57.80
		300.00
June	Same as above	300.00
July	Same as above	300.00
August	Same as above	300.00
September	Yellow Pages	35.20
	Greensheet Weekly	97.20
	Metro City Penny Power	110.00
	Grandburg Daily News	23.80
	Manville Daily Star	39.60
	Suburban News	24.29
	Eastworth Daily News	29.57
	Hand Circulations	40.34
		400.00
October	Yellow Pages	35.20
	Greensheet Weekly	194.40
	Metro City Penny Power	110.00
	Business & Professional Gazette	47.76
	Manville Daily Star	39.60
	Suburban News	24.29
	Eastworth Daily News	29.57
		500.82

GENERAL: Layout of ad is based on 2" x 2" (See Exhibit 2) copy for hand circulations, boldface lettering in Yellow Pages and Metro City Penny Power (2½" x 3 5/8"). All costs have been adjusted upward 10% for rate increases.

1., 2., 3., 4., 5., 6., 7. See Notes to Year 1 Advertising Schedule.
8. Based on a weekly rate of 48.60 for six weeks with seventh week free. Circulation 50,000.

APPENDIX O

Equipment & Supplies List

Equipment

Hurricane $2\frac{1}{2}$ HP Vacuum Sweeper (includes filter)	$ 782.00
Used Chevrolet Panel Van, $\frac{1}{2}$ Ton, 350 Stnd.	2,175.00
Total Capital Assets	2,957.00

Small Tools and Supplies

3" Vacuum Hose	42.09
1½" Hose Attachment Kit	78.26
Hose Terminus Flange. 4" x 4"	11.18
Flue Brushes:	
6" Round	12.12
8" Round	14.22
8" x 8"	20.47
8" x 12"	27.32
12" x 12"	26.13
10—Fiberglas Rods, 0.440 Diameter x 10'	64.10
1—30" Fiberglas Rod, 0.480 Diameter x 30"	5.31
Quick Disconnect Fittings	8.31
6" Round Scraper	20.20
Hand Brushes:	
Duster Milbury	2.59
U–Brush	5.16
Scratch N' Scrape	2.56
Wire and Scratch	2.56
Pot Brush–Scout	3.26
Safety Goggles	2.74
Drop Cloths—9' x 12', 12 oz.	22.86
Respirator, B–40–128	23.00
Respirator Prefilters (box of 10)	9.71
Soot Cloth (48" x 48")	13.40
Rope with Snap Fitting	10.13
Weight	32.86
Pipe Thread Loop	1.35
Adapters:	
3/8" to 1/4" female PT	1.10
3/8" PT	2.60
Cold Chisel	3.14
Nut Driver Set	17.85
Coal Hod and Fire Shovel	11.42
12 oz. Ballpeen Hammer	8.91
Drop Light—25'	9.86
Light Bulbs (4—75 watt)	1.04
Inspection Mirror	5.02
20' Type II Extension Ladder	94.49
Roof Hook	12.42
Fire Extinguisher—5# CO_2	35.00
Polyethylene Bags	4.50
Total Small Tools and Supplies	$ 653.20

1. Vacuum system recommended by Amfab Chimney Sweeps Intl., Inc., Bakersville, Massachusetts. Their cost including freight was $1,014. However, system is in stock and available in Metro City at a Hurricane distributor for $782.
2. Cost of small tools and supplies is based on most competitive prices among: (1) Fincher Hardware, Grandburg, Missouri; (2) Sears & Roebuck, Grandburg, Missouri; and (3) Amfab Chimney Sweeps Intl., Inc. The list of recommended tools and supplies was published by Amfab.
3. Savings of $500 was affected by purchasing vacuum system and necessary supplies and hand tools locally.

APPENDIX P

Loan Amortization Schedule

Month	Payment	Interest	Repayment of Principal	Remaining Balance
1	$ 249.62	$ 75.00	$ 174.62	$ 4,825.38
2	249.62	72.38	177.24	4,648.14
3	249.62	69.72	179.90	4,468.24
4	249.62	67.02	182.60	4,285.65
5	249.62	64.28	185.34	4,100.31
6	249.62	61.50	188.12	3,912.20
7	249.62	58.68	190.94	3,721.26
8	249.62	55.82	193.80	3,527.46
9	249.62	52.91	196.71	3,330.75
10	249.62	49.96	199.66	3,131.09
11	249.62	46.97	202.65	2,926.44
12	249.62	43.93	205.69	2,722.72
13	249.62	40.84	208.78	2,513.96
14	249.62	37.71	211.91	2,302.05
15	249.62	34.53	215.09	2,086.97
16	249.62	31.30	218.32	1,868.65
17	249.62	28.03	221.59	1,647.06
18	249.62	24.71	224.91	1,422.15
19	249.62	21.33	228.29	1,193.86
20	249.62	17.91	231.71	962.15
21	249.62	14.43	235.19	726.96
22	249.62	10.90	238.72	488.24
23	249.62	7.32	242.30	245.95
24	249.62	3.69	245.95	—0—

APPENDIX II: BAHNHOF-X

Business Plan for a Contracting Business

BAHNHOF—X, INC.

Business Plan

Prepared by

George C. Scarsdale
Bahnhof—X, Inc.
Suite 203
124 Main Street
Ceredo, Texas 76301
(241) 891—6574

FOR <u>INFORMATION</u> ONLY

TABLE OF CONTENTS

Business Plan

BUSINESS CONCEPT

Bahnhof–X, Inc. will provide rotary drilling services to
oil and gas operators in the western Texas and eastern New
Mexico areas. Two of the company's major goals are
controlled growth and capital accumulation through
profits from independent contract drilling.

Location of Operations

Operators and drillers typically exist as separate
entities because operators normally have leases all over
the country and transporting drilling rigs over long
distances is not economical. Independent drilling
contractors like Bahnhof–X generally restrict their
rigs' operations to within 100 miles of a specified base.
They thereby add the benefits of specialization in a
given area.

Bahnhof–X, Inc. will tap the Paleostrata Basin, the
largest subsurface geological formation in the targeted
area. The company's first operation base will be in the
northwest area of the formation, at Ceredo, Texas, in
Dillon County. The target area within 100 miles of Ceredo
is ideal for initial operations because of: (1) the
demand for rigs, (2) the availability of supplies and
labor, (3) the lack of natural interruptions, and (4) the
depths to which drilling takes place.

The Service to Be Offered

Aside from the fact that the current market is a driller's
market in which a condition of excess demand exists,
Bahnhof–X will concentrate on dependability and
efficiency. Furthermore, Bahnhof–X drilling equipment
will permit work conforming to the highest industry
standards.

During the initial phases of the company's
operations, management will endeavor to reduce the firm's
risk by working on a daily rate basis and will avoid
responsibility for trucking, mud, fuel, and bits to
concentrate on the efficiency of the rigs and crews. The
management of Bahnhof–X feels that conditions during the
initial stages will allow it to secure 365–day contracts
of this type. A sample drilling contract with data from an
actual 12,500–foot contract for a rig operating in the Texas
Panhandle having a capacity similar to that of the proposed
Bahnhof–X Rig #1. Note that the contract has an industry
standard escalation clause of 1% per month or the escalation
rate of the driller's direct costs, whichever is higher.

Because of the risks they impose on the driller,

turnkey and footage contracts on deep or exploratory wells will be avoided by Bahnhof–X for the foreseeable future. Some operators are even reducing driller's risk by letting daywork contracts for up to three years with the above–mentioned features.

Some major firms have been so desperate for rigs as to assist in financing the construction of new ones. It is a realistic assumption that a new independent driller, such as Bahnhof–X, with equipment of the proposed capacity will be able to secure with a major oil company a contract.

Drilling Equipment

An emphasis will be placed on acquiring or creating highly competitive equipment that will retain its value relatively better than competing rigs. Each purchase of equipment will be approved only after extensive cost–benefit and market feasibility analysis by management. However, the desire to reduce costs will not be allowed to interfere with the construction of an efficient and high–quality rotary rig system.

The firm's first rig will be assembled under the supervision of Bahnhof–X and will have a capacity of 12,500 feet total depth. The components listed in Appendix D have been proposed for Bahnhof–X Rig #1. Additional rigs will be purchased or constructed if future conditions so warrant. Present indications suggest that a second rig of a similar capacity to Rig #1 could be utilized in the near future.

MARKET CONSIDERATIONS

Drilling activity in our market area is particularly high and should continue strong well into the future. Domestic drilling has been on an upward trend for a number of years and should remain on this trend until reserves become exhausted or an alternative power source is developed.

Industry Economic Factors

Before the raising of oil prices by the OPEC nations in 1973, domestic drilling was at a low point. Major oil companies had a supply of cheap foreign oil, which discouraged costly domestic drilling activity. Independent investors' interest in domestic drilling was extremely low, because a government ceiling created artificially low prices on oil, which no longer justified the risks of drilling at unregulated rising costs. It was

338

an operators' market in which operators could impose
demanding requirements on independent drillers.

With the decontrol of prices, oil well drilling has
become an independent drillers' market. The drilling
capacity of the rotary rigs in operation is far exceeded
by the demand for holes.

Domestic oil prices have increased tenfold since
1973, and the supply of rigs has yet to meet the demands
for their services. The majority of current drilling
activity is still infilled drilling--most rigs are still
being used for expanding production in fields where
production is already taking place. Rigs are still being
used in this manner to expand production in fields that
were being underproduced before decontrol. It is
generally accepted that infilled drilling will retain its
prominence for another three to four years, after which
operators will begin to expand into more wildcat and
exploratory activity. Though rigs are entering the market
at a rate of 70 per month, investors, major suppliers, and
government officials do not visualize supply meeting
demand within the near future. Many feel the demand for
medium- and larger- size rigs will not be met for a number
of years.

Though the current demand for rigs is artificially
high because of the effects of former price controls, rig
utilization should continue to be strong even after
supply meets demand and the market becomes more
competitive. Drilling activity will be stimulated as the
price of crude continues to climb relative to other
prices and oil becomes more difficult to find. Strong
popular trends toward less government and further
decontrol suggest that efforts to boost domestic
production will not be hindered by price controls.
Forecasts of major oil companies indicate a strong up
trend for spending on exploration activity with no
downward trends in the foreseeable future. Until an
alternative fuel is developed or our national reserves
are depleted, the demand for drilling activity should
continue upward.

Target Area Demand and Competition

The target area is a drillers' market. The Hughes Tool
Count, considered to be the most accurate measure by the
industry, indicates that there were 70 rotary drilling
rigs in the area during the past year. The rigs are all
owned by the 14 independent drillers in the area, the
largest of which owns 13 rigs and the smallest of which
owns one. Of these rigs, none was reported idle except for
repairs, and the only reason why any had backlogs of less
than six months was gross negligence by the drilling
company.

Most of the activity is on wells of 8,000-11,000 feet; however, some drilling is starting to take place in the lower levels of the basin at depths of 12,000-12,500 feet. Though the demand for all the rigs operating near Ceredo will remain strong in the near future, rigs capable of reaching the deeper levels will retain their value longer than lesser rigs. Bahnhof-X rigs will be capable of competing for 12,500 foot holes.

The demand for drilling comes from private investors, independents, and major oil operators. Along with numerous smaller ventures, the major oil companies are extremely active in the target area. Bidding for drilling services is led by Diamond-Shamrock and Amalgamated Petroleum, which own the vast majority of the area's mineral rights, but other major operators looking for drillers include Gulf, Texaco, Socal, Arco, Exxon, and Mobil. Sales appear to be limited in the near future only by our ability to find and finance equipment.

Other Attractive Qualities of Target Area

From the standpoint of supplies and labor the target area is particularly attractive. The commitment to continued drilling operations near Ceredo is evidenced by a high level of local investment. Supply companies, machine and repair shops, and trucking companies have been plentiful in the area since 1928. Ceredo and the surrounding towns of Lubbock, Smithville, Centerburg, Madden, and Dekalb in Texas and Hobwell in New Mexico all offer supplies and repair services available 24 hours per day, within 100 miles of base. Access to pipelines is readily available, and Ewing Petroleum is currently constructing a new refinery in Smithville.

Even with the construction of the refinery requiring 1,200 men, Hughes Tool reports none of the drillers or operators has difficulty procuring crews. Although Ceredo has a population of less than 4,500, it is centrally located to the oil towns mentioned above, and the company could draw from all of them for crew members. Facilities in the town itself now include one of the region's better school systems, a YMCA, several fast-food restaurants, a family restaurant, and three hotels, including a newly-built Holiday Inn. Current housing construction should provide space for incoming laborers.

MANAGEMENT

Bahnhof-X, Inc. recognizes that success depends on its management. Outstanding individuals will be selected for all key slots. Four crucial members of the management team have been identified.

President

The founder and president of Bahnhof–X, Inc. is Mr.
George C. Scarsdale. Mr. Scarsdale, age 38, grew up with his
family's oil and well drilling and exploration business. He
received a B.S. degree in geology from the University of
Texas and an M.B.A. from Wharton. He worked for five years
with Mobil Oil in various positions related to the management
of oil well exploration and drilling activities. His next
position was with Texaco. As a manager with Texaco he
supervised up to 15 drilling projects at one time. For the
last four years he has served as Chief Operating Officer of
Cecil M. Cartwright Drilling Corporation, an established
drilling contractor based in the Texas Panhandle. As Chief
Operating Officer, Mr. Scarsdale built the business from
four drilling rigs to ten. During his tenure profits
quadrupled, and each of Cartwright's rigs is under contract
for at least two years.

Tool Pusher

The assistant will be an experienced tool pusher. The
individual must have at least five years' experience as a
tool pusher with a minimum of two years' work experience
on a rig of the capacity of the proposed Bahnhof–X rig.
The individual must have spent at least one year working
in the target area and be able to move into the area within
two weeks after he is hired.
   Mr. Scarsdale and his assistant will supplement
their capabilities with expert consultation as it is
needed.

Management and Financial Consultant

Mr. C. B. Finch, President of Finch Drilling and C. B.
Finch, Inc., has offered to assist in the start–up
operations and provide advice regarding future large
investment decisions. He has over 44 years' experience in
the petroleum industry, including 21 years as head of his
own companies, which now operate nine rotary drilling
rigs in Kansas and New Mexico.

Technical Consultant

Mr. Harry Davis has offered his services as a petroleum
engineer. He received his engineering degree from the
University of Texas and has since accumulated 28 years of
experience in exploration, well completion, reservoir
design, and equipment design in Kansas, Oklahoma, and
Texas oil regions. Mr. Davis is a registered professional
engineer in the states of Texas and Oklahoma and is
familiar with operations in the target area. He is highly

respected for his work in rig design and will collaborate
with Mr. Finch on the construction of Rig #1.

Résumés and references for any of the members of the
management team are available on request.

FINANCIAL PERFORMANCE

The financial forecasts provide an estimate of results of
operations and changes in financial position for the
first two years of the firm's existence. The estimates
are based on corporate formation before next July and
include timely data derived from similar operations in
the Northern Texas Panhandle and West Texas areas. Market
and other industry information was obtained from highly
reliable sources and it reflects a realistic outlook.

The projections are based on 30-day months and all
data is computed on full months to highlight trends and
fluctuations in unit figures. The forecasted interim
start-up period runs from next July through December with
initial operations of Rig #1 beginning in the following
January. Additional rigs are added to the projections in
October and April of Fiscal Year 2; however, no
exploration or diversification is included within the two
years. It should be noted that contributions from
shareholders are assumed to be in the form of stock only
and that no dividends are distributed.

Pro Forma Income Statements

Monthly Income Statements have been projected for the
first 24 months of Bahnhof-X, Inc. These detailed
forecasts are presented in Appendix A, together with
explanatory footnotes. A summary of the Pro Forma Income
Statements follows.

	Fiscal Year 1	Fiscal Year 2
Total Operating Revenue	$ 1,205,580	$ 5,310,980
Total Operating Expense	765,690	2,897,350
Net of Other Revenue & Expense	[229,800]	[730,600]
Net Profit Before Taxes	210,090	1,683,030
Income Tax	77,420	754,870
Net Profit	132,670	928,160

Solid profitability is achieved in month 7 of Fiscal
Year 1, and no monthly losses are projected thereafter.

Pro Forma Cash Flow Statements

In addition to the Pro Forma Income Statements, monthly
Cash Flow Statements have been projected for the first 24

months of Bahnhof–X, Inc. These Cash Flow forecasts are presented in Appendix B, along with explanatory footnotes. An overview of the Pro Forma Cash Flow Statements follows.

	Fiscal Year 1	Fiscal Year 2
Total Receipts	$ 1,844,820	$ 4,914,970
Total Disbursements	1,308,620	3,817,590
Net Cash Flow	536,200	1,097,380
Ending Bank Balance	536,200	1,633,580

Substantial liquid assets will be available at the end of Fiscal Year 2 permitting the opportunity for expansion, diversification, or distribution.

Pro Forma Balance Sheets

Pro Forma Balance Sheets have been prepared as of the end of Fiscal Year 1 and Fiscal Year 2. A brief summary of the detailed Balance Sheets presented in Appendix C is provided below.

	Fiscal Year 1	Fiscal Year 2
Assets		
Current Assets	$ 759,240	$ 2,382,440
Investments	296,800	314,560
Fixed (Net of Depreciation)	1,989,640	6,439,230
Total Assets	3,045,680	9,136,230
Liabilities		
Current Liabilities	225,700	1,254,910
Noncurrent Liabilities	1,887,310	6,020,490
Stockholders' Equity		
Paid–in Capital	800,000	800,000
Retained Earnings	132,670	1,060,830
Total Liabilities + Capital	$ 3,045,680	$ 9,136,230

FINANCING THE PLAN

Bahnhof–X, Inc. will issue $ 1 par, Section 1244 stock to its incorporators in exchange for their capital contributions. Initial capital of $800,000 is forecasted as necessary to provide working capital for operations and an adequate reserve for unforeseen difficulties. The incorporators may wish to contribute a portion of this capital in the form of disproportionate loans and thus provide for tax–free withdrawal of funds after the start–up period and successful operations; the form of the contributions will depend on the incorporators' final agreement on shareholder objectives.

The first rotary drilling rig will be financed through an agreement with DRICO Leasing Company (the highlights of which are exhibited in Appendix E.) The incorporators may choose at their discretion to form Bahnhof–X Leasing Company to take advantage of interest and depreciation deductions and investment tax credit. Formation of such an additional company could provide tax advantages to the participating investors and financial advantage to the drilling company.

The final financial structure will be determined by the incorporators in consultation with legal counsel.

PHASES OF THE PLAN

Timing is crucial for sound planning and analysis of drilling operations. Bahnhof–X will enter the market under ideal conditions in which sales are limited only by the ability to find and finance additional equipment. The corporation will have an optimal situation in which to accumulate experience and establish a quality track record, so that it will be able to operate profitably in later years when conditions become more competitive.

The plan for taking advantage of today's conditions may be separated into five phases: (a) corporate formation, (b) interim start–up, (c) rapid experience accumulation, (d) equipment expansion, and (e) vertical expansion.

Corporate Formation

This phase encompasses the actual incorporation process, the securing of employment agreements, production of the necessary contracts, and procurement of insurance policies to begin construction of a rig.

Interim Start–up

Construction of Rig #1 and broadening contacts with various operators would be the primary activities of the interim period before operations begin. Under the offer outlined in Appendix E, DRICO Leasing would offer Bahnhof–X a $2.8 million line of credit for the construction of Rig #1. During this period, expenses incurred for the construction of the rig, such as yard rental, tool pusher/foreman salary, and supplies, may be charged to DRICO Drilling. The incorporators will work out of their homes throughout this period, for an office will not be established until a positive cash flow warrants it.

Rapid Experience Accumulation

Upon construction of the first rig and the commencement
of operations, the firm will be able to gain operating
experience rapidly, as its rigs will be virtually assured
of full 24-hour operation. The firm will be able to move
into a highly competitive position on its experience
curve before competition for work becomes a challenge.

Equipment Expansion

The management of Bahnhof-X will endeavor to expand the
equipment line, for there are definite economies of scale
to be had when managing large equipment. Under the
present outlook, it is desirable to add at least two
additional rigs to utilize administrative capabilities
fully and to justify the purchase of a yard. With the
three rigs, Bahnhof-X will be able to accumulate and use
some major spare parts and further minimize downtime
caused by equipment failure. A profitability study will
be made in detail before each equipment purchase.
Conditions may indicate the need for additional rigs and
personnel, and, if so, every effort will be made to
acquire them.

Vertical Expansion

The firm may find it desirable to enter into exploration
programs and expand its services. As the supply of rigs
nears their demand, Bahnhof-X will gradually take on
greater responsibility from the operator and will need to
purchase its own supplies, fuel, etc. It may be best for
the firm to enter into or form oil exploration programs to
diversify its revenue sources and take advantage of
available tax benefits.

APPENDIX A

Pro Forma Income Statements & Explanatory Footnotes

Approximate Month	July 1	Aug 2	Sept 3	Oct 4	Nov 5
OPERATING REVENUE					
1 Drilling Tool Revenue	-	-	-	-	-
TOTAL OPERATING REVENUE	-	-	-	-	-
OPERATING EXPENSES					
2 Depreciation Expense-Rig	-	-	-	-	-
3 Rig Maintenance & Supplies	-	-	-	-	-
4 Direct Labor-Wages	-	-	-	-	-
5 DL Payroll Taxes	-	-	-	-	-
6 DL Expense Allowance	-	-	-	-	-
7 Insurance Expense	210	210	210	2,690	2,690
8 Truck & Auto Maintenance	-	40	40	40	40
9 Depreciation Expense-Truck	-	190	190	190	190
10 Depreciation Expense-Radio	-	-	-	-	-
11 Yard Rental	-	-	-	-	-
12 Administrative Salaries	2,000	2,000	2,000	2,000	2,000
13 Admin-Payroll Taxes	200	200	200	130	130
14 Admin-Expense Allowance	2,500	2,500	2,500	2,500	2,500
15 Office Rental	-	-	-	-	-
16 Depreciation-Office Equip	10	10	10	10	10
17 Office Supplies	270	-	-	-	-
18 Telephone	300	300	300	300	300
19 Legal & Accounting	500	-	-	-	-
20 Consulting	2,800	-	-	-	-
21 Advertising	70	30	30	30	40
TOTAL OPERATING EXPENSE	8,860	5,480	5,480	7,890	7,900
OPERATING PROFIT	(8,860)	(5,480)	(5,480)	(7,890)	(7,900)
OTHER REVENUES & EXPENSES					
22 Interest Revenue	6,420	6,410	6,410	6,340	6,340
23 Interest Expense	-	-	-	-	46,010
TOTAL OTHER REV & EXP	6,420	6,410	6,410	6,340	(39,670)
NET PROFIT BEFORE TAX	(2,440)	930	930	(1,550)	(47,570)
25 INCOME TAX EXPENSE	(900)	340	340	(570)	(17,530)
NET PROFIT (LOSS)	(1,540)	590	590	(980)	(30,040)

	Dec 6	Jan 7	Feb 8	Mar 9	Apr 10	May 11	June 12	TOTAL FY1
	–	195,960	197,930	199,910	201,900	203,910	205,970	$ 1,205,580
	–	195,960	197,930	199,910	201,900	203,910	205,970	1,205,580
	–	25,230	25,230	25,230	25,230	25,230	25,230	151,380
	–	30,000	30,000	30,000	30,000	30,000	30,000	180,000
	–	33,570	33,570	33,570	35,100	35,100	35,100	206,010
	–	3,520	3,520	3,520	3,690	3,690	3,690	21,630
	–	8,640	8,640	8,640	8,640	8,640	8,640	51,840
	2,690	5,770	5,770	5,770	5,770	5,770	5,770	43,320
	40	40	40	40	40	40	40	440
	190	190	190	190	190	190	190	2,090
	–	–	–	130	130	130	130	520
	–	120	120	120	120	120	120	720
	2,000	5,000	5,000	7,100	7,100	7,100	7,100	50,400
	130	500	500	580	510	510	510	4,100
	2,500	2,500	2,500	2,500	2,500	2,500	2,500	30,000
	–	–	–	1,520	1,520	1,520	1,520	6,080
	10	10	10	140	140	140	140	640
	80	50	50	50	30	30	30	590
	300	300	300	580	380	380	380	4,120
	250	–	–	–	–	–	–	750
	–	2,800	1,400	1,400	700	700	700	10,500
	40	40	120	40	40	40	40	560
	8,230	118,280	116,960	121,120	121,830	121,830	121,830	765,690
	(8,230)	77,680	80,970	78,790	80,070	82,080	84,140	439,890
	6,340	3,780	3,770	4,440	4,940	5,420	6,110	66,720
	46,010	34,550	34,370	34,180	33,990	33,800	33,610	296,520
	(39,670)	(30,770)	(30,600)	(29,740)	(29,050)	(28,380)	(27,500)	(229,800)
	(47,900)	46,910	50,370	49,050	51,020	53,700	56,640	210,090
	(17,650)	17,290	18,560	18,080	18,800	19,790	20,870	77,420
	(30,250)	29,620	31,810	30,970	32,220	33,910	35,770	132,670

Pro Forma Income Statement
Fiscal Year 2

Approximate Month	July 1	Aug 2	Sept 3	Oct 4	Nov 5
OPERATING REVENUE					
1 Drilling Tool Revenue	208,030	210,110	212,210	428,240	432,520
TOTAL OPERATING REVENUE	208,030	210,110	212,210	428,240	432,520
OPERATING EXPENSES					
2 Depreciation Expense-Rigs	25,230	25,230	25,230	53,170	53,170
3 Rig Maintenance & Supplies	30,000	30,000	30,000	60,000	60,000
4 Direct Labor-Wages	35,100	35,100	35,100	73,260	73,260
5 D.L. Payroll Taxes	3,690	3,690	3,690	7,360	7,360
6 D.L. Expense Allowance	8,640	8,640	8,640	17,280	17,280
7 Insurance Expense	5,800	5,800	5,800	12,330	12,330
8 Truck & Auto Maintenance	540	40	40	40	40
9 Depreciation Expense-Truck	190	190	190	190	190
10 Depreciation Expense-Radio	130	130	130	160	160
11 Yard Rental	120	120	120	500	120
12 Administrative Salaries	8,000	8,000	8,000	8,000	8,000
13 Admin-Payroll Taxes	570	540	530	530	80
14 Admin-Expense Allowance	2,750	2,750	2,750	2,750	2,750
15 Office Rental	1,600	1,600	1,600	1,600	1,600
16 Depreciation Office Equip.	140	140	140	140	140
17 Office Supplies	30	30	30	30	30
18 Telephone	380	380	380	380	380
19 Legal & Accounting	250	200	700	200	200
20 Consulting	1,400	1,400	2,800	2,800	1,400
21 Advertising	40	40	40	40	40
TOTAL OPERATING EXPENSE	124,600	124,020	125,910	240,760	238,530
OPERATING PROFIT	83,430	86,090	86,300	187,480	193,990
OTHER REVENUES & EXPENSES					
22 Interest Revenue	6,910	6,950	7,700	6,550	6,550
23 Interest Expense	33,410	33,210	33,000	71,040	70,630
24 Loss on Sale of Truck	–	–	–	–	–
TOTAL OTHER REV & EXP	(26,500)	(26,260)	(25,300)	(64,490)	(64,080)
NET PROFIT BEFORE TAX	56,930	59,830	61,000	122,990	129,910
25 INCOME TAX EXPENSE	25,530	26,830	27,360	55,160	58,260
NET PROFIT (LOSS)	31,400	33,000	33,640	67,830	71,650

348

	Dec 6	Jan 7	Feb 8	Mar 9	Apr 10	May 11	June 12	TOTAL FY2
	436,840	438,440	442,820	447,240	678,050	684,830	691,650	$5,310,980
	436,840	438,440	442,820	447,240	678,050	684,830	691,650	$5,310,980
	53,170	53,170	53,170	53,170	82,930	82,930	82,930	643,500
	60,000	60,000	60,000	60,000	90,000	90,000	90,000	720,000
	73,260	73,260	73,260	73,260	114,570	114,570	114,570	888,570
	7,360	7,360	7,360	7,360	11,510	11,510	11,510	89,760
	17,280	17,280	17,280	17,280	25,920	25,920	25,920	207,360
	12,330	12,700	12,700	12,700	18,930	18,930	18,930	149,280
	40	40	40	40	40	40	40	980
	190	210	210	210	210	210	210	2,400
	160	160	160	160	190	190	190	1,920
	–	–	–	–	–	–	–	980
	8,000	8,000	8,000	8,000	8,000	8,000	10,920	98,920
	80	840	840	660	660	660	950	6,940
	2,750	2,750	2,750	2,750	2,750	2,750	3,750	34,000
	1,600	1,680	1,680	1,680	1,680	1,680	2,400	20,400
	140	140	140	140	130	130	180	1,700
	30	30	30	30	30	30	180	510
	380	420	420	420	420	420	420	4,800
	200	200	450	700	200	200	200	3,700
	700	700	1,400	2,800	2,800	1,400	1,400	21,000
	40	40	120	40	40	40	110	630
	237,710	238,980	240,010	241,400	361,010	359,610	364,810	2,897,350
	199,130	199,460	202,810	205,840	317,040	325,220	326,840	2,413,630
	8,080	9,630	10,430	12,200	13,120	13,120	15,950	117,190
	70,220	69,790	69,360	68,910	109,200	108,550	107,880	845,200
	–	2,590	–	–	–	–	–	2,590
	(62,140)	(62,750)	(58,930)	(56,710)	(96,080)	(95,430)	(91,930)	(730,600)
	136,990	136,710	143,880	149,130	220,960	229,790	234,910	1,683,030
	61,440	61,310	64,530	66,890	99,100	103,070	105,390	754,870
	75,550	75,400	79,350	82,240	121,860	126,720	129,520	928,160

BAHNHOF-X, INC.

Footnotes to the Pro Forma Income Statements
Fiscal Years 1 and 2

1. Drilling Tool Revenue is based on 365 day contracts on a
   daywork basis for each rig with three four-man crews per rig.
   Contracts are expected for Rig #1 starting in January of year
   1 and 2 at $7100/day and $7900/day respectively, for Rig #2
   starting in October of year 2 at $7750/day, and for Rig #3
   starting in April of year 2 at $8200/day. These projections
   are derived from contracts for similar equipment and service
   in the West Texas region and are escalated 1% per month as is
   customary. Fees are assumed to include day's drilling and moving
   plus a downtime allowance; however, estimated revenue is
   discounted 8% each month to allow for additional downtime.

2. Depreciation Expense—Rigs is computed on a straight-line
   basis for each rig over its seven-year lease period. Rig #1
   is depreciated at $25,230/mo. starting in January year 1,
   Rig #2 at $27,940/mo. starting in October year 2, and Rig #3
   at $29,760/mo. starting in April year 2. (Note 23, which
   follows, and Note 4 to the Cash Flow Forecast provide
   additional background and supporting information.)

3. Rig Maintenance and Supplies includes minor repairs,
   supplies, and parts used consistently to maintain the
   drilling rig. $1000/day per rig is estimated based on the
   highest allowances budgeted for rigs in the Ceredo area.

4. Direct Labor is computed for each rig at three crews of four
   men each (on eight-hour tours). For one rig in January '82:

3 drillers	x 12.00/hr x 8 hrs =	288/day
3 derrick men	x 10.50/hr x 8 hrs =	252/day
6 floor hands	x 10.50/hr x 8 hrs =	504/day
		1044/day
Add: overtime adjustment for six-day week (seventh-day relief crews)		75/day
		$1119/day

   Wages are based on present rates in the West Texas area with
   an additional $0.50/hr. added to each worker's rate in April
   year 1 for $1170/day, October year 2 for $1221/day, and April
   (month 10) year 2 for $1273/day per rig.

5. Direct Labor—Payroll Taxes computed for FICA at 6.65% on the
   first $29,700 annually per employee and for federal and
   state unemployment at 3.4% on the first $6000. Due to the
   transient nature of the labor, the combined rate of 10.05% of
   wages is estimated throughout the year.

6. Direct Labor—Expense Allowance is limited to 30¢ per mile
   for transportation from here to the rigs. An estimated 80
   miles of travel per day is used to calculate the monthly
   expense of $8640 per rig, and no change in rates is
   forecasted for the two-year period.

7. Insurance Expense is expected to be
   $1,070 semiannually for general liability starting in
   month 1, year 1.

350

$7,443 quarterly for each rig for $25,000 deductible
against fire and loss. Starts in month 4, year 1,
under assumption of insurable interest in Rig #1
at that time. New policies are added in the first
month of operations for the other two rigs.

$37,000 annually for each rig for workmen's
compensation. Added in the first month of each
rig's operations.

$190 semiannually for $250 deductible truck liability.
Starts in month 1, year 1.

The cost of each policy is prorated over its term, and each
new policy in year 2 is increased by 12% in price.

8. <u>Truck</u> <u>and</u> <u>Auto</u> <u>Maintenance</u> or allowance for repairs and
   maintenance of $40/mo. is started in month 2, year 1, and
   continued for the two years with an additional $500 for tires
   in month 1, year 2.

9. <u>Depreciation</u> <u>Expense—Truck</u> is calculated on a
   straight—line basis for tool pusher's pickup truck. First
   truck bought at the end of July of year 1 for $8820 and
   depreciated at $190/mo., but is traded in for $3000 on a
   similar pickup in January of year 2. The new truck with value
   of $9880 is depreciated straight—line at $210/mo.

10. <u>Depreciation</u> <u>Expense—Radio</u> is calculated on a
    straight—line basis for five years for each piece of
    equipment. One base and two mobile units (base at office, one
    mobile unit in truck and other on rig) are purchased in the
    beginning of March, year 1, at a combined cost of $7700 for
    the three and depreciated at $130/mo. Two more mobile units
    are purchased for the other rigs in months 4 and 10 of year 2
    at $1850 each. They are individually depreciated at $30/mo.
    beginning in the month of acquisition.

11. <u>Yard</u> <u>Rental</u> is for a portion of a trucking yard in Ceredo,
    Texas, in which parts may be safely stored and rigs may be
    assembled. A rate of $120/mo. is expected with an additional
    $380 in month 4 of year 2 for the increased activity of the
    new rig. This facility will not be needed after month 5 of
    fiscal year 2.

12. <u>Administrative</u> <u>Salaries</u> are for
    1 officer @ $2000/mo. during mos. 1–8 of year 1, $3000/mo.
        during mos. 9–12 of year 1, and $3500 throughout
        year 2.
    1 tool pusher @ $3000/mo. during second half of year 1 and
        $3300/mo. during year 2.
    1 secretary @ $1100/mo. during months 9–12 of year 1 and
        $1200 throughout year 2.
    1 landman @ $2920/mo. added in the last month of year 2.

13. <u>Administrative—Payroll</u> <u>Taxes</u> are computed at the current
    rate of 6.65% of the first $29,700 per employee calendar year
    income for FICA and 3.4% of the first $6,000 per employee
    calendar year income for unemployment. Both taxes are
    computed on the calendar year basis and no turnover is
    assumed (income limits are computed to the nearest half
    month).

14. <u>Administrative—Expense</u> <u>Allowance</u> includes luncheons,
    travel, dues and subscriptions, etc. The officer's allowance

is expected at $1500/mo. during year 1 and $1650/mo. in year 2. The tool pusher's allowance is estimated at $1000/mo. to be paid by Bahnhof-X in both halves of year 1, and $1100/mo. to be paid in year 2. The landman's allowance is estimated at $1000/mo.

15. Office Rental is budgeted for "A" grade space in Dallas. High-quality space is customary and helpful in drilling operations. Estimates are based on 1400 sq. ft. in First Equity Towers at $13/sq. ft. in January with an escalation of 5% in month 1 and month 7 of FY 2. Another 600 sq. ft. is added in June of year 2.

16. Depreciation—Office Equipment is calculated on a straight-line basis. Two used answering machines and one adding machine purchased in month 1, year 1, for $210 are depreciated at $10/mo. over 21 months. Upon leasing an office in March of FY 1, an estimated $7830 will be spent on used furniture and equipment of "A" quality for one secretary and one officer. This equipment will be depreciated straight-line at $130/mo. starting in the month of purchase. $5200 will be spent in June of FY 2 for office expansion and depreciated at $50/mo.

17. Office Supplies for year 1 are projected as $270 in month 1, $80 in month 6, $50/mo. in the third quarter, and $30/mo. in the fourth quarter. The $30/mo. replenishment allowance is maintained through year 2 with an additional $150 in the last month. The figures fluctuate because of the stockpiling of items and the initial purchases of accessories for the office.

18. Telephone expenses for the first year projections include a $300/mo. long distance allowance through the eighth month and $380/mo. for long distance and office phones thereafter, with a $200 installation charge in the ninth month, Year 2 includes $380/mo. for the first six months with a 10% hike to $420/mo. for the second six months.

19. Legal and Accounting expenses are variable, depending on the timing of leasing agreements and the searches for equipment. Legal fees in year 1 include $500 in month 1 and $250 in month 6. For year 2 the legal expense is forecasted at $250 in months 1 and 8 and $500 in months 3 and 9. Accounting services are presumed to be needed starting in month 2, year 2, at $200/mo. to provide computerized bookkeeping and payroll tax preparation.

20. Consulting expense estimates are projected for a high-quality petroleum engineer to assist in rig design at rates of $50/hr. or $350/day. Periods of greatest assistance will be near rig acquisitions, therefore two days per week or $2800/mo. is estimated for month 7 of year 1 and months 3, 4, 9, and 10 of year 2. $1400/mo. is projected for inspection and planning in months 8 and 9 of year 1 and months 1, 2, 5, 8, 11, and 12 of year 2. $700 is budgeted during months 10, 11, and 12 of year 1 and months 6 and 7 of year 2 to allow for the review of potential equipment for acquisition.

21. Advertising will be minimal for Bahnhof-X, Inc. $30/mo. will be used every month for Yellow Pages advertisements. $10/mo. is budgeted for handbills, which will be used monthly starting in November of year 1 to attract employees.

Advertising will consist of

$30/mo. for ads in the Yellow Pages of Dallas, Lubbock, Smithville, Ceredo, and Centerburg, Texas.

$40 for business cards in July of year 1 and $70 in June of year 2.

$80 for truck signs in February of both years.

$10/mo. for handbills to assist the tool pusher in finding help starting in November of year 1.

22. Interest Revenue is composed of two major components. The first is interest earned and available from prudent investment in a ready asset fund. A rate of return of 12% is assumed, and earnings are estimated from that portion of the company's balances that management chooses not to keep in the checking account at the bank. The second component is the 6% return compounded annually and recognized monthly on the $280,000 of DRICO debentures purchased in the first month of year 1.

23. Interest Expense for the first six months of FY 1 consists of $46,010 in months 5 and 6 to finance the rig during assembly per the base agreement with DRICO Leasing (see Appendix E), calculated under the assumption that virtually all materials will be acquired by month 5 at the maximum value of $2.8 million. Interest expense thereafter consists of amortization under the interest method of each rig's lease payments. 19 1/2% is used as the lessee's incremental borrowing rate to capitalize the lease payments (see note 4 of the Cash Flow Forecast in Appendix B at calculated values of $2,119,640 for Rig #1, $2,397,580 for Rig #2, and $2,552,740 for Rig #3).

24. Loss on Sale of Truck (year 2 only) of $2590 is used to account for the difference between book value and trade-in value of the truck described in Note 9.

25. Income Tax is computed on the net income before taxes at the current federal corporate tax rates. The year's average rate (36.85% year 1, 44.85% year 2) is used to compute the monthly tax or tax benefit. It should be noted that under a business plan for investment in exploration and operating ventures in year 2 the tax would be substantially less; however, this projection does not include any exploration programs.

353

APPENDIX B

Pro Forma Cash Flow Statements
& Explanatory Footnotes

BAHNHOF-X
Projected Cash Flow
Fiscal Year 1

Approximate Month	July 1	Aug 2	Sept 3	Oct 4	Nov 5	Dec 6
RECEIPTS						
1 Drilling Tool Revenue Rec'd	–	–	–	–	–	–
2 Interest Revenue Received	–	5,020	5,010	5,010	4,940	4,940
3 Proceeds From Stock Issue	800,000	–	–	–	–	–
TOTAL RECEIPTS	800,000	5,020	5,010	5,010	4,940	4,940
DISBURSEMENTS						
4 Equipment Rental-Rig #1	–	–	–	–	–	–
5 Rig Maintenance & Supplies	–	–	–	–	–	–
6 Direct Labor Wages	–	–	–	–	–	–
7 D.L. Payroll Taxes	–	–	–	–	–	–
8 D.L. Expense Allowances	–	–	–	–	–	–
9 Insurance	1,260	–	–	7,440	–	–
10 Truck & Auto Maintenance	–	40	40	40	40	40
11 Yard Rental	–	–	–	–	–	–
12 Administrative-Salaries	2,000	2,000	2,000	2,000	2,000	2,000
13 Admin-Payroll Taxes	200	200	200	130	130	130
14 Admin-Expense Allowance	2,500	2,500	2,500	2,500	2,500	2,500
15 Office Rental	–	–	–	–	–	–
16 Office Supplies & Service	270	–	–	–	–	80
17 Telephone	–	300	300	300	300	300
18 Legal & Accounting	–	500	–	–	–	–
19 Consulting	2,800	–	–	–	–	–
20 Advertising	70	30	30	30	40	40
21 Interest Expense	–	–	–	–	–	–
22 Income Tax	–	–	–	–	–	–
23 Purchase of DRICO Debntrs.	280,000	–	–	–	–	–
24 Purchase of Pickup Truck	8,820	–	–	–	–	–
25 Radio Equipment	–	–	–	–	–	–
26 Office Furniture & Equip	210	–	–	–	–	–
TOTAL DISBURSEMENTS	298,130	5,570	5,070	12,440	5,010	5,090
NET CASH FLOW	501,870	(550)	(60)	(7,430)	(70)	(150)
END-OF-MONTH BANK BAL.	501,870	501,320	501,260	493,830	493,760	493,610

Jan 7	Feb 8	Mar 9	Apr 10	May 11	June 12	TOTAL FY1
–	195,960	197,930	199,910	201,900	203,910	$ 999,610
4,940	2,380	2,370	3,040	3,540	4,020	45,210
–	–	–	–	–	–	800,000
4,940	198,340	200,300	202,950	205,440	207,930	1,844,820
45,760	45,760	45,760	45,760	45,760	45,760	274,560
30,000	30,000	30,000	30,000	30,000	30,000	180,000
33,570	33,570	33,570	35,100	35,100	35,100	206,010
3,520	3,520	3,520	3,690	3,690	3,690	21,630
8,640	8,640	8,640	8,640	8,640	8,640	51,840
36,460	–	–	10,520	–	–	55,680
40	40	40	40	40	40	440
120	120	120	120	120	120	720
5,000	5,000	7,100	7,100	7,100	7,100	50,400
500	500	580	510	510	510	4,100
2,500	2,500	2,500	2,500	2,500	2,500	30,000
–	–	1,520	1,520	1,520	1,520	6,080
50	50	50	30	30	30	590
300	300	300	580	380	380	3,740
250	–	–	–	–	–	750
2,800	1,400	1,400	700	700	700	10,500
40	120	40	40	40	40	560
92,020	–	–	–	–	–	92,020
–	–	–	14,370	–	–	14,370
–	–	–	–	–	–	280,000
–	–	–	–	–	–	8,820
–	–	7,770	–	–	–	7,770
–	–	7,830	–	–	–	8,040
261,570	131,520	150,740	161,220	136,130	136,130	1,308,620
(256,630)	66,820	49,560	41,730	69,310	71,800	536,200
236,980	303,800	353,360	395,090	464,400	536,200	536,200

BAHNHOF-X
Projected Cash Flow
Fiscal Year 2

Approximate Month	July 1	Aug 2	Sept 3	Oct 4	Nov 5	Dec 6
RECEIPTS						
1 Drilling Tool Revenue Rec'd	205,970	208,030	210,110	212,210	428,240	432,520
2 Interest Revenue Rec'd	4,710	5,430	5,470	6,220	5,070	5,070
TOTAL RECEIPTS	210,680	213,460	215,580	218,430	433,310	437,590
DISBURSEMENTS						
4 Equipment Rental	45,760	45,760	45,760	147,100	96,430	96,430
5 Rig Maintenence & Supplies	30,000	30,000	30,000	60,000	60,000	60,000
6 Direct Labor-Wages	35,100	35,100	35,100	73,260	73,260	73,260
7 D.L. Payroll Taxes	3,690	3,690	3,690	7,360	7,360	7,360
8 D.L. Expense Allowances	8,640	8,640	8,640	17,280	17,280	17,280
9 Insurance	11,930	–	–	50,840	–	–
10 Truck & Auto Maintenance	540	40	40	40	40	40
11 Yard Rental	120	120	120	500	120	–
12 Administrative-Salaries	8,000	8,000	8,000	8,000	8,000	8,000
13 Admin-Payroll Taxes	570	540	530	530	80	80
14 Admin-Expense Allowance	2,750	2,750	2,750	2,750	2,750	2,750
15 Office Rental	1,600	1,600	1,600	1,600	1,600	1,600
16 Office Supplies & Service	30	30	30	30	30	30
17 Telephone	380	380	380	380	380	380
18 Legal & Accounting	–	450	200	700	200	200
19 Consulting	1,400	1,400	2,800	2,800	1,400	700
20 Advertising	40	40	40	40	40	40
21 Income Tax Payments	47,570	–	15,480	19,360	–	–
22 New Purchase of Pickup Truck	–	–	–	–	–	–
23 Radio Equipment	–	–	–	1,850	–	–
24 Office Furniture & Equip	–	–	–	–	–	–
25 Purchase Yard & Improvements	–	–	–	–	11,800	14,000
26 Spare Rig Parts Purchased	–	–	–	–	–	–
TOTAL DISBURSEMENTS	198,120	138,540	155,160	394,420	280,770	282,150
NET CASH FLOW	12,560	74,920	60,420	(175,990)	152,540	155,440
END-OF-MONTH BANK BAL	548,760	623,680	684,100	508,110	660,650	816,090

356

Jan 7	Feb 8	Mar 9	Apr 10	May 11	June 12	TOTAL FY2
436,840	438,440	442,820	447,240	678,050	684,830	$4,825,300
6,600	8,150	8,950	10,720	11,640	11,640	89,670
443,440	446,590	451,770	457,960	689,690	696,470	4,914,970
96,430	96,430	96,430	202,670	149,550	149,550	1,268,300
60,000	60,000	60,000	90,000	90,000	90,000	720,000
73,260	73,260	73,260	114,570	114,570	114,570	888,570
7,360	7,360	7,360	11,510	11,510	11,510	89,760
17,280	17,280	17,280	25,920	25,920	25,920	207,360
52,500	–	–	63,000	–	–	178,270
40	40	40	40	40	40	980
–	–	–	–	–	–	980
8,000	8,000	8,000	8,000	8,000	10,920	98,920
840	840	660	660	660	950	6,940
2,750	2,750	2,750	2,750	2,750	3,750	34,000
1,680	1,680	1,680	1,680	1,680	2,400	20,400
30	30	30	30	30	180	510
380	420	420	420	420	420	4,760
200	200	450	700	200	200	3,700
700	1,400	2,800	2,800	1,400	1,400	21,000
40	120	40	40	40	110	630
19,360	–	–	19,360	–	–	121,130
6,880	–	–	–	–	–	6,880
–	–	–	1,850	–	–	3,700
–	–	–	–	–	5,200	5,200
–	–	–	–	–	–	25,800
15,700	–	–	–	–	94,100	109,800
363,430	269,810	271,200	546,000	406,770	511,220	3,817,590
80,010	176,780	180,570	(88,040)	282,920	185,250	1,097,380
896,100	1,072,880	1,253,450	1,165,410	1,448,330	1,633,580	1,633,580

BAHNHOF—X, INC.

Footnotes to the Projected Cash Flow Analysis
Fiscal Years 1 and 2

1. Drilling Tool Revenue Received is based on payment within 25 days of completion of a hole with an estimated 30 days per hole to allow for wells to the maximum depth of 12,500', thus, payment is recognized in the month following the month earned.

2. Interest Revenue Received consists of interest from the ready asset fund, which is recognized as received one month after it is earned. Interest from the DRICO debentures is accrued and compounded but not paid until end of the seven-year lease.

3. Proceeds from Stock Issue received in month 1, year 1, consist of $800,000 received for 20,000 shares of common stock with $1 par value. Refer to the section entitled "Financing the Plan" for further details and alternatives on the subject of ownership.

4. Equipment Rental—Rigs is projected using the terms of an offer to lease Rig #1 from DRICO Leasing Co. per the outline exhibited in Appendix E. The payments are specified as 1.6344% of total rig cost, which is assumed to be the maximum of $2.8 million for Rig #1; thus, payments on this rig are estimated at $45,760/mo., commencing on the same day as the rig's operations. Rigs #2 and #3 are assumed to be on the same terms, only the costs of these rigs are adjusted for an increase of 1% per month. Rig #2 cost is estimated at $3.1 million with payments of $50,670/mo. starting in October of year 2, and Rig #3 cost is estimated at $3.25 million with payments of $53,120/mo. starting in April (month 10) of year 2. There are double payments made on Rigs 2 and 3 in the first month of each rig's operation.

5. Rig Maintenance and Supplies are paid in the month expensed.

6. Direct Labor—Wages are paid in the month incurred.

7. Direct Labor—Payroll Taxes are assumed to be deposited in the month incurred.

8. Direct Labor—Expense Allowances are assumed to be paid as incurred.

9. Insurance is paid at the beginning of each term period as specified in Note 7 of the Income Statement, with the exception of the workmen's compensation policies on which 75% is paid in the first month and 8 1/3% paid at the beginning of each of the following three quarters.

10. Truck and Auto Maintenance is assumed to be paid as expensed.

11. Yard Rental is expected to be paid as incurred.

12. Administrative—Salaries are expected to be paid as incurred.

13. Administrative—Payroll Taxes are expected to be deposited in the month incurred.

14. Administrative Expense Allowance is assumed to be paid as expensed.

15. Office Rental is expected to be paid as expensed.

16. Office Supplies are paid in month expensed.

17. Telephone expenses are expected to be paid in the month following their incurrence.

18. Legal & Accounting. Legal expenses are paid in the month following their incurrence, and accounting expenses are paid as incurred.

19. Consulting fees are expected to be paid as incurred.

20. Advertising is expected to be paid as expensed.

21. Interest Expense of $92,020 for interim construction of Rig #1 is paid in month 7 of year 1. The remaining interest expense shown on the income statement reflects an accounting treatment of the equipment rental fee.

22. Income Tax estimated payments are made in the first month following each profitable quarter. The first payments for the third and fourth quarters of year 1 are calculated at 80% of the tax liabilities for these quarters. The balance of 20% is paid the following September. Estimated payments for year 2 are based on year 1 total liability paid on a quarterly installment basis.

23. Purchase of DRICO Debentures is expected in July of year 1 per the lease offer from DRICO Leasing Co. The seven-year 6% subordinated debentures would be purchased for $280,000 to establish a $2.8 million line of credit with DRICO Drilling Supply to which Bahnhof-X would charge the expense of constructing Rig #1.

24. Purchase of Pickup Truck occurs in month 1 of FY 1 and month 7 of FY 2. A $3000 trade-in assumed at the time of acquisition of the second truck, yielding a net cost of $6880.

25. Radio Equipment purchases are explained in Note 10 of Income Statement Forecast.

26. Office Furniture and Equipment purchases are explained in Note 16 of the Income Statement Forecast.

27. Purchase of Yard and Improvements is made in month 5 of year 2. With more than one rig the company will start to build an Inventory of major parts. A five-acre yard is purchased in month 5 for $2360/acre (in Ceredo, Texas). $10,000 is spent for security fence and $4000 for gravel and leveling in month 6.

28. Spare Rigs Parts Purchased include $15,700 for a spare rotary table in month 7 of year 2 and $94,100 spent for a spare mud pump in month 12 of year 2.

APPENDIX C

Pro Forma Balance Sheets

BAHNHOF–X, INC.

Pro Forma Balance Sheets
Fiscal Years 1 and 2

	Ending Balances Fiscal Year 1		Ending Balances Fiscal Year 2	
Assets				
Current Assets				
Cash and Securities	$ 536,200		$1,633,580	
Accounts Receivable	205,970		691,650	
Interest Receivable	4,710		14,470	
Prepaid Expenses	12,360	759,240	42,740	2,382,440
Investments: Debentures		296,800		314,560
Property & Equipment				
Land and Improvement				25,800
Drilling Rig #1	2,119,640		2,119,640	
Less: Accum. Depr.	[151,380]	1,968,260	[454,140]	1,665,500
Drilling Rig #2	––		2,397,580	
Less: Accum. Depr.	––		[251,460]	2,146,120
Drilling Rig #3	––		2,552,740	
Less: Accum. Depr.	––		[89,280]	2,463,460
Yard Equipment and Parts	––		109,800	
Less: Accum. Depr.	––		––	109,800
Trucks and Autos	8,820		9,880	
Less: Accum. Depr.	[2,090]	6,730	[1,260]	8,620
Radio Equipment	7,770		11,470	
Less: Accum. Depr.	[520]	7,250	[2,440]	9,030
Furniture & Equipment	8,040		13,240	
Less: Accum. Depr.	[640]	7,400	[2,340]	10,900
Total Assets		3,045,680		9,136,230
Liabilities & Equity				
Current Liabilities				
Accounts Payable	380		420	
Current Portion of Lease	162,270		557,700	
Income Tax Payable	63,050	225,700	696,790	1,254,910
Noncurrent Portion of Lease		1,887,310		6,020,490
Stockholders' Equity				
Common Stock $1 Par	20,000		20,000	
Additional Paid-in Capital	780,000		780,000	
Retained Earnings	132,670	932,670	1,060,830	1,860,830
Total Liability & Equity		3,045,680		9,136,230

APPENDIX D: RIG DESCRIPTION

Bahnhof-X, Inc.--Rig 1

Drawworks--U-IS Modified

Rig Engines--Two Cat 353 Diesels

Derrick--Covco 132' x 650,000# gross

Substructure--12' x 24' x 45', 800,000# gross

Boock & Hook--Crosby McKissick 250T Combo w/W. W. Hook

Links--2 3/4 x 108"--250T

Drilling Line--1 1/8" x 5000'

Swivel--Ideco 250T

Rotary Table--National 20 1/2"

Kelly--4 1/4" Baash Ross w/Varco Bushing

Rotary Hose--3" x 55', 8000# Goodall

Tongs--B. J. Type B

Automatic Driller and Recorder--Totco

Weight Indicator--Totco

Halliburton measuring line & Totco slope test instrument

Pump--20" Gardner-Denver GXR with Pulsation Dampener, compounded

Pump--14" G.D.--FXK, with Cat 353 Diesel Engine

Mud tanks & Premix--7' x 10' x 60', 550 bbls.
                --7' x 10' x 50', 200 bbl. working
                & 130 bbl premix

Mud house--8' x 30'

Water tank/Generator house--10' x 12' x 50', 600 bbl. capacity

Generators--Two Cat 130 kw, diesel powered

Diesel fuel tank--8' x 16', 6000 gal. capacity

Blowout preventors--10" x 5000# Hydril Hydraulic Double
                   --10" x 5000# Hydril GK Annular

Drilling Spool--10" x 5000#

Closing Unit--Hydril 80 gal. 4 position

BOP Choke Assembly

Drill Pipe--12,000' 4 1/2" x H 16.6 #/ft. Grade E, w/Reed "Casing
        Plus" handbanding

Drill collars--21 6 1/4" x 2 1/4" x 31' Drilco

Miscellaneous--Doghouse, crew change room, parts room, bunk
          house, propane tank, mud bucket, drill pipe
          slips, & elevators, water pumps, compressors,
          walkway, pipe racks, pipe baskets, tarps,
          derrick climber, and geronimo.

Offer of Lease Agreement

DRICO
LEASING COMPANY

MARTIN V. SHEFFIELD
EXECUTIVE VICE PRESIDENT
AND TREASURER

George C. Scarsdale
Bahnhof-X, Inc.
124 Main, Suite 203
Ceredo, Texas 76301

Dear Mr. Scarsdale:

Thank you for your recent inquiry regarding the possibility of our company assisting you in the procurement of an oil and gas drilling rig. We would like to offer the following quotation for your consideration:

LESSOR: DRICO Leasing Company

LESSEE: Bahnhof-X, Inc.

PROPOSED LINE OF CREDIT: $2.8 million (for new equipment and related rig-up expense)

TERM OF LEASE: Seven (7) years

CANCELLABILITY: Lease is non-cancellable

RENTAL CHARGES:

(a) Monthly: Computed using the factor 1.6344%; First month's rent due on commencement date: Monthly rental payments due each month thereafter

(b) Interim: From date of lease execution until rental commencement date upon completion of rig fabrication; Rate computed at Dallas State Bank prime plus 2%; Payment due within ten (10) days of billing and billing to be on lease execution date.

INSURANCE: (a) Evidence from insurance carrier of
                                      intent to insure completed drilling
                                      rig must be submitted to DRICO
                                      Leasing Company prior to any funding

                                  (b) Evidence of insurance during fabri-
                                      cation must be satisfactory to
                                      DRICO Leasing Company.

DRILLING CONTRACT ASSIGNMENT: Bahnhof-X, Inc. shall provide an assignment
                                  of a drilling contract from an acceptable
                                  petroleum company (no less than one-year
                                  term)

DRICO DEBENTURES: Bahnhof-X, Inc. agrees to buy the
                                  following:

                                  DRICO Leasing Company Subordinated
                                  Debentures

                                  • $280,000 Principal Amount
                                  • 7 years and 1 month Term
                                  • 6% per annum compounded Interest

                                  Debentures are to be purchased within one
                                  week after execution of lease agreement
                                  and will be repaid (with accrued interest)
                                  upon satisfactory completion of lease.

If you would like to proceed based on the terms and conditions stated
above, please sign below and return to me at your earliest convenience.

                                  Sincerely,

                                  DRICO Leasing Company

                                  Martin V. Sheffield

                                  Martin V. Sheffield
                                  Vice President

LLG/cm

Agreed to and accepted.

Bahnhof-X, Inc.

_____   _____
George C. Scarsdale, President   Date

APPENDIX III: THERMOS-TOTE, INC.

Business Plan for a Manufacturing Business

THERMOS-TOTE, INC.

Prepared by

Rex J. Powers
1620 Pinehurst Street
Mackworth, Kansas 81504
(913) 228-6277

FOR INFORMATION ONLY

Table of Contents

Business Plan

COMPANY

Thermos–Tote, Inc. is a proposed corporation for
manufacturing and marketing an innovative new product,
the Thermos–Tote™

THE PRODUCT

Thermos–Tote™, a product designed for truckers by a
trucker, is a thermos bottle holder that fastens securely
to the interior of the cab of a truck. It is available in
three sizes, pint and quart thermos bottle and one–half
gallon water jug.

Advantages

The Thermos–Tote™ offers a number of advantages to its
users.

Money Savings   Unsecured thermos bottles and jugs
frequently roll about in the cab of a
truck and fall out on the pavement when
the cab door is open. It is not uncommon
to break three thermos bottles in a
year. The savings could easily pay for
Thermos–Tote™.

Safety   Unsecured thermos bottles that are free
to move about in the cab of a truck
present a potential safety problem. By
securing these bottles, Thermos–Tote™
eliminates this safety problem.

Convenience   If thermos bottles are securely
fastened in a predetermined place, the
convenience to the truck driver is
greatly increased.

In addition, the neat appearance and rugged steel
construction of the Thermos–Tote™ make it an attractive
product with a long useful life.

FINANCIAL OBJECTIVES

Thermos–Tote, Inc. has defined its objectives for the
future.

	Sales	Net Profit after Tax
1st Year	$ 833,466	$ 162,728
2nd Year	1,781,136	393,460

Furthermore, sales for year 3 are expected to increase
$900,000.

CAPITAL REQUIRED

In order to achieve its financial objective, Thermos-
Tote, Inc. will require $100,000.

MARKETING

Market

Every truck driver, heavy equipment operator, boat owner,
and camper owner is a potential user of the Thermos-Tote™.
    Every truckstop, heavy equipment dealer, boat shop,
and camper dealer is a potential distributor of the
Thermos-Tote™.

Market Survey

In an attempt to verify the demand for the Thermos-Tote™
and whether the marketplace would pay the price, a stainless steel prototype of each of the three sizes of the
Thermos-Tote™ was constructed for and demonstrated by
Mr. Powers. Next, an order form was prepared and an effort was
made to obtain firm, written orders for the Thermos-Tote™.
    The reception was very favorable among both truck
drivers and truckstop owners. In a few weeks' time,
signed orders for 726 units were obtained. Approximately
one-half of those potential distributors contacted
placed orders for the Thermos-Tote™. Additional orders are
expected before production actually begins.
    Orders were taken for the deluxe stainless steel
model at the following dealer prices:

Pint size	$13.50 each
Quart size	$14.50 each
1/2 gallon size	$14.00 each

    Furthermore, those surveyed expressed an interest in
a less expensive model of the Thermos-Tote™. Such a unit
can be constructed using cold rolled steel instead of
stainless steel and can be sold at the following dealer
prices:

Pint size	$ 9.90 each
Quart size	$10.90 each
1/2 gallon size	$10.40 each

    Mr. Powers' appraisal of the survey response is that
in the long run, the cold rolled model will comprise 80%
of the number of Thermos-Tote™ units sold.

Competition

There is no product known to Thermos–Tote™ management that directly competes with the Thermos–Tote™.

MARKETING PLAN

The marketing plan centers around a well–organized series of activities aimed at capturing a significant portion of the market. The plan will be coordinated by the president, Mr. Powers, who has approximately twenty years' experience in the trucking and shipping industry. He knows the market, and he knows the people and their needs.

Resources

Thermos–Tote™ plans to use a variety of resources to capture the desired share of the market.

Advertising, Magazines	Commitments for the first year have already been obtained for free advertising in the form of feature stories and new product descriptions in magazines such as Open Road and Overdrive. A budget of $13,200 is allocated for the second year.
Advertising, Radio	Radio spots on stations such as WBAP (Dallas), WHO (Des Moines), WSM (Nashville) will be sponsored during the first year by various truckstops. During the second and subsequent years, Thermos–Tote™ will be running its own series of coordinated radio commercials on radio stations selected as truck driver favorites.
Salesmen	Individual truck drivers will be recruited to promote and service accounts along their regular routes. They will be paid a commission on each unit they sell.

Displays & Posters	Attractive and quality displays and posters depicting the three sizes of Thermos–Tote™ will be given to all distributors in an effort to promote and sell the product at the point of purchase.
Cover Letters & Brochures	Professional cover letters and brochures will be prepared to solicit distribution and sales by mail.
Conventions	Conventions and exhibitions such as the National Truckstop Operators Convention and the Local and Short Haul Carriers National Conference Convention will be attended and utilized for promoting the Thermos–Tote™. It is estimated that three conventions will be attended the first year, and four of these conventions will be attended each year thereafter. Over 2,000 pieces of promotional material will be given away at each convention.

SALES FORECAST

Sales can be made through four distribution channels

1. Truckstops
2. Heavy equipment dealers
3. Boat shops
4. Camper dealers

Sales forecasts, presented herein, however, are based only on truckstops' sales. Projected sales are

First Year	$ 833,466
Second Year	$1,781,136

These projections should be attainable, because they assume that there are only 360 truckstops distributing Thermos–Tote™ by the end of the second year. The Mid–

Continental truckstop system alone has over 600
truckstops.

An additional and significant source of revenues
will result from shipping. The Company will lease a truck
and will combine delivery of products with selling
activities. The shipping revenues are expected to be

First Year	$	53,933
Second Year	$	116,348

MANAGEMENT

President

The president and general manager is Mr. Rex J. Powers.
Mr. Powers has been involved in the trucking and shipping
industry for almost twenty years. He is familiar with
accounting, selling, reporting, maintenance, loading and
unloading activities, and procedures.

Mr. Powers was also vice-president and general
manager of the Alaska Kansas Express Company. His
experience with this company included coordination of
equipment and personnel, hiring, solicitation of
freight, establishment of terminals, instruction of
drivers, and maintenance of equipment (see Appendix A for
résumé).

Sales Manager

A sales manager will be hired in the sixth month of the
first year. This individual will be a professional truck
driver who owns a truck. Initially, this person will help
service and solicit accounts. Later, responsibilities
will include coordinating and managing the sales
organization.

Assistant Sales Manager

An assistant sales manager will be hired in the first
month of the second year. This individual will be a
professional truck driver and will help service and
solicit accounts.

Route Supervisor

A route supervisor will be hired in the first month of the
third year. This person will also be a professional truck
driver and will help service and solicit accounts.

Management Services

Planning Associates, Inc. will provide management
services on a consulting basis. The president of the
company is Dr. Andrew J. Burns, who is an experienced and
accomplished executive (see Appendix B for biographical
data).

FINANCIAL STATEMENTS

Income Statement

Thermos-Tote, Inc. projects a profit in its second month
of operations, as indicated in the detailed two-year pro
forma income statement shown in Appendix C. The company's
net profit after tax may be summarized as follows:

Year	Net Profit after Tax
First	$ 162,728
Second	393,460

Cash Flow Statement

A detailed monthly pro forma cash flow statement was
prepared for the first year to determine the sources and
allocations of cash and the total financing needed (see
Appendix D). As may be seen in this detailed statement, a
maximum cash deficit of $86,297 is realized in the ninth
month of operations.

Balance Sheet

A pro forma balance sheet was prepared for the first year
of operations (see Appendix J). This balance sheet
portrays the financial position of the company after 12
months in business. A summary follows.

	End of Year 1
Assets	$ 328,458
Liabilities	65,730
Capital	262,728

This statement of financial position assumes the
desired capital is secured in return for the issuance of
common stock.

371

ITEMIZED USE OF CAPITAL

Thermos-Tote, Inc., desires $100,000 of initial financing. This capital will be used as follows:

Tooling	$ 6,390
Additional Patent Work	2,400
Organizational Costs	1,000
Marketing Materials Layout	1,000
Office Equipment	1,300
Study and Planning Fee	1,500
Operating Capital	72,920
Contingency Allowance	13,490
Total Capital Used	$ 100,000

APPENDIX A

Résumé of Rex J. Powers

Rex J. Powers

Address
: 1620 Pinehurst Street
Mackworth, Kansas 81504
(913) 228-6277

Experience
: 1974 to present—independent contract trucking with local Mackworth firms.

1969-1974—partner in a company that owned one truck. Transportation company operated truck and drove between Kansas and Florida. Responsibilities included: managing truck, accounting, maintenance records, hiring and instructing drivers, and preventing cargo claims and accidents.

1969—driver with ABC Company of Mackworth, Kansas, routine driving duties, hired and supervised a second driver.

1968-1969—driver for Fast Food Express, Salina, Kansas. Responsibilities included checking product temperature to make sure that it was at the prescribed setting and was working properly and defrosting automatically, logging, filling out trip sheets, attending safety seminars.

1967–1968––founder, vice-president, and general manager of Alaska Kansas Express Company, formed to transport oil field machinery and equipment and other heavy and cumbersome freight between Kansas and Alaska. Activities in forming the company included obtaining ICC permits, attending ICC hearings, answering protests, and soliciting investment capital.

1965–1967––employed by B&N Transportation Company, Inc., Lawrence, Kansas, as their Alaska sales representative, home based in Anchorage, Alaska. Coordinated picking up and delivering freight. Responsible for interlining approximately 530,000 pounds in a four-month period between Alaska and Seattle.

1963–1964––attended Mackworth State College and worked on the freight docks part-time for Ryder Truck Lines and also part-time for Roadway Express. Duties included loading and unloading trucks, checking freight, handling claims, and troubleshooting lost shipments.

1957–1963––rejoined the U.S. Navy. Worked in a Naval supply agency. Duties included handling shipments of general commodities and other heavy shipments from the United States through Japan to ships and bases in the Far and Mid East.

1957––employed by Haverty Trucking Company in Salina, Kansas. Duties included coordinating receiving orders for shipments, making sure that the trucks were properly loaded and at the proper time, dispatching, billing, rating, and operating Teletype.

1954–1957––enlisted in the U.S. Navy. Worked with the USN Postal Service. Duties included loading and unloading. Progressed to dispatcher of 14 trucks, which delivered mail to ships, aircraft, and trains. Was in charge of preventive maintenance program for 14 trucks. Other duties included rating, handling claims, handling government bills of lading, keeping records of tonnage, and working 26 Japanese nationals as freight handlers. Was qualified to handle registered mail.

Military	Military service completed with honorable discharge. No reserve obligation.

Personal	U.S. Citizen; Born August 4, 1940, in Bixby, Kansas. Height 5'11"; Weight 242#; Graduated from Bixby High School, Bixby, Kansas. Hobbies: flying, fishing, calf roping. Other interests: Mason, 32nd Degree, Scottish Rite, and member of the First Baptist Church in Mackworth. Excellent health, married, three children.

374

APPENDIX B

Biographical Summary
Andrew J. Burns, Ph.D.

Experience

1975–Present Adjunct Professor of Finance at Kansas State University. Principal in the management consulting firm of Planning Associates, Inc. Author of two books on starting and managing your own business.

1966–1975 Founder, president of Burns Industries, Inc., a diversified manufacturer and marketer of productivity-improving equipment.

Founded six subsidiaries in four foreign countries.

Company is an industry leader and a dominant competitor in its field.

Company's stock is traded publicly in the O.T.C. market. Current year's sales will top $50 million.

1960–1966 President of Jonathan Damo & Company, Boston, Massachusetts. Sophisticated mechanical engineering services company. Increased sales each year by an average of 30%. Sales in 1966 topped $10 million.

Education
1953–1960 Bachelor's Degree in Mechanical Engineering at Massachusetts Institute of Technology. Master's and Doctor's degrees in Business Administration at Wharton.

Military
1950–1953 U.S. Air Force, fighter pilot. Served in Philippines, Okinawa, and Japan. Honorable discharge.

Personal
Born 1932, U.S. Citizen. Excellent health, happily married, two children.

PRO FORMA INCOME STATEMENT

Thermos-Tote, Inc.
2-Year Pro Forma Income Statement

Month	1	2	3	4	5
(1) Sales	17829	30564	34487	44630	52744
(2) Shipping revenue	930	1595	2258	2922	3454
Total Revenue	18759	32159	36745	47552	56198
Cost of Goods Sold					
Direct Materials					
Stainless Metalwork					
(3) Half gallon	2094	3590	1019	1319	1557
(4) Quart	3616	6199	1756	2273	2686
(5) Pint	1431	2454	693	897	1062
(6) Steel (stainless)	1638	2808	796	1030	1217
Cold Roll Products					
(7) Half gallon	0	0	2951	3819	4514
(8) Quart	0	0	5214	6748	7975
(9) Pint	0	0	2068	2675	3161
(10) Mounting screws	252	432	612	792	936
(11) Screw bag	25	43	61	79	94
Containers (Individual)					
(12) Half gallon	70	120	170	220	260
(13) Quart	124	212	300	389	459
(14) Pint	49	85	120	155	184
(15) Master	123	211	299	387	458
(16) Mailing labels	14	24	34	44	52
(17) Misc. Ship. Supplies	25	43	61	79	94
Total	9461	16221	16154	20906	24709
Direct Labor					
(18) Packaging	76	130	184	238	281
Total	76	130	184	238	281
Overhead					
(19) Storage	20	34	48	62	73
(20) Tooling amortization	805	1380	1955	2250	0
(21) Patent amortization	12	12	12	12	12
Total	837	1426	2015	2324	85
Total Cost of Goods Sold	10374	17777	18353	23468	25075
Gross Profit	8385	14382	18392	24084	31123

376

6	7	8	9	10	11	12	Total	Year 2
64916	75058	85202	93317	101430	111573	121716	833466	1781136
4251	4915	5579	6110	6642	7306	7971	53933	116348
69167	79973	90781	99427	108072	118879	129687	887399	1897484
1917	2216	2515	2753	2992	3291	3590	28853	52521
3306	3823	4339	4753	5166	5683	6199	49799	90694
1306	1511	1715	1880	2045	2249	2454	19697	35899
1498	1732	1966	2153	2340	2574	2808	22560	41081
5556	6424	7292	7988	8683	9552	10420	67199	152442
9815	11349	12882	14109	15336	16870	18403	118701	269239
3891	4499	5106	5592	6077	6684	7292	47045	106684
1152	1332	1512	1656	1800	1980	2160	14616	28728
115	133	151	166	180	198	216	1461	2873
320	369	419	459	499	549	599	4054	7968
565	654	742	813	883	972	1060	7173	14098
226	261	297	325	353	389	424	2868	5639
563	651	739	810	880	968	1056	7145	14045
64	74	84	92	100	110	120	812	1596
115	133	151	166	180	198	216	1461	2873
30409	35161	39910	43715	47514	52267	57017	393444	826380
346	400	454	497	540	594	648	4388	8618
346	400	454	497	540	594	648	4388	8618
90	104	118	129	141	155	169	1143	1600
0	0	0	0	0	0	0	6390	0
12	12	12	12	12	12	12	144	144
102	116	130	141	153	167	181	7677	1744
30857	35677	40494	44353	48207	53028	57846	405509	836742
38310	44296	50287	55074	59865	65851	71841	481890	1060742

Thermos-Tote Pro Forma Income Statement — Years 1 & 2

Month	1	2	3	4	5
Gen. & Administrative Expense					
(22) General manager	1500	1500	1500	1500	1500
(23) Sales manager	0	0	0	0	0
(24) Assistant sales manager	0	0	0	0	0
(25) Route supervisor	0	0	0	0	0
(26) Clerical	950	950	950	950	950
(27) Bookkeeper	0	0	0	0	950
(28) Fringe & payroll tax	368	368	368	368	510
(29) Rent, office	0	0	0	0	188
(30) Phone	250	250	250	250	250
(31) Utilities	0	0	0	0	100
(32) Postage	50	50	50	50	50
(33) Office Eqpt. Dep.	7	7	7	7	7
(34) Legal fees	100	100	100	100	100
(35) Audit	417	417	417	417	417
(36) Organizational costs	83	83	83	83	83
(37) Insurance –general	200	200	200	200	200
(38) Insurance –key man	75	75	75	75	75
(39) Bad debt allowance	357	611	690	893	1055
(40) Study and planning fee	125	125	125	125	125
(41) Franchise tax	30	30	30	30	30
(42) Office supplies	80	80	80	80	140
(43) Management assistance	0	0	0	0	0
Subtotal G&A	4592	4846	4925	5128	6730
(44) Miscellaneous	230	242	246	256	337
Total G&A	4822	5088	5171	5384	7067
Marketing					
(45) Posters	46	33	33	33	26
(46) Displays	70	50	50	50	40
(47) Brochures	50	50	50	50	50
(48) Cover letters #1 & #2	15	21	6	6	6
(49) Advertising	0	0	0	0	0
(50) Personnel costs – conv.	75	75	75	75	75
(51) Pins	50	50	50	50	50
(52) Brochures	50	50	50	50	50
(53) Booth cost	175	175	175	175	175
(54) Marketing Materials Layout	83	83	84	83	83
(55) Commissions	0	0	740	1980	2340
(56) Bonus	0	0	0	0	0
(57) Truck Lease Exp.	2700	2700	2700	2700	2700
(58) Car Lease Expense	0	0	0	0	0
(59) Maint. & Opr. Exp.	1667	1667	1667	1667	1667
(60) Travel	600	600	600	600	600
Total Marketing	5581	5554	6280	7519	7862
Total Op. Exp.	10403	10642	11451	12903	14929
Net Profit before Tax	(2018)	3740	6941	11181	16194
(61) Income Tax Allowance	0	654	2638	4249	6154
Net Profit after Tax	(2018)	3086	4303	6932	10040

378

6	7	8	9	10	11	12	Total	Year 2
1500	1500	1500	1500	1500	1500	1500	18000	24000
1500	1500	1500	1500	1500	1500	1500	10500	19050
0	0	0	0	0	0	0	0	16800
0	0	0	0	0	0	0	0	0
950	950	950	950	950	950	950	11400	12600
950	950	950	950	950	950	950	7600	12200
735	735	735	735	735	735	735	7127	12698
188	188	188	188	188	188	188	1504	3000
250	250	250	250	250	250	250	3000	3900
100	100	100	100	100	100	100	800	1800
50	50	50	50	50	50	50	600	600
22	22	22	22	22	22	22	189	264
100	100	100	100	100	100	100	1200	1400
417	417	417	417	417	417	417	5004	5004
83	83	83	83	83	83	83	996	0
200	200	200	200	200	200	200	2400	2400
75	75	75	75	75	75	75	900	900
1298	1501	1704	1866	2029	2231	2434	16669	35623
125	125	125	125	125	125	125	1500	0
30	30	30	30	30	30	30	360	420
140	140	140	140	140	140	140	1440	2160
0	600	600	600	600	600	600	3600	7200
8713	9516	9719	9881	10044	10246	10449	94789	162019
436	476	486	494	502	512	522	4739	8101
9149	9992	10205	10375	10546	10758	10971	99528	170120
39	33	33	26	26	33	33	394	78
60	50	50	40	40	50	50	600	120
50	50	50	50	50	50	50	600	600
6	6	6	6	6	6	6	96	72
0	0	0	0	0	0	0	0	13200
75	75	75	75	75	75	75	900	1200
50	50	50	50	50	50	50	600	800
50	50	50	50	50	50	50	600	800
175	175	175	175	175	175	175	2100	2800
84	83	83	84	83	83	84	1000	0
2880	3330	3780	4140	4500	4950	5400	34040	71820
1152	1332	1512	1656	1800	1980	2160	11592	28728
2700	2700	2700	2700	2700	2700	2700	32400	32400
310	310	310	310	310	310	310	2170	3720
1867	1867	1867	1867	1867	1867	1867	21404	22404
1200	1200	1200	1200	1200	1200	1200	11400	21600
10698	11311	11941	12429	12932	13579	14210	119896	200342
19847	21303	22146	22804	23478	24337	25181	219424	370462
18463	22993	28141	32270	36387	41514	46660	262466	690280
7016	8737	10694	12263	13827	15775	17731	99738	296820
11447	14256	17447	20007	22560	25739	28929	162728	393460

Notes to Two-Year Pro Forma
Income Statement

(1) During the first two months, sales will reflect an assortment of stainless units only (cold rolled not available for 60 days). Sales are assumed to be 80% cold rolled units and 20% stainless units after the first two months. 30% of <u>all</u> sales are 1/2 gallon sizes, 50% are quart, and 20% are pint. Sales volume is based on each dealer that carries Thermos-Tote™ selling 36 units/month during years 1 and 2. The company will begin operations with 35 truckstops and will have 300 by the end of the 1st year; 360 by the end of the 2nd year. The following are the prices charged for the product by the company (i.e., dealer cost):

	Stainless (each)		Cold Rolled (each)	
	Year 1	Year 2	Year 1	Year 2
1/2 Gallon	$14.00	$15.40	$10.40	$11.40
Quart	14.50	16.00	10.90	12.00
Pint	13.50	14.90	9.90	10.90

For detailed sales calculations, see Appendix E, which itemizes year 1.

(2) Thermos-Tote™, by utilizing its own truck for delivery, will be paid the equivalent shipping rates the same as if the order were shipped by the post office or other carrier. Shipping rates are based on each order's size and weight. Pint and quart units are the same size and weight, therefore they produce the same shipping revenue. The present established commercial shipping rate for a nearby outlet and that of the most distant geographic outlet were averaged to produce the following rates (a COD surcharge was not added). Amounts increase 10% in year 2:

> 1/2 Gal., 1/2 doz. order--wt. 20 lb.--$6.40/order
> 1/2 Gal., 1 doz. order--wt. 37 lb.--$11.00/order
> Pint/Quart, 1/2 doz. order--wt. 12 lb.--$4.24/order
> Pint/Quart, 1 doz. order--wt. 21 lb.--$6.66/order

Detailed calculations for year 1 are illustrated in Appendix F.

(3) Metalwork cost of 1/2 gallon stainless is $5.54/unit in year 1 and increases 10% in year 2.

(4) Metalwork cost of quart stainless is $5.74/unit in year 1 and increases 10% in year 2.

(5) Metalwork cost of pint stainless is $5.68/unit in year 1 and increases 10% in year 2.

(6) Cost of stainless steel raw material is $1.30/unit for all three units in year 1 and increases 10% in year 2.

(7) Metalwork cost of 1/2 gallon cold rolled is $4.02/unit, including raw material cost in year 1, and increases 10% in year 2.

380

(8) Metalwork cost of quart cold rolled is $4.26/unit, including raw material cost in year 1, and increases 10% in year 2.

(9) Metalwork cost of pint cold rolled is $4.22/unit, including raw material cost in year 1, and increases 10% in year 2.

(10) Mounting screws to install the product cost $.20 per Thermos-Tote™ and are enclosed in each individual container. Cost is same for both years.

(11) The plastic bag that holds the mounting screws is budgeted at $.02/unit. Cost is same both years.

(12) Individual packaging containers for all 1/2 gallon size costs $.1849/unit. Cost is same both years.

(13) Individual packaging containers for all quart size costs $.1963/unit. Cost is same both years.

(14) Individual packaging containers for all pint size costs $.1963/unit. Cost is same both years.

(15) A master container holds a maximum of 12 individual Thermos-Totes™. It is assumed that 50% of all sales are in 1/2 dozen quantity orders and 50% are in one-dozen quantity orders. Master containers for each of the three sizes cost

$$
\begin{array}{ll}
\text{1/2 Gallon} & \text{--\$.9354/unit} \\
\text{Quart} & \text{--\$.8581/unit} \\
\text{Pint} & \text{--\$.8581/unit}
\end{array}
$$

The weighted average cost per master container is $.88. Cost is same both years.

(16) Mailing labels cost $.10/master container shipped. Cost is same both years.

(17) Miscellaneous shipping supplies cost $.02/unit shipped. Cost is same both years.

(18) Packaging labor is allocated @$.06/unit. Cost is same both years.

(19) Storage cost based on floor space is $.50/ft.^{2}/month.

(20) Tooling cost of $6,390 is amortized over the first 10,000 units sold.

(21) Patent cost of $2,400 is amortized over its 17-year life.

(22) General manager starts drawing salary at $1,500/month in month 1 for the 1st year. Second year salary is $24,000.

(23) Sales manager starts in the 6th month of the 1st year at $1,500/month and gets a 20% raise one year later.

(24) Assistant sales manager starts in month 1 of year 2 at $1,400/month and continues at this rate.

(25) Route supervisor does not start until month 1 of year 3.

(26) Clerical employee is paid $950/month in year 1 and $1,050/month in year 2.

(27) Bookkeeper is paid $950/month in year 1 and $1,050/month after 12 months' employment. Bookkeeper is hired in 5th month of year 1.

(28) Fringe benefits and payroll taxes will be 15% of salaries.

(29) Office is estimated to be 225 ft.^{2} in year 1 and 300 ft.^{2} in year 2, and will cost $10 per ft.^{2} per year.

(30) Phone expense is assumed to be $250/month in year 1 and $325/month in year 2.

381

(31) Utilities are estimated to be $100/month in year 1 and $150/month in year 2.

(32) Postage is estimated to be $50/month.

(33) Office equipment includes the following and is depreciated over 60 months:

1 calculator	$ 400	acquired in month 1
2 desks & chairs	700	acquired in month 6
1 filing cabinet	200	acquired in month 6

Total $1,300

(34) Legal fees are assumed to average $100/month in year 1 and total $1,400 in year 2.

(35) An audit will be performed each year at an approximate cost of $5,000.

(36) Costs to incorporate plus other miscellaneous organizational costs will be approximately $1,000 in the first year.

(37) General inventory insurance is estimated at $2,400/year.

(38) Key man life insurance on the president will be a five-year term $100,000 policy and will cost $900/year.

(39) Bad debts are estimated at 2% of sales of the units.

(40) Planning Associates, Inc. will be paid $1,500 for business study and business planning fee.

(41) Franchise tax is estimated at $360 for year 1 and $420 for year 2. Payment is in the following year.

(42) Office supplies are estimated at $80/month in year 1 and $120/month in year 2. Typewriter rental of $60/month beginning the 5th month is included in this category.

(43) Planning Associates, Inc. will provide ten hours' post-incorporation management consultation each month, beginning in the 7th month of operation.

(44) Miscellaneous is computed at 5% of subtotal general and administrative.

(45) Advertising posters will be placed in every truckstop that carries Thermos-Tote™. Cost is $654 for the first 500 and $234 for each additional 500.

(46) Point-of-purchase displays will also be installed in every truckstop that carries Thermos-Tote™. Cost is $102 for the first 50 and $100 for each additional 50.

(47) Five hundred brochures will be dispensed per month at a cost of $.10 each.

(48) Cover letter #1 is a promotional solicitation mailed out by large trucking chains. It is an introductory letter and costs $.03/letter. Five hundred will be mailed in month 1, 200 in month 2, and 100/month will be mailed thereafter. Cover letter #2 is a follow-up letter supporting the first mailing. Cost is also $.03/letter. Five hundred will be mailed out in month 2 and 100/month thereafter. Distributor will provide envelope and postage.

(49) Advertising is composed of magazine and radio advertising as outlined below:

Magazine—first year will be at no expense, new product
announcements and feature stories will be adequate
during this period. During the second year, one $500 ad
will be run every three months in each of three
magazines.

Radio—sponsored advertising will suffice during the first
year. During the second year, $200 worth of advertising
per month will be obtained on each of three select
stations that are truck driver favorites.

(50) The president will attend three trucking/truckstop—related
conventions in the first year and four every year
thereafter. One person can attend a convention for $300.

(51) At the conventions, promotional pins will be handed out.
One thousand will be given away at each convention at a cost
of $.20 each.

(52) Two thousand promotional brochures will be passed out at
each convention at a cost of $.10 each.

(53) Booth cost for each convention will be $700.

(54) Initial marketing materials layout work cost of $1,000 is
amortized over the first year of business.

(55) Commissions will be $.50/unit and will be paid after the
first 5,000 units are sold.

(56) A bonus of $.20/unit will be paid at the end of each year to
the sales manager. Bonus starts to accrue after the sales
manager becomes an employee in month 6 of year 1.

(57) Lease payments on the company's tractor/trailer are
forecast at $2,700/month.

(58) A car is leased in the 6th month at $310/month. Lease price
includes all expenses except gas and oil. (See Note 59.)

(59) The truck will cost $.40/mile to operate and will travel
50,000 miles the first year and 100,000 miles each year
thereafter. Beginning in month 6 of year 1, an allowance of
$200/month is made for gas and oil for the car.

(60) Travel allowance is projected at $600/month for each of the
following: general manager, sales manager, and assistant
sales manager.

(61) Federal income tax is computed on an estimated rate of 38%
in year 1 and 43% in year 2. Taxes are accrued monthly and
paid quarterly. Losses are carried forward and applied
against profits in subsequent months. Tax is calculated on
the positive difference (note start—up losses).

PRO FORMA CASH FLOW STATEMENT

Thermos–Tote, Inc.
Pro Forma Cash Flow
    Year 1

Month	1	2	3	4	5
RECEIPTS					
(1) Sales revenues	17829	30564	0	0	34487
(2) Shipping revenues	930	1595	2258	2922	3454
Total	18759	32159	2258	2922	37941
DISBURSEMENTS					
Direct Materials (stainless)					
(3) Raw stainless steel	4550	1300	0	650	1300
(4) Metal work half gallon	8310	0	0	0	2770
(5) Metal work quart	11480	2870	0	0	2870
(6) Metal work pint	5680	0	0	0	2840
(Cold Roll)					
(7) Metal work half gallon	0	4020	4020	0	4020
(8) Metal work quart	0	6390	6390	0	8520
(9) Metal work pint	0	2110	4220	0	2110
(10) Mounting screws	400	400	600	800	0
(11) Screw bag	200	0	0	200	0
Containers					
(12) Half gallon (individual)	185	185	0	0	370
(13) Pint/quart (individual)	196	393	393	589	0
(14) Masters	880	0	0	880	0
(15) Mailing labels	500	0	0	0	0
(16) Misc. Shipping Supplies	25	43	61	79	94
Total materials	32406	17711	15684	3198	24894
Direct Labor					
(17) Packaging	76	130	184	238	0
Total	76	130	184	238	0
Overhead					
(18) Storage	20	34	48	62	0
(19) Tooling	6390	0	0	0	0
(20) Patent	1400	0	0	0	0
Total	7810	34	48	62	0
(21) General manager	1500	1500	1500	1500	1500
(22) Clerical	950	950	950	950	950
(23) Bookkeeper	0	0	0	0	950
(24) Manager (sales)	0	0	0	0	0
(25) Assistant sales manager	0	0	0	0	0
(26) Route supervisor	0	0	0	0	0
(27) Fringe & Payroll Taxes	368	368	368	368	510
(28) Office rent	0	0	0	0	188
(29) Phone	0	250	250	250	250
(30) Utilities	0	0	0	0	0
(31) Postage	50	50	50	50	50
(32) Legal	0	0	0	0	0
(33) Audit	0	0	0	0	0
(34) Organizational costs	1000	0	0	0	0
(35) Insurance (general)	200	200	200	200	200
(36) Insurance (key man)	75	75	75	75	75
(37) Study and planning fee	500	0	0	0	500
(38) Office supplies	80	80	80	80	140
(39) Management contract	0	0	0	0	0
(40) Misc. & bad debts	587	853	936	1149	1392
Total G&A	5310	4326	4409	4622	6705

6	7	8	9	10	11	12	Total
44630	52744	64916	75058	85202	93317	101430	600177
4251	4915	5579	6110	6642	7306	7971	53933
48881	57659	70495	81168	91844	100623	109401	654110
1300	1950	1950	1950	2600	2600	2600	22750
2770	0	2770	2770	2770	5540	2770	30470
2870	5740	2870	5740	5740	5740	5740	51660
0	2840	0	2840	2840	2840	0	19880
6030	6030	8040	8040	8040	10050	10050	68340
8520	12780	12780	12780	17040	17040	17040	119280
4220	4220	6330	4220	6330	6330	8440	48530
1000	1000	1400	1600	1600	1800	2000	12600
0	200	0	200	200	200	200	1400
185	370	370	370	555	370	555	3515
589	785	982	982	1178	1178	1374	8639
0	880	880	0	880	880	880	6160
0	0	500	0	0	0	0	1000
115	133	151	166	180	198	216	1461
27599	36928	39023	41658	49953	54766	51865	395685
281	346	400	454	497	540	594	3740
281	346	400	454	497	540	594	3740
73	90	104	118	129	141	155	974
0	0	0	0	0	0	0	6390
1000	0	0	0	0	0	0	2400
1073	90	104	118	129	141	155	9764
1500	1500	1500	1500	1500	1500	1500	18000
950	950	950	950	950	950	950	11400
950	950	950	950	950	950	950	7600
1500	1500	1500	1500	1500	1500	1500	10500
0	0	0	0	0	0	0	0
0	0	0	0	0	0	0	0
735	735	735	735	735	735	735	7127
188	188	188	188	188	188	188	1504
250	250	250	250	250	250	250	2750
100	100	100	100	100	100	100	700
50	50	50	50	50	50	50	600
600	0	0	0	0	0	600	1200
0	0	0	0	0	0	0	0
0	0	0	0	0	0	0	1000
200	200	200	200	200	200	200	2400
75	75	75	75	75	75	75	900
0	0	0	500	0	0	0	1500
140	140	140	140	140	140	140	1440
0	0	600	600	600	600	600	3000
1734	1977	2190	2360	2531	2743	2956	21408
8972	8615	9428	10098	9769	9981	10794	93029

385

Thermos-Tote Pro Forma Cash Flow - Year 1

Month	1	2	3	4	5
Marketing					
(41) Posters	654	0	0	0	0
(42) Displays	102	100	0	0	100
(43) Brochures	100	200	100	0	0
(44) Cover letter #1	15	6	3	3	3
(45) Cover letter #2	0	15	3	3	3
(46) Personnel cost (conventions)	0	0	0	300	0
(47) Pins	0	200	0	0	0
(48) Booth cost	0	700	0	0	0
(49) Commissions	0	0	740	1980	2340
(50) Marketing materials layout	1000	0	0	0	0
(51) Travel	600	600	600	600	600
(52) Bonuses	0	0	0	0	0
(53) Truck lease	2700	2700	2700	2700	2700
(54) Auto lease	0	0	0	0	0
(55) Maint. & opr. expense	0	1667	1667	1667	1667
Total Marketing	5171	6188	5813	7253	7413
Taxes					
(56) Federal Income	0	0	0	3292	0
Total F.I.T.	0	0	0	3292	0
Capital Expenditures					
(57) Office equipment	400	0	0	0	0
Total equipment	400	0	0	0	0
Total Disbursements	51173	28389	26138	18665	39012
Total Cash Flow	(32414)	(3770)	(23880)	(15743)	(1071)
Beginning Cash Balance	0	(32414)	(28644)	(52524)	(68267)
Ending Cash Balance	(32414)	(28644)	(52524)	(68267)	(69338)

Notes to Pro Forma Cash Flow Statement

(1) Sales for months 1 and 2 are COD. Thereafter, all sales are assumed to be collected on a 60-day basis.

(2) Dealer will pay the shipping costs within seven days of receipt of order. (See Note 2, Pro Forma Income Statement for shipping rates.)

(3) The raw stainless steel is picked up at the mill by Thermos-Tote, Inc. and delivered to Spring Steel Company. Four weeks are required for preparation at the mill for an order. Orders in months 1 and 2 are COD at the mill. Thereafter, all transactions carry 30-day terms. Detailed calculations are shown in Appendix G.

(4), (5), (6) Spring Steel Company must have a commitment for 10,000 units of which the first 5,000 ordered will be COD. Thereafter, Thermos-Tote will have 30-day terms. Minimum order quantity for the 1/2 gallon, quart, and pint size models is 500 units. (See Pro Forma Income Statement Notes 3, 4 and 5 for cost of three sizes.) Detailed calculations are shown in Appendix H.

(7), (8), (9) Arrangements and terms for cold rolled steel products are the same as stainless except Thermos-Tote, Inc. does not procure the steel. Costs for the three sizes of cold rolled products are shown in Notes 7, 8 and 9 of the Pro Forma

6	7	8	9	10	11	12	Total
0	0	0	0	0	0	0	654
0	0	100	0	100	0	100	602
100	0	300	0	100	0	300	1200
3	3	3	3	3	3	3	51
3	3	3	3	3	3	3	45
0	0	0	300	0	0	0	600
0	200	0	0	0	200	0	600
0	700	0	0	0	700	0	2100
2880	3330	3780	4140	4500	4950	5400	34040
0	0	0	0	0	0	0	1000
1200	1200	1200	1200	1200	1200	1200	11400
0	0	0	0	0	0	11592	11592
2700	2700	2700	2700	2700	2700	2700	32400
310	310	310	310	310	310	310	2170
1667	1867	1867	1867	1867	1867	1867	19537
8863	10313	10263	10523	10783	11933	23475	117991
17419	0	0	31694	0	0	47333	99738
17419	0	0	31694	0	0	47333	99738
900	0	0	0	0	0	0	1300
900	0	0	0	0	0	0	1300
65107	56292	59218	94545	71131	77361	134216	721247
(16226)	1367	11277	(13377)	20713	23262	(24815)	(67137)
(69338)	(85564)	(84197)	(72920)	(86297)	(65584)	(42322)	
(85564)	(84197)	(72920)	(86297)	(65584)	(42322)	(67137)	

Income Statement. Detailed calculations are shown in Appendix I.

(10) Mounting screw cost is $.20/Thermos–Tote™ unit. Minimum order is 1,000. Cash is paid in the first four months of operation. Thereafter, 30–day terms will be available.

(11) The plastic bag to hold the mounting screw costs $.02/unit. Cash is paid for this relatively small expense through the first four months. Thereafter, 30–day terms will be available. Purchases are in multiples of 10,000.

(12) One–half gallon individual containers cost $184.90/1,000 and are ordered in increments of a thousand. Cash is paid for the first two orders. Thereafter, 30–day terms are available.

(13) Quart and pint individual containers cost $196.30/1,000. The same payment terms as 12 apply.

(14) Master containers (1/2 gallon, quart, and pint sizes) must be ordered in quantities of 1,000. Cash is paid for the first two orders. Thereafter, 30–day terms are available.

(15) Five thousand mailing labels are ordered in month 1 at a cost of $.10/each. Five thousand more are ordered in month 8. Both transactions are for cash.

(16) Miscellaneous shipping supplies are paid for within the month that the expense occurs.

(17) Packaging is done by Acme Packing, Inc. and costs $.06/unit. In the first four months the terms are cash. Thereafter, 30-day terms are available.

(18) Storage costs $.50/ft.^{2}/month and will vary according to the inventory that is stored. Cash is paid the first four months, and 30-day terms are available thereafter.

(19) Spring Steel Company must be paid $6,390 in cash during month 1 for the tooling to make the Thermos-Tote™.

(20) Patent work will cost $2,400. Fourteen hundred dollars will be disbursed in month 1 for filing, etc. One thousand dollars will be paid in month 6 for the remainder of the patent work.

(21) The general manager will be paid $1,500/month. Salary is paid beginning in month 1.

(22) The clerical employee is paid $950/month. Disbursement is in month expensed.

(23) Bookkeeper starts in month 5 at $950/month. Disbursement is in month expensed.

(24) Sales manager is hired in 6th month of year 1 at $1,500/month. Disbursement is in month expensed.

(25) Assistant sales manager is hired in month 1 of the 2nd year at $1,400/month.

(26) Route supervisor is hired in month 1 of year 3 at $1,400/month.

(27) Fringe benefits and payroll taxes are 15% of salaries; disbursement is made within the month expensed.

(28) An office is rented beginning in month 5. Rent payment is made in month in which rent expense occurs.

(29) Telephone bill is paid in the month following the expense.

(30) Utilities are paid in the month following the expense.

(31) Postage is paid within the month expensed.

(32) Miscellaneous legal work in the amount of $600 will be paid in the 6th and 12th months.

(33) An audit is performed at the close of the first year and disbursement is made in month 2 of the 2nd year.

(34) Cost to organize the corporation (filing fee, registration of company name, legal fees, etc.) will be $1,000 and will be disbursed in month 1.

(35) Premium payment of $200 is disbursed each month for general insurance coverage.

(36) Key man life insurance premium will be paid monthly.

(37) Study and planning fee of $1,500 is paid to Planning Associates, Inc.; 1/3 is disbursed in month 1, 1/3 in month 5, and 1/3 in month 9.

(38) Office supplies are paid for in cash each month as expensed.

(39) Management consultant fee of $600/month is paid in month after it is expensed.

(40) Miscellaneous is computed at 5% of subtotal general and administrative and is paid in month expense is incurred.

388

(41) Advertising posters to be placed in each truckstop carrying Thermos-Totes® are $654/500 units; 500 are ordered and paid for in month 1.

(42) Point of purchase displays placed in each truckstop carrying Thermos-Totes® must be ordered in quantities of 50. Cost for first 50 is $102 and $100 for each 50 thereafter. Cash is paid for the first three orders and 30-day terms are available thereafter.

(43) Brochures cost $100/1,000. Cash is paid for the first three orders. Thereafter, 30-day terms are available. This includes both the brochures passed out monthly and the 2,000 passed out at each convention.

(44), (45) Cover letters #1 and #2 are on COD terms.

(46) Personal costs to go to conventions will be $300/convention. Conventions will be attended in the 3rd, 8th, and 12th months. Expense will be charged on a credit card and paid in the month following the convention.

(47) Promotional pins costing $.20 each will be handed out at the conventions and will be paid for in cash the month preceding the convention; 1,000 will be ordered for each convention.

(48) Booth cost for the three conventions will average $700 and must be paid one month in advance of the convention.

(49) After the first 5,000 units, $.50 commission/unit is paid to those who bring in orders. Disbursement is made in the month the order is taken.

(50) Disbursement of $1,000 in month 1 is for marketing materials layout.

(51) Travel allowance for general manager and sales manager is disbursed weekly.

(52) Upon hiring of the sales manager, a $.10/unit bonus is accumulated and paid in the 12th month.

(53) Truck lease payments are in the month of the expense.

(54) Auto lease payments will be $310/month and include maintenance and insurance.

(55) Maintenance and operating expenses for the truck and gasoline expense for the car are paid in month following the expense.

(56) Federal income taxes will be paid quarterly in the 4th, 6th, 9th, and 12th months of the year.

(57) A calculator is purchased for cash in month 1 and two desks and two chairs are purchased and paid for in month 6.

SALES FORECAST FOR THERMOS-TOTE:
ILLUSTRATION OF CALCULATIONS (YEAR 1)

Month		1	2	3	4	5
Year 1						
Number of Dealers		35	60	85	110	130
Total Units Sold		1260	2160	3060	3960	4680
COLD ROLL						
1/2 Gallon (Units)		0	0	734	950	1123
Quart (Units)		0	0	1224	1584	1872
Pint (Units)		0	0	490	634	749
SALES						
1/2 Gallon ($10.40 ea.)	$	0	0	7634	9880	11679
Quart ($10.90 ea.)		0	0	13342	17266	20405
Pint ($9.90 ea.)		0	0	4851	6277	7415
Cold Roll Sales	$	0	0	25827	33423	39499
STAINLESS						
1/2 Gallon (Units)		378	648	184	238	281
Quart (Units)		630	1080	306	396	468
Pint (Units)		252	432	122	158	187
SALES						
1/2 Gallon ($14.00 ea.)	$	5292	9072	2576	3332	3934
Quart ($14.50 ea.)		9135	15660	4437	5742	6786
Pint ($13.50 ea.)		3402	5832	1647	2133	2525
Stainless Sales	$	17829	30564	8660	11207	13245
TOTAL SALES	$	17829	30564	34487	44630	52744

SHIPPING REVENUE FORECAST:
ILLUSTRATION OF CALCULATIONS (YEAR 1)

Month		1	2	3	4	5
Year 1						
Total Units Sold		1260	2160	3060	3960	4680
Number of 1/2 Gallon		378	648	918	1188	1404
Number of Pints & Quarts		882	1512	2142	2772	3276
SHIPPING REVENUE						
1/2 Gallon*	$	374	642	909	1176	1390
Pints & Quarts**		556	953	1349	1746	2064
Total Shipping Revenue	$	930	1595	2258	2922	3454

*The 1/2 dozen rate of $6.40 and the 1 dozen rate of $11.00 were converted to their respective per unit rates and then averaged to arrive at an average per unit shipping rate of $.99 per 1/2 gallon unit.

6	7	8	9	10	11	12	Total
160	185	210	230	250	275	300	N/A
5760	6660	7560	8280	9000	9900	10800	73080
1382	1598	1814	1987	2160	2376	2592	16716
2304	2664	3024	3312	3600	3960	4320	27864
922	1066	1210	1325	1440	1584	1728	11148
14373	16619	18866	20665	22464	24710	26957	173847
25114	29038	32962	36101	39240	43164	47088	303720
9128	10553	11979	13118	14256	15682	17107	110366
48615	56210	63807	69884	75960	83556	91152	587933
346	400	454	497	540	594	648	5208
576	666	756	828	900	990	1080	8676
230	266	302	331	360	396	432	3468
4844	5600	6356	6958	7560	8316	9072	72912
8352	9657	10962	12006	13050	14355	15660	125802
3105	3591	4077	4469	4860	5346	5832	46819
16301	18848	21395	23433	25470	28017	30564	245533
64916	75058	85202	93317	101430	111573	121716	833466

6	7	8	9	10	11	12	Total
5760	6660	7560	8280	9000	9900	10800	73080
1728	1998	2268	2484	2700	2970	3240	21924
4032	4662	5292	5796	6300	6930	7560	51156
1711	1978	2245	2459	2673	2940	3208	21705
2540	2937	3334	3651	3969	4366	4763	32228
4251	4915	5579	6110	6642	7306	7971	53933

**The pint and quart 1/2 dozen rate of $4.24 and the 1 dozen rate of $6.66 were converted to their respective per unit rates and then averaged to arrive at an average per unit shipping rate of $.63 per pint and quart unit.

STAINLESS RAW MATERIAL INVENTORY FOR THERMOS-TOTE:
CALCULATIONS FOR YEAR 1 DISBURSEMENTS

Month	1	2	3	4	5
Year 1					
(Units)					
Beginning Inventory	0	2240	1080	968	1176
(−) Units Shipped	1260	2160	612	792	936
(+) Units Received*	3500	1000	500	1000	1000
Ending Inventory**	2240	1080	968	1176	1240
(Dollars)					
Value of Purchases***	$ 4550	1300	650	1300	1300
Disbursements for Purchases****	$ 4550	1300	0	650	1300

---

*Stainless material purchased in 500 unit quantities and multiples of 500 units

**It is desired to have enough material on hand at the end of a month
to be sure that the next month's anticipated volume can be shipped.

***At $1.30 per unit.

****Payment terms are C.O.D. for months 1 and 2 and net 30 days
thereafter. These numbers are transferred to the Cash Flow Projections.

APPENDIX H
STAINLESS FINISHED GOODS INVENTORY SCHEDULE:
CALCULATIONS FOR YEAR 1 DISBURSEMENTS

Month	1	2	3	4	5
Year 1					
Stainless: 1/2 Gallon					
Beginning Inventory (Units)	0	1122	474	290	552
(−) Units Shipped (Units)	378	648	184	238	281
(+) Units Received (Units)	1500	0	0	500	500
Ending Inventory (Units)*	1122	474	290	552	771
Value of Purchases ($5.54 ea.)	$ 8310	0	0	2770	2770
Disbursements for Purchases	$ 8310	0	0	0	2770
Stainless: Quart					
Beginning Inventory (Units)	0	1370	790	484	588
(−) Units Shipped (Units)	630	1080	306	396	468
(+) Units Received (Units)	2000	500	0	500	500
Ending Inventory (Units)*	1370	790	484	588	620
Value of Purchases ($5.74 ea.)	$ 11480	2870	0	2870	2870
Disbursements for Purchases	$ 11480	2870	0	0	2870
Stainless: Pint					
Beginning Inventory (Units)	0	748	316	194	536
(−) Units Shipped (Units)	252	432	122	158	187
(+) Units Received (Units)	1000	0	0	500	0
Ending Inventory (Units)*	748	316	194	536	349
Value of Purchases ($5.68 ea.)	$ 5680	0	0	2840	0
Disbursements for Purchases	$ 5680	0	0	0	2840

---

*Inventory policy is to have enough units on hand at the end of a month to be cert
the following month's anticipated shipment's can be made from units on hand.

6	7	8	9	10	11	12	Total*
1240	1588	1756	1744	2088	2288	2308	
1152	1332	1512	1656	1800	1980	2160	17352
1500	1500	1500	2000	2000	2000	2500	20000
1588	1756	1744	2088	2288	2308	2648	
1950	1950	1950	2600	2600	2600	3250	
1300	1950	1950	1950	2600	2600	2600	22750

6	7	8	9	10	11	12	Total
771	425	525	571	574	1034	940	N/A
346	400	454	497	540	594	648	5208
0	500	500	500	1000	500	500	6000
425	525	571	574	1034	940	792	N/A
0	2770	2770	2770	5540	2770	2770	33240
2770	0	2770	2770	2770	5540	2770	30470
620	1044	878	1122	1294	1394	1404	N/A
576	666	756	828	900	990	1080	8676
1000	500	1000	1000	1000	1000	1000	10000
1044	878	1122	1294	1394	1404	1324	N/A
5740	2870	5740	5740	5740	5740	5740	57400
2870	5740	2870	5740	5740	5740	5740	51660
349	619	353	551	720	860	464	N/A
230	266	302	331	360	396	432	3468
500	0	500	500	500	0	500	4000
619	353	551	720	860	464	532	N/A
2840	0	2840	2840	2840	0	2840	22720
0	2840	0	2840	2840	2840	0	19880

COLD ROLLED FINISHED GOODS INVENTORY SCHEDULE:
CALCULATIONS FOR YEAR 1 DISBURSEMENTS

Month	1	2	3	4
Year 1				
Cold Roll: 1/2 Gallon				
Beginning Inventory (Units)	0	0	1000	1266
(−)Units Shipped (Units)	0	0	734	950
(+)Units Purchased (Units)	0	1000	1000	1000
Ending Inventory (Units)*	0	1000	1266	1316
Value of Purchases ($4.02 ea.)	0	$ 4020	4020	4020
Disbursements for Purchases	0	$ 4020	4020	0
Cold Roll: Quart				
Beginning Inventory (Units)	0	0	1500	1776
(−)Units Shipped (Units)	0	0	1224	1584
(+)Units Received (Units)	0	1500	1500	2000
Ending Inventory (Units)*	0	1500	1776	2192
Value of Purchases ($4.26 ea.)	0	$ 6390	6390	8520
Disbursements for Purchases	0	$ 6390	6390	0
Cold Roll: Pint				
Beginning Inventory (Units)	0	0	500	1010
(−)Units Shipped (Units)	0	0	490	634
(+)Units Received (Units)	0	500	1000	500
Ending Inventory (Units)*	0	500	1010	876
Value of Purchases ($4.22 ea.)	0	$ 2110	4220	2110
Disbursements for Purchases	0	$ 2110	4220	0

---

*Inventory policy is to have enough units on hand at the end of a month
to be certain the following month's anticipated shipments can be made from
units on hand.

5	6	7	8	9	10	11	12	Total
1316	1693	1811	2213	2399	2412	2752	2876	
1123	1382	1598	1814	1987	2160	2376	2592	16716
1500	1500	2000	2000	2000	2500	2500	2500	19500
1693	1811	2213	2399	2412	2752	2876	2784	
6030	6030	8040	8040	8040	10050	10050	10050	78390
4020	6030	6030	8040	8040	8040	10050	10050	68340
2192	2320	3016	3352	3328	4016	4416	4456	
1872	2304	2664	3024	3312	3600	3960	4320	27864
2000	3000	3000	3000	4000	4000	4000	4500	32500
2320	3016	3352	3328	4016	4416	4456	4636	
8520	12780	12780	12780	17040	17040	17040	19170	138450
8520	8520	12780	12780	12780	17040	17040	17040	119280
876	1127	1205	1639	1429	1604	1664	2080	
749	922	1066	1210	1325	1440	1584	1728	11148
1000	1000	1500	1000	1500	1500	2000	1500	13000
1127	1205	1639	1429	1604	1664	2080	1852	
4220	4220	6330	4220	6330	6330	8440	6330	54860
2110	4220	4220	6330	4220	6330	6330	8440	48530

APPENDIX J

Pro Forma Balance Sheet
Thermos-Tote, Inc.
as of End of Year 1

Assets

Cash*		$ 32,863
Accounts Receivable		233,289
Materials and Supplies		5,173
Inventory—Finished Goods		53,766
Equipment	$ 1,300	
Less Accumulated Depreciation	189	1,111
Intangible Assets	2,400	
Less Accumulated Amortization	144	2,256
Total Assets		328,458

Liabilities

Accounts Payable	65,370
Taxes Payable	360
Total Liabilities	65,730

Capital

Common Stock*	100,000
Retained Earnings	162,728
Total Capital	262,728
Total Liabilities and Capital	328,458

*Assumes desired capital of $100,000 is incorporated into the financial position as a purchase of common stock.

Notes

Chapter 2

[1]Al Ries and Jack Trout, *Positioning: The Battle for Your Mind* (New York: McGraw-Hill Book Company, 1981), p. 6.

[2]Ibid., p. 18.

[3]John A. Welsh and Jerry F. White, "A Small Business Is Not a Little Big Business," *Harvard Business Review*, July–August 1981, pp. 18–32.

Chapter 7

[1]Byron Williamson, Personal Communication.

[2]The firm of Rohrer, Hibler & Replogle, Inc., Chicago, Ill.

[3]David C. McClelland, J. W. Atkinson, R. A. Clark, and E. L. Lowell, *The Achievement Motive* (New York: Appleton-Century-Crofts, 1953).

[4]Orvis F. Collins, David G. Moore, and Darab B. Unwalla, *The Enterprising Man* (East Lansing, Mich.: Michigan State University Press, 1964).

[5]*Statistical Abstracts of the United States: 1979*, 100th edition (Washington, D.C.: U.S. Bureau of the Census, 1979), p. 555.

[6]Ibid.

[7]Ibid., p. 682.

Chapter 8

[1]Byron Williamson, "A Profile of the Successful Entrepreneur," in *Investing in the Entrepreneur*, Proceedings of the Second Annual Seminar, Staff of the Caruth Institute of Owner-Managed Business, Southern Methodist University, Dallas, 1974.

[2]John A. Hornaday and John Aboud, "Characteristics of Successful Entrepreneurs," *Personnel Psychology* 24 (1971), pp. 141–153.

[1]Albert Shapero, "Who Starts New Businesses? The Displaced, Uncomfortable Entrepreneur," *Psychology Today* 9, no. 6 (November 1975), pp. 83–88.

[2]David C. McClelland, "As I See It," *Forbes*, June 1, 1969, pp. 53–57.

Chapter 11

[1]Richard F. Tozer, "Economic Experience and the Entrepreneur," in *Investing in the Entrepreneur*, Proceedings of the Second Annual Seminar, Staff of the Caruth Institute of Owner-Managed Business, Southern Methodist University, Dallas, 1974.

[2]Albert Shapero, "Who Starts New Businesses? The Displaced, Uncomfortable Entrepreneur," *Psychology Today* 9, no. 6 (November 1975), pp. 83–88.

[3]Arnold C. Cooper, "The Founding of Technologically-Based Firms," Center for Venture Management, Milwaukee, Wis., 1971.

[4]Richard F. Tozer, "1975 SMU National Venture Capital Industry Survey." The Caruth Institute of Owner-Managed Business, Southern Methodist University, Dallas, 1975.

Chapter 12

[1]R. Gene Brown and Kenneth S. Johnston, *Paciolo on Accounting* (New York: McGraw-Hill Book Company, Inc., 1963).

[2]Abraham H. Maslow, *Motivation and Personality* (New York: Harper & Row Publishers, Inc., 1954).

Chapter 13

[1]*The Journal of Business Strategy*, published quarterly by Warren, Gorham & Lamont, Inc., 210 South Street, Boston, MA 02111.

[2]International Association of Strategic Planning Consultants, Post Office Box 5198-B, Akron, Ohio 44313.

[3]Michael E. Porter, *Competitive Strategy: Techniques for Analyzing Industries and Competitors* (New York: The Free Press, 1980). Copyright © 1980 by The Free Press, a Division of Macmillan Publishing Co., Inc.

[4]Al Ries and Jack Trout, *Positioning: The Battle for Your Mind* (New York: McGraw-Hill Book Company, Inc., 1981).

Chapter 16

[1]Frederick W. Taylor, *Shop Management* (New York: Harper & Brothers, 1911).

[2]Miguel A. Reguero, *An Economic Study of the Military Airframe Industry*, Department of the Air Force, Wright-Patterson Air Force Base, Ohio, October 1957, p. 213.

[3]T. P. Wright, "Factors Affecting the Cost of Airplanes," *Journal of Aeronautical Science*, February 1936, pp. 122–128.

[4]Frank J. Andress, "The Learning Curve as a Production Tool," *Harvard Business Review*, January–February 1954, pp. 87–97.

[5]Winifred B. Hirschmann, "Profit from the Learning Curve," *Harvard Business Review*, January–February 1964, pp. 125–139.

[6]The Boston Consulting Group, Inc., *Perspectives on Experience*, 1968.

[7]Ibid., pp. 70–100.

[8]Walter Kiechel III, *Fortune* (series) "The Decline of the Experience Curve," October 2, 1981, pp. 139–146; "Three (or Four, or More) Ways to Win," October 19, 1981, pp. 181–188; "Oh Where, Oh Where Has My Little Dog Gone? Or My Cash Cow? Or My Star?" November 2, 1981, pp. 148–154; "Playing the Global Game," November 16, 1981, pp. 111–126.

[9]See Michael E. Porter, *Competitive Strategy* (New York: The Free Press, 1980); and *The Journal of Business Strategy*, published quarterly by Warren, Gorham & Lamont, Inc., 210 South St., Boston, Mass. 02111.

[10]Kiechel, November 16, 1981.

Chapter 17

[1]*Design-to-Cost: An Introduction*, Vectors Pamphlet V-10, Texas Instruments Incorporated, Dallas, Tex., 1977.

[2]"Texas Instruments Shows U.S. Business How to Survive in the 1980's," *Business Week*, September 1978, pp. 66–92.

[3]Abraham H. Maslow, *Motivation and Personality* (New York: Harper & Row Publishers, Inc., 1954).

[4]John A. Welsh and Jerry F. White, *Administering the Closely Held Company* (Englewood Cliffs, N.J.: Prentice-Hall, Inc., 1980), p. 307.

Chapter 18

[1]The Boston Consulting Group, Inc., *Perspectives on Experience*, 1968.

[2]Richard F. Tozer, "Economic Experience and the Entrepreneur," in *Investing in the Entrepreneur*, Proceedings of the Second Annual Seminar, Staff of the Caruth Institute of Owner-Managed Business, Southern Methodist University, Dallas, 1974.

Chapter 20

[1]Richard F. Tozer, "Economic Experience and the Entrepreneur," in *Investing in the Entrepreneur*, Proceedings of the Second Annual Seminar, Staff of the Caruth Institute of Owner-Managed Business, Southern Methodist University, Dallas, 1974.

[2]Personal communication, W. W. Caruth, Jr., who conceived of and funded the Caruth Institute of Owner-Managed Business, Edwin L. Cox School of Business, Southern Methodist University, Dallas, in 1970.

[3]Gene Bylinsky, *The Innovation Millionaires* (New York: Charles Scribner's Sons, 1976), p. 205.

[4]Personal communication, Morris B. Zale.

[5]Bylinsky, p. 183.

[6]Edwin A. Gee and Chaplin Tyler, *Managing Innovation* (New York: John Wiley & Sons, 1976), p. 149.

Chapter 21

[1]John A. Welsh and Jerry F. White, "Finding Opportunities to Be Your Own Boss," *The Executive Female*, January–February 1982, p. 22.

Chapter 24

[1]Richard F. Tozer, "Entrepreneurial Experience and the Investor," in *Investing in the Entrepreneur*, Proceedings of the Second Annual Seminar, Staff of the Caruth Institute of Owner-Managed Business, Southern Methodist University, Dallas, 1974.

[2]This is a very common method of approximating the number of units represented by a sixty-day inventory. Note that it is only an approximation and may not necessarily be the best one. In this example, where sales doubled during the year, a day's sales at the end of the year should be quite a bit larger than a day's sales at the beginning of the year. We have overlooked this difference to simplify the example. Once the principle is clear you may wish to recalculate the numbers with a different approximation.

[3]The expense of the median unit produced is easy to find on the graph and is a reasonable approximation. To find the exact average expense under an exponential curve requires a calculation involving calculus.

[4]If price declined throughout the year in proportion to unit expense, the receivables at the end of the year might be even smaller. Invoices for shipments during the last two months would be for inventory produced at about the beginning of the third quarter. For S, the competitor who established the price, the unit expense, from Figure 24-2, is approximately 83¢. Price would be 91¢. Then receivables at the end of the year for D would have been [$2/12 \times 100 \times \$0.91$] or $15.17. The price established by S at the beginning of the year would be about $1.10. The receivables at the beginning of the year for D would have been about [$2/12 \times 50 \times \$1.10$] or $9.17. The increase in receivables would be $6.00 and in inventory $4.00, for a total increase of $10.00. The profit of $27.00 would be unchanged.

As you can see, the numbers don't produce exact results unless they represent exactly what happened. If these numbers represent reasonable approximations of price and expense declines, then the results are a reasonable approximation of the inventory and receivables growth. The conclusions drawn remain unchanged; dominance provides a working capital advantage.

[5]Some readers may note that the value of the receivables at the beginning of the year is determined by the sales price during the prior year. Presumably the price in year 1 was $1.10. Then receivables at the beginning of year 2 would be [$2/12 \times 50 \times 1.10$] = $9.17 for D and [$2/12 \times 25 \times 1.10$] = $4.58 for S. Working capital needed by D would be $11.00 instead of $14.75 while profit would remain $27.00. Working capital needed by S would be $6.00 instead of $6.54 and profit would remain $4.50.

[6]As shown in footnote 5 the value of the receivables at the beginning of the year is determined by the sales price during the prior year. If this is taken into consideration then the receivables at the beginning of year 3 would be $[2/12 \times 100 \times 0.97] = \$16.17$ for D and $[2/12 \times 50 \times 0.97] = \$8.08$ for S. Working capital needed by D would be $\$15.83$ instead of $\$19.17$ while profit would remain $\$42.00$. Working capital needed by S would be $\$8.75$ instead of $\$10.41$ and profit would remain $\$7.00$.

Chapter 25

[1]John A. Welsh and Jerry F. White, *Administering the Closely Held Company* (Englewood Cliffs, N.J.: Prentice-Hall, Inc., 1980), p. 303. © 1980 by Prentice-Hall, Inc.

[2]*Encyclopedia of Associations*, 16th edition, vol. I (Detroit, Mich.: Gale Research Co., 1981).

[3]Bruce D. Henderson, "The Experience Curve-Reviewed, IV. The Growth Share Matrix or the Product Portfolio," The Boston Consulting Group, Inc., 1973.

[4]Ibid.

Chapter 26

[1]William J. Abernathy and Kenneth Wayne, "Limits of the Learning Curve," *Harvard Business Review*, September–October 1974, p. 111. Reprinted by permission of the *Harvard Business Review*. Copyright © 1974 by the President and Fellows of Harvard College; all rights reserved.

Chapter 27

[1]John A. Welsh and Jerry F. White, "A Small Business Is Not a Little Big Business," *Harvard Business Review*, July–August 1981, pp. 18–32.

Chapter 28

[1]Calvin A. Kent, Donald L. Sexton, and Karl H. Vesper, *Encyclopedia of Entrepreneurship* (Englewood Cliffs, N.J.: Prentice-Hall, Inc., 1982), table 7, p. 176.

Chapter 29

[1]Gene Bylinsky, *The Innovation Millionaires* (New York: Charles Scribner's Sons, 1976), p. 212.

[2]Personal communication, William P. Clements, Jr.

[3]Personal communication, M. Lamar Muse.

[1]*Securities Act of 1933,* U.S. Securities and Exchange Commission (Washington, D.C.: Superintendent of Documents, U.S. Government Printing Office, 1933).

[2]David L. Ratner, *Securities Regulation* (St. Paul, Minn.: West Publishing Co., 1978); James S. Mofsky, *Blue Sky Restrictions on New Business Promotions* (Albany, N.Y.: Matthew Bender & Company, Incorporated, 1971); and the securities act of your state, usually available from the state office having a name similar to State Securities Commissioner or State Securities Board.

Chapter 31

[1]U.S. Bureau of the Census, *Statistical Abstracts of the United States: 1980* (101st ed.) Washington, D.C., 1980, Table No. 927, p. 556.

[2]Ibid.

[3]Ibid.

Chapter 32

[1]"The Venture Capital 100," *Venture* Special Report, June 1982, pp. 80–89; and *Venture Capital Journal,* published monthly by Capital Publishing Corporation, Wellesley Hills, MA, 02181.

[2]Stanley E. Pratt, ed., *Guide to Venture Capital Sources,* 5th ed. (Wellesley Hills, MA: Capital Publishing Corporation, 1981).

[3]Calvin A. Kent, Donald L. Sexton, and Karl H. Vesper, *Encyclopedia of Entrepreneurship* (Englewood Cliffs, N.J.: Prentice-Hall, Inc., 1982), pp. 140–192.

Chapter 33

[1]John A. Welsh and Jerry F. White, *Administering the Closely Held Company* (Englewood Cliffs, N.J.: Prentice-Hall, Inc., 1980). © 1980 by Prentice-Hall, Inc.

[2]John A. Welsh and Jerry F. White, "A Small Business Is Not a Little Big Business," *Harvard Business Review,* July–August 1981, pp. 18–32.

Chapter 34

[1]John A. Welsh and Jerry F. White, *Administering the Closely Held Company* (Englewood Cliffs, N.J.: Prentice-Hall, Inc., 1980), p. 39. © 1980 by Prentice-Hall, Inc.

[2]*Profit Forecasting,* That's Business™ Educational Films, Produced by John A. Welsh and Jerry F. White, The Owner-Managed Business Center, Inc., Dallas, 1978.

Notes   ³Congress and the Internal Revenue Service change the permissible methods of depreciation from time to time. The IRS publication *Depreciation Guidelines* is free for the asking; it is very clearly written and describes the latest rules for depreciation.

Chapter 35

¹John A. Welsh and Jerry F. White, *Administering the Closely Held Company* (Englewood Cliffs, N.J.: Prentice-Hall, Inc., 1980), p. 42. © 1980 by Prentice-Hall, Inc.

²*Cash Flow Forecasting*, That's Business™ Educational Films, Produced by John A. Welsh and Jerry F. White, The Owner-Managed Business Center, Inc., Dallas, 1978.

Chapter 36

¹John A. Welsh and Jerry F. White, *Administering the Closely Held Company* (Englewood Cliffs, N.J.: Prentice-Hall, Inc., 1980), pp. 39, 41. © 1980 by Prentice-Hall, Inc.

²*Financing Growth*, That's Business™ Educational Films, Produced by John A. Welsh and Jerry F. White, The Owner-Managed Business Center, Inc., Dallas, 1978.

Chapter 37

¹*The Accounting Process*, That's Business™ Educational Films, Produced by John A. Welsh and Jerry F. White, The Owner-Managed Business Center, Inc., Dallas, 1978.

²R. Gene Brown and Kenneth S. Johnston, *Paciolo on Accounting* (New York: McGraw-Hill Book Company, Inc., 1963).

³John A. Welsh and Jerry F. White, *Administering the Closely Held Company* (Englewood Cliffs, N.J.: Prentice-Hall, Inc., 1980), p. 258. © 1980 by Prentice-Hall, Inc.

⁴*The Balance Sheet*, That's Business™ Educational Films, Produced by John A. Welsh and Jerry F. White, The Owner-Managed Business Center, Inc., Dallas, 1978.

Chapter 38

¹John A. Welsh and Jerry F. White, *Profit and Cash Flow Management for Non-Financial Managers*, School of Business Administration, Southern Methodist University, Dallas, 1974, p. 37.

Index